DATE DUE

DEMCO 38-296

Peter Sculthorpe

Peter Sculthorpe. Photograph courtesy of Perry Andronos, Sydney.

Peter Sculthorpe

A Bio-Bibliography

Deborah Hayes

Bio-Bibliographies in Music, Number 50
Donald L. Hixon, Series Adviser

Greenwood Press
Westport, Connecticut • London

Library of Congress Cataloging-in-Publication Data

Hayes, Deborah.
    Peter Sculthorpe : a bio-bibliography / Deborah Hayes.
        p.   cm.—(Bio-bibliographies in music, ISSN 0742-6968 ; no.
    50)
    Discography: p.
    Includes indexes.
    ISBN 0-313-27742-7 (alk. paper)
    1. Sculthorpe, Peter, 1929—Bibliography.   2. Sculthorpe, Peter,
    1929—Discography.   I. Title.   II. Series.
    ML134.S415H4   1993
    780'.92—dc20
    [B]   93-56774

British Library Cataloguing in Publication Data is available.

Library of Congress Catalog Card Number: 93-56774
ISBN: 0-313-27742-7
ISSN: 0742-6968

First published in 1993

Greenwood Press, 88 Post Road West, Westport, CT 06881
An imprint of Greenwood Publishing Group, Inc.

Printed in the United States of America

The paper used in this book complies with the
Permanent Paper Standard issued by the National
Information Standards Organization (Z39.48-1984).

10 9 8 7 6 5 4 3 2 1

To Peter Sculthorpe

and Edna Sculthorpe

Contents

Preface

This volume documents the work of Australian composer Peter Sculthorpe (b. 1929), one of today's truly original composers, an influential teacher, and a beloved public figure. Sculthorpe's music is well known in Australia and continues to find wider audiences overseas, especially in England and the United States. Australian musicians and audiences also know him for his ideas about music, his commitment to his art, to Australia and to the earth, and for his enthusiasm, wit, and humor. Since 1963 he has been a member of the distinguished Department of Music of the University of Sydney, teaching composition, ethnomusicology and the history of Australian music. He makes frequent public appearances. He is on stage at concerts to introduce his music or someone else's music. He speaks on radio and television and participates in panel discussions. He presents public lectures on music and various aspects of composing and related subjects. He is interviewed by the press. He makes himself available to musicians and to students of all ages at his home and studio in the Sydney suburb of Woollahra.

I first met Peter Sculthorpe in the course of preparing the volume in this series about Australian-American composer Peggy Glanville-Hicks (1912-1990). When I was in Sydney, Melbourne, and Canberra in July and August of 1988, Australians continually recommended Sculthorpe to me as a source of information about Glanville-Hicks. He, however, was in Colorado then as composer-in-residence at the Aspen Music Festival. After I returned home to Colorado, we finally met in Telluride where he had been invited to participate in the first Composer-to-Composer conference. He was indeed able to supply valuable information and insights about Glanville-Hicks. It was some time before I understood his appreciation of her contributions as part of his larger commitment to increasing the understanding and recognition of contemporary music and musicians, especially Australian musicians.

Peter Sculthorpe: A Bio-Bibliography is a record of this composer's work and of its reception by composer colleagues, performers, critics, and audiences. I am often asked why I, an American, chose to write about an Australian. My principal reason is that I love his music. When I began, I knew only a half dozen works, from recordings, and one of the pleasures of the research has been getting to hear more—though some of my original favorite works, like the Louisville Orchestra's recording of **Sun Music III** and the Kronos Quartet's recording of **String Quartet No. 8**, are still among my favorites. Another reason for my interest—in both Glanville-Hicks and Sculthorpe—is that a significant branch of my family is Australian. I grew up hearing about Australia and reading books sent from Australia. One of my aunts is, like Peter Sculthorpe, a Tasmanian, and we have discovered that one of her cousins was Sculthorpe's classmate at grammar school. (Tasmania is a small island state, and Tasmanians are used to discovering such connections.) Finally, as an American, I am intrigued by the way in which Australian composers, like American composers, have established international musical languages that are true to their European origins and to unique, indigenous origins as well. I continue to be fascinated by the cross-currents among musical cultures in what is often referred to as our shrinking world—though my confidence in world-wide communication may have diminished somewhat during the preparation of this volume.

Much of my research and writing occurred in Boulder, Colorado. Basic sources included Michael Hannan's 1982 book, *Peter Sculthorpe: His Music and Ideas 1929-1979*, Andrew McCredie's articles on Sculthorpe in the *New Grove Dictionary of Music and Musicians* (1980) and M. G. G. (suppl., 1979), James Murdoch's chapter on Sculthorpe in his book *Australia's Contemporary Composers* (1972), and Roger Covell's *Australia's Music: Themes of a New Society* (1967). In early 1991, Sculthorpe sent me updated lists compiled by one of his undergraduate students, Philip Percival. Some of the sources were in the University of Colorado libraries and others were available through our interlibrary loan service. None of the bibliographies, however, included concert reviews, which are a mainstay of this volume.

In mid-1991 I worked in Sydney with Sculthorpe's files, which he made completely available to me (as he had done with Hannan and Murdoch). The files included hundreds of concert reviews and other press cuttings, many of them sent to him by family, friends and colleagues in other parts of the world. Many of the cuttings, especially those from the 1960s, had been pasted onto large sheets, some of them identified by month and year, often erroneously. In preparation for my first visit, Sculthorpe and his secretary, Adrienne Askill, reorganized the material, filing either by work (in the case of reviews) or by event (in the case of such things as honorary degrees and overseas symposia). When I arrived, there were still boxes of materials that had yet to be filed. There were further materials that had been sorted into files separate from the main files. Books and magazines in the composer's studio and in other parts of the house contained substantial material about him. I was told about boxes of letters, simply accumulated in the order received, telling him that his music was to be performed at a school or a private concert of some kind or was being used for a dance performance. Twenty years earlier, in 1972, Murdoch had written that Sculthorpe had so many performances that he could not keep track of them. Since then, performances have only become more frequent.

While all researchers face the problem of identifying press cuttings, I was fortunate in that Sculthorpe himself could usually identify the source by the typeface or contents, and he could almost always recall the year, sometimes the month and even the exact date. For the cuttings that remained unidentified I was able to use the State Library of NSW in Sydney, with its vast collection of newspapers and other periodicals, to corroborate an educated guess. In some cases, however, I have had to be satisfied with an educated guess. There are no real indexes to the daily newspapers, even the *Sydney Morning Herald*, a principal source. (That is roughly the same as if a researcher into American music had no *New York Times Index*.) The State Library staff has compiled an index of the *Sydney Morning Herald* under broad topics, but the index included almost no reviews of music, concerts, or recordings.

I investigated the Sculthorpe collections in the library of Sounds Australian, formerly the Australian Music Centre, in Sydney, and at the Denis Wolanski Library and Archives of the Performing Arts at the Sydney Opera House. I used bibliographic databases available at the National Library in Canberra, such as the *Australian Bibliographic Network (ABN)* and the *Australian Public Affairs Information Service (APAIS)*. In Boulder I collected materials through the *Music Index, RILM,* and the "Reuter's index" or Nexis/ Lexis database. I used such bibliographic tools as Storm Bull's *Index to Biographies of Contemporary Composers* (Metuchen NJ, 1987), Deborah Crisp's *Bibliography of Australian Music* (Armidale NSW, 1982), and Philip J. Drummond's *Australian Directory of Music Research* (Sydney, 1978). I found items that were not part of Sculthorpe's files at the time. Still, I do apologize to performers, critics, and others whose work has escaped my attention.

As would be expected with such a public figure, there is an overwhelming amount of material. My initial bibliography, consisting of almost 3,000 items, amounted, with annotations, to almost 300 printed pages—a whole volume in itself. While a steady stream of information, however repetitive and redundant, has clearly contributed significantly to the reception of Sculthorpe's work over the years, this bio-bibliography, according to the established format for this series, required a more concise account. The contents of the volume, then, are arranged as follows:

Biography. The biography chapter examines Sculthorpe's consistent aims and interests and provides a chronological account of the phases of his work so far. The chapter depends on the sources listed in later chapters: "Works" (**W** numbers), "Discography" (**D** numbers), "Performances" (**P** numbers), "Bibliography" (**B** numbers), and Appendices. Sculthorpe has continued to affirm the influence of critics' opinions, both positive and negative, on his work, and thus it is especially suitable that the biography call on critics to help define his place in the history of twentieth-century music. Here and throughout the volume I have allowed Australian and US spellings and terminology to coexist.

Works. The second chapter, "Works," with the mnemonic **W** before each catalog number, is a chronological listing of Sculthorpe's compositions from 1945 through 1992. Included for each work is descriptive information in the manner of a *catalogue raisonné*—genre, instrumentation, duration, contents, dedication, publishing information, composer's note, and details of first performance, with references to recordings (**D** numbers), other performances (**P** numbers), and bibliographical items (**B** numbers). For the composer's notes I drew on a variety of sources, including concert programs, interviews, lectures, scores, and recordings. For this volume, the composer revised the existing material to emphasize interrelationships among works as well as to explain more fully the sources of his ideas; for a few titles, he wrote a new note. While many other work lists have been published over the years, this one, which has been done in collaboration with the composer, should be taken as definitive—as of early 1993.

While Sculthorpe wrote many works before 1945, that is, before the age of sixteen, he considers them to be *juvenilia* and they are not part of this catalog. The large number of early works (1945-54) may seem out of proportion to their musical significance, but there was no alternative to giving them separate W numbers, no way of combining them without creating confusion as to their separate identities. And although the catalog only goes through 1992, at this writing (early 1993) Sculthorpe is at work on several commissions and can be expected to continue to produce several new works a year.

Peter Sculthorpe's music is available from his publisher: Faber Music Ltd., 3 Queen Square, London WC1N 3AU, England; telephone 71-278-7436; fax 71-278-3817. The US/Canadian office is: Faber Music Inc., 50 Cross Street, Winchester MA 01890; telephone (617)-756-0323; fax (617)-729-2783. Overseas hire agents for Faber Music Ltd. are based around the world. Readers outside the UK, US, and Canada are advised to contact the local Faber representative or a music retailer for information on purchase or hire (rental) of scores and parts.

Discography. The third chapter, with the mnemonic **D**, is the "Discography" of commercial recordings of Sculthorpe's work, both in and out of print, in alphabetical order by title. References are given to the work's main listing in the catalog (W number) and to bibliographical items (**B** numbers). Australia is now enjoying the same increase in the production of CDs as the rest of the world, and the chapter includes a few CDs whose release is imminent. Readers outside Australia will be dismayed that it is often difficult and usually impossible to obtain Australian labels. One solution is to order from Sounds Australian or some other Australian retailer; another is to contact a Faber representative who may be able to supply tapes. It should be added that Australians, too, are dismayed by the lack of circulation outside Australia, and the situation is likely to improve soon.

Performances. The fourth chapter, "Performances," with the mnemonic **P**, is a chronological listing of performances of Sculthorpe's works other than first performances (first performances are listed in the **W** catalog). The **P** numbers denote the year and month: P79-4 designates 1979-April. Reference is made to reviews and publicity items in the "Bibliography" chapter (**B** listings); in a few cases, the reference is at the end of the **P** listing itself. The separate "Performances" chapter is provided to help clarify the chronology of the reception of Sculthorpe's work over the years and to indicate the depth and breadth of this reception. For concerts devoted to Sculthorpe's work alone, it was much less cumbersome to list a concert once (one **P** number) than under each of the works performed (several **W** numbers). The **P** listings help identify most (as many as possible) of the performers, ensembles, orchestras, and conductors who perform certain Sculthorpe works virtually countless times. These artists, especially the many who have been able to work closely with the composer, can be sources of further information themselves.

The listings, though extensive, are not to be taken as a complete record of concerts. Included are only a few of the increasingly frequent performances at schools, private concerts, and dance recitals, and almost none of the even more frequent uses of his music in films, television programs, commercials, Qantas airlines' in-flight entertainment, and the like.

Bibliography. The fifth chapter, "Bibliography," with the mnemonic **B**, lists published sources by and about Sculthorpe from 1945 through 1992, numbered **B1-B1200**. Items **B1-B1186**, listed chronologically and annotated, include books, book chapters, encyclopedia entries, journal articles, performance and score reviews, interviews, films, and miscellaneous news items about the composer. Related citations are listed at the ends of some of the annotations, to convey an idea of the number and kinds of references to his work. Of the hundreds of passing references to Sculthorpe, I have included only a few—enough to indicate that his name is almost certain to be found in any history of Australia, in any discussion of Australian culture or Australian music, and in anything published by or about any performer or performing group that has played his music, or has thought of playing it, or may play it some day.

The **B** listings for each year begin with books and other sources that are dated by year. For the remainder of each year, for periodicals published in the southern hemisphere the spring issue is listed in September, summer in December, and autumn in March; for northern hemisphere periodicals the spring issue is listed in March, summer in June, and autumn in September.

Australian dissertations, theses, and papers about Sculthorpe are listed at the end of the chapter, **B1187-B1200**, in chronological order from 1969 to 1991. I have separated these documents from the other bibliographical material because access to them may be problematic. At the same time these documents contain technical discussion of the music, and most, especially those by the composer's students, are full of highly informative quotes from his conversations, correspondence, lectures and seminars.

I have not listed in-house publications such as *Faber Music News, Fanfare* (Faber Music), *Accent* (Boosey and Hawkes Australia, agent for Faber Music), the *Musica Viva Bulletin,* and World Record Club brochures, all of which have provided performance listings and review excerpts. I have not listed the entries in the *International Who's Who 1992-93* (London, 1992) and *Who's Who in the World 1993-94* (New Providence NJ, 1992); the information they provide on Sculthorpe has not changed since the seventies. I have not included unpublished material—correspondence, notes on librettos and historical subjects, lecture notes, and the like. Michael Hannan's book, however, provides a list through 1979.

Appendix, Index. Finally, three appendices contain a classified list of works, a list of awards, degrees, and positions, and a list of works dedicated to Sculthorpe. Of the two indices, the title index lists titles of Sculthorpe's works, titles of movements and sections, and alternate titles. The subject index lists authors, critics, librettists, poets, names of publications, performers, performing groups, and other significant categories. References to the "Biography" are indicated by the actual page number, while items located in the other chapters are identified with the relevant mnemonic (**W, D, P**) and catalog number.

I am indebted to all the Sculthorpe experts in Australia whose writings have greatly contributed to this volume. Sculthorpe's assistant Graeme Skinner organized several mailings to me and helped answer questions. Another Sculthorpe expert, Australian composer, conductor, and commentator Vincent Plush, living in the United States, was always ready to provide invaluable information. Adrienne Askill assisted by correspondence and in person, tirelessly pursuing crucial bits of information that could only be obtained through persistent questioning of the appropriate people. Joel Crotty deserves special credit for discovering, at the eleventh hour, in the library of the Melbourne Conservatorium, the autograph manuscript of a work that the composer had almost forgotten.

Many other people provided information and assistance: Virginia Boucher, Reggie Ahram, and Martha Jo Sani of the University of Colorado Libraries; David Garrett, Sue Tronser, and other staff members at the ABC, Sydney; Ann Jeremy, CSM concert manager; Jean Hasse of Faber Music Inc., Boston; Richard Letts, former director of Sounds Australian, and the Sounds Australian staff; Henry Liles, general manager of the Paul Taylor Dance Company; Edward Pask, archivist of the Australian Ballet; Evelyn Portek of the Melbourne Conservatorium library; Melissa Smith of the Kronos Quartet staff; Don Tharp, librarian of the Austin (TX) Symphony Orchestra; Steven Tomlinson of the Bodleian Library; staff members of the ACO and the Australia Ensemble; Anne Boyd; Anthony Fogg; Andrew Ford; Jeannie Marsh; Wilfrid Mellers; Prudence Neidorf; Peter Platt; Larry Sitsky; Penelope Thwaites; and Daniel Welcher. John Douglas Gray assisted in Boulder, Hannelore Stupp in Sydney, and Barbara and Kevin Fitzpatrick in Launceston.

The University of Colorado provided support in the form of research travel funds, computer facilities, and a sabbatical leave which allowed me to complete the book.

Thanks are due my editors at Greenwood Press, especially Ann E. LeStrange, Alicia S. Merritt, and Jane Lerner.

Jane de Couvreur, Sculthorpe's former secretary, longtime neighbor and close friend, contributed immeasurably to my life in Sydney during each visit.

The composer's mother, Mrs. Edna Sculthorpe, was a cheerful and charming hostess; she offered many valuable recollections and was patient with my seemingly constant need to keep working on "the book."

Finally, I would like to thank Peter Sculthorpe for his abiding confidence that this volume would see completion. He helped assure its completion by spending many hours answering my questions, offering suggestions, correcting my several attempts to compile a valid worklist, and reading the final drafts of the other chapters as well. At the same time, I take full responsibility for the contents of the volume, particularly for any errors that remain.

Readers wishing further information are encouraged to contact me through Greenwood Press.

Abbreviations

Abbreviations for musical instruments and for months of the year are as in the *New Grove Dictionary of Music and Musicians* (London, 1980); for states in the USA and publication terms they are as in the *Chicago Manual of Style*. Other frequently-used words and phrases in this volume are abbreviated as follows:

A. A. P. = Australian Associated Press
ABC = Australian Broadcasting Commission, now Corporation
ACO = Australian Chamber Orchestra
ACT = Australian Capital Territory
AFR = Australian Financial Review
ANU = Australian National University, Canberra
AO = Officer of the Order of Australia
APRA = Australasian Performing Right Association
ASO = Adelaide Symphony Orchestra
Aud. = Auditorium
AYO = Australian Youth Orchestra
c = copyright
c = circa (about)
CAAC = Commonwealth Assistance to Australian Composers
CBC = Canadian Broadcasting Corporation
CH = Concert Hall
choreog. = choreographed by
Clancy Aud. = Sir John Clancy Auditorium, Univ. of NSW, Kensington
CO = Chamber Orchestra (*or* Colorado)
Con. = Conservatorium
CSM = Canberra School of Music
dir. = director, directed by
dur. = duration
H = Hall
HK = Hong Kong
HS = High School
ISCM = International Society for Contemporary Music
ISME = International Society for Music

Education
LA Times = Los Angeles Times
lit. = literature (about the event)
MS = manuscript
MSO = Melbourne Symphony Orchestra
Mtg Rm = Meeting Room
narr. = narrator
NE = New England (NSW, Australia) *or* Nevada
NLA = National Library of Australia, Canberra (*usually* **Aus**: CAnl)
NSW = New South Wales
NT = New Territory
NTO = National Training Orchestra
NY = New York
NYC = New York City
NZ = New Zealand
NZCO = New Zealand Chamber Orchestra
OH = Opera House (Sydney)
OHCH = OH Concert Hall
OHMR = OH Music Room
OHRH = OH Recording Hall
PA = Performing Arts (*or* Pennsylvania)
PAC = Performing Arts Centre/Center
perf. (perfs.) = performance(s)
PO = Philharmonic Orchestra
Post Aud. = Joseph Post Auditorium, NSW State Conservatorium of Music, Sydney
PS = Peter Sculthorpe
QEH = Queen Elizabeth Hall, London
QLD = Queensland
Qnt = Quintet
QPAC = Queensland Performing Arts Complex, Brisbane

QSO = Queensland SO
Qt = Quartet
QTO = Queensland Theatre Orchestra
SA = South Australia
SACEM = Société des Auteurs, Composi-
teurs et Éditeurs de Musique (Society for
Authors, Composers and Publishers of
Music), Paris
SASO = South Australian SO (*now* ASO)
SF = San Francisco
SMH = Sydney Morning Herald
SO = Symphony Orchestra
SQ = String Quartet

SSO = Sydney Symphony Orchestra
TAS = Tasmania
TH = Town Hall
TSO = Tasmanian Symphony Orchestra
UNESCO = United Nations Educational,
Scientific, and Cultural Organization
VIC = Victoria
WA = West Australia
WASO = West Australian Symphony
Orchestra
Ww = Woodwind
YSO - Youth SO
YO = Youth Orchestra

Peter Sculthorpe

Biography

Peter Sculthorpe is Australia's most prominent composer and one of the most important composers on the international scene. In a body of work that so far includes orchestral and chamber music in many genres and mediums, opera and other theatre music, songs and choral music, and music for documentary and commercial films, radio, and television, he has established a personal musical style and public presence that have shaped the history of twentieth-century music in Australia and the larger world. Owing to circumstances of place and time—Australia in the twentieth century—he has been defining, or re-defining, the role of composer for himself and his audiences.

AN AUSTRALIAN COMPOSER

Peter Joshua Sculthorpe was born on April 29, 1929, in Launceston, Tasmania, the island state just south of the eastern end of continental Australia. He grew up in St. Leonards, a small village outside Launceston; the Launceston area remained his home, or home base, until he moved to Sydney in 1963. His younger brother, Roger, still lives in Launceston. His mother, Edna Sculthorpe, née Moorhouse, lived there until a few years ago when she came to live with the composer in Sydney. His father, Joshua Tasman Sculthorpe (1900-1961), was fourth-generation Australian of English ancestry; the name Sculthorpe is of Viking origin. His mother, born in England in 1901, came to Tasmania from Yorkshire with her parents at the age of twelve.

Sculthorpe is among the generation of Australian composers who came to prominence as Australia became an influential force, economically and culturally, after World War II. He was educated in Launceston and at the University of Melbourne, where he earned a Bachelor of Music degree in 1950. During the nineteen-fifties, his work first became known outside Australia through several important overseas performances in England and Europe. From 1958 to 1960, he lived in England and pursued doctoral studies at Oxford. He returned to Tasmania and by the early sixties was recognized in Australia as an outstanding composer with a brilliant future. He was appointed to the Department of Music at the University of Sydney in 1963 and helped create an active new-music scene.

Sculthorpe has exhibited an extraordinary consistency of purpose from his earliest years to the present. He sees himself as an Australian composer, in the deepest sense. "My life has been devoted to the idea of a culture appropriate to Australia," he wrote in the seventies. His use of the word *life* rather than simply *work* is significant, as is the reference to *culture* rather than simply *music*, for his music is part of a broad vision of Australian culture. Unlike several other famous Australian composers of earlier times (Peggy Glanville-Hicks [1912-1990] and Percy Grainger [1882-1961] among them) who made their careers overseas, Sculthorpe decided to live permanently in Australia. A non-Australian may be surprised at the number of references in the literature to the fact that Sculthorpe chose to stay home, but Australians have seen many of their famous people choose to leave.

As late as 1955, in fact, Sculthorpe was the first *resident* Australian to have a work performed at an International Society of Contemporary Music festival. (Glanville-Hicks, in 1938, living in England, was the first Australian.) Five years later, in 1960, when he returned from Oxford, the press reported, ominously, that "Mr. Sculthorpe said he would rather stay in Australia but there are more opportunities overseas" (**B36**, in the "Bibliography"). During the sixties, with Australia's increasing prosperity came increased federal and other support for new music, while improvements in world communication stimulated the musical community's desire to achieve international recognition. By 1965, it looked as though Sculthorpe and many other Australian composers of his generation would stay (**B119**). Opportunities seemed virtually endless. By 1967, he was calling Australia the "last paradise" (**B196**), and in 1969, the place "where I can be most happy" (**B321**). A Sydney journalist asked, "shouldn't we thank the dear Lord for the important Australians" like Sculthorpe "who came back?" (**B324**). In 1971 reference was made to his "uncontrollable, permanent love affair with elemental Australia" (**B404**).

In recent years, his love for Australia has only intensified. "I've felt for the last five years or so that everywhere else is the end of the line and this is the centre of the world," he said in Sydney in 1988. "I used to feel that we were cut off from the world, but now I feel more that the rest of the world is cut off from us" (**B900**). Overseas, such expressions of identity can bring unexpected reactions, as when a Denver, Colorado, critic the same year found it remarkable that Sculthorpe called Australia the center of the world "with a straight face" (**B828**). At home, he has become something of an "icon" of Australian music (**B965**), although he says, "I see myself as a fairly simple, modest person just trying to write better music" (**B1025n**).

Perhaps manifesting Australian democratic ideals, Sculthorpe is accessible—as a person and as a composer. Anxious for audiences and critics to know what he is "on about," he supplies informative, elegantly-phrased program notes for his published works and willingly revises them for subsequent performances. Also effective are his pre-concert lectures and informal talks. Years of study, teaching, writing, and lecturing have contributed to making him an inspiring and popular speaker. Australians' appreciation of his public appearances goes back at least to the sixties. In 1971, a Sydney critic noted that "Peter Sculthorpe has only to walk on stage and listeners cheer and applaud madly" (**B422**). Overseas audiences are impressed as well, as at the

Aspen Music Festival in Colorado in 1988, where a local critic reported that the "charm and warmth" of Sculthorpe's explanations of his new orchestral work, **Kakadu**, won over an audience, many of whom had come primarily to hear Brahms; at the end of **Kakadu** "they stood for a prolonged ovation for the composer and the musicians" (**B901**).

Sculthorpe, in turn, has always been extremely gratified by audience response, especially emotional response, and concerned with critical reaction. Critics quote his program notes and pre-concert lectures, and interviewers recount his stories and his plans. Says Sydney journalist Jill Sykes, "He makes good copy" (**B972**). Composing is solitary work, and public attention helps provide balance. In 1966 fellow-Tasmanian composer Felix Gethen wrote that "some future historian of the Australian world of music will have little difficulty in finding information on Peter Sculthorpe" (**B155**)—a prophetic statement indeed, as most of the bibliography listed in this volume was still to come.

Sculthorpe's work has been controversial, especially in Australia, once a colony of Britain and thus susceptible, as an emerging New World power, to what Australians describe as a kind of inferiority complex in the face of Old World traditions. Part of the colonial legacy throughout the New World has been the habit of cringing from one's own country's art for fear of being labelled untutored or uncivilized. The Australian expression, *cultural cringe,* or simply *the cringe,* refers to an Australian tendency to feel embarrassment at things Australian—unless they meet with European approval. Sculthorpe's statements that Australia is the center of the world, which express his deepest feelings about his country, challenge this national inferiority complex.

When he returned to Australia from England in 1960, he was known to have established a strong reputation overseas; this reputation served to protect him from the cringe. Australian musicians who were counting on him to help establish an international reputation for Australian music commended his innovative writing. A continuing theme in the bibliography of the sixties is Sculthorpe's contribution to Australia's "emergence from a cult of musical cobwebs" (**B89**, in 1964) and to creating "music for the export list" (**B97**, 1965), "catching the world's ear" (**B144**, 1966), and "showing the world our mettle" (**B199n**, 1967). At the same time, during these years of what Sculthorpe calls Australia's "post-Webern era," when many thought that only the prevailing European, post-Webernian sound was of international significance, Sculthorpe was making controversial public statements about his Australianism and his lack of interest in imitating European trends. A few critics began noticeably to cringe. As his popularity increased, his success suggested to some that he had risen too far and needed to be cut down to average height—what Australians call the "tall poppy syndrome," explaining it as another aspect of the national inferiority complex.

In Australia much support for new music comes from public funds, mainly through the federally-funded ABC (Australian Broadcasting Corporation, originally Commission) and the Australia Council. The ABC records studio and concert performances and broadcasts them on radio and television; it also commissions works and supports a professional orchestra in each of the six state capitals—Sydney, Melbourne, Hobart, Adelaide, Perth, and Brisbane (the

SSO, MSO, TSO, ASO, WASO, and QSO, respectively). As the "Works" (**W**) catalog and "Performances" (**P**) listings in this volume show, Sculthorpe began receiving ABC commissions in the sixties and the ABC orchestras have performed his work with extraordinary frequency, in regular series concerts and at schools concerts—concerts for schoolchildren—in the capital cities and in surrounding country towns. "Teaching kits" are prepared for classroom study of the music. (In 1991, he wrote **From Uluru [W216]** especially for schools concerts, explaining the work's connection to a very bumpy road between Uluru [Ayers Rock] and the Olgas in central Australia. "Draw a picture of Peter Sculthorpe driving to Uluru," the teaching kit suggested [**B1151**], and the children did.) In 1992, a survey of ABC orchestral programming since 1988 revealed that his works had been performed more often than those of any other Australian composer. This has aroused some resentment, as might be expected, often in the form of a questioning of artistic merit and integrity.

Sculthorpe has also written for other performers and ensembles regularly for many years. Sydney's Seymour Group, Synergy percussion, the Australian Chamber Orchestra (ACO), and the Kronos Quartet in the US are but a few of the groups who program his music repeatedly. His music is also programmed by the Australian Youth Orchestra (AYO) and other youth orchestras, by conservatorium ensembles, and by high school and even younger students. In early 1980, Sydney critic Fred Blanks reported that Sculthorpe was the most-performed Australian composer in 1979—and in his 35 years of concert diaries as well (**B632**). In 1991, he made a similar report (**B1138**). Sculthorpe has demonstrated an extraordinary ability to inspire performers, reach audiences, and generate excitement about new music.

AN AUSTRALIAN MUSIC

Sculthorpe explains his music as a response to his experience of being Australian. "I write music about Australian themes because that is what I know" (**B965**). Inspiration, he often says, comes from everything he experiences (**B854**). Composer Anne Boyd, his student at the University of Sydney in the sixties and now Professor of Music there, recalls that he "introduced composition as something that one not only studied, but that one lived—one *was* a composer. Therefore, everything that one thought, felt, listened to, looked at and read, affected what one did as a composer" (**B982**, quoted in **B1199**). Sculthorpe believes that "music must have a sense of place and leap up from there" (**B1096**). "People should be able to hear Australian music and immediately identify it with this country" (**B684**).

In citing his sources of inspiration, he usually begins with the Australian landscape, a sensitivity he ascribes to the experience of growing up in a country village. The generally flat, unchanging landscape of continental Australia, he believes, is related to the flatness of Australian speech, whether Aboriginal languages or English spoken with an Australian accent. This flatness enters into Australian music as well. "Aboriginal music is flat and dronelike," he explained to an American critic in 1983. "We [Anglo-Saxons] likewise flattened out any interesting leaps in the folk music we imported" (**B737**).

As the "Works" catalog shows, Sculthorpe's music reflects several Australian traditions. He uses Aboriginal words as titles (**Irkanda** means "a remote and lonely place"). He uses Aboriginal myths (as in **The Loneliness of Bunjil** and **How the Stars Were Made**) and Aboriginal texts (**The Song of Tailitnama, Rites of Passage**). He names his pieces after ancient sacred sites (**Nourlangie**). He crafts his music from Aboriginal melodic shapes (**Djilile**), rhythmic patterns (**String Quartet No. 9**), and instrumental sounds such as didjeridu and rhythm sticks (**The Fifth Continent, Jabiru Dreaming**). He finds inspiration in the musics of Australia's Asian neighbors, particularly the traditional music of Indonesia (**Tabuh Tabuhan**) and Japan (**Mangrove**). He makes reference to the music of the English colonials in Australia (**Port Essington**) and to the European art music tradition, including Chopin, Rachmaninov (**Piano Concerto**) and Mahler (**Lament for Strings**). There are musical references to Anglican and other Christian missionaries (**Songs of Sea and Sky**), to the Roman Catholic Mass (**Requiem** for solo 'cello), and to Spanish and Portuguese explorers (**Quiros**). Sculthorpe's music also reflects other sounds of Australia, especially flocks of birds and insects; his scores direct string players to produce these sounds with very high glissandi or by rubbing the wood of the instrument. He also uses the sounds of blowflies and wind—sounds that he notes are also in Aboriginal music. "In other places, there is either wind or no wind. In Australia, there is always a wind, and its character changes continually" (**B911**).

He has adapted many twentieth-century European avant-garde techniques to his own language, including **Musique Concrète** (**W71**), sound mass and tone-clusters (**Sun Music I**), tone rows and other kinds of serialism (**Music for Japan**), rock-classical fusion (**Love 200**), collage (**Love 201**), aleatory performance (**Dream**), and live-tape combination (**Landscape**). Modern vocal techniques—glissandi, chanting, whispering, percussive sounds—are used, particularly in works of the sixties and seventies (**Night Piece, Rites of Passage**). Much of the piano music, especially in works of the seventies, involves playing on the strings with fingers, plectra, and mallets, drumming on the crossbars, and preparing the strings with hardware and amplification (**Koto Music I, II**). The violinist in **Alone** is called on to whistle or hum while playing, and the flautist in **Eliza Fraser Sings** also sings while playing.

He also invents some techniques of his own. An effect that he calls *fuori passo* requires instrumentalists playing the same melody to change pitches at slightly different times, resulting in a hauntingly reverberant quality (**Landscape II, Mangrove**). To produce an effect *come organo*, wind players are asked to sustain a chord imitating the precise attacks and cut-offs and even sound of the pipe organ (**Quiros, Nangaloar**). For percussion, subtle gong effects are a Sculthorpe trademark, as well as less subtle congas and bongos; the sound of crotales strung together and shaken is among his innovations. Players are his main source of ideas for new sounds and effects, and several of his notations—including symbols for birdsong and insect noises—have not yet found their way into the northern hemisphere's reference books of new devices. Critics and colleagues often remark on his "enquiring and open mind" (**B402**) and his "tireless investigation of new timbres, rhythms, and forms" (**B628**).

From these and other sources, Sculthorpe has created a musical language that is individual and immediately reconizable, made up of his own distinctive melodies, rhythmic patterns, textures, and tone colors. As more than one critic has noted, his style is almost impossible to categorize. It is romantic in its emotional content, classical in its formal clarity, avant-garde in its sound materials, exotic in its references, and postmodern in its accessibility. He is an artist all of whose work springs from a consistent artistic vision—an *inner* landscape—that he has known since his earliest years. While he almost always reports feeling excitement over a work in progress, and great satisfaction in whatever work he has just completed—he is essentially a happy person— he has yet to feel that he has expressed all that he is, that he has shared his vision in its entirety.

He describes himself as a melodist, and as a tonal composer. "I like writing tunes" (**B1021**). In melodic and non-melodic passages alike, one tonal center remains for a long time before moving to another, a feature that Sculthorpe explains as the musical representation of Australia's vast and somewhat static landscape. "This country we Australians live in has an austere simplicity, and our music should be long and flat, to match it," he said in 1968. "This is a quality that Japanese music has, and that the European avant-garde with its leaps and jumps, hasn't " (**B273**). His harmonies are likewise somewhat static

Kakadu. Copyright © 1992 by Faber Music, Ltd., London. Reproduced by permission of the publishers. Horns in F. Trumpets in C. *Key* [birdsong]—*Vln. I*, rapid continuous quarter-tone vibrato; *Vln. II*, rapid continuous glissando played on upper half of string indicated; *Vla.*, rapid upward glissando from any very high note; *Vc.*, *seagull sound, produced by making glissandi without changing hand position.

or non-directional and sparse. Chord voicings typically convey a feeling of openness and vastness. Rhythms are clear and coherent, usually occurring in repeated patterns with subtle variations and interpolations. Listeners often describe quick passages as "ritualistic" and slow passages as "meditative, lamenting, incantatory" (B976).

His music contains little of the *development* which has been an important concept in the European tradition, especially the Germanic academic tradition from romantic and post-romantic to avant-garde. Instead, a Sculthorpe work typically dwells upon one idea, then withdraws from this idea and goes on to something else. "Quite early on I found, say, the development sections in Beethoven symphonies rather corny," he explained to the Sydney writer and recording executive Belinda Webster in 1989. "The greatest music doesn't develop at all—Victoria, Palestrina, Monteverdi, Bach, *gagaku*, Balinese music" (B964). Dynamics, rhythms, and tone colors shape his music within tightly-controlled formal outlines for a sophisticated and disciplined musical architecture. His larger forms typically alternate sections or movements based on contrasting ideas. He terms this the *duality* of his work, or "two things playing against each other, rubbing against each other" (B800)—Australian and European styles (**Kakadu**), Australian and Asian (**Sonata for Viola and Percussion**), old and new (**String Quartet No. 10**), objective and subjective (**Requiem**). This duality, he notes, is in keeping with his "schizophrenic" situation as a European Australian with "one foot in Australia and one back in Europe, or one foot in Australia and one in Asia."

Sculthorpe's music is typically playable by reasonable forces, a feature that he sometimes attributes to Australian pragmatism. He writes for particular players. "I like to write for human beings," he says (**B722**). "I can't write a work unless I know the performer, the instrument, and the player's strong and weak points." Further, "a performance failing, with wrong notes, wrong tempi, is interesting to me. I learn about the work" (B1071). "I write with love for each particular person; or I am thinking of my friends in a particular orchestra" (B964). **Sun Music II**, critics noted in 1969, showed off the newly-improved percussion section in the Sydney Symphony Orchestra; the 'cello solo in **Love 200** (1970) was for a 'cellist who was playing her final concert with the same orchestra. Performers often request new arrangements of favorite works (**Irkanda IV, Songs of Sea and Sky**). He has occasionally written for a particular publishing project (he wrote **Saibai** for a new hymn book, for instance), but most often he writes for particular performers and performance circumstances.

His music is almost always programmatic, and it is often dramatic. "I love the theatre," he says (**B282**). He has written film scores and incidental music for dramatic productions at every stage of his career. In the fifties, when he was fresh from university, writing incidental music and revues helped develop his melodic gifts while providing the experience and discipline of writing for particular performers, directors, and situations. Larger, more serious theatrical works like **Rites of Passage** (1972-73) and the opera **Quiros** (1982) embody significant aspects of his own vision of Australia.

Sculthorpe is a composer who revises almost constantly, owing partly to the frequent performances of his music. The **W** and **P** listings demonstrate what Prudence Neidorf, the distinguished music librarian of the National Library of Australia (who has been dealing with his work for years), calls the "evolving" nature of the Sculthorpe canon. Several of the *official* first performances are preceded by earlier performances; revision has typically followed each hearing. He may make slight revisions in the published manuscript (Faberprint) score before the final printed version. All versions must be considered "authentic" representations of his wishes, but at different times. He withdraws the occasional work, but seldom for good—**Callabonna** (1989), for instance, reinstates a movement of the earlier **Sonata for Piano** (1963). In some cases he withdraws a work because he has revised it to the point that it is replaced by, or absorbed into, a new work (**Irkanda II** into **Irkanda IV**). He also revises his system of naming works. A work may be performed under different names (**Ketjak**, now **Sun Music II**), and different works may have the same name—**Sun Song** and **Sun Music** are favorite names because of his abiding concern with the Australian sun.

Of his characteristic, recurring sounds, the melodies are perhaps the most readily identifiable. The Japanese-derived melody in **Landscape II** (1978) reappears in the **Piano Concerto** (1983). The Aboriginal-derived melody of **The Song of Tailitnama** (1974) reappears in the several instrumental versions of **Tailitnama Song** and in the orchestral work **Earth Cry** (1986). The melody called **Djilile** reappears frequently, most recently in **Dream Tracks** and **Tropic** (both 1992). In 1972, the Australian musician, writer, and arts administrator James Murdoch in his chapter on Sculthorpe in *Australia's Contemporary Composers* (**B432**), noted that "a chart of the cross fertilization within his works looks like a maze"; in a humorously irreverent metaphor, Murdoch likened the "new contexts" Sculthorpe discovers for "the cells of his musical sources" to "the infinite varieties of sensation that can be obtained from worrying a nerve in a tooth." In 1990, the Sydney critic and historian Roger Covell, an outspoken champion of Sculthorpe's work since the sixties, suggested that "somebody is going to have a lot of fun piecing together the interrelationships of Sculthorpe's pieces and making a kind of family tree of them" (**B1030**). Sculthorpe makes no secret of these interrelationships.

Sculthorpe has devoted much attention to the underlying philosophy or cultural "meaning" of his Australian music. "I trace the history of the human race in terms of its art, not its wars" (**B547**). The classical composer voices the "feelings and aspirations of society," he observes. "Many people have always aspired, and will always aspire, to make great art. The aspirations are more than enough to keep one going. I aspire to make great art" (**B900**). His concern with the spiritual basis of his music surfaces in published interviews even though it is rarely the main topic. He considers himself to be a religious composer, using the word *religion* in the broad sense to mean a deeper meaning, a spiritual significance, beyond the notes themselves. In an essay from the late sixties on the American composer Charles Ives (1874-1954), he quotes Ives on the deeper meaning of a national consciousness in music: "If local color, national color, any color is a true pigment of the universal color, it is a divine quality. And it is part of substance in art, not of manner" (**B266**). Sculthorpe believes that "all the greatest art is founded on faith of some kind" (**B979**). For him, the sacred is in natural forces. **Rites of Passage** "is a religious work, a statement of my belief in the divine, the sacred in nature" (B469); music and ritual celebrate "the love that orders and unites the universe."

SCULTHORPE'S AUSTRALIA

Sculthorpe feels that he, like other Australian artists, has had to make his own way in creating the intellectual framework of his art. As he noted in 1975 (B516), "because we have produced so few serious writers on our music and the society from which it stems, the composer here is forced to create his own view of himself as a composer and as an Australian." In program notes and interviews, he cites the books, paintings, artefacts, architecture, and ideas which seem to him to point to the essence of the country. He composes surrounded by books (B861). Critics have reported, with some surprise, that he adopted Japanese musical and philosophical concepts before visiting Japan in 1968 (B268, B273), and used Indonesian textures and melodic shapes before visiting Indonesia in 1974 (B457). He named a work **Teotihuacan** without visiting Mexico. He wrote **Kakadu** the year before he first visited Kakadu National Park, the area of northern Australia after which the work is named. "I have lots of books and photographs," he explains. "The rest is in my imagination" (B972).

Henry Tate's *Australian Musical Possibilities* (1924), encountered early in his career, suggested birdsong as an authentic Australian sound (notes to **W62**). English author D. H. Lawrence's poems and his Australian novel *Kangaroo* provided the texts for **Sun** (1958) and **The Fifth Continent** (1963) and led Sculthorpe to develop his own ideas about "the Mexican sun, the Japanese, Asian and Australian—and my own sun" (**W94**). He usually names Joseph Conrad as a favorite author—a source of musical ideas in some unexplainable way—and *Lord Jim* as his favorite book (B964). It "is a good adventure story and, beneath the surface, a penetrating examination of the human condition. Persistent themes in Conrad, such as primeval terror of wilderness, anguish of alienation and hazards of colonization are also themes of my music" (B1127).

His program notes refer to the Australian painters Russell Drysdale (1912-1981) and Sidney Nolan (1917-1992). "I'm rarely inspired by a painting but when I'm working I often think of a painting" (B964). His program notes for **String Quartet No. 7 (W99)** refer to Drysdale's depiction of the "sun-drenched and drought-ridden land." The title **Callabonna (W197)** is the name of an outback lake depicted by Drysdale in a painting which he gave to Sculthorpe in appreciation for **String Quartet No. 6** (which Sculthorpe had dedicated to the memory of Drysdale's first wife). In his note for **Lament for Strings (W135)** the composer refers to a "melancholic convention" in Australian painting and literature, corresponding to the sense of loss and loneliness experienced by European-Australians confronted with the vast deserts of the continent, the harsh and unforgiving landscape. "The persistent theme of my music has been the lonely figure in the landscape," he wrote in 1979 (**W132**). His attraction to Nolan's depictions of Mrs. Fraser and the convict Bracefell are related to his writing of both the theatre piece **Eliza Fraser Sings** (1978), which focuses on the historical events, and the orchestral work **Mangrove** (1979), which refers to his feelings about Nolan's mangrove images and to the life-force of the "man-woman" meaning that he ascribes to the word mangrove.

Sculthorpe's exploration of Aboriginal songs and chants introduces the almost timeless spirituality of music that "has grown from, is a part of, our landscape" (**B623**). Aboriginal culture is thought to be at least 40,000 years old, the oldest culture on earth. Sculthorpe cites as his particular sources the recordings, transcriptions, and translations of A. P. Elkin, T. G. H. Strehlow, and others. In writing the score for the film **Manganinnie** (1980), Sculthorpe's source was the Aboriginal actress playing the title role, and her singing of a traditional *lament*. He cites as precedent the use of Aboriginal material by Isaac Nathan (1790-1864), one of the first well-known composers to live in Australia; in 1991, Sculthorpe made an arrangement of Nathan's **Kooee**. (The "coo-ee" is an Aboriginal call or cry.) In his program notes for **Dream Tracks** (1992), Sculthorpe uses the words of Strehlow's recent interpreter, Bruce Chatwin, the English writer whose book *The Songlines* (1987) has been a bestseller. The Aboriginal chants are *songlines* or *dreaming tracks* that form "the labyrinth of invisible pathways that are created by the totemic ancestors of all species as they sing the world into existence." Australian writers occasionally compare Sculthorpe's Aboriginal borrowings to "jindyworobakism" (meaning annexing or joining), referring to the Jindyworobak movement in Australian literature in the late thirties and forties whose writers sought a closer identification with the continent.

Sculthorpe uses outside sources not as decoration or local color but to uncover or reveal aspects of his own vision. "I'm a melodist, so I've looked to Asia for melodic ideas," he said in 1968 (**B273**). He cites precedent in Percy Grainger's advice to "look to the north," to the islands of Indonesia. (Most other Australians, it should be noted, still refer to Asia in the European manner, as "the east" or "the orient"—as Americans do, even though Asia could be considered to be west of the Americas.) Sculthorpe has frequently described the three stages in his use of Balinese music, as in a 1979 interview (**B623**): first, imitation of actual *gamelan* sounds (**Tabuh Tabuhan**); next, the use of Balinese compositional techniques in pieces that do not sound Balinese (**String Quartet No. 8**); and finally, "I approach the heart or essence of Balinese music, and that remains today." He uses Japanese music in a similar way. "The glissandi in **Sun Music I** derive from Buddhist chant and *Noh*; **Koto Music I and II** derive from music associated with the koto but don't sound particularly Japanese. I'm especially interested in the Japanese mind and am influenced by Japanese concepts." In Aboriginal music, too, he responds to, and appropriates into his own language, what is essential to his own art. For **Kakadu**, "I took an Aboriginal melody and for some months hummed it over and sang it to myself, and eventually it became something else entirely, my sort of melody" (**B964**).

THE PHASES OF SCULTHORPE'S WORK

While Sculthorpe's work exhibits a consistent artistic and cultural vision, it is also evident that his views have developed in changing circumstances and through the influence of critics, colleagues, friends, and family.

Early years to 1950. Sculthorpe has always described his childhood in Tasmania as happy, busy, and somewhat lonely. His parents ran a general store, becoming highly successful. He and his brother, provided with few distractions and little entertainment, invented their own activities and projects. As he recalled later, "of course I was happy to wander around in the bush and to have my canoe in the river," but, when he was eight years old, "it was decided that I must take piano lessons" (**B290**). As often happens with the musically gifted, he found composing his own music more interesting than learning to play other people's. His creative efforts so annoyed his first teacher that she rapped him across the knuckles with a feather-duster. His mother found other piano teachers for him and supported his composing. He presented another teacher with a piece "without melody, harmony, or rhythm," expressing his fear that the world might run out of tunes. "Does God ever run out of faces?" she asked—a thought that he continues to find quite reassuring. At age ten, he composed a "Chinese opera" (referred to in **B1**), inspired by his hearing of Chinese music. He later recalled that "once a week, when I was very young, my father took me to a Chinese market garden, and there a small open-air concert would be mounted for our benefit" (**B804**); he liked the "twanging, whining, extraordinary sounds" (**B994**). From an early age, he recalls, he was interested in Asia in general, and in things visual; through relatives he began to acquire books about Japan, and he began to collect Japanese Buddha figures.

In Tasmania in the thirties and forties, he felt quite isolated from the larger world of music. He knew no composers, and recalls that it was considered rather "un-Australian" to be a composer (**B718**). Yet, as he wrote in 1988 for a young people's encyclopedia (**B872**), "before I reached my teens, I decided that I was going to be a composer. The grown-ups said that all composers were dead, and so I decided I'd be the first living composer. It was comforting to discover later that the grown-ups were wrong." He has recalled overhearing a conversation in which "Dad said to Mum, 'Why is he always inside writing music; why isn't he outside with the other boys?' And Mum replied, 'There are thousands of boys out there playing football, and only one in here writing music. We should be grateful' " (**B597**). Urged by his father to excel in athletics, and also demonstrating a penchant for the solitary work that composing entails, Sculthorpe chose individual rather than team sports and became a state champion in swimming—much to his father's delight. His creative energy and his competitive spirit, encouraged by his parents, proved invaluable as he continued to win prizes, competitions, and recognition in music.

He began at an early age to search for his own musical language, as Michael Hannan has shown in his 1982 book *Peter Sculthorpe: His music and ideas 1929-1979* (**B702**). His early works are, understandably, songs and piano pieces, and there was another dramatic work, "Fleur de Valle" (quoted in **B979**). As a teenager, he acquired a copy of Ernst Krenek's *Studies in Counterpoint* (New York, 1940), a study of Schoenberg's twelve-tone serial technique, and tried writing some serial music—without having heard any. His knowledge of music, especially the late romantics, increased through his favorite radio program, the Sunday evening "Enjoyment of Music," presented by the famed English expert on music (and cricket), Neville Cardus, who spent the years 1941 to 1947 in Sydney.

In 1942 he was awarded the Magistrate's Scholarship to Launceston Church Grammar School (*see* Appendix II), where he was an exemplary student. The senior-school masters were impressed with his literary interests, pursued with his mother's guidance—English literature and poetry, French symbolist poetry, some philosophy. One of the masters, Wilfred Teniswood (d. 1983), heard him playing the piano and organized his first concert on ABC radio. The first bibliography entry (**B1**) is a broadcast announcement in the national radio guide, *ABC Weekly*, in 1945; "his favourite composers are Chopin and Debussy," the announcement noted, but besides his classical tastes "he obligingly plays boogie-woogie for his schoolmates at Launceston Church Grammar School, and enjoys playing swing music."

The earliest work in his catalog is the 1945 **Nocturne, W1** (the **W** numbers are chronological); he performed it often in the forties and fifties and it was revived in 1982 in a recital at the Sydney Opera House. In **Elegy for a Clown** (**W18**)—Hannan quotes this song in full—and **Two Reveries** (**W31**), Sculthorpe set his own poetry; in other songs he set poetry of Shakespeare, Thomas Campion, Joyce, Sitwell, and other Europeans. He was able to play some of his compositions for J. A. Steele of the Melbourne Conservatorium, who visited Tasmania to examine piano students for the Australian Music Examinations Board (AMEB).

He played recitals at every opportunity, usually programming some of his own pieces and works by established Australian composers such as Frank Hutchens and Alfred Hill, as shown in the first performance listings (**P45, P46**). He won piano competitions, he later recalled, "only through sheer love and wanting to get through to the world" (**B279**). In the rural community people took notice of his talent. His mother reported his musical activities to a friend at the Launceston *Examiner* and the newspaper kept its readers informed. The *Examiner* has continued to this day to report on the achievements of one of Launceston's favorite sons (**B455, B1101, B1157**).

In 1945, when he was sixteen, the results of his AMEB examination gained him a scholarship to the University of Melbourne. He became a full-time student the next year, completed his studies in 1950, and was awarded the B. Mus. at commencement ceremonies in 1951. He studied composition with Steele, counterpoint with A. E. H. Nickson, and piano with Raymond Lambert. He continued to play piano recitals, often programming the same work under different names—**Sketch**, **Scherzo**, and **Prelude**, for example, were used for **W3, W4, W7**, and other works. He won several prizes for his music, including the J. A. Steele Composition Prize for the **Chamber Suite** in 1946. The *Examiner* reported that conductor Sir Bernard Heinze, Ormond Professor of Music and director of the Conservatorium, said, "I was struck by the promise and unusual talent exhibited in the work" (**B2**). In 1948, Sculthorpe was runner-up in the Victorian School Music Association's song writing competition, "placing equally" with established composers (**B5**). Indeed, his early works exhibit an originality and intensity beyond his years.

In a 1980 interview Sculthorpe named as early musical influences Delius,

Vaughan Williams, and the English pastoral composers, "because much of their music is quite appropriate to the Tasmania landscape." In Melbourne "I became acquainted with a different landscape; Bartók and other European composers, including Bloch, who was a very popular composer," became an influence. "I equated Bloch's biblical wilderness with the Australian wilderness and loneliness. When I left home and went to Melbourne and began to discover something of the ways of the world, I was drawn to the psychodrama of the music of Mahler" (B646). He continued to adopt, and transform, bits of musical technique, including Debussy's parallelism, Mahler's way of writing harmony that is slightly out-of-step with its melody ("my music does that all the time"), and Copland's spacious-sounding chords (B979).

As part of a bohemian circle gathering at the home of composer Felix Werder and his wife Minna, he heard music of the Melbourne composers and of Europeans such as Bartók and Schoenberg. At the same time, like most young composers, he resisted what seemed like domination by others. He found inspiration not only in Varèse's writing for percussion but also in his independence of mind in the face of prevailing European ideas. He found himself drawn to the landscape of mainland Australia as depicted in Steele's collection of Australian paintings, a landscape of desert and harsh bushland quite unlike Tasmania. He heard his first Japanese music and other non-Western works recorded on the multi-volume *History of Music in Sound* that accompanies the *Oxford History of Music*. (He continued to be disturbed that there was no mention of Australian Aboriginal music in this series.) He recalls being affected by a recording of an arrangement of *Etenraku*, a work from the Japanese *gagaku* repertoire, performed by the Philadelphia Orchestra. He was attracted to what seemed to be a serenity in Japanese art; for awhile, through the sixties, he considered himself to be a Zen Buddhist.

He wrote music for fellow-students to perform, including pianists Max Olding (from Launceston) and Harriet Nemenoff, bassoonist and composer George Dreyfus, and violinist Wilfred Lehmann. (Today he continues to advise his composition students to "adopt a performer" as he "adopted" his fellow-students.) He took lessons on the double bass and played in a string orchestra at the Conservatorium led by Henri Touzeau, which played his **Elegy** (W29), **To Meadows** (P49-5), and other works; he developed a lasting fondness for writing for string orchestra. The *Examiner* reported from time to time that Mr. and Mrs. J. T. Sculthorpe, or Mrs. Sculthorpe alone, had gone to Melbourne to hear a concert of son Peter's music. From the first, Melbourne critics noted his originality and his interest in melody and uncluttered textures. In 1948, a critic described his songs as depending on the "vocal line for the expression of his meaning," seldom aided by the accompaniment (B4). In 1949, Melbourne critic and composer Linda Phillips, reviewing a performance of **String Quartet No. 3**, evidently became the first to note, in print, that his music "lacked thematic development" (B8). In 1950 the Launceston *Examiner* reported that **String Quartet No. 4** had been favorably received in Melbourne (B9). Phillips found that it was "rather thin in texture but showed promise and some original ideas" (B10). As indicated by his description of the quartet, "Recollections of holidays spent in a country village in Tasmania," Sculthorpe had discovered in Melbourne his identity as a Tasmanian composer.

Launceston, 1950-1958. After university, Sculthorpe returned to Launceston. He went into partnership with his brother Roger in the Outdoor Sports Supplies shop, a "huntin', fishin' and shootin' store," he has called it (**B290**). Photographs in the local press showed him helping customers choose fishing rods for fishing season and hunting rifles for hunting season. The experience may have increased his sensitivity to business considerations in music as well as to community sensibilities—useful attributes for an artist. Earlier, he had earned some income teaching music at the Hagley Area School (grammar school) and as a lecturer for the Council for Adult Education. He investigated Aboriginal music, listening to the few recordings available in the Tasmanian Museum in Hobart, and he collected Australian artefacts. In Melbourne, Bernard Heinze continued to be an important contact, a mentor. "Sir Bernard introduced me to the music of Webern, to Indonesian music and to musique concrète," Sculthorpe wrote in 1982, on Heinze's death (**B718**).

He became active with the local theatre group, the Launceston Players, writing incidental music for about one production a year and playing the piano—giving expression to his love of theatre and his search for opportunities to "get through to the world." The group's mimeographed newsletter, *News-'n-Views*, welcomed him as a new member in August 1951, commenting that his music for **Much Ado About Nothing** "is more than incidental music; it links the varying scenes and moods throughout." Enthusiastic reports continue about his musical efforts and his friendliness. For Molière's **The Miser** in 1952, he used drawing-pins (thumbtacks) to make the piano sound like the harpsichord appropriate for the seventeenth century. For **Life with Father** in 1954, he wrote tonal music fitting for the 1880 setting. The program for *Waters of the Moon* in November of 1955 thanks "R. and P. Sculthorpe" for supplying sporting equipment. Sculthorpe remembers these years as a happy time, largely because of his association with people who "really cared about" the theatre.

He became active in the Launceston Subscriber's Association (LSA) Committee, which organized receptions for the ABC's touring arists from overseas—Victoria de los Angeles, Paul Badura-Skoda, Isaac Stern, and others. The chance to talk to such people at length in the informal setting of an after-concert party helped him to overcome the musical isolation of Launceston. Yet he seemed a long way from being a composer. He later recalled, in an interview on the occasion of his fiftieth birthday (**B597**), that on his twenty-fifth birthday (April 1954) he sat on his parents' bed and "bawled my eyes out. I can remember saying, 'I'm a quarter of a century old and I have done nothing.' " It was decided that he would work only part-time at the store and spend most of his time on music. From this time on, he made substantial progress. His brother Roger's success as a businessman has been legendary as well.

The **Sonatina** for piano (**W59**), which has entered the repertoire of virtually every Australian pianist and many non-Australians as well, dates from this year, 1954. He regards it as "the first of my [non-theatrical or "serious"] works that seems to be not a bad piece" (**B290**). Though its subtitle refers to Aboriginal legend, it does not draw on Aboriginal musical materials. The string trio **The Loneliness of Bunjil**, also from 1954, refers to Aboriginal legend in its title. In later years Sculthorpe viewed this period as one of aggressive Australianism, or "banging the kerosene tin" (B290)—a period of jindyworobakism—though, as he told a journalist in 1965, even then he was using "the sieve of my mind to make all impulses entirely mine" (B103). He submitted the Sonatina to the ABC in 1954, and again in 1956, but it was turned down as "far too modern to be programmed" (B290). In 1954 he submitted it to the ISCM Festival jury in Melbourne; it was accepted and was performed in Baden-Baden in June 1955. Pianist Maria Bergmann reported to Sculthorpe a favorable audience response. (Sculthorpe, already an accomplished publicist, told an Australian critic that Stravinsky had asked for a copy; he says now that he made up the story.) The one review that mentions the work, that of H. H. Stuckenschmidt in *Musical America* (B16), called it "naive" and "folkloric" in relation to the prevailing dissonant, complex music of the European avant-garde. (Boulez's *Le marteau sans maître* in first performance, which required something like fifty rehearsals, was probably the most-discussed work at that festival.)

In an autobiographical essay in the late sixties (B290), he defined seven stylistic features of the Sonatina that are, "on the whole, still characteristic of the music that I write today": (1) the opening chord, the sound of two major sevenths separated by a major third; (2) symmetrical bar-patterns; (3) repetition of rhythmic and melodic patterns (in accordance with the world's increasing industrial repetitiveness); (4) symmetrical melodic patterns; (5) exploitation of a specific instrumental colour (here, the piano's percussive quality); (6) characteristic intervals of the falling minor second and falling minor third; and (7) the work's programme (Australians are a *visual* people, he believes, and find programmatic music more suitable than abstract music). Indeed, by the seventies Sculthorpe's composition students were calling the opening chord (item no. 1) the "Woollahra chord," referring to the Sydney suburb in which he lives. The Australian pianist and composer Miriam Hyde, when introducing her performances of the work (as in P92-8), calls this the "Sculthorpe chord."

In 1954 and 1955 he wrote two more works for Wilfred Lehmann: Sonata for Violin Alone and Irkanda for solo violin (now called Irkanda I, the first of four Irkanda pieces). Hannan's discussion of the Sonata in 1978 (B566), illustrated with excerpts from the score, indicates the work's importance to Sculthorpe's creation of his musical language—Hannan calls attention to its texture of melody with rhythmic, tonally-based, open-string pizzicato accompaniment. Sculthorpe's fondness for the material is indicated by his return to it in the Sonata for Viola and Percussion (1960) and, even later, in String Quartet No. 6 (1964-65). Lehmann performed the Sonata for Violin Alone in Melbourne in March 1955 to mixed reviews which perhaps reflected conservative Melbourne tastes. Composer and critic Dorian Le Gallienne in the *Age* heard "many attractive and unexpected sounds"; it holds the listener's attention, he noted, "despite a certain monotony in the melodic lines (or rather their harmonic implications) and the frequent use of repeated figures" (B14). John Sinclair (like Sculthorpe, a Heinze protegé) found that it might want "less tricks and more substance" (B15).

While the Sonata for Violin Alone is no longer available, Irkanda I has remained in the violin repertoire and has been recorded twice in Australia for commercial release. In 1956, in a brief summary of Sculthorpe's career, *Canon: Australian Music Journal* reported that the composer considered **Irkanda** to be his finest work to date, and "truly Australian" (**B18**). The "irkanda" of the title—the "remote and lonely place"—refers in one sense to Australia. "The melody follows a 360-degree contour of the hills around Canberra, where most of the work was written," Sculthorpe wrote (**W62**). The word "irkanda" may also describe the heart and mind of the composer searching for a way to "get through to the world." Wilfred Lehmann played the work in Lisbon in 1956 and in Moscow in 1958; the *Examiner* reported on the success of these overseas performances (**B17, B24, B25**).

Sculthorpe returned to writing music for theatre. The director of the Launceston Players, Anne Godfrey-Smith, moved to the Canberra Repertory Theatre, and Sculthorpe wrote music for her first production, **Twelfth Night** (**B19**). He then worked in Canberra as composer and pianist for a new show, **Ulterior Motifs**, a political satire which follows the repercussions of a missing red (therefore suspected to be communist) shower-room curtain from a student hostel. The show was a hit in the nation's capital where audiences that included many federal officials and bureaucrats could appreciate the humor. In 1992, Anne Edgeworth (formerly Godfrey-Smith), in her history of the Canberra Repertory Society (**B1140**), recalled that Sculthorpe "turned out some catchy tunes." (The Society recently revived one of these, **P92-3**). She also reported that the famed English counter-tenor Alfred Deller later proclaimed Sculthorpe's **Twelfth Night** settings to be "the best he had come across" and performed them several times.

After Canberra, in 1957, Sculthorpe lived in Sydney for a time and wrote incidental music for two ABC radio plays by Launceston playwright Catherine Duncan, **Sons of the Morning** and **Don't Listen Ladies**. He also wrote several songs for a long-running revue **Cross Section**. In his number *Manic Espresso*, satirizing the cult of the coffee bar, the ensemble "brings the house down," reported Sydney's venerable weekly newsmagazine *The Bulletin* (**B23**). Back in Launceston, a production of *Dear Charles* (**P58-6**) used his music. Bernard Heinze wrote glowingly of his promise as a composer in *Vogue Australia* (**B21**)—the first of many articles about him in popular national magazines. The *Examiner* relayed to its Launceston readers Heinze's assessment of Sculthorpe as one of the most important stars on the musical horizon.

Oxford, 1958-1960. In 1958, still anxious for wider knowledge and experience, he applied for and won the first Lizette Bentwich scholarship awarded by the University of Melbourne, for study at any recognized institution. He decided to pursue studies towards the D. Phil. at Oxford, the "fount of wisdom" in the mind of a university-trained Australian, and something his father would, understandably, respect (**B702**). Before he sailed in August, friends and family in Launceston hosted numerous farewell parties, the local press reported (**B27**). He remained in England for over two years, returning to Tasmania in late 1960.

A member of Wadham College, he studied composition at first with Edmund Rubbra (1901-1986), a composer deeply interested in Asian music and philosophy, and a leading exponent of thematic development. Sculthorpe wrote **Prophecy** (now withdrawn) under Rubbra. He next studied with Egon Wellesz (1885-1974), the Schoenberg pupil and Byzantine music scholar. Sculthorpe in his late twenties, however, was even less amenable to strong guidance than he had been as an undergraduate in Melbourne. His view that "you can't teach composition" clearly originates from his experience as a student. Eventually he developed a close friendship with Rubbra, who led him to a deeper understanding of his identity as a composer, mainly, Sculthorpe believes, because Rubbra listened to him. Composing, for Sculthorpe, involves "unlocking the human being"; the music is only the outward sign of a statement of self (**B994**). Much of his own extraordinary success as a composition teacher has from all reports been his ability to lead his own students to discover who they are. To learn to compose, he believes, "you need a willing ear and somebody who really cares for you."

Just as he discovered his identity as a Tasmanian composer while a student in Melbourne, in England he discovered his identity as an Australian composer. He heard much new European music, and found not much of it to be appropriate to his vision of Australia. Though he had been writing Australian music, including the "truly Australian" **Irkanda I**, it was at Oxford that, as he later told the Launceston musician and writer Max Oldaker (**B47**), he could "rationalize the chief source of his stimulus, that is, Australia."

Perhaps the most important and lasting influence of England on Sculthorpe's thinking has been his friendship with the English composer and scholar Wilfrid Mellers (b. 1912), a specialist on the relation between music and the society from which it arises; Sculthorpe has called him the greatest living writer on music. In many writings, such as the book *Caliban Reborn* (1967), Mellers explains his theory that twentieth-century western European music has found much-needed spiritual renewal through a revival of melodic and rhythmic elements—music's "universal" elements—that were lost or discarded in Europe's post-Renaissance "heroic" period, as the element of harmony became of prime importance; an emphasis on harmony reflected a concern with "consciousness and the will" which led to "spiritual impoverishment." Mellers's view of the European tradition in the context of world music and ideas helped reveal to Sculthorpe the intellectual meaning and validity of his own musical path—his refusal to embrace European systems, his vision of an authentic Australian music, and his search for spiritual meaning in ancient musical and cultural sources.

To describe Sculthorpe's non-developing style and his way of building a melody, a phrase, and an entire work by combining separate building-blocks of sound, Mellers coined the phrase "growth by accretion"—a phrase that recurs repeatedly, especially in program notes for works of the sixties. Mellers suggested that Sculthorpe explore his ideas of the Australian sun, and Sculthorpe wrote the song cycle **Sun** (1958), which Mellers and his wife Pauline (Peggy) Lewis premiered (**W74**). "I have no desire any more towards woman or man, bird, beast or creature or thing," the last song begins; Lawrence's expression of "a state of no-desire, and desolation and loneliness before the sombre face of the Pacific Ocean" (as the composer describes the poem in his notes for **W91**) found response in Sculthorpe's philosophy.

During his time in England, Sculthorpe's incidental music for the

Launceston production of **The Miser** was used for a production in the original French (**P59-2**). He won first prize in the Royal Concert Trust Fund competition for **Irkanda II (String Quartet No. 5)** in 1959, and in 1960 another first prize for the **Sonata for Viola and Percussion**. The *Examiner* and the *Australian Musical News* reported the news back home (**B28, B32**). Reviews of **Irkanda II** in Oxford and in the English periodical *Music and Musicians*, mention an "austerity of expression," "sharp rhythmic contrasts," "vitality," and a slight weakness of "structural discipline" (**B29-31**).

In 1960, Mellers invited him to be resident composer and guest lecturer at Attingham Park summer school of music in Shropshire (**B32, B49**), where, in July, **Sun** was performed again and the **Sonata for Viola and Percussion** was premiered; the composer (reluctantly) played percussion because the percussionist's train was delayed. The **Sonata** has become a favorite work, especially of percussionists, with frequent performances in Australia and throughout the world. In October 1960, he provided *musique concrète* for a nontraditional production of **King Lear** in Oxford (**B34**). He presented a lecture-recital on his music to the Contemporary Music Club in June 1959 (**B28**), and in 1960 wrote a report for the *Oxford Magazine* about the presentation to the club by the noted English serial composer Elizabeth Lutyens (**B35**).

Launceston, 1960-1963. Although Sculthorpe had not expected to return to Tasmania before completing his studies, late in 1960 he was suddenly called home because his father was dying of cancer. The return trip was by plane— "BOAC comet"—and he was interviewed on arrival in Sydney in November (**B36**). At this point, busy with requests from performers overseas, he questioned whether there were sufficient opportunities for a composer in Australia. Returning from the Old World, he had a better understanding of why a distinctly Australian music was slower to develop than Australian painting and literature. As he noted some twenty years later (**B691**), "While the painter and the writer need an audience, just as much as the composer, a painting, a novel, a poem can all exist complete in themselves. A piece of music needs a performer, and most of the strongest musical statements need many performers and sympathetic performers." Composers "struggling to be heard" need an audience, and in fact "a whole part of society" oriented to their needs.

Back home in Launceston, he finished the piano trio **Irkanda III** for performance in Birmingham (**B39**). Performances of two works written in Launceston six years earlier occurred in England after his return home—the premiere of **The Loneliness of Bunjil**, and **Irkanda I** in Birmingham, broadcast over the BBC. Birmingham critic J. F. Waterhouse found **Irkanda I** an "impressionistic" and "strikingly original" work that "holds together remarkably well as a musical structure " (**B38**). He reported that Sculthorpe had advised the performers of **Irkanda III** to read the classic descriptions of Australia's "bush-country and loose-clutching civilisation" in D. H. Lawrence's *Kangaroo*. He liked the work's "clear and organic formal design in its thematic recurrences," but disliked the "miscellany" of "special effects" (**B39**). The *Musical Times* reported that in Birmingham "a young Australian composer, Peter Sculthorpe, has shown solid achievement as well as promise" (**B41**).

From this point, his reputation at home grew steadily. The works of 1961 to 1963, **W80-W87**, include concert music, film music, and commercial music, as he continued the pattern of writing in a number of styles, for a number of audiences, in any given period. Although he had worked in Sydney for a time in the fifties, most of his contacts were still in Melbourne, then considered the "hub" of creative music in Australia (**B60**). His first work on his return from England was **Irkanda IV (W80)**, written in memory of his father. "I went quietly on dissonance because that's the way he would have liked it," the composer explained (**B43**). As always, he wrote with the performers in mind, in this case Melbourne's remarkable all-woman Astra Chamber Orchestra. This expressive, rhapsodic work was something they could really put across— and without fifty rehearsals.

Irkanda IV was the first of Sculthorpe's non-theatrical works to "bring the house down." He bounded down the aisle, he later recalled, and took a bow from the platform. "I thought at the time that that's what I wanted all my life" (**B547**). Felix Werder in the Melbourne *Age* found the work "truly Australian" with an "imaginative handling of ideas" that indicated the composer's "touch of genius" (**B45**). *Canon* reported **Irkanda IV** to be a "fine work" (**B42**), and in 1962 published a photo of Sculthorpe as a "leading Australian composer" (**B54**). *Music and Dance* called it "a first-rate piece, thoroughly contemporary" (**B50**). Overseas, the correspondent to *Music and Musicians* described **Irkanda IV** as a work of "fine lyrical intensity" by an "outstanding talent" (**B48**).

In response to materials sent by the composer by way of introduction, "C.M. Prerauer"—the influential husband-and-wife team of Curt and Maria Prerauer—in the fortnightly Sydney newsmagazine *Nation*, described **Irkanda IV** in nineteenth-century European aesthetic terms: "it produces the elation which overcomes one when one is face to face with a great work of art." It is contrapuntal, atonal, and contemporary, they wrote. "The national element must be fully digested for the composer to make an internationally valid musical statement. This is what Peter Sculthorpe has done in **Irkanda IV**" (**B58**). It remains one of his most popular works today; he arranged it for strings and percussion in 1964 and has lately returned to it, arranging it for flute and string trio (1990), string quartet (1991), and flute and string quartet (1992).

For the score of the children's film **They Found a Cave**, set in Tasmania, his first feature film, he used his short piano piece, **Left Bank Waltz** (1958). The recording of the *Theme and Journey's End* (**D72**) by the American harmonica virtuoso Larry Adler (on tour with the ABC in 1961) was the first commercial recording of Sculthorpe's music; the sheet music was his first published work. In late 1962, the Melbourne *Age* gave the film's "little tune" some publicity: "from the way Mr. Sculthorpe whistled it across our desk yesterday, we think it should have a good chance of getting high up on the hit parade" (**B55**).

To complete **The Fifth Continent**, Max Oldaker reported in 1963 (**B62**), the composer spent four months living on the west Tamar (northern Tasmania), his only visitor his mother, who came occasionally to check up on her son's diet. Some critics were disappointed in the work. "Pleiades" in the *Mercury* found that, though advertised as a symphony, it covers a vast quantity of material "but hardly develops what's available" (**B69**). C. M. Prerauer, preferring absolute music, registered disappointment that the work seemed to be a group of symphonic poems, "or rather, symphonic atmospheres. We are waiting for a really major work of Peter Sculthorpe, with large architectural dimensions" (B71). Though the work has had few performances since, the melodious third movement, Small Town, which refers to Lawrence's description of the coastal town of Thirroul, just south of Sydney, became a separate piece in 1976 (W136) and has remained a favorite of professional, amateur, and student orchestras.

Still anxious to develop receptive Australian audiences for new music, Sculthorpe appeared on television in Hobart (the Tasmanian capital) to explain music composition and his own work. At this time, arts coverage was mostly on daytime women's programs, sometimes evening. In March 1961, for his first television appearance in Tasmania, on "Telewives Time," he played the piano and talked about Oxford (B40). "Composer shows how he works" announced an evening television appearance in October 1961 (B49); he demonstrated the creation of a work—an arrangement of Irkanda IV for flute, viola, 'cello, and percussion—from plan through first performance. In September 1962, also in the evening, he appeared with composers Felix Gethen and Ian Harris (B52). In October 1963, on "Women's World," Eileen Ralph played a movement of the new Sonata for Piano (B65). Her husband, Thomas Matthews, conducted the first performances of The Fifth Continent shortly thereafter in Melbourne, Hobart, and Sydney.

Sculthorpe's work became more widely known at the conference on "The role of the Australian composer in contemporary society" held in Hobart on April 18-21, 1963. Composers, critics from major newspapers, and educators travelled to Tasmania for the event; twelve composers played tapes and discussed their work. The inspiration for the conference came from Kenneth Brooks of the Tasmanian Adult Education Board (Sculthorpe's former employer); the Board and the University of Tasmania sponsored it. The topic was one of great concern to Sculthorpe, who has called the conference "one of the most important events in the history of Australian music" (quoted in B840). According to the Hobart Mercury, Professor Donald Peart (1909-1983) of the University of Sydney observed that Australian composers were out of touch with the rest of the world, that modern Australian compositions seemed to belong to the eighteen-nineties rather than the nineteen-sixties, and that Australian music was a long way behind painting and poetry in expressing contemporary feeling; composers needed to exert "greater mental activity" in composing (B59). To remedy these problems, seminar participants produced an ambitious set of recommendations, including federal funding for publishing and recording Australian works for distribution at home and overseas, overseas study and experience for Australian composers, and visits from overseas composers (B61). During the sixties, these goals became reality, due largely to what Sculthorpe has described as "a handful of caring people" (B623).

At Hobart, he presented The Loneliness of Bunjil, Sonatina, Sonata for Viola and Percussion, and Irkanda IV—the only "serious" works, besides Irkanda I, with which he was satisfied at this point. Among the critics present was Roger Covell, who came from Sydney and wrote about Sculthorpe's work in the Sydney Morning Herald for the first time (B59n), naming Sculthorpe,

Richard Meale, and Larry Sitsky as the most interesting composers at the seminar. Composer Mirrie Hill (whom Sculthorpe had met in Sydney when recording **They Found A Cave**) recalled in 1977 (**B545**) that at Hobart she said of Sculthorpe (in a characteristically Australian figure of speech), "If he were a racehorse I'd back him." Perhaps the most important immediate result of the conference for Sculthorpe was his appointment by Donald Peart as Lecturer in Music at the University of Sydney, beginning in November 1963. Tasmanian colleagues congratulated Sculthorpe on his appointment; Tasmania's loss is a gain for New South Wales, Gethen observed gallantly in *Canon* (**B118**).

Sydney, 1963-1965. With the move to Sydney, Sculthorpe entered a new, invigorating milieu. Donald Peart became another mentor or "father figure" to him. In July, Peart prepared the way for the new member of his academic staff by leading a performance of **Irkanda IV** by his Pro Musica Society musicians at the university (**P63-7**). Upon Sculthorpe's arrival, Peart suggested that he introduce himself to Sydney audiences, and he played the new **Sonata for Piano** at an ISCM concert. Fred Blanks of the *Sydney Morning Herald*, reviewing Sculthorpe's work for the first time, found the work concise, with nothing superfluous; "it moves with slow deliberation in an idiom of knotty power," he wrote (**B66**). Lecturing at the university encouraged further articulation of his ideas, as did working with a number of highly gifted students, including, in these first two years, composers Anne Boyd and Ian Cugley, both of whom published analytical discussions of his work in the late sixties. He also met pianist and composer Michael Hannan (b. 1949), then a high school student, who made Sculthorpe's work the subject of his Higher School Certificate thesis (mentioned in **B1187**), his B. A. thesis in 1971 (**B1188**), his Ph. D. thesis in 1977 (**B1190**), a chapter in a study of Australian composers published in 1978 (**B566**), and his landmark 1982 book (**B702**).

Sculthorpe produced seven works in these two years, **W88-W94**, foremost among them being **String Quartet No. 6** (the first of his quartets to remain in the quartet repertoire) and **Sun Music** (now **Sun Music I**, the first of several **Sun Musics**). As the **W, P** and **B** listings show, he wrote increasingly extensive program notes to guide audiences, gave more pre-concert talks and public lectures, and found his music discussed in the press by numerous music critics. In Sydney, Roger Covell emerged as the historian of the group, explaining to readers of the *Sydney Morning Herald* the significance of each new work, performance, recording, commission, and published score. (His 1967 book, *Australia's Music*, **B184**, is a major historical study.) In a feature essay in July 1964 (**B80**), Covell observed that "for the first time in this country, a generation of composers is appearing—and receiving a hearing—that is not working in outmoded styles": Meale, Nigel Butterley, Sculthorpe, Sitsky, Dreyfus, and Helen Gifford (shown in photos), among the "immediate juniors of Werder (who is forging his own style)."

Covell viewed the premiere of **String Quartet No. 6** as an event of historic importance: "the fact that this is the first new Australian work introduced by Musica Viva [Australia's largest concert promotion agency after the ABC] in its nearly 20 years of existence reflects on the society's earlier conservative bias as well as the scarcity of important Australian music" (**B94**). In connection with a performance of the quartet at the 1965 Mittagong Easter Festival (about 80 miles from Sydney), he led a session of "Composers and their music," a panel of Sculthorpe, Butterley, Meale, and Eric Gross. Kenneth Hince of the *Australian* reported that the audience was "impressed by the honesty of the composers," and noted that "this kind of encounter will bring Australians to understand that the new idioms are genuinely expressive and not a disguise for arrogance or self-will in the composers of the *avant-garde* (B102). Covell's review of the score of **Sun Music (B175)** in the daily newspaper was even illustrated by a passage from the score to show the new sound-mass or space-time notation. Performers as well as audiences needed an introduction to the new techniques, and Sculthorpe used all his diplomatic skills in persuading the Sydney Symphony Orchestra members to play **Sun Music.** "Some, in fact, walked out," he recalled in 1990 (B1037). "Some of them claimed that it was damaging their instruments, but they decided to humour me. It was not a sunny beginning." In 1965, however, Sculthorpe tactfully mentioned only the outcome: "The orchestra had it mastered within an hour and at the end of the rehearsal they applauded me. That was my biggest thrill. I knew I was getting across" (B149).

In an interview published in the *Bulletin* in July 1964 (B79)—Sculthorpe's first substantial Sydney interview—his "silence story" first appears, a parable of the irrelevance of the post-Webern style to his own approach; the story reappears several times in the sixties (as in B86, B103, B152, and notes to D54). He says that he decided that serialism, taken to its logical end, would lead to "total silence." (He had in mind the work of a certain European painter, Kasimir Malevich, who, seeking freedom from human expression and imperfection, based his art on complex mathematical calculations, only to end up painting white canvases—the equivalent, to Sculthorpe's way of thinking, of composing silence.) Of course, as the **W** listings and program notes show, Sculthorpe continued to use serialism and other avant-garde techniques, but he used them in the context of his own sound or musical language.

His views engendered some controversy. In particular C. M. Prerauer took the position that only the post-Webern style was of international significance. After the glowing review of **Irkanda IV,** and in spite of a fondness for **String Quartet No. 6,** the Prerauers soon tired of Sculthorpe's "Great Australian Loneliness" theme (referring to the title of a once-popular book). In **Sun Music,** they wrote, "Sculthorpe does not fulfill his great promise. It reminds one of the accompaniment to a science-fiction film" (B136). (Curt Prerauer, in his reports on Australian music to the German periodicals *Melos* and *Neue Zeitschrift für Musik* in 1966 and 1967 [listed in the bibliography of B285] did not mention Sculthorpe at all.) Advanced listeners, the Prerauers wrote, could surely digest a Richard Meale ["richer meal"] of "contemporary music on an international scale" (B136). Although Sculthorpe felt that Covell supported him in the Prerauer controversy—in a later interview he described Covell as "pro-me" (B547)—the reviews show Covell to have been reporting on all new music with the same enthusiasm regardless of composer. He did support Sculthorpe in another way, as did Fred Blanks, in perceiving Sculthorpe's melodic, tuneful pieces to be as interesting and "significant" as his sound-mass and other more avant-garde works—even in the sixties when melodic writing was quite suspect among the musically educated. At any rate, the controversy attracted some welcome attention to new music. Sculthorpe likes controversy, and his music thrived on it. "All publicity, good or bad, is in the long run good for a composer," he noted in 1973 (**B451**). In the sixties, "I really emerged as a known composer through criticism" (**B507**).

Both **String Quartet No. 6** and **Sun Music** were performed in England in 1965 and widely reviewed; the Sydney newspapers reported the views of over-seas critics (as they continue to do today). In the quartet, the *Times* critic heard "finesse" but doubted the sincerity of emotion (**B132**). To Meirion Bowen (**B134**), it sounded like "etiolated Bartók or Schoenberg." He did not enjoy hearing so little concern with the "big struggles within European music over the last hundred years" in Sculthorpe's "static, contemplative, Eastern-like techniques." In **Sun Music** the *Times* critic heard "familiar freak effects" treated with masterly skill. Neville Cardus, whom Sculthorpe had admired since the forties, called the gong vibrations and 59 adjacent string tones con-temporary "formulae" and not particularly Australian. "Maybe after Scul-thorpe has shed one or two acquired sophistications, or drawn them into his instinctive way of feeling and thinking in music, he will lay the foundations of an original and characteristic Australian music" (**B126**). A recording of **String Quartet No. 6** was entered into the Paris International Rostrum, where it received favorable votes by delegates from national radio which would ensure broadcasts in the countries they represented. It was also recorded for distribution at home and overseas on the first volume of *Australian Music Today* (**D54**). Covell, like most Australian critics, viewed the project as "one of the most important events in the history of Australian music" (**B123**).

Visits by overseas composers had been a goal of the Hobart seminar, and the Sydney ISCM members organized a UNESCO conference on school music, held in June 1965, to which they invited Wilfrid Mellers and composer Peter Maxwell Davies (**B103-105**). Mellers, on his return home, published an essay about Australian music in the *New Statesman* in London (**B118**). To him, the Australian artist was a "visionary alien," an outcast from European civiliza-tion, and as such was perhaps the envy of artists the world over who "seem deliberately to be seeking rootlessness." Both Sculthorpe and Meale, he wrote, left to their own devices (as the painters Drysdale and Nolan had been), had caught the major theme of their time, an obsession with "emptiness" which Mellers contrasted to the European post-Renaissance concern with "con-sciousness and the will." Meale's post-Webernism was one way to achieve "an Asiatic immobility," he wrote, and Sculthorpe's "attempts to enter the heart of the Australian experience by way of a static technique of cumulative ostinati and note-clusters" was another.

Mellers also described Sculthorpe's teaching. University students "create serial masses corporately, serial song-cycles, Berio pieces, Cage pieces," he reported. Each student "directs" his own piece written for the other students; they tape one another's work, comment on it, even take it down as dictation excercise. "I've never met students more enthusiastically committed to invention and experiment; and they were so because their work seemed directly relevant to their lives." In Sculthorpe's course in Asian music, he continued, students "make their own Japanese music, not in an attempt to emulate an alien culture, but to discover how far this music may be relevant to them." He described Australia as a meeting-place for Eastern and Western cultures. "Despite the 'Keep Australia White' slogans chalked on walls, [Australia's] future must lie with an acceptance of Asia and a partial rejection of Europe, or at least of the moribund British tradition," he wrote.

In 1965, Sculthorpe signed a contract with the distinguished London publishing house of Faber and Faber, now Faber Music, Ltd. (**B135**), which remains his publisher. In 1990, Donald Mitchell of Faber Music was quoted as recalling that the melodiousness of **Small Town** (in **The Fifth Continent**) "convinced me to sign him on." With Peart's support, Sculthorpe had applied for, and won, a Harkness Fellowship to Yale University; he left for the United States in late 1965 (**B90**). In 1964 he had been commissioned to write an opera for the new Sydney Opera House (under construction)—a major commission—and he thought he would write it in the US (**B93**). (This became **Rites of Passage**, finally produced ten years later, in 1974.) As when he left for England in 1958, a farewell party was held; this one was filmed (**B150**). Larry Sitsky published an article in the American journal *Perspectives of New Music* (published by Yale's rival school, Princeton) introducing Sculthorpe and other Australians and their music (**B119**).

United States, 1966-67. In 1966 Sculthorpe was a fellow of Branford College of Yale University in New Haven, Connecticut. He also stayed for six months, from September 1966, to February 1967, at Yaddo, an artists' colony near Saratoga Springs, New York. Spending over a year away from Sydney just as he had begun to be established may seem to have been unwise, but again here was the opportunity to gain experience and enhance his reputation overseas. His name was kept alive at home by many performances of his work, including, in July of 1966, the new **Sun Music for Voices and Percussion (W96)**, written at Yale for Donald Peart.

In December 1965, on his way to the US, he stopped over in England. Henry Raynor published an extensive interview in the London *Times* headed "Australian composer with something new to say" (**B152**). "A little conversation with Mr. Peter Sculthorpe is enough completely to explode the myth of the New World's artistic dependence on the Old," Raynor wrote, although, he added, Sculthorpe speaks of his lack of interest in serialism "quietly and with a good deal of affection for the Old World." Sculthorpe's phrase "Asia is the future, Europe the past" was widely quoted—in the Sydney press and elsewhere. During 1966, Donald Peart published two articles in English journals about the newly-emerging Australian composers (**B162, B177**).

At Yale, Sculthorpe completed **String Quartet No. 7** which was premiered in July by the acclaimed Yale Quartet. Colin McPhee's *Music in Bali* was published by Yale University Press that year; the transcriptions of Balinese music were a revelation to Sculthorpe (as Hannan has shown, **B702**). At Yaddo, inspired by Mc Phee's book, he began work on **Anniversary Music (Sun Music III)**. According to the "Yaddo story," a parable of the labor of composing music, he saw artists, writers, and sculptors finish their work during the day, whereas "we composers struggled back to our huts at night to copy out and arrange our meagre lines" (**B496**). In Alice Springs in August 1990 (**B1056**), he recalled that at Yaddo "the composers worked long after dinner and still had only black dots on paper."

Sydney, 1967-1971. Sculthorpe returned to Sydney in early 1967. Interviewed for the *Bulletin* by David Salter (a former student), he reported that money—"dough"—is the big thing in the American arts and academic climate. The "mathsmusic works" of the academic in-group of American composers, led by Princeton's Milton Babbitt, he reported, are performed in splendid university auditoriums but hardly anywhere else. His period at Yaddo in a centrally-heated cabin by the lake was "idyllic" **(B195)**. He found America more exciting visually than Europe, he said in a later interview. "I would like to write music like the American road systems—enormous, wonderful roads" **(B321)**.

Over the next five years in Sydney, from 1967 until he left for England in late 1971, he tried new ways of writing serious music with even greater popular appeal. The new works, W100-W121, include three new **Sun Music** pieces, the **Sun Music** ballet, **Tabuh Tabuhan**, **String Quartet No. 8** (for an English competition), the pop-rock **Love 200**, **Music for Japan**, **Night Pieces** for piano, and **How the Stars Were Made**, his first work for percussion ensemble. He visited Japan for the first time, an experience that brought more revelation **(B547, W145)**. At the university he was promoted from Senior Lecturer in Music to Reader, which freed him of some lecturing responsibilities so that he would have more time for composing **(B278)**. Some new critics' names appear in the bibliography, and press coverage of all sorts increases markedly.

Sculthorpe continued to be active in the ISCM, and his studio became a kind of resource and information center—it continued to do so, he recalls, until the seventies when James Murdoch founded the Australia (later *Australian*) Music Centre, now Sounds Australian. In 1968, he was awarded the prestigious, and generous ($10,000), Australian Encyclopedia Britannica award for outstanding merit in the arts. He was delighted, Meredith Oakes (a former student) reported in the *Telegraph*, and not only for the personal triumph. "Painters and writers and sculptors have had recognition in Australia for some time. But it's only now that this sort of award is beginning to go to people who write music" **(B281)**. He told the *Age* that he appreciated "the honor, the glory, and the cash" and that he would be using the money to extend his house **(B280n)**. In 1970, he was made MBE; he told a journalist that the award means that Australia "is coming of age musically."

In 1967, **Anniversary Music (Sun Music III)**, with its placid Balinese melody and delicate sounds, initiated a new phase in Sculthorpe's work. Covell described "gamelan noises, a gorgeous ripple of antique cymbals on a string and all kinds of tender shocks for strings" which "set the greenery of the work in motion," followed by "an unabashed tune" **(B218)**. Hince liked its "beautiful sound" but added, "it has none of the dramatic power of **Irkanda IV** or the syntactic logic of the **Sixth Quartet**" **(B211)**. Bernard Heinze conducted the work, commissioned for the twentieth anniversary of the ABC youth concerts, in each of the six state capitals **(W100, P67-6, -7, -8, -10)**. "How we both enjoyed the first performances, and cutting the birthday cake on the stage in each capital city," Sculthorpe recalled later **(B718)**. In Sydney, "the orchestra played Happy Birthday in at least three keys at once" (B219). As the P listings show, all of the Sun Music pieces continued to be performed widely and regularly. Maria Prerauer, writing on her own after her husband's death, noted that "no radio program or concert schedule seems complete without its quota" (B254).

Sculthorpe became popular with the "stampede of young listeners" (B234) in their late twenties and early thirties at the summer (February) SSO Promenade concerts—the "Proms." They heard Sun Music I in 1966, Irkanda IV in 1967, Sun Music IV in 1968, Ketjak (Sun Music II) in 1969, Love 200 in 1970 (Sculthorpe wrote these last two especially for the Proms), and Music for Japan in 1971. Conductor John Hopkins, like Sculthorpe a popular figure, introduced the programs, for which he chose much contemporary Australian music. Sculthorpe was "cheered like a hero," wrote Frank Harris in 1968 (B231); listeners were packed shoulder-to-shoulder on the cleared ground floor of the Town Hall, he reported, and only a forceful dozen or so "insisted on their Prom lie-down rights." Love 200 perhaps marked the height of Sculthorpe's efforts so far to bring the excitement and immediacy of popular music into the concert hall. "I haven't enjoyed writing a piece so much for years," he said (B335). "In a sense, Love 200 is my lightest and most tuneful work; yet in another sense it is my most serious. I went all out to win over the audience to a sense of involvement and personal pleasure in the music" (B340). As in Sun Music II (Ketjak) the preceding year, he used amplification to surround the audience with sound, to "make people feel it's worthwhile to get up and go to a concert" (B308). "I'm against the two-dimensional concept of having the audience here, the performer there. You can have that at home with the stereo," he said (B381). Love 200 also featured a light show, swirls of fog, and brass choirs in the balconies. The press the next morning reported a smashing success. "About 2,000 cushion-carrying, blanket-bearing people streamed into the Sydney Town Hall last night and, by their enthusiasm, forced the orchestra to repeat the world premiere of Love 200. Members of the orchestra said they had never before seen such enthusiasm," the Sunday Mirror reported (B366n).

Critics registered hearty disapproval. Meredith Oakes in the Telegraph was perhaps the most emotional (B337). "Peter Sculthorpe writes about love—in 1970 what else is there?" Yet "his music, his own sound, is not about love. And Tully's [rock band] sound cannot readily be put at the service of an outsider's musical conception." Kenneth Robins called it "a barren monster" that lacked sensitivity; the amplification almost obscured the "first class sophisticated pop tunes" (B342). Eva Wagner in the Australian suggested that Sculthorpe was overwhelmed by university responsibilities; "it is time he settled down and gave us a sample of what he can really do" (B339). Composer David Ahern in the Telegraph urged him to "define his position vis-à-vis the avant-garde," and decide whether to discover new sounds or continue this "trendiness" (B363). Donald Peart defended his younger colleague: "Love 200 has had to atone for the warmth of its acceptance in the Town Hall by a cold and uncomprehending press reception. Rather than a piece for the concert hall, it is theatre. The audience appreciated the interweaving of the pop idiom and symphonic style, which must be reconciled so as to restore the wholeness of music as an art." (B345).

Even Sculthorpe had second thoughts about working with pop groups. He contrasted the "free-wheeling" world of rock with the discipline of composing—the discipline one needs "to make a shape in time articulate" instead of just an amorphous sound (B335n). Further performances of **Love 200**, plus working with another rock band on **Love 201** in 1971, left him even more frank. He told Suzanne Gartner (a former student), in *Vogue Australia* (B430), "I'm sick to death of working with unprofessional pop groups. Most of the local ones are high all the time; you'd rehearse them and then they'd forget. But I love listening to pop. I admire Paul McCartney, and Frank Zappa is brilliant." He salvaged two "first-class tunes" from **Love 200**: **The Stars Turn**, a "folk-soul-Mahler-type piece" ("I loved writing every note of that," B335), which exists in several arrangements; and **It'll rise again** (or **Boat Rise**).

Already by 1968, Sculthorpe was noticeably enjoying his success and an increasingly fashionable image. It was a wonderful feeling, he admitted with charming candor, to have famous artists calling "and with money involved in their artistic wishes" (B237). *Australian Home Journal* published pictures of the interior of his "tiny house" in fashionable Woollahra and talked about its "warmth of atmosphere" and Asian touches. "I love collecting things," he told the magazine (B256). *Vogue Australia* called him "probably the most important musical talent we Australians have ever produced," and published a large photo of this "friendly, cheerful and unassuming composer" (B271). In 1968 in Sydney, the **Sun Music I** recording was used in an Industrial Design exhibition opened by Prince Philip, Duke of Edinburgh; photos of Prince Philip, Sculthorpe, and others appeared on the front page of the *Sydney Morning Herald* (B252). In 1969, Sculthorpe was one of the subjects of an elegant book about artists at work called *In the Making* (B287); the book-launching party was covered in the society pages. In 1970, an interviewer described him "chortling with delight" over new clothes (B354). "It was all part of an effect I was trying to create," Sculthorpe says now (B1101), a kind of "insecurity."

In 1968, Paul Frolich commented in the *Bulletin*: "By common consent, Peter Sculthorpe's dominant trait is charm; he charms artists into playing his music, discussing it, and liking it" (B246). David Ahern remarked in 1970, upon hearing **Rain** for orchestra (now withdrawn), that the audience had accepted it "hook, line and sinker. That alone should cause Mr. Sculthorpe some consternation" (B368). Fred Blanks put Sculthorpe's dilemma into some perspective after a 1970 performance of **Tabuh Tabuhan**: "the ethos of modern art has, sad to relate, conditioned us to distrust anything we like on first encounter," he wrote. Although on first hearing this work "I distrusted its ready appeal," this performance "revealed an emotional sensitivity beyond the work's immediate aural accessibility" (B366).

Sculthorpe redeemed himself in the eyes of almost all critics with **Music for Japan** (1970) and **How the Stars Were Made** (1971). **Music for Japan** is "my best work so far," he told Ahern in 1970. The AYO was to perform it in Japan in "way-out buildings and a futuristic setting, and I decided the piece should match this atmosphere, at the same time blending with the idea of youth." His admiring words for the AYO were quoted more than once in the press: "There may be more technically excellent and highly polished orchestras, but

I'd rather have it play my work than any other orchestra, because everything these players do is touched with love" (**B359**). In **How the Stars Were Made**, Kenneth Hince (**B423**) heard a new enthusiasm and "confidence in himself," plus the "perennial charm" and "the tact of the golden boy who can't put a foot wrong." Here, Sculthorpe was writing for first-class performers (Les Percussions de Strasbourg) and in a favorite medium, percussion. Critics liked the theatricality of the presentation, the lighting effects and choreography of the six percussionists. "Their performance must have been a composer's dream," wrote Kenneth Robins (**B425**).

England, 1971-1973. In late October of 1971, Sculthorpe left Sydney for England to be visiting professor at the University of Sussex. Besides his teaching duties, he devoted his energy to completing **Rites of Passage**. Of the three new titles from this time, **W122-124**, only **Ketjak** is a new work. To Martin Cooper in the *Daily Telegraph* it conveyed an "extraordinary impression of authenticity by the combination of rhythmic and consonantal precision with the harsh, impersonal tone typical of primitive religious utterance" (**B441**)—the "ritualistic" effect that Sculthorpe achieved in **Rites of Passage** as well. In June 1972, publicity appeared back home in Australia about **Rites of Passage** that could only be called sensational. The rituals will be "straightforward and frank," Sculthorpe said in England (**B443**). In December the London *Times* announced that the work would not open the Sydney Opera House in 1973 after all. It was postponed to the 1974 season because of a change of director, said the press release (**B446**).

Sydney, 1973-1979. Sculthorpe's return to Sydney in March 1973 was reported in the press. Journalists waited to greet him, probably wanting to hear more about **Rites of Passage**. Through an airline error in the spelling of his name (as "Mr. Scuthorse," said the reporter, **B450**), they only caught up with him at home. He returned to welcome students at the university (the report continued), and he bought a new red sports car—the same MGB he still drives today, or, more precisely, drives occasionally. In 1977, after four years, it had a mere 12,000 miles on the clock (**B547**). In 1992, after almost 20 years, it had just over 40,000 miles, due to the composer's increased penchant for staying home.

A national contest was launched to choose an Australian national anthem; asked to be one of the contest judges, he consented "so that people entering the contest would stop phoning him" (**B455**). Ironically, on the morning after the opening of the Opera House (with Prokofiev's *War and Peace* instead of Sculthorpe), Sculthorpe's photo, in connection with the national anthem contest decision, appeared on the front page of the *Sydney Morning Herald* alongside news of the Opera House opening. The contest judges recommended familiar and established songs (**B458**).

In 1974 he made his first trip to Bali, for the filming of *Tabuh Tabuhan: Peter Sculthorpe in Bali*, for which he wrote the script and composed **Crimson Flower** for performance by Balinese musicians in the film. Before Bali, he spent two days in Launceston; the *Examiner* reported that he would be in a remote Bali village for three weeks, and his mother, travelling with a friend, would join him for a few days (**B455**).

Rites of Passage is the main topic of the Sculthorpe bibliography in 1973-74. As Michael Hannan has shown (**B702**), and as Sculthorpe explained in *Opera Australia* and *Music Now* (**B465, B468, B499**), it was intended to be a truly Australian theatre work, not a drama in the "European post-Renaissance sense" but "world theatre." Texts, chosen by the composer, are in the ritual languages of two cultures, Latin (from European culture) and Aranda (an Australian Aboriginal language). It is impossible to know exactly what audiences experienced, as many effects that were crucial to Sculthorpe's conception were changed or even discarded. In over forty reviews, critics either loved it or hated it; few discussed the music or its effects. *Opera Australia* eventually published excerpts from the contradictory critical opinion and audience members' reactions, under the apt heading "Rites or Wrongs?" (**B501**). Though the *Chorales and Rebirth* have been performed and recorded commercially, with favorable response, **Rites of Passage** has not been revived.

Completing **Rites of Passage** seems to have unleashed new creativity in Sculthorpe, with 29 titles, numbered **W126-154**, dating from 1973 to 1979. In a sense, he was able to return to the melodic style of **Sun Music III** and carry it further to solidify his own melodic language. As the W listings and program notes show, it was during this period that he began to use Aboriginal melodic material (with the blessing of Aboriginal leaders [**B801**]), Australian colonial music, Japanese *gagaku* melodies, and traditional North American Indian music. He continued to write avant-garde instrumental works, including **Koto Music I and II**, and he wrote his first work for guitars. Several works touch on subjects that he had contemplated during the years of planning **Rites of Passage**—the Eliza Fraser story, Aztec and Spanish cultures in Mexico, and the Catholic Mass. In 1977, he received further civic honours: he was made OBE for services to music, and was awarded the Queen's Silver Jubilee Medal.

After the controversial **Rites of Passage**, reviews and other press coverage are relatively few in 1975, picking up in 1976, 1977, and 1978 and then becoming more numerous in 1979, the composer's fiftieth-birthday year. A certain weariness, or wariness, towards Sculthorpe's music after **Rites**, plus what Covell (**B616**) perceived as a quieter contemporary music "mood" in the seventies, may explain the comparatively subdued reaction of Sydney critics in 1975 to the new **String Quartet No. 9** (Maria Prerauer, never much of a fan, called it "as Aussie as kangaroo butter" [**B515**])—especially when compared to its enthusiastic reception overseas by critics in London (**B519-520**) and the Americas (**B536-538**), or even, for that matter, its reception by Sydney critics in later years. In 1989, when the **Rites** controversies were a distant memory, Laurie Strachan wrote that, though the quartet seems "too slender in terms of material to support its length," it "cleverly maintains interest by beautifully judged tonal shifts and athletic ostinato rhythms" (**B1001**).

Just as in 1960, when Sculthorpe returned to Australia from England with a concept of a philosophy of Australian musical culture, so in 1973 he returned from England with renewed conviction of the need for more Australian music in the schools. As he recently remarked, "our secondary and tertiary institutions tend to concentrate on Western European music—they are the last bastion of the cultural cringe" (**B914**). He planned to write an elaborate program of music education, called the Peter Sculthorpe World Music Books

(B450). He spoke of a series of piano works, music theatre works for tertiary students and others for primary and secondary schools, a percussion book, and an instrument-making book for adults and children illustrating instruments created by himself and schoolchildren. In August 1974, he was awarded a three-year grant, the first Australia Council grant, in recognition of his contribution to Australian music (B472). In 1975-1977, he was able to take leave from the university to begin work on these long-term projects.

In 1976 he moved house, to a nearby one-room shepherd's cottage built in the eighteen-forties. He proceeded to rebuild it, restoring the Georgian architectural features that have remained a favorite style from his years in Tasmania, noted for its Georgian houses, and adding a studio at the back and small gardens at front and back. David Marr, in 1977 (B547), mentioned that the renovation was about half-completed. In April 1979, Maria Prerauer, interviewing Sculthorpe for his fiftieth birthday (B593), described a palatial dwelling, a largely fictional description (perhaps reflecting some resentment of his success) which was picked up by the Launceston *Examiner* (B596). With the completion of the renovation, many photo-essays have been published, beginning with house photos in *Vogue Living* in 1981 (B690, B696) and garden photos in *Australian Home Beautiful* in 1983 (B734). In describing his house and gardens, Sculthorpe takes the opportunity to introduce elements of his aesthetic, such as noting how, in music and in garden design, symmetry is given tension and interest through the introduction of asymmetry.

The seventies saw the formation of two performing groups that have continued to perform Sculthorpe's music repeatedly—the ACO in 1975, and the

Mangrove. Copyright ©1982 by Faber Music, Ltd., London. Reproduced by permission of the publishers.

Kronos Quartet. In 1976, he began to supply the ACO with works for string orchestra, **Port Essington** (1977) being perhaps the most loved both at home and overseas. In late 1977, the Kronos Quartet included the eight-year-old **String Quartet No. 8** in their first two San Francisco Bay area concerts; it "looks like it will become a classic," wrote a San Francisco critic (**B561**). Since then, the work has become the group's "signature piece," as they have performed it hundreds of times, and have performed the second movement, as "Rice Pounding Music," as an encore countless more.

Two new works of 1979, **Requiem** for solo 'cello and **Mangrove** for orchestra, have become major additions to the concert repertoire. **Mangrove** placed fifth at the Paris International Rostrum and earned a commendation—Australia's best showing to that date. Instead of the empty desert landscapes of **Sun Music, Mangrove** "is concerned with my feelings about growth and life, an abundance of life" (**B623**). Mellers calls it Sculthorpe's "masterwork" (**B1112**). If Covell found a quieter mood in the seventies than in the sixties, nevertheless by 1979 Sculthorpe could say that more was happening in new music, with more young composers, more performances of Australian music, teaching of Australian music in the schools, and university theses on Australian topics (**B623**). "A number of composers in Australia write music that stems very much from Australian beliefs and attitudes, that could be written only by an Australian," he noted.

1980-1989. Of the forty-seven new titles in the eighties (**W155-201**), about a dozen are new works, including such major achievements as the opera **Quiros**, the **Piano Concerto, Kakadu**, and **Nourlangie**. He wrote scores for two feature films based on Australian history, **Manganinnie** (1980), set in Tasmania, and **Burke and Wills** (1985). The remainder of the works are arrangements, reflecting his increased popularity among performers. He was busier than ever. Interviewed in 1985 (**B800**), he reiterated the long hours needed for composing. There is no "good life." You simply decide that "certain things have to go," like reading fiction or going to the cinema. "You become ruthless." Many more works were recorded in the eighties, and CDs began to be released that were devoted exclusively to his music (**D35, D38**).

He talked about a new passion in his music, in place of the anguish of the seventies. In 1980 (**B671**), he noted a general trend towards more accessible music, romantic and melodic. The eighties seemed newly conservative, now that "we have got through the post-Webern period" (**B769**). The **P** listings show a large increase. Groups adopted a work or two into their repertoires and went on tour, as the ACO toured Asia with **Port Essington** and **Lament for Strings** in early 1980 and 1983. For some dates, two, three, even four performances are listed in different locations in the world, and occasionally more than one performance in the same city.

Critics continued to note Sculthorpe's immersion in Australian music history. The program notes for **W155-201**, besides the expected remarks on instrumentation and form and ideas, provide a veritable panorama of Australian history and culture, largely due to his intensive work during the seventies. Historical references even occur in the preamble to his recipe for pancakes found in a Sydney celebrities' recipe book (**B845**), and in his designing of a garden that combines blue with red and white, as red and white alone have been thought unlucky "since the Wars of the Roses" (B753). His statements about Asian influences were no longer described as "provocative" but were part of his historical lectures on Australian music. He could now see Australians as belonging to a new twentieth-century "Pacific culture" (B784). He discussed the work of Asian-influenced Australian composers from Grainger and Glanville-Hicks to Meale, Boyd, Ross Edwards, Barry Conyngham, and others (B804). As his love and appreciation of Australia deepened, he decided that he had been using Japan and Bali as "surrogates for Australia."

In 1980, he was awarded an honorary doctorate by the University of Tasmania; the university's music department presented a concert of his works during his visit, and Launceston honored him with a civic reception. In 1989 came two more honorary doctorates, from the University of Melbourne and the University of Sussex.

In the television opera **Quiros** (1982), he fulfilled a longstanding dream of writing "an enormous work for chorus and soloists and orchestra," as he had described it five years earlier (B547), on the poem "Captain Quiros" by James McAuley. After **Rites of Passage**, he wanted "a writer he could level with" (B496), and found one in Brian Bell. The opera is passionate, said Sculthorpe; it is not about landscape but about the "horizons of the human mind." Work was delayed when he almost killed himself in a car accident; recovery was slow but complete. The opera, screened in July, was acclaimed as a masterpiece by virtually all critics. Sculthorpe undoubtedly felt a kinship with its hero, the sixteenth-century explorer Quiros who thought he discovered Australia; he is presented as a man of faith and vision thwarted by people who do not share his vision (B708).

In 1984, Sculthorpe began a book, "a sort of autobiography," he described it to critic Laurie Strachan in 1986 (B821), which he now (early 1993) considers only half completed, at four substantial chapters. He intended to incorporate his collected writings, public addresses, and lectures on Australian music in the book, which he hoped would prove useful in schools, colleges and universities and provide a springboard for further research. In 1986 (B821), he observed that even the great historian Manning Clark (d. 1991), who "knows what's happening at the moment in poetry, painting, literature, the footy," is not up to date in music. "I just want to take away a little of that mystique."

Critical attention and audience enthusiasm in Australia were less intense than in the sixties or even the seventies. The premiere of the **Piano Concerto**, for instance, did not draw big crowds (B743). A comment by Fred Blanks in 1982 appears to come to Sculthorpe's defense in the face of some hostility: "for proving that contemporary music can be enjoyable and significant, many find it hard to forgive the influential Peter Sculthorpe" (B685). Overseas, however, there is a noticeable increase in performances and reviews. **String Quartet No. 10**, hailed by US critics in 1983, though not the first Sculthorpe work to have its premiere overseas, was unusual in that it was not performed in Australia for five years. In 1984, **String Quartet No. 6** was enthusiastically received in Moscow, as was **Mangrove** in New York; in 1988, US audiences enjoyed **Port Essington** by the ACO, **Mangrove** by the SSO, and the **Kakadu** premiere. Bernard Holland of the *New York Times* heard in **Mangrove** a welcome "new way of dealing with tradition" (B930).

The three-fold increase in P listings from 1987 to around 90 in 1988 is due in part to the Australian bicentenary which brought commemorative concerts overseas as well as at home. In 1989, there is further increase as Australian musicians virtually everywhere observed the composer's sixtieth-birthday year with special all-Sculthorpe concerts. The composer traveled to Paris with Synergy to introduce **Sun Song (W196)**, Australia's gift to France for the bicentenary of the Revolution. The year 1989 also brought several commemorative essays. In Sydney, composer and critic Andrew Ford analyzed Sculthorpe's music and aesthetic in a series of radio talks, later published (B1021). In England, composer David Matthews, Sculthorpe's friend and collaborator, published an analytical essay concentrating on the works since 1979 (B1007); "Sculthorpe has not suffered from our present [European] inhibitions about melody, and here he may have most to teach us," Matthews concluded.

Much information about Sculthorpe's home life appears in the bibliography of the eighties. While he has not married or reared children, he has created and nurtured a loving "family" of students, colleagues, and close friends. He says that part of his emotional life is in the continuity of composing and guiding students (B704). Sydney writer Nadine Amadio calls him a "model composer" for the country, for his generosity to students and his commitment to his art (B719). He is a great host, talker, and thinker, but has an almost disturbing ability to shut himself off to work, writes composer Barry Conyngham, a former student (B963). Sculthorpe is described as "not lonely, merely solitary" (B715). Still, "my house is a bit like Central Railway," he says (B821). His "indefatigable" housekeeper, Dot Hockley (d. 1991), receives several mentions in the eighties; she was succeeded in the nineties by Birgit Siegel and then by Mary Devine. Joe Faust, "on call to repair the house" (B972), provided a number of the photographs in Hannan's book. A 1982 interview mentions the composer's then-secretary, Jane de Couvreur, "who protects him and makes him meals when he's working and who has just taken off for six months" (B715); she returned from France after four years. She was succeeded by Adrienne Askill, who is his secretary, friend, and confidante. In the late eighties, having lived alone for most of his life, Sculthorpe invited his mother, Edna, a frequent visitor over the years, to move into his house; he is able to adjust his schedule to her interests. He keeps long hours, but does not compose according to a set daily routine (B752). Nights are working time, when it is "still and quiet" (B861).

In 1989, filming began for a television documentary about his work, and the filmmaker took him to Kakadu and Port Essington, sites which had inspired his music though he had known them only from books. "There's no time," the title of the film (B1026), became his byword.

INTO THE NINETIES

"There's no time" is still the byword, as Sculthorpe appears to be continuing the intense work schedule of the eighties. Interviewed in August 1990, on a visit to Alice Springs to meet the AYO, which was playing **Kakadu** on tour, he described a life less glamorous than the composers' lives he remembered seeing depicted in movies in his childhood. "The phone is always ringing with requests for commissions, writing forewords, openings—the things you dream about when you are young. When you get older and they do happen, there's no time" (**B1076**). In 1990, even without a bicentenary as in 1988, or an important birthday as in 1989, concert activity did not decrease markedly. In March in Adelaide, the Kronos Quartet premiered **String Quartet No. 11, Jabiru Dreaming,** and, as with **No. 8,** they have performed it dozens of times since. A performance in Tucson, Arizona, in 1991, "was rewarded with hoots, whistles, shouts and thunderous applause, from a packed house" (**B1094**), a reaction reminiscent of the Sydney Proms concerts in the sixties. He wrote more of the "straightfoward, joyful music" that he believes could only be written today in Australia (**W201**).

A new generation of Australian critics is noticeably cooler than Australian critics in the expansive sixties, or even than contemporary critics overseas. In contrast to the attention given the earlier works, his newer works may be given only brief mention at home, as happened with **Nangaloar (B1085),** or even ignored (**B865n**). *Sydney Morning Herald* critic Peter McCallum protests the landscape aesthetic as requiring too little effort (**B1061**), much as Maria Prerauer earlier tired of Australian themes. At the same time, overseas, Mellers, in an essay in the US magazine *The Atlantic* (**B1112**), also published in the UK (**B1155**), calls Sculthorpe "one of the most important living composers" for his discovery of "the universal within the topical and local."

Accolades and civic honors continue. In 1990, Sculthorpe was appointed AO (Order of Australia). In 1991 the *Bulletin* included him in a list of Australia's fifty-five "human assets." At the university he was promoted to the distinguished title of Personal Chair. His music and ideas are apparently integrated into the cultural fabric to an extent that a bibliography does not always reflect. Sculthorpe's studio is becoming familiar to television viewers as the site of filmed interviews. He speaks on the radio on a variety of topics, musical, environmental, and cultural. His music is used by dance companies and as background for innumerable Australian radio and television programs, commercials and films; **Small Town** is a favorite for nostalgic topics and country scenes, and **Irkanda IV** and **Mangrove** for matters of Aboriginal culture. In March 1993, he delivered the inaugural Stuart Challender Memorial Lecture sponsored by the ABC and the NSW Ministry for the Arts (and published in the *Age* and *24 Hours*), which is a profound yet accessible statement of his deepest beliefs. In a series of seemingly casual recollections, he draws together, within the concept of duality, his own musical experience, the Australian experience, and the human experience.

Peter Sculthorpe is defining the role of composer in unexpected ways. He provides exciting music for appreciative performers and audiences, while carrying out the responsibilities of a distinguished academic with dedication and enthusiasm. He has achieved greatness as an artist, and has made the sacrifices attendant on greatness, but remains basically optimistic and quite happy. He maintains a dialogue with critics and journalists, but is still a very private person pursuing his own course. He demonstrates uncompromising artistry and integrity in his work and in his life.

Works

This is a chronological list from 1945 through 1992, according to date of composition. References to items with a **D** refer to entries in the "Discography," with a **P** to "Performances," and with a **B** to entries in the "Bibliography," including reviews and other literature. Instrumentation for larger works is listed in the customary pattern of woodwinds, brasses, timpani, percussion, and strings. For example, 2.2.2.2., 4.3.2.1., timp, 3 perc (instruments named), strings, means that the work calls for 2 flutes, 2 oboes, 2 clarinets, and 2 bassoons (alternate piccolo, English horn, bass clarinet, contra-bassoon are indicated in parentheses); 4 horns, 3 trumpets, 2 trombones, and 1 tuba; timpani, 3 percussion players; and a full string section of first and second violins, violas, cellos, and double basses. All vocal and choral works are in English unless otherwise stated.

Sculthorpe's publisher is Faber Music Ltd., London. Works that carry a six-digit Faber ISBN number (50752-2, for example) are available for purchase through music retailers; the Faber ISBN prefix is 0-571. Other works, unless "withdrawn" or "not available," may be obtained through Faber Music for perusal or hire (rental). The publisher also makes some material available for sale in "Faberprint," which is a facsimile of the manuscript awaiting printing, or a copy of an earlier printing that has gone out of print (OP). Works without publishing information are not ready for publication. Autograph manuscripts are in the composer's possession unless otherwise stated.

W1   Nocturne (no. 1) (1945)
For piano. Revised version of an earlier work. 4 p.
Performances: **P45-8, -9, P48-8, -12, P49-6** (x2), **-12, P51-7, P53-8, P82-11**. *Reviews:* **B4, B6, B7, B723**.

W2   It's dark down the street (1945)
For speaker and piano. Text: the composer. 4 p.

W3   Falling Leaves (1945)
For piano. Inscribed at the beginning "Op. 5, no. 1." Revised version of an earlier work. Sometimes called **Sketch** or **Scherzo**, and sometimes performed with the 1946 **Evocation** under the title **Two Evocations**. 3 p.

Performances: P45-9, P46-8 (as **Evocation**), P47-10 (as **Sketch**), -12 (as **Scherzo**), P48-8, P49-6. *Reviews:* **B4, B7.**

W 4 **Short Piece for Pianoforte No. 1** (1945)
Inscribed at the beginning "Op. 6, no. 1." Sometimes called **Sketch** or **Scherzo**, but more often **Prelude** as one of **Two Preludes.** 3 p.
Performances: P46-8, P47-10 (as **Sketch**), -12 (as **Scherzo**), P48-8, P49-6, P50-11 (these three as **Prelude**). *Reviews:* **B4, B7.**

W 5 **Short Piece for Pianoforte No. 2** (1945)
Inscribed at the beginning "Op. 6, no. 2." Sometimes called **Sketch** or **Scherzo**, but more often **Prelude**, as above. 3 p.
Performances and reviews: same as **W4.**

W 6 **Slow Movement from Sonata no. 1** (1945)
For piano. Inscribed at the beginning "2nd movement." Uses material from earlier **Prelude to a Puppet Show** and **Winter Woodland**, both for piano. Other movements were not completed. 4 p.

W 7 **Short Piece for Piano (No. 1)** (1945)
Inscribed at the beginning "To W. T." (Wilfrid Teniswood, the composer's English teacher; he organized the first ABC broadcast performances of the composer's music); inscribed at the end "Sept. 1945" and "(40 secs)." Sometimes called **Sketch** or **Scherzo**, this work is a refinement of **W5.** 3 p.
Performances: P47-10 (as **Sketch**), P47-12 (as **Scherzo**).

W 8 **Aboriginal Legend** (1946) not available
For piano. Sketches only. 5 p.
Performances: P46, P47-10, -12, P49-6, P50-11, P53-5. *Review:* **B7.**

W 9 **Evocation** (1946)
For piano. Inscribed at the end "2 mins." and "March 1946." 4 p.
Performance: **P46-8.**

W10 **Chamber Suite** (1946) not available
For high voice, bassoon and piano. This work is missing. The composer believes it to be a setting of his own translations of poems by Paul Verlaine. Awarded the J. A. Steele Composition Prize at Melbourne Conservatorium (**B2**).
Performance: 1946 (May). Melbourne (Conservatorium).

W11 **Sonatina no. 1** (1946) not available
For piano. In two movements. This work is missing, apart from some sketches for the first movement.
Performances: P46-8, P49-6. *Review:* **B7.**

W12 **New Hampshire** (1946)
For unaccompanied chorus and solo soprano. Text: T. S. Eliot. Inscribed at the beginning "Landscapes," and at the end "August 1946." 4 p.

W13 Epigram (1946)
For piano. Inscribed at the end "(80 secs)" and "August 1946." Sometimes called **Sketch** or **Scherzo**. 3 p.
Performance: **P47-10** (as **Sketch**), **P47-12** (as **Scherzo**).

W14 Gardener Janus Catches a Naiad (1946)
For voice and piano. Text: Edith Sitwell. Inscribed at the end "Sept. 1946." 2 p.
Performance: **P47-10**.

W15 Siesta (1946)
For piano. Inscribed at the end "Sept. 1946." 3 p. A copy of the score is in the Sounds Australian library in Sydney.
Performance: **P49-6**. *Review:* **B7**.

W16 Come Sleep (1946)
For mixed chorus. Text: John Fletcher. 2 p. MS is titled "Part-Song."

W17 The Olive (1946)
For voice and piano. Text: A. E. Housman. Inscribed at the end "October 1946." 3 p.
Performance: **P47-10** (?)

W18 Elegy for a Clown (1946)
For voice and piano. Text: the composer, from "Collected Poems (1944-50." MS is inscribed at the beginning "To —" (Frances Cowper, soprano and fellow-student), and at the end "November 1946." 2 p. Quoted in full in **B702** (Hannan), p. 7-8.
Performances: **P47-10, P48-8**. *Review:* **B4**.

W19 Siesta, arr. bassoon and piano (1946)
An arrangement by the composer of **Siesta, W15**. Inscribed at the beginning "To my friend G. D." (George Dreyfus, composer and fellow-student). Sketches only, headed "Piece for Bassoon & Piano." 4 p.

W20 Monsieur Miroir (1946)
For voice and piano. Text: Philippe Soupalt, in French. Inscribed at the beginning "Founded on the following eight-tone series," and series given. 2 p.

W21 In the morning (1947)
For voice and piano. Text: A. E. Housman. Inscribed at the end "Feb. 1947." 2 p.
Performance: **P47-10** (?)

W22 Wenn zwei voneinander scheiden (1947)
For voice and piano. Text: Heinrich Heine, translated into English by Robert Garran ("When two that have loved are parting"). Inscribed at the beginning "Parting" and at the end "Feb. 1947." 2 p.
Performances: **P47-10, P48-8** (both as **Parting**). *Review:* **B4**.

W23 To Meadows (1947)
For three female voices (unaccompanied). Text: Robert Herrick. Inscribed at the beginning "April 1947" and "From the poem by Herrick." 3 p.
Performance: **P47-10**

W24 Song (1947)
For voice and piano. Text: Shakespeare, *Take, O take those lips away* from *Measure for Measure*. Inscribed at the end "May 1947." 2 p.
Performance: **P47-10, P48-8.** *Review:* **B4.**

W25 Hughley Steeple (1947)
For voice and piano. Text: A. E. Housman. 3 p.
Performance: **P47-10** (?)

W26 Aspatia's Song (1947)
For voice and piano. Text: Beaumont and Fletcher. MS is inscribed at the end "May 1947." 2 p.
Performances: **P47-10, P48-8.** *Review:* **B4.**

W27 Jack and Joan (1947)
For voice and piano. Text: Thomas Campion (1565-1620). 3 p.
Performance: **P47-10, P48-8.** *Review:* **B4.**

W28 To Meadows, arr. soprano and strings (1947)
An arrangement by the composer of **To Meadows, W23.** Text: Robert Herrick. Inscribed at the beginning "1947." 5 p.
Performance: **P49-5** (for string orchestra)

W29 Elegy (1947)
For string orchestra. MS is inscribed at the beginning "June 1947" and "Opus 24, no. 6." 7 p.
First performance: 1947 (July). Melbourne (Melba Hall). Melbourne Conservatorium String Orchestra; Henri Touzeau, conductor.

W30 Jack and Joan, arr. soprano and strings (1947)
An arrangement by the composer of **Jack and Joan, W27.** Text: Thomas Campion. 4 p.

W31 Two Reveries (1947)
For voice and piano. Text: the composer, from "Collected Poems (1944-50." Contents: *A dryad murmurs in trembling tones* (2 p.), and *O who is she who kissed thy brow* (2 p.).

W32 Trio (1948) not available
For oboe, viola and 'cello. 4 p.

W33 How should I your true love know? (1948)
For voice and piano. This is the only remaining song from a cycle of four Shakespeare settings. 2 p. Known as *A Glimpse of Seventeenth Century England*, the work was runner-up in the 1948 Victorian School

Music Association Competition for a vocal work. *Lit.:* **B5**.

W34   Aubade (1948)
For strings. 4 p.

W35   O cool is the valley now (1948)
For voice and piano. Text: James Joyce. While the title on the MS is given as **Reverie**, the work is known by the above first line of the text. Inscribed at the beginning "For Mrs. Dixon" (Gwynneth Dixon, soprano, who performed many of the composer's early songs), and at the end "1948." Also performed as a piano solo. 3 p.
Performances (as **Reverie**): **P48-5, -8, -12** (piano solo), **P52-4**. *Review:* **B4**.

W36   String Quartet No. 2 (1948) not available
In one movement. The score is missing.
Performance: **P48-8**. *Review:* **B4**.

W37   Untitled piano piece (1948)
Inscribed at the beginning "in a nauseating lavender-&-lace manner." 2 p.

W38   Seascape (1948)
For piano. While the title on the MS is given as **Nocturne**, the work is known as **Seascape**. 3 p.
Performances: **P48-8, P49-6, P50-11, P51-12**. *Reviews:* **B4, B7**.

W39   Three Songs (1948) not available
For voice and piano. Contents: *Mushrooms; Sleep; The Children's Minuet*.
Performance: **P48-12**

W40   Prelude to Suite for String Orchestra (1948)
For strings. The suite itself was not completed. 2 p.

W41   Nocturne (1949)
For piano. Inscribed at the beginning "For Hetty" (Harriet Nemenoff, pianist and fellow student); also inscribed incorrectly as "(no. 5)." The work was usually performed with the 1945 **Nocturne** (**W1**) under the title **Two Nocturnes**. 2 p.
Performances: **P49-6** (x2), **-12, P50-11, P51-7, -12, P53-8**. *Reviews:* **B6, B7**.

W42   Nocturne, arr. violin and piano (1949)
Composer's arrangement of **Nocturne, W41**, for Wilfred Lehmann. 3 p.

W43   Two Aboriginal Songs (1949)
For solo voice (or voices in unison) & orchestra. Contents: *Maranoa Lullaby; Warrego Lament*. Both are melodies collected by H. G. Lethbridge, with accompaniments by Arthur S. Loam. 8 p.

W44   String Quartet No. 3 (1949)

In three movements: *Pastorale; Interlude; Fantasy*. The score is missing, but the *Pastorale* forms the basis of the second movement of **String Quartet No. 4 (W47)**.
Performance: 1949 (October 26). Melbourne. Guild of Australian Composers (Victorian Branch). Wilfred Lehmann, Geoffrey Fegent, violins; Florence Barber, viola; Marjorie Thoms, 'cello. *Review:* **B8**.

W45 Overture (1949)
For theatre orchestra. Written for performance at the National Theatre, Melbourne, to open a program given by the Indian dancer Shivaram. It was rehearsed, conducted by James Penberthy, but not performed. 27 p. The complete work exists in piano score, 5 p.

W46 Country Dance (1950)
For piano. 1 p.

W47 String Quartet No. 4 (1950)
Inscribed at the beginning "Recollections of holidays spent in a country village in Tasmania." In three movements: *Prelude; Pastorale; Country Dance*. The last movement is missing. 22 p. The complete work exists in piano score, 13 p.
First performance: 1950 (June 14). Melbourne (British Music Society's Rooms, 465 Collins Street). British Music Society of Victoria recital by young Melbourne musicians. Brenda Cullity and Barbara Young, violins; Lesley Kerr, viola; Marjorie Thoms, 'cello. *Lit.:* **B9, B10**.
Other performances: **P50-6, -10**.

W48 Elegy (1950)
For strings. Inscribed at the end "South Yarra, 1950." 3 p. Written at the request of Henri Touzeau, the work was not performed, due to lack of rehearsal time.

W49 Suite (1950)
For piano. Inscribed "from the background music to an experimental documentary film on Tasmanian life. The names I have given the five sections are: *Introduction; Aubade; Interlude; Eclogue; Finale*." The work uses material from **To Meadows (W23)**, **Jack & Joan (W27)**, and **Overture (W45)**. The film was not made. 10 p.

W50 The White Bird (1950)
For high voice and piano. Text: the composer. Inscribed at the end "Devonport Dec., 1950. For Gwen" (Gwynneth Dixon, as in **W35**).
Performances: **P50-6, P52-4**.

W51 Music I-VII (1950-54) not available
A group of works for various instrumental ensembles. Experiments in serial techniques, the works were destroyed by the composer. *Music VI*, for wind quartet, is said to have been performed, but the composer (in 1992) has no recollection of this. *Lit.:* **B184, B285**.

W52 Much Ado About Nothing (1951)
Incidental music for the Shakespeare play specially composed for the
Launceston Players. Includes setting of song *Sigh no more, ladies.*
First performances: 1951 (August 22-25). Launceston TAS (National
Theatre). Launceston Players production; Anne Godfrey-Smith, direc-
tor. Mrs. Kurt Rodgers, violin; Peter Anstey, cello; Peter Sculthorpe,
piano. Launceston performances also included a recorder player.
Other performances by Launceston Players, 1951: September 6, Laun-
ceston (National Theatre), Tasmanian State Finals of the 1951 Jubilee
Amateur Theatrical Groups Competition (it won the prize); and
October, Devonport (performances sponsored by the Tasmanian Adult
Education Dept.), and other locations in TAS; November 17, Hobart
(Theatre Royal), Commonwealth Jubilee Drama Festival.

W53 Strings in the Earth and Air (1952)
For voice and piano. Text: James Joyce. Inscribed "Jan. 25, 1952." 2 p.

W54 The Miser (1952) not available
Incidental music for the Molière play.
First performances: 1952 (October 7-11). Launceston (National Theatre).
Launceston Players production. Peter Sculthorpe, piano. *Lit.:* " 'Miser'
pleased L'ton audience," *Examiner.*
Other performances: **P59-2**

W55 Ballet (1953)
For piano. Autograph manuscript score, 20 p., in Baillieu Library, University of Melbourne Conservatorium. Dated at the end "May 1953."

W56 Overture (1953)
For orchestra. Submitted to the ABC as an entry in the 1953 overture
competition. Sketches are in the composer's possession.

W57 The Girl Who Couldn't Quite (1953) not available
Incidental music for the Leo Marks play.
Performances: 1953 (October 7-10) Launceston (National Theatre).
Launceston Players.

W58 Life With Father (1954) not available
Incidental music for the Lindsay and Grouse play.
Performances: 1954 (March 31-April 3) Launceston (National Theatre).
Launceston Players. Peter Sculthorpe, piano. *Lit.:* "Family life in
Players' comedy" (both period and mood of 1880 will be underlined by
incidental music, played by the Launceston pianist PS).

W59 Sonatina for Piano (1954)
In three movements. *Dur.:* 7:30. *Pub.:* Sydney: University of Sydney
Music Publications, 1964, distributed by Leeds Music Pty Ltd. *Reviews:*
B88, B91. Composer's analysis: **B290.**
Composer's note: "The **Sonatina** is subtitled 'For the journey of Yoonecara to the land of
his forefathers, and the return to his tribe.' The work follows the Aboriginal legend

'The Adventures and Journey of Yoonecara, the Head Man,' from W. E. Thomas, *Some Myths and Legends of the Australian Aborigines* (Melbourne, 1923). The legend is a simple tale, not unlike the Ulysses myth. Following his journey (in the first movement), Yoonecara arrives at the land beyond the setting sun (in the second movement), and meets Byama, the Great Spirit, and his two beautiful daughters. He returns to his tribe (in the last movement) and there is much rejoicing."

First performance: 1955 (June 19). Baden-Baden (SW Radio). ISCM Festival. Maria Bergmann, piano. *Lit.:* B11, B12, B81, B728. *Review:* B16.

Other performances: P56-1, -3, P57-3, P76-4, P79-5, -11, P80-7, -8, -9, -10, P81-7, P82-11, P83-10, P84-5, -8, -12, P87-11, P88-1, -2, -6, -10, -11, P89-4, -7, P90-6, P91-5, P92-4, -6, -8, -10. *Reviews:* B17, B22, B53, B530, B605-606, B723, B758, B897, B1003, B1156, B1164.

Recordings: D38-39, D43, D46-47. *Reviews: see* "Discography."

W60 The Loneliness of Bunjil (1954)

For string trio. *Dur.:* 10:00. Written in Tasmania in 1954; revised in 1964. Uses intervals made up of 1, 3, 5 . . . (odd numbers) of quarter-tones. *Notes in score:* "In the beginning the Great Spirit Bunjil created the earth and all things in it except man. He became lonely . . . ." Playing score, 6 p., 1964, for sale.

First performance: 1960 (November 30). London (Recital Room, Royal Festival Hall). Haydn Trio—Sylvia Cleaver, violin; Rosemary Green, viola; Olga Hegedus, 'cello. *Also:* P61-1. *Lit.:* B33. *Reviews:* B39, B41.

W61 Sonata for Violin Alone (1954-55) not available

Composed for violinist Wilfred Lehmann. *Dur.:* 18:00.
Contents: I. *Prelude;* II. *Five aspects of a slow theme;* III. *Postlude.* Movement I is dated at the end "Feb-March 1955," movement II is marked "ostinato" and "S. T.," and movement III is inscribed at the end "PS Feb 1955."

First performance: 1955 (March 28). Melbourne (Assembly Hall). Wilfred Lehmann, violin. *Reviews:* B13-B15. Lehmann performed movement II in 1954 as *Variations for violin* and later as *Five aspects of a slow theme.*

Also performed: P56-4

W62 Irkanda I (1955)

For violin alone. *Dur.:* 10:00. Written at the invitation of Wilfred Lehmann. In one movement. Inscribed at the beginning "To Wilfred Lehmann" and at the end "Canberra, 1955." Score 50524-4, c1977.

Composer's note: "**Irkanda I** is in one movement, and in it, long, melodic lines and bird-sounds are contrasted with brittle, rhythmic sections. The opening melody follows a three hundred and sixty degree contour of the hills around Canberra, where most of the work was written. It might be added that my use of birdsong stems from suggestions in the writings of Henry Tate. *Irkanda* is an Australian Aboriginal word meaning "a remote and lonely place."

First performance: 1955 (June 30). Melbourne (British Music Society's Rooms). British Music Society farewell concert for Wilfred Lehmann. Wilfred Lehmann, violin. *Reviews:* B17-18.

Other performances: P56-2, P57-11, P58-4, P61-2, P65-11, P66-5, P73-3, P76-4, P79-4, P81-3, P81-6, P82-11, P83-4, P86-3, P89-10, P90-9, P91-3, -8.

Reviews: **B17, B24-25, B38, B80, B145-147, B165-169, B449, B530, B694.**
Recordings: **D15-16.**

W63   Junius on Horseback (1956) not available
"Curtain music" (incidental music) for solo piano, for the Launceston
Players production of a comedy by the local playwright Walter
Sutherland.
Performance: 1956 (March 17). Hobart TAS (Hobart Playhouse). Third
Hobart Drama Festival. Sculthorpe plays "A Footman."
Also performed: 1956 (April 10). Launceston (National Theatre). Tenth
Tasmanian Drama Festival.

W64   Twelfth Night (1956)
Incidental music for the Shakespeare play, including four songs: *O
mistress mine; Come away, death; I am gone, sir;* and *When that I was
a little tiny boy.*
Performances: 1956 (June 29-July 28). Canberra ACT (Riverside Theatre).
Canberra Repertory Society. Anne Godfrey-Smith, director. *Review:*
B19. *Lit.:* **B1140.**
Also performed: 1956 (December), Launceston High School; three songs,
ABC broadcast, June 27, 1956, and April, 1957; **P70-5.**

W65   Ulterior Motifs (1956)
Overture and songs for a musical farce in two acts. For: 2 pianos, solo-
ists, chorus. *Dur.:* 120:00. Book by Ric Throssell, lyrics by Anne Godfrey-
Smith.
Performances: 1956 (Fridays and Saturdays, November 9-December 8).
Canberra (Riverside Theatre). Canberra Repertory Society. Peter Scul-
thorpe and Margaret Cooke, pianists. *Lit.:* **B20, B1140.** *Also performed:*
December 16, 1956, ABC broadcast of four numbers; and **P92-3** (song).

W66   Sons of the Morning (1957) not available
Incidental music for ABC radio play by Catherine Duncan. *Broadcast:*
1957 (March 27).

W67   Don't Listen Ladies (1957) not available
Incidental music for ABC radio play by Catherine Duncan. *Broadcast:*
1957 (June 19).

W68   Cross Section (1957)
Six songs for a revue satirising Life at "the Cross" (King's Cross,
Sydney's bohemian quarter): *Truth in advertising; Manic espresso*
(satirises the cult of the coffee bar, in "send-up samba rhythm" [score
annotation]); *Redleaf revelations; Shooting a lion; I knew a fella;* and
Something you can't pin down. Texts: John McKellar.
Performances: 1957 (Thursday September 27-October 20, 1958). Sydney
(Phillip Street Theatre). William Orr, producer. Dot Mendoza and Ray
Cook, piano; Carl Mehden, drums. *Reviews:* **B23.** *Excerpt:* **Manic
espresso** (1958), ballet music for ABC television production, *broadcast:*

1958 (January 6, Sydney, and March 29, Melbourne). Withdrawn.

W 69 Three Movements for Jazz Band (1957) not available
Arrangements of Sculthorpe's music for **Cross Section** for Louis
Armstrong's touring jazz band. *Dur.:* 7:00. The arrangements were
probably made by Ray Cook or Eric Razdell. The score is missing.
Performance: 1958 (August). Sydney (Sydney Stadium). Louis Armstrong
and his band.

W 70 Left Bank Waltz (1958)
For piano. *Dur.:* 1:30. Score, Allans Music Pty Ltd [Australian Music
Examinations Board publication], *c*1962. Also published as no. 2 of **Two
Easy Pieces (W104)**; *see* **Two Easy Pieces** for *performances*.
Recordings: **D21, D38-39 (Two Easy Pieces)**. *Reviews: see* "Discography."

W 71 Musique Concrète (1958) withdrawn
For animated film *Man from Outer Space*. *Lit.:* **B74**.

W 72 Some New Moon (1958) not available
Incidental music for a play by Catherine Duncan. Song *Moon after
midnight* is available.
Performance: 1958 (July 28). Hobart TAS. Fifth Hobart Drama Festival.
Production entered into original play section for *The Mercury*
perpetual trophy. Peter Sculthorpe, piano. *Also:* adapted for radio,
broadcast 1958 (August 5), ABC, Sydney.

W 73 Prophecy (1958) withdrawn
For unison voices and piano. Text from Isaiah 34. Contents: *The Laying
Waste; The Blossoming*. 6 p.

W 74 Sun (1958) withdrawn
Song cycle for medium voice and piano. *Dur.:* 9:00. Text: D. H.
Lawrence. Contents: 1. *Sun in me;* 2. *Tropic;* 3. *Desire goes down into
the sea.* "For Wilfrid and Peggy Mellers" (Wilfrid Mellers and Pauline
Lewis).
Performance: 1960 (February). Birmingham UK (Birmingham Art
Gallery). Pauline Lewis, mezzo-soprano; Wilfrid Mellers, piano.
Repeated: July. Shropshire (Attingham Park Summer School), with the
Sonata for Viola and Percussion (W77). *Also:* P67-7 on tape (**B208**).

W 75 Irkanda II (String Quartet no. 5) (1959) withdrawn
For string quartet. *Dur.:* 10:00. Written in Oxford. Awarded First Prize
(£100) in the 1959 Royal Concert Trust Fund Composers' Competition
conducted by the Australian Musical Association, London. *Lit.:* **B28**.
Performance: 1960 (February 29). Oxford (Lincoln College). Concert in aid
of World Refugee Year. Wilfred Lehmann Quartet. *Reviews:* **B29-31**.

W 76 Sonata for 'Cello Alone (1959) withdrawn
In one movement, several sections. Material was taken from **Sonata
for Violin Alone (W61)**, movements I and III.

Composer's note (1980): "The work was written in Oxford in 1959 upon the request of an Australian 'cellist then living in England. Unfortunately, it was never performed; the 'cellist found it unplayable. Thus, I later decided to re-think the music, and in 1960 it became the **Sonata for Viola and Percussion**. The 'cello sonata is in one movement. It could be said that it is a free set of variations upon three ideas—the first a *quasi*-Mahlerian melody accompanied by plucked open strings, the second a rapidly-repeated rhythmic figure, and the third a martial-like motive punctuated by percussive sounds. My 'cellist friend took the most objection to the percussive sounds. I have resisted the temptation to revise the original score."

First performance: 1980 (October 12), as "Sonata for Unaccompanied Cello." Sydney (Cell Block Theatre). Megan Garner, cello. *Review:* **B677**.

W77   Sonata for Viola and Percussion (1960)
For solo viola and percussion (1 player)—tam tam, large susp. cymbal, Chinese cymbal, triangle, bass drum, side drum, tom tom, bongos. *Dur.:* 12:00. Awarded First Prize (£100) in the 1960 Royal Concert Trust Fund Composers' Competition conducted by the Australian Musical Association, London. In one movement: *Animato—Poco lento—Animato—Risoluto—Poco lento—Lento* (then *Alla marcia funebre)—Quasi cadenza—Risoluto.* Inscribed at the end "Oxford July 1960." The work is based upon the **Sonata for Cello Alone (W76)**. Playing score 50554-6, 1979, 12 p., inscribed "To Peter Komlos" (he championed the work in the seventies). Publication of the score was assisted by a grant from the Music Board of the Australia Council. *Lit.:* **B32, B288**.

Composer's note (1962): "The work was written with feelings of longing for Australia and also with feelings of apprehension towards Asia. It is in one continuous movement. Formal growth is through a succession of architectonic blocks based on a martial figure heard at the outset, and an expressive melody for viola."

First performance: 1960 (July). Shropshire, England (Attingham Park Summer School). Rosemary Green, viola; Peter Sculthorpe, percussion.

Other performances: **P62-3, P64-8, P65-10, P67-7, P70-11, P71-10, P72-5, P73-11, P76-1, -4, P79-4, P80-3, P81-12, P86-3, -11, P88-6, -8, -10, P89-10** (x2), **P90-9, P91-7.** *Reviews:* **B82-82n, B83-83n, B84-86, B137-138, B208, B255, B525, B530, B830, B910, B925.**

Recordings: **D44-45.**

W78   King Lear (1960)
Incidental music for the Shakespeare play. Musique concrète.
Performances: 1960 (October 24-29). Oxford, England (Oxford Playhouse). Lincoln College Players production. *Reviews:* **B34**. Some of the music was used in a later production at Stratford-upon-Avon.

W79   Irkanda III (1961) withdrawn
For piano trio. Commissioned by the Birmingham Chamber Music Society in 1960. Uses material from **Irkanda II (W75)**. Inscribed "Music to be always austere … Australian. Jan. 1961, Launceston, Tasmania."
Performance: 1961 (February 18). Birmingham UK (Birmingham Art Gallery). London Czech Trio: Lisa Marketta, piano; Jack Rothstein, violin; Karel Horitz, 'cello. *Lit.:* **B33**. *Reviews:* **B41**.
Also performed: **P65-2**. *Reviews:* **B93**. Performed, early sixties, in Hobart: Beryl Sedivka, Jan Sedivka, Sela Trau; tape broadcast in 1981 (**B691**).

W80 Irkanda IV (1961)

For solo violin, 1 percussion (bass drum, tom tom [or side drum without snares], gong, 2 susp. cymbals [large, small], triangle), strings. *Dur.:* 11:00. In one movement. Uses material from **Sun (W74)**, **Irkanda II (W75)**, and **Sonata for Viola and Percussion (W77)**. Score is inscribed at the beginning "Written upon the death of my father," and at the end "Launceston, Tasmania, June, 1961." Composed for the Astra Chamber Orchestra and Wilfred Lehmann. The solo part of this work may be performed by the leader of the orchestra, sitting at his/her desk. Full score, 50128-1, 1968; 19 p.; parts for hire. *Review:* **B313.** Excerpt used in orchestration book, **B506.**

Composer's note: "This work is a plain and straightforward expression of my feelings upon the death of my father. The one predominantly slow movement is made up of a ritual lamentation heard at the outset, alternating with contrasting sections growing from that material. Following the climax an extended song-like coda suggests an affirmation of life and living, and the work ends in a haze of wind and sea and sun. There is little development in the nineteenth-century sense, but rather, growth by accretion, almost, it might be said, like the manipulation of building blocks made of sound. *Irkanda* is an Australian Aboriginal word meaning 'a remote and lonely place.' " *Addenda, 1984,* **D35:** "Looking back, I now regard **Irkanda IV** as my first mature work. It also marks the beginning of my preoccupation with solar symbolism. The coda is an instrumental setting of D. H. Lawrence's poem *Sun in Me.* The poem is a clear statement of Lawrence's doctrine concerning the dark sun, 'the same that made the sun and the world, and will swallow it again like a draught of water.' ([**B286**, 1969]: The melisma of the solo violin is, in fact, a reflection of the poem: thus in the final bars there is a high white 'c', and Lawrence, in his poem, relates sun and atom to God and atom. The high white 'c', which must be the whitest note of all is the word 'God'.) In subsequent works, I might add, this dark sun was transformed into my own sun, a Pacific sun."

First performance: 1961 (August 5) Melbourne (Nicholas Hall). Wilfred Lehmann, violin; Astra Chamber Orchestra; George Logie-Smith, conductor. *Lit.:* **B43.** *Reviews:* **B42, B44-B46, B48, B50, B58.**

Other performances: P63-7, -9, -11, P65-6, -9, P67-2, -3 (x2), -11, P68-2 (& March), -8, P69-8, P70-3, P71-1, -3, -4, -6, P73-2, -3, -4, P74-6, P75-7 (dance), -10, P76-4, P77-9, P80-3, P83-3, P86-6, P87-2, P88-1, -3, -5, -7, P89-4, -5, -7, -12, P90-1, -4, -7, -9, P91-5, P92-9 (& Oct), -12. *Reviews:* **B61, B65, B68, B112-113, B121, B188-190, B193-193n, B235, B400-401, B406, B530, B816-817, B850, B973-974, B983, B989, B1005.** *Performed by string sextet and perc:* P74-6; **B470-471.**

Recordings: **D31, D35-36.** *Reviews: see "Discography."*

W81 Three Songs (1962)

For voice and piano. Text: Edna and Peter Sculthorpe. Contents: *Fallen for you; Why don't you make your mind up?; Tell me you love me.* With the need to earn a living through his work, the composer wrote these somewhat commercial songs with the intention of making what is now called a "demonstration tape." The songs were not recorded. 9 p.

W82 They Found a Cave (1962)

Film score (Chappell and Co.). Columbia Pictures; a Visatone Island production; Andrew Steane, director; Charles Wolnizer, producer. *Dur.:* 63:00. Main theme is the melody of **Left Bank Waltz (W70)**, and it

is heard in a number of variations. Film is also on video recordings: captioned version, Melbourne: Syme Home Video and Australian Council for Children's Films and Television, 1988? Excerpt in **B982**.
Plot: four English orphans staying at their aunt's farm in Tasmania, and their friend Tas, the farm boy, foil a plan to swindle the aunt. The story is from a book by Tasmanian author Nan Chauncy (whose property was used for the film's outdoor scenes).
Film premiere: 1962 (December 20), Hobart. *Lit.:* **B55-55n, B56-57**. Launceston premiere earlier. *Revival:* 1978 (January), Sydney Filmmakers' Cooperative, for Festival of Sydney. *Lit.:* **B569**.
Recording of *Theme and Journey's End* (1961): **D72**.

W83 Two Shakespeare Songs (1962)
For voice and piano. Text: Shakespeare. Contents: I. *Take, O take those lips away* (**W24**); II. *O mistress mine* (from **W64**). Revisions of two early songs, prepared especially for Max Oldaker, to whom they are dedicated. Inscribed "To Max." 5 p.

W84 The Splendour and the Peaks (1963)
Documentary film score. Commonwealth Film Unit.

W85 Sonata for Piano (1963) withdrawn
Inscribed at the end "October 1963." Uses material from **Sun** (**W74**), **Irkanda II** (**W75**), and **Irkanda III** (**W79**). First movement was reinstated in 1989 as **Callabonna** (**W197**).
First performance: 1963 (November 3). Sydney (Cell Block Theatre). Peter Sculthorpe, piano. *Review:* **B67**. *Also:* movement I on TV, **P63-10** (**B66**).

W86 Kings Cross Overture (1963) not available
For orchestra: 2.2.2.2., 4.2.2.1, timp, perc, strings. Orchestral arrangement of material from revue **Cross Section**. Mentioned in **B62** (the composer is writing it for Thomas Matthews). The score is missing.

W87 The Fifth Continent (1963)
Radiophonic. For speaker and orchestra: 0.1.0.0., 0.1.0.0., timp, 2 perc, harp, strings. Also requires occasional use of continuous tapes of didgeridoo and high wind. *Dur.:* 45:00. Text culled from D. H. Lawrence's novel *Kangaroo*. In five movements: *Prologue, Outback, Small Town, Pacific, Epilogue*. Commissioned as an ABC Italia Prize entry and composed in Tasmania. *Lit.:* **B63**.
Composer's note (1968): "Owing partly to the scoring and partly to a personal style in the process of being established, a feeling of distance and loneliness pervades the entire work. Each movement is introduced by the speaker; the narrative concerns the coming of a man to Australia, and his changing feelings for this country. The *Prologue* sets the mood and states the basic thematic material; *Outback*, the longest movement, is concerned with a land 'hoary and lost,' with charred bush and raw silences; *Small Town* is tender and relaxed, with its recollection of the bell sounding from the yellow stucco church and *The Last Post*; *Pacific* is richly oceanic, in turn both storm-torn and calm; the brief *Epilogue*, warm and sunbaked, completes the work with feelings of hope and optimism: 'the bush was in bloom, the wattles were out . . . it was August and spring, the hot, hot sun in a blue sky.' "
First performance = recording: **D9**. 1963 (December 10). Melbourne (ABC

Recording Studio). Frederick Parslow, speaker; Melbourne Symphony Orchestra; Thomas Matthews, conductor.
First live performance: 1963 (December 13). Hobart (City Hall). ABC Hobart Summer Music Festival. James McAuley, speaker; Tasmanian Orchestra; Thomas Matthews, conductor. *Reviews:* **B69.**
First Sydney performance: 1964 (January 26). *Review:* **B71.** *Paintings:* **B70.**
Also performed: **P68-9.** *Reviews:* **B75, B77.** *See also:* **Small Town, W136.**

W88 El Alamein Fountain (1964)
Documentary film score. Written for the UNESCO seminar Music for Film, March 1964, Adelaide Festival (University of Adelaide), as the soundtrack of a short film that shows the fountain in Sydney's King's Cross. *Lit.:* **B73**

W89 The Troubled Mind (1964)
Documentary film score. Commonwealth Film Unit. Also known as *Under Stress.*

W90 Irkanda IV, arr. strings and percussion (1964)
An arrangement by the composer of **Irkanda IV (W80).** *Pub.:* Melbourne: Australian Music Fund, 1964. *Review:* **B87.**
First performance: 1964 (March 20). Adelaide Festival. ISCM concert. *Reviews:* **B76-76n.**

W91 String Quartet No. 6 (1964-65)
Dur.: 15:00. First Alfred Hill Memorial Award administered by the Musica Viva Society of Australia. Dedicated to Bonnie Drysdale; inscribed "For Bonnie." In three movements: I. *Lento molto;* II. *Lento—con moto—lento—con moto;* III. *Lento—moderato assai—con moto—lento.* Uses material from **Prophecy (W73), Sun (W74), Irkanda III (W79),** and **Sonata for Piano, 2nd movt (W85).** Score 50050-1 and parts 50051-X, 1966. *Lit.:* **B62-62n** (award), **B314.** *Reviews:* **B164, B176, B191.**
Composer's note (1965): "The quartet, which is freely atonal, is based completely on several motifs heard at the outset. It is dominated by falling minor seconds and falling minor thirds. There is little formal growth in the nineteenth-century sense, but rather growth by accretion, almost, it might be said, like the manipulation of building blocks made of sound. The first movement is tense and introspective, almost funereal, having been written upon the death of a close friend. The second movement is hard and rhythmic in its outer sections, and in its central section again tense and introspective, but with the loneliness of some secret desert place. The last movement, the longest of the three, draws out the original motifs in yearning melodic lines, until finally the tension is resolved, or almost resolved. The movement revolves around recollections of phrases and fragments from both a short poem by D. H. Lawrence and the novel *Kangaroo.* The passages concern a state of no-desire, and desolation and loneliness before the sombre face of the Pacific Ocean. On the title-page of the score, one reads: 'always austere . . . . . Australian.' "
First performance: 1965 (April 1). Sydney (Town Hall). Musica Viva Subscription Concert. Austral String Quartet: Donald Hazelwood and Ronald Ryder, violins; Ronald Cragg, viola; Gregory Elmaloglu, 'cello. *Lit.:* **B92, B94-94n.** *Reviews:* **B95-B101.**
Other performances: **P65-4** (x2), **P65-6, -9** (x2), **-11, P67-7, -9, P68-6** (x2), **-9,**

P69-9, -10 (dance), P72-5, P73-11, P74-6, P75-3, -9, P76-11, P79-4, P80-2, -7, P84-5, -7, P85-6, P86-6, -10, P89-3, -4 (x2), P91-9. *Reviews:* B102, B104, B120, B122, B128, B141-142, B144, B208, B214-215, B258, B267, B318-320, B467, B595, B607, B759, B765, B767, B769, B796, B818, B827, B962, B966, B968, P976-977. Paris Rostrum: B110, B114.
Recordings: D54-55. *Reviews: see* "Discography."

W92 **South by Five** (1965) withdrawn
A group of pieces for girls' voices and instruments. Text: Roger Covell.
First performance: 1965 (May 21). Sydney (NSW Conservatorium).
UNESCO seminar on school music. Cremorne Girls' High; Merle Berriman, conductor. *Reviews:* B107-B109.
Other performances: B224 (schools).

W93 **Haiku** (1965)
For piano. The music is based upon the row from Webern, *Variations for piano*, op. 27 (1936). Originally, the work was part of a set of pieces, *Three Haiku* [P66-4]. Two of these are missing. **Haiku** reappears as mm. 63-70 of **Sun Music I** (W94), and as mm. 5-20 of *Night* in **Night Pieces** (W118). Published in B228, with discussion.

W94 **Sun Music I** (1965)
For orchestra: 0.0.0.0., 4.3.3.1., timp, 2 perc (chimes, crotali, bass drum, tenor drum, side drum, gong, 2 susp. cymbals [large, small] guiro, maracas, sand block, triangle, whip), strings. *Dur.:* 10:00. Written upon the invitation of Sir Bernard Heinze for performance by the Sydney Symphony Orchestra at the 1965 Commonwealth Arts Festival in London. Inscribed at the end: "Sydney, August 1965." Third printing (1985) of the work is inscribed at the beginning "for Bernard and Valerie Heinze." Mm. 63-70 use serialized pitches, rhythms, and attacks, as in **Haiku** for piano (W93). Score 50752-2, 1966; 28 p.; parts for hire. *Lit.:* B117-117n, B226, B282 *Reviews:* B175-176. *Analysis:* B228, summarized in B629. *Educational materials:* B683.
Composer's note [B286, B290, 1969]: "Unlike **Irkanda IV** and the Sixth String Quartet, **Sun Music I** is without specific literary reference. But the sun of D. H. Lawrence, the Mexican sun, the Japanese, Asian and Australian—and my own sun—are ever present. This is a sun which is more concerned with the mystery, fear and lonely glare of sun and space than about the pleasures of warmth. This work might be called a sound-piece, a post-impressionistic piece. Certainly **Sun Music I** has little rhythm, melody and harmony in the conventional sense. The brass instruments represent terrestial forces, while the strings are associated with celestial activities. The tempo of the piece is not quick, but it isn't really slow; rather, the piece is motionless, static."
First performance: 1965 (September 30). London (Royal Festival Hall). Commonwealth Arts Festival. Sydney Symphony Orchestra; John Hopkins, conductor. *Lit.:* B183, B269, B728. *Reviews:* B124-134, B139-140. Broadcast in Australia, ABC, October 7, with introduction by the composer; *review:* B136.
Other performances: P65-11, P66-1, -2, -5, -10, P67-7 (recording), P68-5 (x2), P69-9, P70-4, P71-6, P74-9, P76-5, -7, P77-7, -9, P78-8, P79-4, -9, P84-3, -4, P87-6, P88-7, P89-2, -9, P91-5 (several). *Reviews:* B148-149, B156-160,

B175, B182, B208, B248-254, B531, B856-857, B954-955, B1104. Paris
Rostrum: B200, B225.
Recordings: D31, D34. *Reviews:* B252, B619, B624.

W95 Night Piece (1966)
For SATB chorus and pianoforte (one or two players). *Dur.:* 2:30. Text:
Chris Wallace-Crabbe. *Note:* "The pianoforte part is for the strings only,
to be played with a large soft stick, a pair of wire brushes, and a rubber
eraser. Throughout, alto, tenor and bass parts should be whispered, and
placed in the middle register, except where glissandi are indicated."
Inscribed at the end "New Haven, Connecticut, Feb. 1966." *Published
by:* Novello and Co. Ltd.; 8 p. **Night Piece** was the supplement to the
Musical Times 107 (July 1966), with **B171** (Henderson).
Performances: **P69-4, P90-7.**

W96 Sun Music for Voices and Percussion (1966)
For SATB chorus, piano (all sounds on the strings using soft stick, hard
stick, any other assorted sticks, wire brush), 3 perc (susp. cymbal, tom-
tom, gong, maracas, bongos, bass drum, guiro, sandblock). *Dur.:* 9:00.
Originally called "Sun Music II" for voices and percussion, the work
was replaced in 1969 by the orchestral **Sun Music II** (*Ketjak*) so that all
the **Sun Music** series are orchestral works. Later, for a while, renamed
Canto 1520 (the year that the Aztec king Moctezuma was killed). Inscribed at the beginning "to Donald Peart" and at the end "New Haven,
Connecticut." Score 50172-9; 15 p.; perc part for sale. *Reviews:* **B534-535.**
Composer's note (from **B290**): "As with **Sun Music I**, this work is made up of long waves
of sound."
First performance: 1966 (March 13), as "Sun Music II." Adelaide (Elder
Hall, University of Adelaide). Second ISCM concert, Adelaide Festival
of Arts. Pro Musica Choir of the University of Sydney; Donald Peart,
conductor. Repeated at end of concert. *Reviews:* **B163.**
Other performances: **P66-5, P69-2, -4, P76-1, P90-10.** *Reviews:* **B165-169,**
B291, B525, B1068. *Recording:* **D62.**

W97 News Theme (1966)
For piccolo, percussion and strings. *Dur.:* 0:19. Written upon the invitation of the ABC, but not used. Score is in time-space notation and the
music is not unlike **Sun Music I** in sound. Inscribed "May 1966." 2 p.

W98 Morning-Song for the Christ Child (1966)
Carol for unaccompanied SATB chorus. *Dur.:* 3:00. Text: Roger Covell.
Note: "A deep gong, if available, may be rolled softly on the rim during
each verse." Arranged by the composer from **South by Five** (W92), in
response to a request from Faber Music for a Christmas carol. Score for
sale, Faberprint, 1988. *Review:* **B187.**
Performances: **P68-3, P69-3, P71-7, P80-1, P91-8.** *Reviews:* **B642, B987.**
Recordings: **D26-29.**

W99 String Quartet No. 7 (1966)

Dur.: 7:00. Commissioned by the Ellen Battell Stoeckel Trust of Norfolk, CT, for the Yale Summer School of Music. In one movement. Original title **Teotihuacan** refers to the Mexican town of that name, famous for its Pyramids of the Sun and the Moon; a later title **Red Landscape** refers to a particular painting by Russell Drysdale, and also to a large area of Drysdale's work, which is characterised by sun-drenched and drought-ridden land. Playing score for sale.

First performance: 1966 (July 29) Norfolk CT (Music Shed). Yale University Summer School of Music and Art concert. Yale Quartet: Broadus Erle, Yoko Matsuda, violins; David Schwartz, viola; Aldo Parisot, 'cello. (Announced as "Three Pieces" for string quartet.) *Reviews*: **B172-173.**
Other performances: P67-5, P68-4, -10, P72-12, P76-1, P81-6. *Reviews*: **B244-245, B247, B274, B525, B693.**
Recordings: D25. *Reviews*: **B429, B492.**

W100 **Sun Music III** (1967)
For orchestra: 2(pic). 2.2.2., 3.2.2.0., timp, 2 perc (vibraphone, chimes, bass drum, side drum, tom toms, bongos, large gong [tam-tam], small susp. cymbal, large susp. cymbal, triangle, maracas, claves, guiro, crotales), strings. *Dur.*: 13:00. Originally called **Anniversary Music**, it replaces "Sun Music III" for string orchestra (1966), now withdrawn. ("Sun Music III" for string orchestra was commissioned by George Logie-Smith for the Astra Chamber Orchestra in Melbourne; *performed* November 18, 1966, Melbourne [Assembly Hall]; *reviewed*: **B178-180.**) **Anniversary Music (Sun Music III)** was commissioned by the ABC to mark the occasion of the twentieth anniversary in 1967 of Youth Concerts in Australia. Work was begun in 1966 at Yaddo, an artists' colony in Saratoga Springs, NY, and completed in Australia in 1967. Score is inscribed at the beginning "for Donald and Kathleen Mitchell" and at the end "Saratoga Springs—London—Sydney, 1967." Study score (1973, 32 p., OP) for sale; full score and parts for hire. *Lit.*: **B269, B309, B511.**

Composer's note: "**Sun Music III** is to me a very important piece; this is the first work in which I really did something about my interest in Asian music. Parts of **Sun Music III** are written exactly in the style of Balinese gamelan, but instead of the music being played by gongs, the textures are created through the use of conventional Western instruments, mainly woodwind. The work opens with the shimmering sound of sixteen adjacent notes, in strings, followed by a pentatonic section written in the manner of music for a Balinese shadow play. This gently-flowing section is interrupted by another shimmering sound, here consisting of thirty-two adjacent notes, which leads to the central part of the work. Suggested by *gamelan arja*, music used in a form of Balinese popular theatre, the central section is dominated by an extended melody [by I Lotring], the repeated notes of which are reminiscent of the sound of gongs. The oboe announces the melody and the strings state it more fully, the whole section being decorated with brief bird-like sounds, trombone glissandi, and percussion. Following this, the timpani elaborate upon material heard at the outset and continue until the climax, after which the vibraphone, flute, and clarinets quietly recall the *gender wayang* or shadow-play music. Above these characteristic figurations the main melody enters, again in the strings, and leads, after its complete statement, into the final bars of the work."

First performance: 1967 (May 16). Perth (Winthrop Hall). West

Australian Symphony Orchestra; Bernard Heinze, conductor. *Review:* **B194**.
Other performances: P67-6, -7, -8, -10, P68-1, -3, -9, P69-2, -3, -4, -6, -11, P70-7 (several), -8 (x3), -10 (& Nov), P71-2, -4, -5, -6, P72-4, -6, -8, -12, P73-8, -10, P74-3 (x5), -5, -10, -11, P75-3, -4, P77-10, P78-4, -7, P79-6, P80-10, P83-1, P84-7, -12, P85-4, P86-5 (& June), P87-3, -7, -9, -11, P88-7, -11, P89-3, P91-8, P92-5. *Reviews:* B201-202, B209-211, B216, B218-219, B222, B291, B361, B376, B583, B701, B726, B732-733, B933-934, B956, B1115. *Recordings:* D34, D64-67. *Lit. & reviews: see* "Discography."

W101 Sun Music IV (1967)
For orchestra: 2(pic). 2.2.2., 4.3.3.1., timp, 2 perc (bass drum, side drum, large gong [tam-tam], susp. cymbal, triangle, temple bells, maracas, guiro), strings. *Dur.:* 9:00. Commissioned by the Australasian Performing Right Association (APRA) Music Foundation in April 1967 for performance at Expo '67 in Montreal. Based principally on material originally in **String Quartet No. 7** (**W99**), and then transferred into "Sun Music III" for string orchestra (*see* **W100**). Score is inscribed at the end "New York—London—Sydney, 1967." Study score (1973, 24 p., OP) for sale; full score and parts for hire. *Lit.:* **B195n, B269**. *Review:* **B509**.
Program note: The first few sentences of the note for **Sun Music I** are used for this work ("the mystery, fear and lonely glare of sun and space"). Descriptions of **String Quartet No. 7** ("sun-drenched and drought-ridden land") also apply.
First performance: 1967 (May 29). Melbourne (Town Hall). ABC Subscription concert. Melbourne Symphony Orchestra; Willem van Otterloo, conductor. (The composer attended.) **B196-199n, B207**.
North American premiere: 1967 (June 6). Montreal, Quebec (Salle Wilfrid Pelletier). Expo '67. MSO; van Otterloo. *Lit.:* **B198n**. *Reviews:* B203-206; mentioned in B247. Also CBC radio and TV studio broadcast.
Other performances: P67-7, -9 (recordings), P67-11, P68-2 (x2), -3, -6 (x6), -8, P69-3, -5, P70-1 (? for dance), -3, -4, -6, -11, P71-7, P73-10, P74-8, -9, P75-11, P76-4, P77-6, P79-7, P88-5, P89-11, P91-5. *Reviews:* B208, B230-234, B240, B255, B259, B261, B272, B287, B305-306, B474, B476, B701, B518-518n, B530.
Recordings: D34, D68. *Reviews:* B619, B624.

W102 Age of Consent (1968)
Film music. Columbia Pictures. Written for a feature film based on Norman Lindsay's novel of the same title. Commissioned by the director Michael Powell. Score has theme music for the stars James Mason and Helen Mirren, and pop music emanating from the transistor of one of the characters; Helen Mirren's theme, influenced by *gamelan* music, was said to have popular hit potential. Uses material from **The Fifth Continent** (**W87**: *Small Town*), and **Tabuh Tabuhan** (**W106**). *Lit.:* **B269**. Owing to the poor quality of the sound recording, the music was not used in the film after its Australian season.
Premiere: 1969 (March 27). Brisbane (Odeon Theatre). *Also screened:*

Sydney (Rapallo Theatre).

W103 **Sea Chant** (1968)
For unison voices and piano, with optional parts for high instruments and percussion. *Dur.:* 2:00. Arranged from **South by Five** (**W92**). Text: Roger Covell. **Sea Chant** was the supplement to the *Australian Journal of Music Education*, no. 3 (1968) with **B270** (Covell). Score for sale.
Composer's note: "The descant may be played by flutes, recorders or chime bars. Suggested percussion instruments are bass drum, gong, suspended cymbal, side drum, triangle, jingles and maracas. The cymbal should always sound like breaking waves, and percussion players may improvise in verses 4 and 5."
Performances: **P70-9, P87-11, P91-4.** *Reviews:* **B1100-1101.**

W104 **Two Easy Pieces** (1968)
For piano. *Dur.:* 3:00. Contents: I. **Sea Chant** (**W103**), arr. piano; II. **Left Bank Waltz** (**W70**). Score for sale. **Sea Chant** is to be in *Australian Piano Music*, vol. 2, by Sally Mays (Sydney: Currency Press, 1994).
Performances: **P81-7.**
Recordings: **D38-39.** *Reviews: see* "Discography."

W105 **Autumn Song** (1968)
For unaccompanied SATBarB chorus. *Dur.:* 3:00. Arranged from **South by Five** (**W92**) in response to a request from Faber Music. Text: Roger Covell. Score for sale.
Composer's note: "The text speaks, almost as in a nursery rhyme, of the Australian landscape."
Performances: **P68-3, P79-4, P81-6, P88-5, P90-7, P92-6, -9.** *Review:* **B607.**

W106 **Tabuh Tabuhan** (1968)
For wind quintet (flute, oboe, clarinet, bassoon, horn), and percussion (2 players—timpani, vibraphone, chimes, tam-tam, 2 susp. cymbals, bass drum, tom-toms, bongos, guiro, maracas, sand block, whip, triangle). *Dur.:* 24:00. In five movements: I. *Grave;* II. *Pieni di sogni;* III. *Lento;* IV. *Pieni di sogni;* V. *Lento.* First John Bishop Memorial Award funded jointly by the Adelaide Festival Trust and Advertiser Newspapers Ltd. Dedicated "to my mother because she liked it so much." Score for sale; parts for hire. *Lit.:* **B216, B269, B299.**
Composer's note: "**Tabuh Tabuhan** is a Balinese word meaning 'all kinds of *gamelan* music.' Movements I, III, and V are 'Dream' movements based on Indonesian textures; II and IV are in the style of the **Sun Music** pieces. The idea of the piece stems from a love poem written by a Balinese boy about his girl. The music incorporates traditional Japanese aesthetic concepts and Balinese musical ideas."
First performance: 1968 (March 20). Adelaide SA (Town Hall). John Bishop Memorial Concert, Fifth Adelaide Festival of Arts. University of Adelaide Wind Quintet; Richard Smith and Bevan Bird, percussion. *Lit.:* **B217, B223.** *Reviews:* **B239, B241-243, B246.**
Other performances: **P68-11, P69-3, -7, P70-10, P71-5** (dance), **-6, P72-1, P73-3, -10, P76-1, P77-8** (x3), **P78-4, P79-4, -6 , -10, P88-2, P89-3, -9** (& Oct), **P91-4, P92-6** (x2). *Reviews:* **B244-245, B247, B275-277, B279, B302-303, B315-317, B366, B373, B409, B411-414, B525, B548, B610, B884, B962,**

B966.
Recordings: D70-71. *Review:* B415.

W107 **Music for Mittagong,** or **Fun Music I** (1968)
For any wind, string and percussion instruments, with bell and massed voices. Written for audience participation, the sung part consisting of nonsense syllables and imitations of bird calls. Verbal score is in time-space notation. 2 p.
Performance: 1968 (April 14, Easter Sunday). Mittagong Festival.
Reviews: B244-245, B255.

W108 **From Tabuh Tabuhan** (1968)
For orchestral strings and perc (2 players—timpani, vibraphone, gong, large susp. cymbal, bass drum). *Dur.:* 4:00. Written at the invitation of the ABC for its radio programme marking the 86th birthday of Igor Stravinsky. Based on a section of the last movement of **Tabuh Tabuhan** (W106). Study score for sale, 4 p.; full score and parts for hire.
First performance = recording: D11. 1968 (May 2). Hobart (ABC Orchestral Studios) Tasmanian Orchestra; Patrick Thomas, conductor. Broadcast in June. *Review:* B260.
Also performed: P76-4. *Review:* B530.

W109 **Sun Music** (1968)
Ballet in five parts. For orchestra: 3.2.2.2., 4.3.3.1., timp, 3 perc, strings; and SATB chorus. *Dur.:* 44:00. Music is based on the **Sun Music** series: (1) *Soil,* **Sun Music I;** (2) *Mirage,* "Sun Music II" (**Sun Music for Voices and Percussion**); (3) *Growth,* **Sun Music III;** (4) *Energy,* new *Interlude* for percussion (this became the basis of **Sun Music II**); and (5) *Destruction,* **Sun Music IV.** Composed for the Australian Ballet. Score and parts for hire.
First performance: 1968 (August 2). Sydney (Her Majesty's Theatre). Australian Ballet. Robert Helpmann, choreographer; Kenneth Rowell, designer; Elizabethan Trust Orchestra; Robert Rosen, conductor. *Lit.:* B226, B257-257n, B282, B1074. *Reviews:* B262-265. *Photos:* B226, B523, B539, B567.
Other performances: P70-5, P71-1, P73-10. *Reviews:* B350. The ballet had over 100 performances in Australia.

W110 **Sun Music II** (1969)
For orchestra: 2(pic).2.2.2., 4.2.3.1., timp, 3 perc (bass drum, gong, large susp. cymbal, bongos [high, low], timbales [medium], maracas, whip), strings. *Dur.:* 6:00. Commissioned by the ABC for the 1969 Sydney Promenade Concert Series. Inscribed at end "Gosford—Sydney, 1969." Study score 50307-1, 1973; 19 p.; parts for hire.
Composer's note: "The inspiration for this short piece was the Balinese *ketjak* or 'monkey dance' in which the dancers fall into a kind of trance. It is a rhythmic and vital piece, without melodies or harmonies; the whole orchestra is used percussively. The music isn't oriental and the scoring is for a normal Western orchestra, but without Asia the work wouldn't have existed."
First performance: 1969 (February 22), as *Ketjak.* Sydney (Town Hall).

ABC Sydney Promenade Concert. Sydney Symphony Orchestra; John Hopkins, conductor. *Lit.:* **B308.** *Reviews:* **B292-296, B301, B304.** Broadcast April 10.
Other performances: P69-10, P70 (dance), P70-1, -2, -7, P71-2, -9, -10, P72-3, -4 (several), -5, P74-2, P75-1, P76-7, P78-8, P80-10, P81-4, -6, -8, -11 (several), P84-8, P87-3, P88-3, P89-7, P90-5, P92-2. *Reviews:* **B347-348, B772-777, B999.**
Recordings: **D34, D62-63.** *Reviews:* **B619, B624.**

W111   String Quartet No. 8 (1969)
Dur.: 16:00. Commissioned by the Radcliffe Trust (Music Award 1969). Contents: I. *Con dolore;* II. *Risoluto;* III. *Con dolore;* IV. *Con precisione;* V. *Con dolore.* Inscribed at the beginning "To Lilian and Donald Peart." Originally titled **String Quartet Music** (published 1974), and inscribed at the end "Sydney 1968" [1969]. The composer made minor revisions to the work in 1975. Study score 50513-9, 1979; parts 50530-9. *Reviews:* **B602, B617.** *Educational materials:* **B562.**

Composer's note: "In this work, the basic ideas stem from the rice-pounding music, *ketungan,* of Bali, and the popular song play, *arja.* This music, however, serves as a starting point only, although the work does retain the basic simplicity of Balinese folk-idioms. **String Quartet No. 8** is in five movements, the first and last being almost entirely for solo cello. These shorter movements, together with the third movement, are writen in a spatio-temporal notation in order to create a feeling of improvisation, and also to form a contrast with the strict meters, in the second and fourth movements, of the quicker *ketungan* sections. The actual metrical patterns in these, extremely limited in the number of notes employed, are characteristically Indonesian. These two movements, in fact, seem to have a static, ritualistic quality that is very much in keeping with the ideals of Asian music, and not unrelated, in the West, to present-day popular music. The scarcity of climaxes, and the work's symmetrical shape which could never function as an intense dramatic structure, are indicative of a compositional aim which has obsessed me. I have consistently tried to purge the European heroic gesture from my music."

First performance: 1970 (January 15). London (Wigmore Hall). Macnaghten Concert Series. Allegri Quartet: Hugh Maguire and David Roth, violins; Patrick Ireland, viola; Bruno Schrecker, 'cello. *Reviews:* **B329-334, B343-344.**
Other performances: P69-11, P70-8, -9 , P71-3, -7, -11, P72-5, -6, -12, P73-4, P75-5, -11, P77-8, -10 (x2), P77-11 (x2), P78-4, P79-3, -4, -6, P80-2, -7 (x2), -10, P81-11, P82-9, P83-9, -10, P84-3, -8, -10, P86-3, -9, -11, -12, P87-1, -2, -3 (1, & dance [& 1989]), -4 (dance x2), -7, P88-2 (x3, & dance), -3 (x2, & dance), -4 (dance, & May 1990), P88-5, -8, -10, -11, P89-4, -5, -9 (dance), -10 (x2, +2 [dance, & 1991]), P90-5 (1, & dance [& June]), -9, P91-6, -9 (dance), P92-5. Kronos Quartet frequently performs the **2nd movement** alone, as *Rice Pounding Music. Reviews:* **B328, B362, B403, B416-417, B444-445, B560-561, B608, B644, B699, B746, B755, B785, B811, B813, B825, B834, B837-839, B848-849, B852, B863, B882-883, B891, B909, B937, B990, B1044, B1107, B1160, B1179.**
Recordings: **D25, D56-59.** *Reviews:* see "Discography."

W112   Love 200 (1970)
For orchestra: 2.2.2.2.cbn., 4.3.3.1., timp, 3 perc (bass drum, timbales,

bongos, gong, 2 susp. cymbals, vibraphone, chimes, maracas, guiro, cymbals), strings; 2 vocalists; rock band (drum kit, electric piano, bass guitar, electric guitar). *Dur.:* 18:00. Text: Tony Morphett. Contents: I. *Prelude;* II. *It'll rise again;* III. *Interlude;* IV. *The stars turn;* V. *Interlude;* VI. *Love.* Commissioned by the ABC for the 1970 Sydney Promenade Concert Series. Title refers to the 200th anniversary in 1970 of the landing of Capt. Cook whose voyage was planned to watch the transit of the planet Venus, Venus being the goddess of love. Full score for hire.

First performance: 1970 (February 14). Sydney (Town Hall). ABC Promenade concert. Jeannie Lewis, singer; Tully rock band (Terry Wilson, singer; Michael Carlos, keyboards; Richard Lockwood, reeds; Robert Taylor, bass); Ellis D. Fogg, Light Show Environmentalist; Sydney Symphony Orchestra; John Hopkins, conductor. *Lit.:* **B327, B335-335n.** *Reviews:* **B336-336n, B337, B338-338n, B339, B341-342, B345.**

Other performances: **P70-7** (TV film), **P70-9, P71-3, P72-3.** *Reviews:* **B363, B399.** Mentioned in **B402.**

Recording: **D23;** excerpts, arr.: **D4, D17.** *Review:* **B465.**

W113   **Music for Japan** (1970)

For orchestra: 2 (optional fl3 or pic).2.2.2., 4.4.3.1., timp, 3 perc (crotales, timbales, tam tam, side drum, bass drum, 2 bongos, whip, maracas, sand block, guiro, susp. cymbal, claves—all amplified), strings. *Dur.:* 12:00. Inscribed at the beginning "To John Hopkins" and at the end "Sydney, March-April 1970." Commissioned for the Australian Youth Orchestra by the National Music Camp Association for performance at Expo '70, Osaka. Full score 50535-X, 1979; 27 p.; parts for hire. *Analysis:* **B1189.** Score excerpt in **B751.**

Composer's note: "I wanted the AYO to take to Japan music that says something of my own country. If the view of desert and sea, bush and city seems to be a personal one, it is because I wanted also to send music that says something about me. Some of the most memorable times of my life have been in Australia and Japan. **Music for Japan** is quite adventurous in its sonorities and in the means required to produce these. It might be called a 'sound piece' because, like my **Sun Music** series, it's made up of sound-impressions. Much as I enjoy writing melodies, in this work I've used no conventional melodic shapes, in order to give more fully an abstraction of my feelings."

First performance: 1970 (May 25). Melbourne (Town Hall). ABC Youth Concert. AYO; John Hopkins, conductor. *Reviews:* **B351-353.** *Lit.:* **B354, B359-359n.** Concert was also broadcast June 23 by ABC radio on second network (*lit.: ABC Radio Guide,* 16 June).

Other performances: **P70-7** (x2, including Expo '70), **P71-2, P71-12** (dance, & March 1972), **P72-4, P74-2, P76-1, -8, -9, P77-5, P78-4, 11.** *Reviews:* **B359-359n, B392-396, B434-436, B463, B525**

Recording: **D30.** *Reviews:* **B383-384, B390.**

W114   **Dream** (1970)

For any instruments and any number of performers. Any duration. Written for the ISCM, Sydney. Playing score for sale.

First performance: 1970 (September 21-22). Sydney (Cell Block Theatre). ISCM Music Now Proms Series concert. Jeannie Lewis, singer; Peter

Richardson, flute; students and staff of the Department of Music, the University of Sydney; various ethnic instruments; Peter Sculthorpe, conductor. *Reviews:* **B364-365, B372.**
Other performances: **P70-11, P71-11, P89-1, P90-6, -9, P91-11.** *Reviews:* **B375, B1047.**

W115 Morning Song, arr. string quartet (1970)
This work was arranged especially for the Austral String Quartet.
First performance = recording: **D25.** *Reviews:* **B429, B492.**

W116 Rain (1970) withdrawn
For orchestra: 2(pic).2.2.2.cbn., 4.2.3.1., timp, 3 perc (marimba, vibraphone, glockenspiel, bongos, sand block, timbales, crotales, maracas, antique cymbal, susp. cymbal, side drum, bass drum, gong), strings. *Dur.:* 14:00. Contents: *Opening music; Water music; Golden rain* [Javanese melody *Udan mas*]; *Waves; Closing music.* "To Barry, Deborah, Meredith and Suzy" [Barry and Deborah Conyngham, Meredith Oakes, Susan Day]. Commissioned by the XVIII International Dairy Congress Committee, Sydney, in 1970.
First performance (as **Music of Rain**): 1970 (October 12). Sydney (Town Hall). Special Concert, XVIII International Dairy Congress. Sydney Symphony Orchestra; Janos Ferenscik, conductor. *Lit. & review:* **B367.** *Repeated:* October 14, SSO subscription series concert. *Reviews:* **B368-371, B373.**

W117 Overture for a Happy Occasion (1970)
For orchestra: 2.2.2.2., 2.2.2.1., timp, 1 perc (susp. cymbal, gong, bass drum), harp, strings. *Dur.:* 4:00. Commissioned by the City of Launceston for the occasion of the re-opening of the Princess Theatre, Launceston. This work is an abbreviated version of the orchestral music of the last movement of **Love 200** without rock band and vocal lines. Full score and parts for hire.
First performance: 1970 (November 16). Launceston (Princess Theatre). Special concert (as above). Elizabethan Trust Orchestra of Sydney; Dobbs Franks, conductor. *Lit.:* **B377, B380.** *Review:* **B379.**
Also performed: **P76-4, P91-2.** *Reviews:* **B530, B1091.**

W118 Night Pieces (1971)
For piano. Also called *Five Night Pieces. Dur.:* 7:00. Commissioned for the Festival of Perth in 1971. Contents: I. *Snow, Moon and Flowers;* II. *Night* (1965/70); III. *Stars.* Score prefaced by *haiku* poem by Masaoka Shiki (1867-1902): "The moon one circle; Stars numberless; Sky dark green." The work may be played directly on the strings, if desired, as in **D43.** *Snow, Moon and Flowers,* and *Night* were first published in 1972 and *Stars* in 1973 by Allans Music (Australia) Pty Ltd. Score 50369-1, 1973; 8 p. *Review:* **B510.**
Composer's note: "The opening bracket of pieces is based on a Japanese concept known as *setsugekka,* which means, literally, 'snow, moon and flowers'. This concept is concerned with metamorphosis: moonlight, for instance, may make snow of flowers, and flowers of snow; and the moon itself may be viewed as an enormous snowflake or a

giant white flower. The music of these three pieces, and of *Stars*, is concerned with transformations of similar harmonic and motivic structures. *Night* is a free transcription of part of **Sun Music I** (1965). It is related to the other pieces in its gong-like punctuation and its harmonic usage. *Snow, Moon and Flowers* is dedicated to Michael Hannan, *Night* to Anne Boyd and *Stars* to Peter Kenny."

First performance (without *Stars*): 1971 (February 28). Perth (Octagon Theatre, University of Western Australia). Festival of Perth, Australian Composers' Workshop Concert. David Bollard, piano.

Other performances: P73-2, -10, P76-4, P77-5, -11, P78-1, -5, -8 (x2), -9 (several), -12, P79-4, P80-1, -3, P81-7, P82-11, P83-10, P84-12, P89-1, -2, -3, -4, -5, -7, -8, P90-9, P91-2, -11, -12. *Reviews:* B460, B530, B543, B577, B584, B586, B642, B723, B951, B953, B962, B966, B1000, B1003, B1113, B1129.

Recordings: D38-39; selections on D21, D32, D43. *Reviews: see* "Discography."

W119 Landscape (1971)

For amplified piano with tape delay and pre-recorded tape loop (made by performer). Performance requirements: piano; microphone or microphone pre-amplifier, 2 potentiometers, two tape recorders (mono), 2 power amplifiers, 2 loudspeakers; wire brushes, timpani sticks, rubber eraser, and a number of thin leather straps. *Dur.:* 13:00. Commissioned by the Department of Music, the University of Western Australia, for the 1971 Perth Festival. In order to make the work more accessible to performers, a simplified performance edition, without tape delay, was prepared by Michael Hannan in 1981. Revised score for sale.

First performance: 1971 (February 28), with **Night Pieces** above.

Other performances: P71-9, P73-10, P74-12, P81-5, P82-11. *Reviews:* B420, B460, B502, B689. Excerpt in B982.

Recordings: D20, D38-39, D43. *Reviews: see* "Discography."

W120 Love 201 (1971) not available

Ballet devised for The Dance Company (New South Wales) for performance at the Aquarius Festival of University Arts, Canberra, May 1971. For rock band (winds, keyboards, bass guitar, drums) and pre-recorded tape of J. S. Bach's Fourth Brandenburg Concerto (for chamber orchestra: 2 flute/recorders, strings, continuo). (Rock band plays countermelodies and harmonies in parallel with the concerto.) *Dur.:* 15:00. Score somewhere in Hungary.

First performances: 1971 (May 21). Canberra (Canberra Playhouse). Aquarius Festival of University Arts. The Dance Company (NSW); Syrius ([*sic*], Hungarian rock band—flute, saxophone, electronic organ, percussion), with pre-recorded tape. *Lit.:* B407. *Reviews:* B408-408n. *Also performed:* P71-5. *Review:* B409.

W121 How the Stars Were Made (1971)

For percussion ensemble of 6 players (vibraphone, marimba, xylophone, tubular bells, glockenspiel, crotales, susp. Chinese and Turkish cymbals, crash cymbals, roto-toms, Aboriginal music sticks, bullroarer, Chinese bell-tree, bass drum, triangle, whip). *Dur.:* 10:00.

Commissioned by the Musica Viva Society of Australia for perform-
ance at the Canberra Spring Festival in 1971 by Les Percussions de
Strasbourg. In seven movements: (1) *Prelude;* (2) *Sea;* (3) *Seashore;* (4)
Interlude; (5) *Fire;* (6) *Interlude;* (7) *Stars.* Playing score, manuscript,
for hire.
Composer's note: "The title and structure are based on an Australian Aboriginal
Dream-time legend of Rolla-Mano and the Evening Star, from W. E. Thomas, *Some
Myths and Legends of the Australian Aborigines* (Melbourne, 1923): One day, Rolla-
Mano, the Old Man of the Sea, saw two beautiful women walking on the seashore. He
chased them and captured one. The other dived into the sea, and vanished. Rolla-
Mano threw his fire stick after her, and the sparks scattered and became stars. Rolla-
Mano then took the captured woman into the kingdom of the sky, and they have both
lived there since that time. The *Prelude* and the two *Interlude* movements, serving as
punctuation to the work, are basically aleatoric. *Sea* consists of an accompanied vibraphone solo, and its music is gently transformed at the end of the work, in *Stars. Seashore* and *Fire,* on the other hand, are more sharply defined rhythmically, and the
metrical patterns and instrumentation used in each are closely related. The climax is
at the beginning of *Stars.* At this point most of the tuned metallic instruments are
amplified, remaining so until the end of the work."
First performance: 1971 (October 4). Canberra (Playhouse). Musica
Viva's Canberra Spring Festival. Les Percussions de Strasbourg.
Reviews: **B421-422.** *Lit.:* **B430.**
Other performances: P71-10, P79-*2, -12, *P81-8, *P82-11, P86-8, P88-8,
P89-3, -*4, -*5 (x3), -*6, -*10 (x2), P90-4, P92-10 (* = arr. Askill for four
players). *Reviews:* **B423-426, B590, B697, B823, B962, B966, B988, B1012.**
Recordings: *D12-14. *Reviews:* **B869, B950.**

W122   The Stars Turn, arr. high voice and piano (1972)
Dur.: 5:00. The work is a reduction of **The stars turn** from **Love 200** for
rock band and orchestra (**W112**). "To my family." Score for sale.
First performance: 1972 (April 4). Sydney (Town Hall). "Gipsy Train:
Jean Lewis in concert with." Jeannie Lewis, singer.
Other performances: P71-2, P80-3, P83-10, P89-5. *Review:* **B989.**

W123   The Stars Turn, arr. high voice, strings, and percussion (1972)
An arrangement of **The stars turn** from **Love 200** (**W112**). Percussion:
timpani, vibraphone, chimes, gong, large susp. cymbal, small susp.
cymbal, bass drum. (Listed in Faber Music catalog, 1979, and in **B876** as
for **high voice and strings** [string orchestra], no percussion.)

W124   Ketjak (1972) not available
For six male voices with tape delay. *Dur.:* 10:00. Text: nonsense
syllables by the composer. Commissioned by the Arts Council of Great
Britain. Composed for the King's Singers. Score, 7 p.
Composer's note: The title derives from a Balinese trance-inducing music sung, usual-
ly, by a number of men sitting in concentric circles around a narrator. The narration is
taken from an episode in the *Ramayana* where Rama enlists the aid of tribes of
monkeys to rescue Sita from the Evil Demon.
First performance: 1972 (July 8). Cheltenham, England (Pittville Pump
Room). 1972 Cheltenham Festival. King's Singers. *Lit.:* **B439.** *Reviews:*
B440-442.

W125 Rites of Passage (1972-73)

Theatre work for dancers, double SATB chorus, 2 onstage orchestras—(1) for *chorales:* 2 tubas, 3 perc (tam tams, cymbals, bass drum, tubular bells, glockenspiel, vibraphone), piano (with optional tape delay), 6 'cellos, 4 double basses; (2) for *rites:* piano (with optional tape delay), 4 perc (small ensemble of skin drums, slit drums, bull-roarers), conch shells played by singers. Choral and orchestral music treated during performance by means of reverberation and tape delay. *Dur.:* 105:00. Contents: *First Chorale; Preparing the Ground; Second Chorale; Ordeal; Third Chorale; Interlude; Fourth Chorale; Death; Fifth Chorale; Rebirth; Sixth Chorale.* Libretto by the composer uses texts from Boethius, *The Consolation of Philosophy* (sung in Latin) for the *chorales,* and from Southern Aranda poetry (sung in Aranda) and nonsense syllables (including sounds from Ghanaian and Tibetan chants) for the *rites.* Dedicated "to my mother." Commissioned in 1965 by the Australian Elizabethan Theatre Trust for the 1973 opening of the Sydney Opera House, but instead produced the following year. *Lit.:* B72-72n, B79-79n, B111-111n, B122n, B267, B312, B355-355n. Score and parts for hire. *See:* Peter Sculthorpe, *Rites of Passage—Text and Pronunciation* (London: Faber Music, 1972), for performance directions and other information. Excerpt published in B447.

Composer's note: **Rites of Passage** is a return to the idea of drama as ritual. The titles refer to Arnold van Gennep's *Les rites de passage,* an anthropological work concerned with the ceremonies which occur at the time of transition from one status to another. The rites and chorales both make a parallel life-affirming statement; the text of the chorales is a hymn of praise to *imperitans amor,* while the rites are concerned with the progression from birth to death to rebirth.

First performance: 1974 (September 27). Sydney (Opera Theatre, Sydney Opera House). Jaap Flier, producer and choreographer; Kenneth Rowell, stage designer; Anthony Everingham, lighting; Australian Dance Theatre; Australian Opera Chorus; Geoffrey Arnold, chorus master; members of the Elizabethan Trust Sydney Orchestra; skin drums (3 players); bells and wind chimes (3 players); Michael Hannan, piano; John Hopkins, conductor. 16 perfs. *Lit.:* B437-438, B443-443n, B446, B466-467, B469-470, B475-475n, B489, B491, B499, B505 (with photos), B508, B540, B679, B873 (with photo), B874, B913, B1077, B1145. *Reviews:* B478-488, B490, B497-498, B500-501.

Other performances: 1974 (November 7-8, 2 performances) in Adelaide (Adelaide Festival Theatre). *Reviews:* B493-494.

Excerpts: Nocturne (1977) [=*Second Chorale*] for SATB chorus and optional bass instruments (performing score hire). The *Chorales* and *Rebirth* may be performed as a concert work, duration 42:30.

Performances of excerpts: P73 (*Nocturne*), P75-9, P89-5 (*Chorales*).

Recording: D42. *Review:* B568.

W126 Crimson Flower (1973)

For *gender wayang* (ensemble of four metallophones that provides the accompaniment to Balinese shadow plays). Written for performance in the ABC TV film *Tabuh Tabuhan: Peter Sculthorpe in Bali* (script by the composer); Stafford Garner, director. In a sequence of the film, the composer teaches the music, which is in traditional style, to Balinese musicians.

Performance = recording for film: 1973 (July). Ubud, Bali. Peter Sculthorpe; Ubud *gender wayang* ensemble. *Screened:* 1974 (November 13), ABC TV "Survey" program. *Lit. & reviews:* **B495**. Excerpt in **B982**.

W127 Koto Music (1973)

With the addition of **Koto Music II** in 1976 the work is usually called **Koto Music I**. For amplified piano and pre-recorded tape loop. Performance requirements: piano interior and pre-recorded tape of same; microphone, mixer, amplifier, tape recorder; *tsume* or plectra. Player makes own tape. *Dur.:* 7:00. Commissioned by the ABC and APRA, with the support of CAAC, to mark the opening of the Opera House, Sydney, in 1973. "To Roger Woodward." "L.H. techniques" and "R.H. techniques" are listed in Japanese with descriptions in English. Published in part in **B571** (with **Koto Music II**). As with **Landscape,** a simplified performance edition was prepared by Michael Hannan in 1981. Revised score for sale.

First performance: 1973 (October 13). Sydney Opera House. "Avant-garde Piano" concert of music commissioned for the opening of the Opera House. Roger Woodward, piano.

Other performances: **P79-10, 81-6, P82-2, P89-4**. *Review:* **B692**. Also: usually performed with **Koto Music II** (see below).

Recordings: **D18, D38-39**. *Reviews: see* "Discography."

W128 Essington (1974)

Film score, with Michael Hannan and David Matthews. Manuscript. Feature film written by Thomas Keneally and directed by Julian Pringle for the ABC.

Broadcast: 1974 (March 6; March 7 in QLD and TAS).

W129 The Song of Tailitnama (1974)

For high voice, 6 'cellos, 2 perc (tam tam, water gong, Chinese cymbal, crotale [high 'e'], Chinese bell tree [may substitute any small set of bells], pair bongos, pair timbales, Aboriginal music sticks [may substitute claves], guiro, wood chimes, sand block). *Dur.:* 11:00. Text from the Northern Aranda poem *The Song of Tailitnama* transcribed by T. G. H. Strehlow, sung in Aranda. Written for an ABC TV documentary film *Sun Music for Film* directed by Stafford Garner. Film is concerned with the composer's conception of the work, its composition, rehearsal and subsequent performance. Score is inscribed at the beginning "To David Matthews," and at the end "Sydney, April/May 1974." Publication assisted by a grant from the Music Board of the Australia Council. Score 50697-6; parts 50698-4; 30 p.

Composer's note: "*Tailitnama* (*Tai* pronounced *tie*) is an Aboriginal totemic centre in Central Australia. For my text I chose four verses, in Aranda, from a rock wallaby song associated with this area. The verses concern the glowing of the mountains, the coming of dawn and the singing of the Ilbirbia bluebirds as they soar to the sky. **The Song of Tailitnama** opens with a slow vocalise, followed by a short episode which leads to the main part of the work, a long dance-like section, in the latter half of which the Aranda verses are sung. These verses lead to the climax, after which follows an expansion of the opening vocalise and a short coda."

First performance = *recording for film:* 1974 (May 5). Melbourne (Bill Armstrong Studios). Halina Nieckarz, soprano; instrumental ensemble from the School of Music, Victorian College of the Arts; John Hopkins, conductor. *Broadcast:* 1974 (September 25), ABC "Survey" program. *Lit.:* **B477.**

Other performances: **P79-2, P89-3.** *Reviews:* **B591, B881, B962, B966.** Excerpts in **B982.** Score excerpts in **B908.**

Recording: **D48-49.**

W130   Alpine (1974)

For string quartet. Television commercial. Recorded by the Austral String Quartet. Not screened: the advertising agency thought that using a string quartet was "too highbrow."

W131   Sea Chant, arr. unison voices and orchestra (1975)

Dur.: 2:30. An arrangement of **Sea Chant (W103)** for unison voices and orchestra: 2.2.2.2., 4.3.2.0., timp., 2 perc, strings. Text: Roger Covell. Score and parts for hire.

First performance: 1975 (June). Melbourne (Town Hall). Massed children's choir; Australian Youth Orchestra; John Hopkins, conductor.

Also performed: **P87-7.**

W132   String Quartet No. 9 (1975)

Dur.: 15:00. Commissioned by the Musica Viva Society of Australia with assistance from the Music Board of the Australia Council, for the Austral String Quartet. In one continuous movement consisting of the sections: *Lontano—Preciso; molto preciso—Calmo—Molto preciso—Grave.* Inscribed at the beginning "To the Austral Quartet and to the memory of Ronald Ryder" and at the end "Sydney 1975." Score 50548-1 (15 p.) and parts 50549-X, 1978. *Analysis:* **B1196.**

Composer's note (1979): "The persistent theme of my music has been man and nature or, more exactly, the lonely figure in the landscape. In my works for string quartet, I have, in addition to this, tended to write with some yearning for the intellectual and emotional climates of Europe; this is perhaps because of the nature of the genre. Thus, **String Quartet No. 9** juxtaposes and combines this yearning with music derived from Australian Aboriginal sources. The structure of the work is: A (Introduction), B, C, B', A' (Coda). Of these sections, A, C and A' are basically slow, with the chant-like, three-note theme first heard in the introduction flowering into what amounts to a twelve-note elegy in the central section. The B sections are quick, the pulse being maintained by an intricate series of overlapping ostinati, a characteristic of much of my more recent music. The ostinati are based on melodies transcribed by Trevor Jones in R. M. Berndt & C. H. Berndt, *Aboriginal Man in Australia* (Sydney, 1965)."

First performance: 1975 (October 17). Sydney (Everest Theatre). Austral String Quartet. *Reviews:* **B514-515.**

Other performances: **P75-12, P76-2, -3, -4, -8, -9, -10** (tour), **P77-4, -8, -10** (x2), **P79-4, -10, P80-2, -3, P87-6, P89-4** (x3), **-5, -7, P90-10** (dance), **P91-6.**

Reviews: **B519-520, B528-528n, B529, B533, B536-538, B548, B595, B609, B647-648, B975-975n, B989, B1001, B1108.** *Lit.* (broadcast): **B663.**

Recording: **D60**. *Review:* **B582**.

W133 **Koto Music II** (1976)
For amplified piano and pre-recorded tape loop. Performance require-
ments as in **W127**. Performer makes own tape. *Dur.:* 5:00. Commis-
sioned by the ABC *Composer Plays* radio broadcast series for Michael
Hannan. Published in part in **B571**. As with **Landscape** and **Koto
Music I**, a simplified performance edition was prepared by Hannan in
1981. Revised score for sale.
First performance: 1976 (January). Sydney (ABC Studio recording).
Michael Hannan, piano.
Other performances: **P76-1, P78-5** (tape), **-7, P81-5, -6, P82-11**. *Reviews:*
B526, B576, B580, B689, B723.
Recordings: **D38-39**. *Reviews: see* "Discography."

W134 **Sun Song** (1976)
For recorder quartet. Uses American Indian material as in **W168**. Pub-
lished in *The Recorder Book*, pieces for recorder consort collected by
Steve Rosenberg. Wellington, NZ: Price Milburn Music, 1976. 2 p.
Performances: **P78-4**.

W135 **Lament for Strings** (1976)
For string orchestra. *Dur.:* 10:00. In one movement: *Desolato—Con
calore—Desolato*. Written especially for the ACO. Score is inscribed at
the end "Sydney, March 1976." Full score 50553-8, 1978; 10 p.; parts for
hire. Publication of the score was assisted by the Music Board of the
Australia Council.
Composer's note: "Although the piece is related in many ways to my threnody **Irkanda IV** (1961), its basic material stems from my theatre work **Rites of Passage** (1972-
73). The opening music, for instance, which gives the piece its title, is a reworking of
the choral lamentation following the section *Death*. This music, however, is extended in a way that was precluded by the formal needs of **Rites of Passage**, revealing in
its yearning song-like structure a characteristic debt to Mahler. The **Lament for
Strings** has three clearly-defined parts: the first is intimate, alternating solos for
violin and 'cello; the second is broader and more impassioned; and the last, dominated by solo 'cello, is again intimate." *Addenda, 1984* (D35): "Most early immigrants
and visitors to Australia were disturbed by what seemed to them to be a hostile landscape. One writer went as far as to suggest that Dante must have had the gum tree in
mind when he wrote his *Inferno*, and, he added, 'the wretched things ... give no
shade.' Even Darwin was troubled by the 'desolate and untidy appearance of the
woods'. During the nineteenth century, then, there developed a melancholic convention in Australian literature and painting. Music, however, remained untouched
by this convention until after the Second World War. At that time, as composers in
Europe began to rebuild their particular worlds, many Australian composers, unaf-
fected by the conflict, began to look more closely at their own world. For some decades, a sense of loss tended to pervade much Australian music. The **Lament for Strings**
is my farewell gesture to this melancholia. Indeed, the downward-turning motives of
the work's central section can be found in their inverted and more optimistic forms in
many subsequent pieces."
Official first performance: 1976 (May 26), as **Lament**. Wollongong,
NSW (City Hall). Australian Chamber Orchestra.
Other performances: **P76-4, -6, P77-7, P79-4, P80-1, P81-12, P82-1** (x4),

P83-1 (& tour), -3; P87-6, -7, P88-9, -10, P89-3, -10, P90-10, P91-2 (ballet), P91-4, -6, -8, P92-8 (tour). *Reviews:* B530, B532-532n, B549, B607, B635, B640-641, B700, B735, B858, B918, B962, B966, B1106, B1170-1174. *Recordings:* D19, D35. *Reviews:* B614, B895, B941.

W136 Small Town (1976)
From **The Fifth Continent** (W87). For small orchestra: 0.1.0.0., 0.2.0.0., timp, 2 perc (bass drum, chimes, triangle, Chinese cymbal, tam tam, vibraphone, tom tom, susp. cymbal, glockenspiel), harp, strings. *Dur.:* 6:00. Dedicated to Russell Drysdale. Score 50274-1; parts for hire.
First performance: 1976 (April 8). Hobart (ABC Odeon Theatre). Tasmanian Symphony Orchestra; Gerald Krug, conductor.
Other performances: P83-5, -11, P84-7, P85-1, -4, P86-3, -7, -8 (x2), -10, P88-4, -5, -6, -11, P90-2, -4, -5, -10, P91-3, -4, -6, -9 (dance), P92-4, -5 (x2). *Reviews:* B530, B896.
Recordings: D34, D36. *Reviews: see* "Discography."

W137 The Stars Turn, arr. string orchestra (1976)
Dur.: 6:00. An arrangement by the composer of *The stars turn* from **Love 200** (W112).
First performance: 1976 (April 8), with **Small Town**, above.
Other performances: P76-5 (tour), P76-6, P86-1. *Reviews:* B530, B532-532n, B809.

W138 Alone (1976)
For solo violin. *Dur.:* 6:00. Player is also asked to whistle or hum. Written for Ronald Woodcock. Score for sale.
First performance: 1976 (August 27). Nuku'alofa, Tonga (L. D. S. Auditorium). Ronald Woodcock, violin.
Also performed: P88-3, -5. *Review:* B892.

W139 The Body is a Concert of Sensation (1976) not available
Radiophonic, for speakers and singer with music improvisations. Text: Japanese poetry, trans. Graeme Wilson. *Broadcast:* 1977 (August 21).

W140 Colonial Dances, arr. two pianos (1977) not available
Dur.: 7:00. Contents: I. *The Randwick Galop* (Essie Thomas); II. *The Volunteers' Polka* (Ernesto Spagnoletti).

W141 Little Serenade (1977)
For string quartet. *Dur.:* 3:00. Based on the title theme of **Age of Consent** (1968), and written especially for the Sydney String Quartet to use as an encore. Inscribed "to Anne and Mal," the composer's niece and husband, in 1992 [*see* W218]. Score and parts for sale.
Performances: P77-8, P83, P90-5. *Review:* B1045.
Recording: D22. *Review:* B582.

W142 Love Thoughts of a Lady (1977) not available

Radiophonic, for speakers and singer with music improvisations. Text: poems, trans. Graeme Wilson, from the *Manyoshu* ("Collection of Ten Thousand Leaves"), a 4,500-poem imperial anthology from the 7th century. Uses the melody *Ise no Umi* from *saibara*, an early vocal form of *gagaku*, traditional Japanese court music. *Broadcast:* 1977.

W143   **Port Essington** (1977)
For string trio (2 violins and 'cello) and string orchestra. *Dur.:* 15:00. Commissioned by Musica Viva Australia for the ACO's 1977 Musica Viva Concert Series. In six sections, played without a break: I. *Prologue* (The Bush); II. *Theme and Variations* (The Settlement); III. *Phantasy* (Unrest); IV. *Nocturnal* (Estrangement); V. *Arietta* (Farewell); VI. *Epilogue* (The Bush). "Dedicated to Ken and Joan Tribe" and inscribed at the end "Sydney, April/May 1977." Score 50579-1, 1980; 27 p.; parts for hire. The cover of the printed score was especially drawn by Russell Drysdale: *Essington*, ink and colour on paper.
Composer's note: "This work tells the story of the attempted settlement of Port Essington in the north of Australia. It appears that the main reason for the abandonment of Port Essington was, simply, that those living there were unable to adapt to the peculiar conditions of the land. Because my life is centred upon the idea of a culture that is appropriate to Australia, the story has, for me, a special importance. The music exists upon two planes: broadly, a string orchestra represents the bush; and the string trio playing what appears to be drawing-room music represents the settlement. During the opening sections of the work, the two planes co-exist, but then the insistence of the music of the string orchestra brings about a withdrawal of the music of the string trio. Then the string trio makes a final statement, and the music is echoed by the string orchestra, suggesting that some kind of agreement could have been possible. The theme heard in the prologue is an adaptation of an Aboriginal melody [*Djilile*] from Arnhem Land collected by Professor A. P. Elkin. This melody serves as a theme for the complete work, which is a double set of variations, one in my own manner and one in a nineteenth-century European manner."
First performance: 1977 (August 16). Brisbane (Mayne Hall, Univ. of Queensland. Australian Chamber Orchestra. *Lit.:* B544. *Review:* B553. *Other performances:* P77-8 (x5), P79-4, -6 (dance), P80-1 (x3, & Feb), -6, -10, P83-3 (tour), P84-7, P85-9, P87-5 (& June), P88-2, -4, -5 (tour) -8, -9, -10, P89-8, -9 (x6), -10 (several), -11 (x2), P90-5 (dance, & June), P91-1, -3 (tour), -5 (& June), P92-9, -10, -11, -12. *Reviews:* B552, B554-559, B607, B634, B636, B639, B798, B879-880, B887, B915, B1098. Used in film, B669. *Recording:* D35. *Reviews:* B895, B941.

W144   **Dua Chant** (1978)
For three recorders (S, A, T). *Dur.:* 2:00. Published in *Recorder Book 2*, pieces for recorder consort collected by Steve Rosenberg (Wellington, NZ: Price Milburn Music, 1978). Especially commissioned "to give players a chance to play some music of our own time." *Dua* is the name of an Aboriginal social unit.
Composer's note: "The melody used in this piece is based upon an Australian Aboriginal melody [*Djilile*] collected in Arnhem Land by Professor A. P. Elkin. If desired, a low 'A' may be sounded from the beginning of the seventh bar to the end. This 'A' drone, as in **Earth Cry** (1986) and other works, is intended to signify Australia."
Performance: **P90-2.**

W145 Landscape II (1978)
For string trio (violin, viola, 'cello) and amplified piano (keyboard and strings). *Dur.:* 18:00. Commissioned for the New England Ensemble by Musica Viva Australia in 1977. Uses the melody *Mushiroda* from *saibara*, an early vocal form of *gagaku*, traditional Japanese court music; this is played in an unsynchronized manner, called by the composer *fuori passo*. Source of transcription of melody: Sukehiro Shiba, *Gagaku*, vol. 2 (Tokyo, 1956). Score for sale.

Composer's note: "In a sense I first thought about **Landscape II** in the late sixties, at a time when I was living in a Zen Buddhist monastery in Japan. After making calls upon the Abbot of a nearby Shinto shrine, I became preoccupied with what seemed to be schizoid behaviour in the Japanese: the embracing of two religions, and the tearing between the two. I related this to my own situation, to the tearing inside me between Australia and Europe. The work, then, is influenced by both Japanese attitudes and music, by the Balinese *gamelan*, and by Australian Aboriginal chant. Its four movements are not unlike meditations, often with a feeling of suspension of time, and the natural world is ever-present, especially through the sounds of insects and the occasional cries of birds. All the same, the music is concerned with landscapes of the heart and mind as much as with their physical presence."

First performance: 1978 (April 27) Sydney (Queen St. Galleries, Woollahra). Programmed as "Desert Places." New England Ensemble—Andrew Lorenz, violin; Robert Harris, viola; Janis Laurs, 'cello; Wendy Lorenz, piano. Musica Viva concert. "The composer, a resident of Woollahra, will introduce the work." *Lit. & reviews:* **B573-575.**
Other performances: P79-4, P81-2, -5, -6, P83-9, P87-5, P92-3. *Reviews:* **B607, B685, B692, B744, B853.**
Recording: **D37** (earlier version, five movements). *Reviews:* **B995-996.**

W146 Eliza Frazer Sings (1978)
Music theatre piece. May be performed as a concert work. For soprano, flute (alto flute & piccolo), and piano. *Dur.:* 22:00. Text from Barbara Blackman's *Eliza Surviver* [*sic*], published in **B542.** Commissioned by the Lyric Arts Trio, a Canadian ensemble specializing in contemporary music with theatrical presentation. Contents: *Prelude; Shipwreck; Capture; Corroboree; Interlude; Escape.* Inscribed at the end "Sydney, Feb/March 1978." Score and part for hire. *Preliminary sketches:* **B542.** *Lit.:* **B679.**

Composer's note: "In 1836 the merchant ship 'Stirling Castle' under Captain Fraser was wrecked in northern Queensland waters. The survivors took to the longboat and, unable to put to shore, sailed southward. After putting ashore on a coastal island, later known as Fraser Island, the captain and his crew were killed by natives. Mrs. Fraser was taken prisoner and held for years. The natives believed white men and women to be returned spirits of the dead, having observed how black flesh pales when burning. They called together a corroboree, to bring about the ritual mating of their She-Ghost, Mrs. Fraser, with a He-Ghost, an escaped convict living with a neighbouring tribe. The corroboree caused Mrs. Fraser to take refuge in a dream that the convict would return as a lover and lead her away into paradisal existence. Immured in this fantasy, she was then able to endure her miseries. Unexpectedly, however, she was rescued and taken to the garrison at Moreton Bay. Her dream shattered and her sanity shaken, she set herself up in a showground booth in Hyde Park, London, where she displayed her scars and told her stories to all and sundry for the price of sixpence apiece. The text of **Eliza Fraser Sings** concerns itself with Mrs.

Fraser soliciting customers to hear her tell of her adventure, her mind wandering between the then-present and the romantically-remembered past. The work, then, is a study in breakdown of personality. While existing in the then-present outside her show-ground booth, Mrs Fraser speaks and declaims in the third person; while dreaming of the past, she sings in the first person. At the climax of *Corroboree* the present begins to elude her; at the end of the work, she exists only in a fantasy-world made up of past realities."

First performance: 1978 (April 29). Toronto (Walter Hall, Edward Johnson Building, University of Toronto). "New Music Concerts." Lyric Arts Trio: Mary Morrison, soprano; Robert Aitken, flute; Marion Ross, piano. *Lit.:* **B873**.

First Australian performance: 1978 (July 1). Sydney (Downstairs Theatre, Seymour Center). "An Evening with Eliza Fraser." Seymour Group: Eilene Hannan, soprano; Geoffrey Collins, flute; David Miller, piano. Vincent Plush, artistic director. Preceded by "Eliza Surviver" [sic] read by Gillian Jones, with music improvised on Sculthorpe themes by flute and piano with electronics—tape delay, feedback, etc. *Reviews:* **B579, B581, B585**.

Other performances: **P81-5** (tour), **-6, P88-9**. *Review:* **B916**.

W147 Exploration North (1978)

Music for an ABC TV series, directed by Ken Taylor. Six films: *The Explorers; Land of Bulloo* [the Mulga]; *The Bush; The Rainforest; The Swamps; The Reef.* From the book *Exploration North: Australia's wildlife from desert to reef*, ed. H. J. Lavery (Richmond VIC, 1978), about the northeast corner of Australia.

W148 The Stars Turn, arr. David Matthews for mixed chorus (1979)

Dur.: 5:00. An arrangement for unaccompanied chorus AATBarBarB, of *The stars turn* from **Love 200 (W112)**. Text: Tony Morphett. Written for Peter Sculthorpe on the occasion of his 50th birthday. Score for sale.

First performance: 1979 (April 13). Mittagong Easter Festival, Musica Viva Australia concert. Leonine Consort. *Review:* **B607**.

Also performed: **P80-1**. *Review:* **B642**.

W149 Four Little Pieces for Piano Duet (1979)

Dur.: 9:00. An arrangement of existing works, written especially for a concert to celebrate Peter Sculthorpe's 50th birthday. Contents: I. **Morning Song (W98)**; II. **Sea Chant (W103)**; III. **Little Serenade (W141)**; and IV. **Left Bank Waltz (W70)**. Score for sale.

Composer's note: "I felt that, to be fully representative of my work, the concert should contain overtly melodious music, as in these pieces, and music that could be played by the very young."

First performance: 1979 (April 28). Sydney (Opera House Recording Hall). "A Concert for Peter Sculthorpe's 50th Birthday." The Seymour Group; Vincent Plush, director. Julianne Reardon and Catherine Neale, piano duet. *Reviews:* **B563, B564, B567**.

Other performances: **P89-4, -5, -7, P90-7** (x2), **-8**. *Reviews:* **B600-601, B989, B1003**.

Recordings: **D10, D37, D39.** *Reviews: see* "Discography."

W150 Night Pieces, arr. harp (1979)
Dur.: 7:00. An arrangement by the composer of **Night Pieces (W118).**
First performance: 1979 (August 10). Sydney (Queen St. Galleries,
Woollahra). Seymour Group concert. Anthony Maydwell, harp.
Review: **B613.** *Also performed:* August 12 (without *Stars*), Pearl Beach
Community Hall. Seymour Group concert. Maydwell.

W151 Koto Music, arr. harp (1979)
An arrangement by the composer of **Koto Music (W127, W133).**
First performance; 1979 (August 5). Sydney (Cell Block Theatre).
Seymour Group's Direction 1980s series. Anthony Maydwell, harp.
Review: **B612.**

W152 Mangrove (1979)
For orchestra: 0.0.0.0., 4.2.3.1., 3 perc (tam tam, large susp. cymbal,
Chinese cymbal, bass drum, bongos, congas, crotales, vibraphone),
strings. *Dur.:* 16:30. Written upon the invitation of the ABC for first
performance at a concert to celebrate the composer's 50th birthday.
Inscribed at the end "Sydney, March/April, 1979." Uses *Ise no Umi* as
in **Love Thoughts of a Lady (W142).** Score 50631-3, 1982; 9 p.; parts for
hire. Publication of the score was assisted by a grant from the Music
Board of the Australia Council. *Review:* **B783.**
Composer's note: "In deciding upon *Mangrove* as the title of this work, I did not wish
literally to describe a mangrove in music but to crystallize my feelings about mangroves. The title finds many resonances in my mind: memories of a time spent among
mangroves; thoughts of Sidney Nolan's rain-forest paintings, in which Eliza Fraser
and the convict Bracefell become, through love, birds and butterflies and Aboriginal
graffiti; even recollections of a beach, mangrove-free, at Ise, in Japan; and thoughts of
a New Guinea tribe that believes man and woman to be descended from mangroves. To
me, the word itself means, in some way, 'man-woman'. The work is in one movement,
consisting of spirited sections scored for brass and percussion, and sections in which a
long, brooding melody becomes a little out of step with itself; this melody is first
played by 'cellos, and later, at the end of the work, by brass. In addition, there are
sections concerning love and loving, scored, for the most part, for strings; and strings
also play bird-sounds, the only music in the work that is specifically descriptive."
First performance: 1979 (April 27) Sydney (Opera House Concert Hall).
Sydney Symphony Orchestra; Louis Fremaux, conductor. *Lit:* **B597.**
Reviews: **B598-599, B604, B625.**
Other performances: **P79-9, P80-4, -9, P81-6, -10, P82-1, -4, P83-5, -6 (&**
July), **P84-6, -9, -12, P85-4, P86-8, -9, P87-4** (dance), **-7, P88-4** (x4), **-7, -10**
(x5); **P89-5, P90-2, P91-7, -11** (dance), **-12, P92-12.** *Reviews:* **B656-657,**
B740-741, B761-763, B766-766n, B778-779, B786-787, B792, B822, B920-
924, B926-930, B935, B938, B949, B989, B1116. Paris Rostrum: **B609;**
review: **B655.** Excerpt in **B982.**
Recordings: **D24, D36.** *Reviews: see* "Discography."

W153 Requiem (1979)
For 'cello alone. *Dur.:* 16:00. In six sections: I. *Introit;* II. *Kyrie;* III. *Qui*
Mariam; IV. *Lacrimosa;* V. *Libera me;* VI. *Lux aeterna.* The work may

be amplified. Commissioned by Musica Viva Australia for performance at the 1979 Mittagong Easter Festival, where concerts were held
to mark the composer's fiftieth birthday. Publication was assisted by a
grant from the Music Board of the Australia Council. Dedicated to
Nathan Waks. Inscribed at the end "Sydney, March-April 1979." Score
50621-6, 1982; 9 p. *Review:* **B783.**

Composer's note: "The idea of using the Plainsong Requiem Mass as source material
for a work has interested me for some years, and it continues to do so. It seemed to be
especially appropriate in writing for the particular timbral and expressive qualities
of the 'cello; and an added richness of sonority is gained by lowering the pitch of the
fourth string [to B-flat]. For the most part, the music reflects the words of the chosen
parts of the Latin text, so that where the text is in the third person, singular or
plural, I have used plainchant, and where it is in the first person I have used a more
personal music. The work, therefore, alternates between the coolness and objectivity
of plainchant, and the warmth, even passion at times, of my own kind of music,
which here is concerned with imploring, with the wanting of forgiveness, and the
wanting of eternal life."

Official first performance: 1979 (April 28). Sydney (Opera House Recording Hall). "A Concert for Peter Sculthorpe's 50th Birthday." Nathan
Waks, 'cello. *Reviews:* **B601-602, B604, B625.**

Other performances: P79-4 (x2), -10, P80-10, P81-3 (x2), -6, P82-6, P83-2,
-11, P84-5, -6, -8, -12, P85-3 (x2), -4 (x2), P85-6, -8, P88-3, P89-3, -6 (x2), -7
(x3), -9, P90-7, -11, P91-3 (x2), -7, -10 (x2), -11, -12, P92-9, -11. *Reviews:*
**B594, B600-601, B607, B618, B677, B688, B764, B771, B785, B793-795,
B962, B966, B1096-1097.**

Recording: **D37.** *Reviews:* **B995-996.**

W154 Cantares (1979)
For guitars (flamenco guitar [solo], classical guitar [solo], 3 acoustic
guitars, 4 electric guitars, electric bass) and string quartet. Amplification required for acoustic guitars, individual amplifiers for electric
and bass guitars. *Dur.:* 20:00 (but variable, depending upon the length
of the flamenco solos). Commissioned by the Spanish Guitar Society
of Sydney for John Williams, Joe Pass, Petra Quartet, and guitarists of
the 1980 Sydney Music Symposium. Dedicated to Peter and Athalie
Calvo. Written with David Matthews. In seven sections: I. *Introit;* II.
Kyrie; III. *Ego sum resurrectio;* IV. *Dies irae;* V. *Sanctus;* VI. *In para-
disum;* VII. *Benedictio.* Uses **Sun Song** (W134) melody, *Dies Irae*
chant, traditional Spanish guitar music. Study score (42 p., c1980) for
sale; full score and parts for hire.

Composer's note: "**Cantares** follows the shape of the Catholic Requiem Mass, and
several sections employ Gregorian Chant. The work is optimistic, though, being
concerned with the death and rebirth of cultures, in this case the consequences of the
Spanish conquest of Mexico. The string quartet could be said to represent native Aztec
culture, and acoustic guitars the Spanish invaders (drawing on plainchant tunes);
electric guitars offer a present-day synthesis."

First performance: 1980 (January 16). Sydney (Seymour Centre). Sydney
Music Symposium Concert. Festival of Sydney. Peter Calvo, flamenco
guiar; John Williams, classical guitar; guitarists of the Sydney Spanish
Guitar Centre; electric guitars led by Joe Pass; the Petra String Quartet,
directed by Janos Starker; Vincent Plush, conductor. Introduced by the

composer. *Reviews:* **B637-638**. *Also performed:* **P87-1** (x2).

W155   Manganinnie (1980)
Feature film. Tasmanian Film Corporation; John Honey, director.
*Dur.: c*90:00. Score includes music for: solo 'cello (a melody based on
an Aboriginal *lament* from the Arafura Sea sung in the film by
actress Mawuyul Yathalway [Manganinnie]); string quartet (*The Journey*); and piano (*The Colonial Family*, written by David Matthews in
the style of Schubert). Score won the Australian Film Institute's Best
Score award, and a Sammy award for the Best Theme Music. *Lit.:*
B622, B649. *Awards:* **B673**. *Analysis:* **B1194**.

Plot summary: Manganinnie, fleeing the Aboriginal genocide of 1830 Tasmania, is
separated from her tribe. In her search for her people, she finds Joanna, a settler's
child, whom she adopts. Joanna learns to survive in the hostile bush environment and
is initiated into the mysteries of the Dream-time. Manganinnie has been a woman of
stature among her people, the Keeper of the Flame, and she passes some of this power
to Joanna. The film is based on a story by Beth Roberts.

Film premiere: 1980 (July 9). Hobart. *Lit.:* **B664**. *Review:* **B668**. Sydney
premiere, August 20; *reviews:* **B672, B675**. London opening, January
1982; **B705**. Video recordings of film: Hobart, TAS: Tasmanian Film
Corporation; and Melbourne, VIC: Syme Home Video distributor,
1980. Captioned version, Moonah, TAS: Tricom Broadcasting Group,
1990?

W156   Small Town, arr. David Matthews for string quartet (1980)
An arrangement of **Small Town (W136)** from **The Fifth Continent
(W87)**.
First performance: 1980 (March 22). Hobart. Petra String Quartet. *Lit. &
reviews:* **B649, B651**.

W157   Boat Rise, arr. Michael Hannan for high voice and piano (1980)
Dur.: 5:00. An arrangement of *It'll rise again* from **Love 200 (W112)**.
Text: Tony Morphett. Score for sale.
First performance: 1980 (March 22). Hobart. Helena Bury, soprano;
Graeme Buchanan, piano. *Lit. & reviews:* **B649, B651**.
Also performed: **P83-10, P84-12**.
Recording: **D4**.

W158   The Visions of Captain Quiros (Guitar Concerto) (1980) withdrawn
For guitar and orchestra. *Dur.:* 32:00. Commissioned by the ABC for
guitarist John Williams. In one continuous movement of seven
sections: *First Vision; Preparation; The Pacific; Second Vision; The
South Land of the Holy Spirit; Disillusionment; Last Vision.*
Based on the Portuguese-born Spanish explorer of James McAuley's
poem *Captain Quiros*, the work also refers to Quiros's prophetic
vision of the history of Australia, a subject often mentioned to the
composer by Dr. H. C. Coombs.

Composer's note: "Stated at the opening is a re-working of an Australian Aboriginal
melody *[lament* as in **Manganinnie (W155)**]; the visions spring from this, and it also
appears in different guises in the other sections."

Performance: 1980 (July 10). Sydney (Opera House Concert Hall). John Williams, guitar; SSO; Niklaus Wyss, conductor. *Lit:* **B650, B659-660, B662.** *Reviews:* **B665-667.** *Radio broadcast:* August 27, ABC.

W159   Nocturne (1980) not available
For guitar. From **Visions of Captain Quiros (W158).**

W160   Overture for a Happy Occasion (1980)
For organ. *Dur.:* 4:00. An arrangement of **Overture for a Happy Occasion (W117),** for the re-opening of Launceston's Albert Hall in 1980. Sometimes called **Overture.** Score for sale.
First performance: 1980 (November 21). Launceston (Albert Hall, Launceston Convention Centre). Chris Ryland, organ. *Lit.:* **B678.**
Other performances: **P89-4, P92-10.**

W161   Nocturnal (1981) withdrawn
For solo piano. Written for the Musical Society of Victoria.
First performance: 1981 (June 28). North Caulfield, VIC (Caulfield Arts Centre). The Musical Society of Victoria, 597th subscription concert; concert by scholarship winners. Ian Munro, piano.
Other performances: **P81-4, -6.**

W162   Mountains (1981)
For solo piano. *Dur.* 5:00. Commissioned as a test-piece by the Sydney International Piano Competition, 1981, with assistance from the Music Board of the Australia Council. Inscribed at the beginning "To Rex Hobcroft" [Director, NSW Conservatorium] and at the end: "Sydney, January 1981." Score 50661-5, 1982; 6 p. *Review:* **B783.**
Composer's note: "Mountains is a test of musicality, rather than a test of technical virtuosity. The work is in three sections: the third is a modified version of the first; and the second is an extension of the opening motive of the work, which is made up of a falling tritone and a rising minor third. The music is a response to the mountainous terrain of Tasmania, so-called 'Isle of Mountains', where I was born."
First performance: 1981 (July 4). Sydney (Verbrugghen Hall, Sydney Conservatorium). Sydney International Piano Competition. Gabriella Pusner, piano (followed by 19 other competitors). *Review:* **B695.**
Other performances: **P81-6, -7, P86-6, P87-7, P88-3, -5, P89-1, -2, -4** (x2), **-5 -7, P91-12, P92-5** (& July). *Reviews:* **B815, B864, B951, B976, B1003.**
Recordings: **D37, D39.** *Reviews: see* "Discography."

W163   Tailitnama Song, arr. chamber ensemble (1981)
For chamber ensemble of 5 players: alto flute, perc (guiro, sand block, wood chimes, maracas, bongos, Chinese cymbal, music sticks, timbales, tam tam), violin, 'cello. *Dur.:* 4:00. An arrangement of part of **The Song of Tailitnama (W129).**
First performance: 1981 (May 15). Sydney (Paddington Town Hall). Seymour Group ensemble; Anthony Fogg, conductor. Concert in support of Aboriginal Land Rights. Didjeridu prelude played by Colin Bright, who organized the concert.
Also performed: **P86-7, P89-7.**

W164 **Quiros** (1982)
Opera for television. For soloists, chorus, orchestra: 0.0.0.0., 4.3.3.1.,
timp, perc (3), strings. *Dur.:* 68:00. Text: Brian Bell. Commissioned and
televised by the ABC for its 50th anniversary celebrations. In three
parts: *First Voyage; Second Voyage; Third Voyage.*
> *Composer's note:* "Following his first voyage in the Pacific Ocean in 1595, Pedro
> Fernandez de Quiros, a Portuguese who sailed for Spain, became completely obsessed
> with the then common belief that there was a great land mass in the Southern
> Hemisphere balancing the continents of the north. Quiros set out from Callao in late
> December, 1605, and arrived at what he believed to be Terra Australis at the end of
> April, 1606. This place he named 'La Austrialia del Espiritu Santo'. It was not, how-
> ever, the south land of which he had dreamed; it was the New Hebridean island
> known since that time as Espiritu Santo. Later, disillusioned, Quiros spent the rest of
> his life vainly trying to raise money for a third voyage. His obsession persisted until
> his death; and his legacy to posterity was that through his published writings sub-
> sequent navigators were more easily able to locate the unknown continent."
Performance: 1982 (July 1). ABC-TV broadcast. Brian Bell, director;
Roger Ford, designer. Jon Weaving, Suzanne McLeod; Gerald
English; Nance Grant; SSO; Myer Fredman, conductor. *Lit.:* **B706-707,
B709, B714-716, B873, B1145.** *Reviews:* **B708, B710-713, B717, B719-720.**

W165 **East of India** (1982) from **Quiros**
For high voice and piano. *Dur.:* 3:00. Text: Brian Bell.

W166 **Three Pieces for Prepared Piano** (1982)
Arrangements of three Balinese melodies transcribed by Colin
McPhee and quoted in his book *Music in Bali* (New Haven, 1966).
Preparation of the piano is achieved by placing manuscript paper on
the strings. 3 p.
Performance: 1982 (November 8). Sydney (Opera House Recording
Hall). Peter Sculthorpe, piano. *Review of concert:* **B723.**

W167 **Piano Concerto** (1983)
For piano and orchestra: 0.2.0.2. cbn., 2.2.3.1., perc (3—tam tam, susp.
cymbal, crotale ['c'], glockenspiel, bongo[s], 3 congas, 3 tom tom, bass
drum), strings. *Dur.:* 23:00. In one movement, consisting of five sections: *Grave—animato—grave; Calmo; Animato—risoluto; Come
notturno (cadenza); Estatico.* Commissioned by the ABC for its fiftieth
anniversary, with assistance given by the Music Board of the Australia Council. Uses material from **Mountains (W162)**, and the *Mushiroda* melody as in **Landscape II (W145)**. Inscribed at the end "completed
Sanur, Bali, August, 1982" [date of rough score]. Dedicated to Helen
and Ross Edwards. Study score, 90 p.; full score and parts for hire.
Teaching kit: **B859.** *Analysis:* **B1193.**
First performance = recording session, **D40:** 1983 (March 9). Melbourne.
Anthony Fogg, piano; Melbourne Symphony Orchestra; Myer
Fredman, conductor. *Lit.:* **B687.**
Other performances: **P83-8, P84-2, -4, P85-film, P86-4, P87-6, -9, -10 (x4),
P88-7 (dance), P89-3, -7, P91-8, P92-5.** *Reviews:* **B742-743, B745, B756,
B859-860, B867-868, B903, B957-960, B1003, B1161.** APRA award: **B800.**

Recordings: **D40-41.** *Lit. & reviews:* **B736, B1051, B1062.**

W168 String Quartet No. 10 (1983)
Dur.: 14:00. Commissioned by the Kronos String Quartet. Contents: I.
Sun Song; II. *Chorale;* III. *Interlude;* IV. *Chorale;* V. *Sun Song.* Move-
ments I, III, and V use the melody of **Sun Song** for recorders (**W134**).
Score in preparation; parts for sale. *Analysis:* **B1197.**

Composer's note: "In writing for the Kronos Quartet, it seemed fitting to use source
material associated with the West Coast of the United States. The outer movements,
then, and the *Interlude*, incorporate transformations of motives and rhythms found in
songs of the Pueblo Indian. Unlike most of my music, **String Quartet No. 10** is not programmatic. The source material, for instance, is not used for extra-musical purposes.
On the other hand, in common with much of my output, the idea of duality is clearly
discernible in the work. It could be said that the New World, in the *Sun Songs* and
the *Interlude*, is juxtaposed with the Old, in the quiet homophonic strains of the
Chorales. The *Sun Songs*, for instance, have a very slow rate of harmonic change, suggesting the breadth of the Australian landscape. The *Chorales*, on the other hand,
have a much more rapid rate of change, and the actual harmonies are much more complex. My overriding intention in writing this work was to fashion music of straightforward line and structure. Such a music, I believe, relates easily to Australia."

First performance: 1983 (April 8). San Francisco (Green Room, Veterans
Auditorium). Kronos Quartet—David Harrington and John Sherba,
violins; Hank Dutt, viola; Joan Jeanrenaud, 'cello. *Reviews:* **B737-738.**
Other performances: **P88-3, -5; P89-1, -2, -7.** *Reviews:* **B894, B905, B951,
B998**

W169 Little Suite for Strings (1983)
For string orchestra. *Dur.:* 10:00. Contents: I. **Sea Chant** (**W103**, arr.); II.
Little Serenade (**W141**); III. **Left Bank Waltz** (**W70**, arr.). Study score
for sale; full score and parts for hire.
Performance: 1983 (September 22). Sydney (Opera House). Australian
Chamber Orchestra.
Also performed: **P91-11, -12.**

W170 Sonata for Strings (1983)
For string orchestra. *Dur.:* 14:00. The work is an arrangement of **String
Quartet No. 10** (**W168**). *See* **W168** for contents and composer's note.
Study score for sale; full score and parts for hire.
First performance = recording: **D35.** 1983 (November 29, completed in
December). Australian Chamber Orchestra. *Reviews:* **B895, B941.**
Other performances: **P86-10** (& Nov), **P87-4** (for dance), **P88-3, -6, P90-6.**
Reviews: **B828-829, B898, B1045.**

W171 The Song of Tailitnama, arr. medium voice and piano (1984)
Dur.: 10:00. An arrangement of **The Song of Tailitnama** (**W129**),
especially for Elizabeth Campbell and Anthony Fogg. Text: Northern
Aranda poem. Score for sale.
First performance: 1984 (September 9). Sydney (Opera House Recording
Hall). "From Nathan to Now" series concert. Elizabeth Campbell,
mezzo-soprano; Anthony Fogg, piano.
Other performances: **P86-1, -6** (x2), **P87-2** (x3, & March x2), **-6, P88-2,**

P90-8, P91-4. *Reviews:* **B808, B814.**
Recordings: **D50-51.** *Review:* **B1046.**

W172 Sun Song (1984)
For orchestra: 2.2.2.2., 2.2.2.1., perc (2—tam-tam, 3 congas [or 1 bongo and two congas], bass drum, susp. cymbal), strings). *Dur.:* 5:00. Composed for "A Concert in Honour of Sir Frank Callaway on his retirement" as Foundation Professor of Music at the University of Western Australia. The work uses the melody of **Sun Song** for recorders (**W134**). Full score and parts for hire.

Composer's note: "During the last year or so I have been committed to the idea of writing a straightforward and extrovert music, the kind of music that Percy Grainger might have defined as Australian. It seems to me that Australia is perhaps the only place in the world where one may now write such a music; and this work demonstrates my commitment. I dedicate **Sun Song** to Professor Sir Frank Callaway, in gratitude and admiration, and in doing so I believe that I represent, if rather inadequately, the feelings of the whole body of Australian composers."

First performance: 1984 (October 20). Perth (Winthrop Hall, University of Western Australia). Members of the West Australian Symphony Orchestra; Frank Callaway, conductor. *Review:* **B781.**
Other performances: **P91-6** (x 2).

W173 Burke and Wills (1985)
Feature film (Hoyts/Edgely), starring Jack Thompson, Nigel Havers, and Greta Scacchi; Graeme Clifford, director. *Dur.:* 140:00. Contents are listed under **D5**. Scores of *The Cricket Quadrille, arr. string trio* and *The Croquet Waltz* and *The Grail, arr. string quartet* are in the Sounds Australian library.

Plot summary: The film tells the story of the first crossing of the Australian continent from south to north. Led by the flamboyant Burke and the steadfast Wills, the expedition encounters enormous difficulties before culminating in triumph and ironic tragedy. In addition to original music, the score includes Aboriginal music, *musique concrète*, British folk material and other music associated with mid-nineteenth-century Australia. (*See also* the notes for **W180**, below.)

Royal premiere: 1985 (November 1). Melbourne (Hoyts Cinema Centre). *Lit.:* **B800-801.** *Reviews:* **B802-803, B862.** Excerpt in **B982.**
Recording: **D5.** Recording was used for **P86-9.**

W174 The Burke and Wills Waltzes, arr. David Matthews (1985)
For flute, clarinet, piano, violin, and 'cello. *Dur.:* 8:00. This is a set of variations upon three themes used in the film **Burke and Wills**: *The Sand Dunes* (Sculthorpe), *The Croquet Waltz* (Matthews), and *The Dream* (Balfe). Dedicated by David Matthews to Vincent Plush and the Magpie Musicians.

First performance: 1985 (September 22). Sydney (Opera House Recording Hall). Magpie Musicians: Anthony Ferner, flute; Catherine Lewis, clarinet; Suzanne Powell, piano; Judith Powell, violin; John Napier, 'cello; Vincent Plush, director. Broadcast direct on the ABC.
Also performed: 1985 (November 6). Sydney (Ervin Gallery). Opening of exhibition by Sidney Nolan, "Burke and Wills." Magpie Musicians, as at first performance.

W175 **Burke and Wills Suite, arr. symphonic band** (1985)
First performance: 1985 (November 1). Melbourne (Hoyts Cinema Centre), at film premiere. Victorian Naval Band.

W176 **The Croquet Waltz, arr. big band** (1985)
For flute, clarinet, 4 trumpets, 4 trombones, and piano. *Dur.:* 5:00. An arrangement by Sculthorpe of *The Croquet Waltz* (by David Matthews and Peter Sculthorpe) from the film **Burke and Wills** (**W173**). Score for sale.
First performance: 1985 (November 1). Melbourne (Southern Cross Hotel Ballroom).

W177 **O Mistress Mine, arr. symphonic band** (1985)
Dur.: 2:00. An arrangement by the composer of the second of **Two Shakespeare Songs** (**W83**).

W178 **The Dream** (1985)
For string orchestra. *Dur.:* 3:00. An arrangement by Sculthorpe of the aria *The Dream* ("I dreamt I dwelt in marble halls") from the opera *The Bohemian Girl* (1843) by Michael Balfe. *Recording:* **D5**, as *Julia*.

W179 **Saibai** (1986)
Hymn for unison voices and organ. Hymn tune *Saibai* (8 7.8 7.), by Sculthorpe, is based on a Saibai Island dance song. Text is a traditional Torres Strait Island hymn, translated by David Thompson (b. 1941), paraphrased by Wesley Milgate (b. 1916): "Father, now we come, well knowing we shall not be turned away" (5 verses). Published in *Sing Alleluia: More Hymns to Sing With One Voice* (A Supplement to the Australian Hymn Book *With One Voice*). London: Collins, 1987.

W180 **Burke and Wills Suite, arr. brass band** (1986)
Contents: *The Sand Dunes; The Cricket Quadrille; The Coolibah; The Dream; The Burke and Wills March.*
Composer's note: "This suite is an arrangement of some of the music written in 1985 for the film **Burke and Wills**. The music used in *The Sand Dunes* and in the *March* is based on my main theme for the film. The music used in the *Quadrille* is a variation of a secondary theme, usually associated with Wills; the Wills theme is based on an English folksong *The Three Ravens*, a song concerned with love and the quest for the holy grail. *The Dream* ("I dreamt I dwelt in marble halls") is an arrangement of the Balfe aria as above. In the film, this is sung by Julia Matthews, the actress with whom Burke was in love. The tragic outcome of the expedition is stated in *The Coolibah*, the music of which is briefly referred to in the final *March*. One of my principal objectives in writing this film score was to fuse my own musical style with that of different kinds of occasional music played in Australia in the mid-nineteenth century."
First performance: 1986 (March 5). Adelaide (St. Peter's Cathedral). "The Wakefield Chronicles" concert, 1986 Adelaide Festival. Elizabeth City Brass Band; Glenn Madden, director. *Reviews:* **B810, B812**.
Other performances: **P87-12, P88-6, P91-12, P92-6**.

W181 **Earth Cry** (1986)
For orchestra: 3.2.3.3., 4.4.3.1., timp, perc (3—tam tam, Chinese

cymbal, 2 bongos, 3 tom toms, bass drum), strings. *Dur.* 12:00. Commissioned by the ABC. Develops the main (Aboriginal-based) melodic material of **The Song of Tailitnama (W129)**. Dedicated, in 1991, to Stuart Challender. Study score for sale; full score and parts for hire.

Composer's note: "My initial idea was to write the second piece of a projected *Mangrove* series. I found, however, that my thoughts were more concerned with Australia as a whole than with particular parts of it. For instance, whenever I have returned from abroad in recent years, this country has seemed to me to be one of the last places on earth where one could honestly write quick and joyous music. It soon became clear that it would be dishonest of me to write music that is altogether quick and joyous. The lack of a common cause and the self-interest of many have drained us of much of our energy. A bogus national identity and its commercialisation have obscured the true breadth of our culture. Most of the jubilation, I have come to feel, awaits us in the future. Perhaps we now need to attune ourselves to this continent, to listen to the cry of the earth, as the Aborigines have done for many thousands of years. **Earth Cry** is a straightforward and melodious work. Its four parts are made up of a quick ritualistic music framed by slower music of a supplicatory nature, and an extended coda. It owes a debt to **The Song of Tailitnama** (1974). The treatment of the orchestra represents a new departure, particularly in the way that instruments are doubled. First and second violins, for instance, sing in unison for most of the work; and lower strings often sing with the lower brass. I have done this in order to summon up broad feelings and a broader landscape."

First performance: 1986 (August 22). Adelaide (Festival Theatre). Adelaide Symphony Orchestra; Jorge Mester, conductor. Repeated August 23. TV broadcast December 17. *Lit.:* **B821**. *Reviews:* **B824, B835**.

Other performances: **P86-11, P87-4, -7, P88-1, -2, -4, -11, P89-10, P90-5** (x2), **P91-2, -3, -6, -9** (dance), **-11** (dance, & concert), **-12, P92-9, -10**. *Reviews:* **B831-833, B865, B1086, B1134**. Excerpt in **B982**. Teaching kit: **B1182**.

Recording: **D36**. *Reviews: see* "Discography."

W182   Djilile (1986)

For 'cello and piano. *Dur.* 4:00. Inscribed "To Ken. Tribe" and dated at the end "Mangrove Mountain, May 1986." Playing score for sale.

Composer's note: "The work is based on an adaptation, with additional material, of the Aboriginal melody *Whistling-duck on a billabong* collected in northern Australia in the late 1950s by A. P. Elkin."

First performance: 1989 (April 3). Brisbane (MOCA). Peter Sculthorpe 60th Birthday concert. 'Cello & piano of the Queensland Piano Trio.

W183   Djilile (1986)

For piano solo. *Dur.:* 5:00. An arrangement of **Djilile (W182)**, above. Revised version inscribed "Sydney, March 1989." Score (4 p.) for sale.

Composer's note (to first performance): "The Liszt theme resembles the contours of a melody used by Australia's nomads, the Aborigines. In keeping with Liszt's transformations in his Rhapsodies of music used by Hungary's nomads, the gypsies, I chose to refer to this melody in my contribution to the set of variations. The melody is known as *Djilile*, which means 'whistling-duck on a billabong'. Although the piece is in my own particular style, I also chose to include passing references to Bartók." (*Note to revised version:*) "I made this piano arrangement of **Djilile**, with additional material, simply for my own pleasure, and perhaps for the pleasure of others."

First performance: 1986 (March). Budapest, Hungary. Sonya Hanke, piano. Work was performed as a Variation on a theme from Liszt's *Hungarian Rhapsody No. 14*, for *Hexaméron 1986*, commissioned by

the South Pacific Liszt Society to mark the centenary in 1986 of Liszt's death. *Other performances:* **P86-10, P88-9, P89-4.**
First performance of revised version: 1989 (May 12). Brisbane (Basil Jones Theatre). Peter Sculthorpe 60th birthday concert in the presence of the composer. Stephen Savage, piano. *Other performances:* **P89-7, P90-5, 8** (x2), **P91-2, -11, P92-10** (x4). *Reviews:* **B826, B989, B1003, B1044.** *Recordings:* **D7, D38-39.** *Reviews: see* "Discography."

W184 Autumn Song, arr. string orchestra (1986) not available
Dur.: 3:00. An arrangement for string orchestra of **Autumn Song (W105).** The score is missing.

W185 Songs of Sea and Sky (1987)
For clarinet and piano. *Dur.* 16:00. Commissioned by the School of Music, Yale University, to honor Keith Wilson upon his retirement in 1987. Score was completed May 30, 1987, and presented by Dean Frank Tirro on behalf of the composer to Professor Wilson at the Alumni Association dinner on June 6. Score and part 51157-0. *Review:* **B1117.**
Composer's note: "Songs of Sea and Sky was inspired by a traditional melody from Saibai, an island just south of Papua New Guinea, in Torres Strait. The melody was collected on Saibai by Jeremy Beckett in May 1961. Although some traditional Torres Strait music still survives in its original form, most of that heard today is strongly influenced by the religious music introduced by missionaries in the nineteenth century. Nevertheless, its themes are still predominantly of sea voyages, flights of birds and changes in sea and sky. This work is in one continuous movement consisting of seven parts: *Prelude,* a somewhat dramatic clarinet solo; *Saibai,* a reworking of the traditional melody; *Interlude,* a second clarinet solo, with piano punctuation; *Mission Hymn,* a variation of *Saibai; Dance Song,* a rhythmic section shared by clarinet and piano, and based upon the opening clarinet solo; *Lament,* a second variation of *Saibai;* and *Postlude,* a brief coda.
First performance: 1987 (October 15). New Haven CT (Sprague Memorial Hall, Yale School of Music). Richard Stoltzman, clarinet; Irma Vallecillo, piano.
Other performances: **P87-8, P88-4, -5, -7, -8, P89-2, -4, -5, -10, P91-2, -4, -11, -12, P92-2** (& March), **-4, -6, -8.** *Reviews:* **B889, B906-907, B951, B976, B989, B1090, B1099, B1132.**
Recording: **D52.** *Reviews:* **B1162-1163.**

W186 Songs of Sea and Sky, arr. flute and piano (1987)
Dur. 16:00. An arrangement by the composer of **W185.** Score and part for sale.
First performance = recording: **D53.** 1987 (July). Geoffrey Collins, flute; David Miller, piano. *Reviews:* **B992, B995.**
Other performances: **P88-1, P89-3, -4, -5, -10, P91-5** (x2), **P92-11.** *Reviews:* **B962, B966, B991, B1103.**

W187 Ballad (1987)
For soprano and orchestra. *Dur.:* 4:00. An arrangement by Sculthorpe of the ballad "Scenes that are brightest" from the opera *Maritana* (1845) by William Vincent Wallace. Also called *The Dream.* Text:

Edward Fitzball. The music is believed to have been written in New Norfolk, Tasmania, in 1835.

W188 Child of Australia (1987)
For speaker, soprano, chorus SATB, and orchestra: 2.2.2.3., 4.4.3.1., timp, perc (3), strings. *Dur.:* 18:00. Text: Thomas Keneally. Commissioned by The Sydney Committee Limited, Organizers of the Festival of Sydney, with funding assistance from the Australian Bicentennial Authority, for performance on Australia Day, January 26, 1988. Originally titled "This Land" etc. Contents: I. *Prelude;* II. *Credo 1;* III. *Motet;* IV. *Credo 2;* V. *Canticle;* VI. *Anthem.* Score for hire.
First performance: 1988 (January 26, Australia Day). Sydney (Opera House Forecourt). Sydney Philharmonia Choir; Joan Carden, soprano; John Howard, narrator; AYO; Carlo Felice Cillario, conductor. TV broadcast direct on ABN2, following live interview of the composer by Helen Wellings. *Lit.:* B841, B870-871. *Reviews:* B878, B885-886, B942.
Other performances: P88-4, -11. *Reviews:* B936
Recording: D6.

W189 Anthem from Child of Australia (1987)
For chorus SATB and piano.

W190 At the Grave of Isaac Nathan (1988) not available
For orchestra: 0.2.0.0., 2.0.0.0., strings. *Dur.:* 18:00. Commissioned by the ACO and funded by the Australian Bicentennial Authority. (Planned for the ACO's 1988 tour of Europe.) Contents: *An Alien Land* (Isaac Nathan muses upon his newly-adopted country); *Song for Rosetta; The Tribute* (Isaac Nathan pays homage to Thomas Mitchell); *Eliza Donnithorne's Song; Australia Felix* (Isaac Nathan recalls the words of Thomas Mitchell). Rehearsed, not performed.

W191 Second Sonata for Strings (1988)
For string orchestra. *Dur.* 13:00. The work is an arrangement of **String Quartet No. 9 (W132)**. Commissioned for the ACO tour of the US and Europe with funding from the Australia Council. Revised in 1990. *See* **W132** for contents and composer's note. Study score for sale; full score and parts for hire. *Lit.:* **B841**.
Official first performance: 1988 (May 19). Brighton UK. (St. Martin's Church). Australian Chamber Orchestra.
Other performances: **P88-2, -4, -5, P89-10, -11, P90-6, -8** (tour), **-10** (tour), **-12, P91-7, P92-7, -10**. *Reviews:* **B1010-1011, B1013, B1048, B1110-1111**.

W192 Kakadu (1988)
For orchestra: 2.2(c.a).2.2(cbn)., 4.4.3.1., timp, perc (3—tam tam, Beijing gong, large susp. cymbal, pair of cymbals, bass drum, bongos, tom toms, congas) strings. (First version, at world premiere, was without flutes, clarinets, and bassoons, but with contrabassoon.) *Dur.:* 15:00. Commissioned by Dr. Emanuel Papper, an Aspen Music Festival trustee, as a present for Patricia Papper, his wife, upon her birthday.

Score is inscribed at the beginning "To Patricia Papper," and at the end "Sydney, July 1988." Full score 51274-7, 1992; 45 p.; parts for hire.

Composer's note: "The work takes its name from the Kakadu National Park in northern Australia. This enormous wilderness area stretches from coastal tidal plains to rugged mountain plateaux, and in it may be found the living culture of its Aboriginal inhabitants, dating back for fifty thousand years. Sadly, today there are only a few remaining speakers of *kakadu*, or *gagadju*. The work, then, is concerned with my feelings about this place, its landscape, its change of seasons, its dry season and its wet, its cycle of life and death. It is in three parts; the outer sections are dance-like and energetic, sharing similar musical ideas. The central section is somewhat introspective, and is dominated by a cor anglais solo, representing the voice of Emanuel Papper, who commissioned the work. Apart from this solo, the melodic material in **Kakadu**, as in much of my recent music, was suggested by the contours and rhythms of Aboriginal chant."

First performance: 1988 (July 24). Aspen CO (Aspen Music Festival Tent). Aspen Festival Orchestra; Jorge Mester, conductor. The composer introduced the work. *Lit.:* **B899, B901n, B904, B943.** *Reviews:* **B901-901n, B902, B904, B949.**

Other performances: P88-11, P89-3, -4 (x2 + Sydney, Austin schools), -7, -9, -11, P90-3, -7 (tour), -9, -10 (x2), -11, P91-3 (& April), -9 (dance), -10, P92-10 (& Nov), -12. *Reviews:* **B931-932, B967, B973-974, B983, B985-986, B1005, B1054-1056, B1058, B1070.** Excerpt in **B982.** Teaching kits: **B970, B1053, B1079.**

Recording: **D36.** *Reviews: see* "Discography."

W193 The Birthday of Thy King (1988)

Carol for unaccompanied mixed chorus. *Dur.:* 5:00. Words after Henry Vaughan (1621-1695), English poet. Written for the choir of King's College, Cambridge, for the annual Service of Nine Lessons and Carols. Sometimes called **Awake glad heart.** Score 51088-4, 1988; 8 p.

Composer's note: "Stephen Cleobury asked me to write a carol for the annual Service of Nine Lessons and Carols. Knowing that composers often have difficulty in finding texts, he sent me a selection from which I could choose, if I wished. I chose a very beautiful poem by Henry Vaughan. It begins with an exhortation to celebrate the birthday of Christ; this is followed first by sadness upon the realization of one's own impurity, and then joy in the knowledge of Christ's cleansing power."

First performance: 1988 (December 24) Cambridge (King's College Chapel). Christmas Eve Service of Nine Lessons and Carols. King's College Choir; Stephen Cleobury, conductor.

Other performances: P89-9, P90-12, P91-8, -9 (tour). *Review:* **B987.**

Recording: **D3.** *Review:* **B1153.**

W194 Tailitnama Song, arr. 'cello and piano (1989)

Dur.: 6:00. An arrangement by the composer of **Tailitnama Song** (W163). Score and part for sale.

First performance = recording: **D37.** 1989 (March). David Pereira, 'cello; Geoffrey Tozer, piano. *Reviews:* **B995-996.**

Other performances: P90-9. *Review:* **B1065.**

W195 It's You (1989)

For chorus SATB. Arrangements of two Gershwin songs, *Somebody*

loves me and *The man I love.*
First performance: 1989 (May 6). Sydney (Opera House Concert Hall).
Sydney Philharmonia presents: Peter Sculthorpe's 60th Birthday
Concert. Sydney Philharmonia Motet Choir; David Miller, piano;
John Grundy, conductor. *Reviews:* **B987.**

W196 Sun Song (1989)
For percussion ensemble of 4 players (vibraphone, 2 marimbas, tam
tam, thunder sheet, 2 rain sticks). *Dur.:* 7:30. Playing score (11 p.) for
sale.

Composer's note: Written as a gift from Australia to France upon the bicentenary of
the Revolution, the work takes its point of departure from three Aboriginal melodies
collected by a member of the Baudin expedition in 1802. These melodies were the first
examples of indigenous Australian music to appear in Western notation.

World premiere: 1989 (June 1). Paris (Ravel-Debussy Auditorium,
Neuilly-sur-Seine [SACEM]). Synergy: Michael Askill; Ian Cleworth;
Rebecca Lagos; Colin Piper. *Lit.:* **B997-997n.**
Other performances: **P89-9, *P90-7, *-10 ,*-11, *P91-3** (*as *Sun Song II*),
P92-8 (as *Jabiru Dreaming*). *Reviews:* **B1008, B1067, B1175-1177.**
Award: **B1040n.**

W197 Callabonna (1989)
For solo piano. *Dur.:* 4:00. The work is a reinstatement and revision
of the first movement of the **Sonata for Piano** (W85). The title refers
to the outback Lake Callabonna, as in a Russell Drysdale painting
owned by the composer. Score for sale.
First performance: 1989 (July 30) (programmed as **Sonata**). Melbourne
(Melba Hall). "Sculthorpe: A Celebration." Linda Kouvaras, piano.
Recording: **D39.** *Reviews: see* "Discography."

W198 Nocturnal (1989)
For solo piano. *Dur.:* 7:00. Uses material from a section of the **Piano
Concerto** (1983). Score for sale.
First performance = recording: **D39.** 1989. Robert Chamberlain, piano.
Reviews: see "Discography."

W199 The Rose Bay Quadrilles (1989)
For piano solo. *Dur.:* 5:00. An edition by Peter Sculthorpe of *The Rose
Bay Quadrilles* (1856) by William Stanley. Contents: *Con brio;
Allegretto; Grazioso; Moderato; Con brio.* Score for sale.

Composer's note: "The music was commissioned by David Cooper to mark the occasion
of the laying of the foundation stone of Woollahra House on December 15, 1856. In
this edition, the only liberties taken were in the name of better voice-leading. Most
of my work was concerned with correcting misprints and inconsistencies in the printed
music."

First performance = recording: **D39.** 1989. Gudrun Beilharz, piano. *Reviews: see* "Discography."
Also performed: **P89-7.** *Review:* **B1003.**

W200 Two Grainger Arrangements (1989)

For percussion (1) and strings. Contents: *Beautiful Fresh Flower; Faeroe Island Song*. Both were originally piano pieces. The first, a Chinese folk song, Grainger arranged in Hobart, Tasmania, in 1935. *Performances:* **P89-4** (first performance of *Faeroe Island Song*), **P91-12**. *Reviews:* **B973-974, B983, B1005**.
Recording of *Beautiful Fresh Flower:* **D2**. *Reviews:* **B1057, B1073**.

W201 Nourlangie (1989)
Concerto for solo guitar, perc (tam tam, thunder sheet, bass drum, Chinese cymbal, bongos), and string orchestra. *Dur.* 20:00. Commissioned by the ACO. Written for John Williams. Uses a Torres Strait melody collected by Jeremy Beckett in 1961. Inscribed at the beginning "To John Williams" and at the end "Paris—Sydney, July-October, 1989." Score and parts for hire. Excerpts: **B1020**.
Composer's note: "Early in 1989, I made my first visit to Kakadu National Park. While there, I spent some time at Nourlangie Rock. A place both powerful and serene, it is clearly a sacred site. Flying over it, I could see across the floodplains to abandoned remains of early white settlement, to the Arafura Sea, to Torres Strait and, in my imagination, to the islands of Indonesia. The musics of these places, and of Kakadu itself, fused in my mind. It was inevitable that I should write a piece about Nourlangie. The work is more concerned with my feelings about the place than with a physical description of it. All the same, I have used many bird sounds in the work; and, while writing it, I often dreamed of a lost guitar in the sea, lying there since the time, in 1606, when a Spanish expedition led by Luis Vaz de Torres vainly sailed through waters to the north. In one movement, basically **Nourlangie** consists of an alternation of two ideas. The first of these, heard at the outset, appears in many different guises. The second almost always takes the form of a somewhat ecstatic melody: it stems from my belief that Australia is one of the few places on earth where one can honestly write straightforward, joyful music."
First performance: 1989 (October 24). Brisbane (Queensland Performing Arts Centre). John Williams, guitar; Michael Askill, percussion; Australian Chamber Orchestra; Richard Hickox, conductor. *Review:* **B1014**. *Lit.:* **B1016**.
Other performances: **P89-10, P90-12**. *Reviews:* **B1015, B1017-1018**.
Recording: **D33** (to be released).

W202 Child of Australia, arr. symphonic band (1990)
Dur.: 18:00. An arrangement by Ken Smith for the Sydney Festival Wind Orchestra.
First performance: 1990 (January 26, Australia Day). Sydney (The Domain). Sydney Philharmonia Choir; Sydney Children's Choir; Joan Carden, soprano; Nick Enright, reader; Sydney Festival Wind Orchestra; Richard Gill, conductor.

W203 Djilile, for percussion ensemble of four players (1990)
For tam tam, 2 rainsticks, thunder sheet, vibraphone, 2 marimbas. *Dur.:* 7:00. An arrangement for Synergy of **Djilile** for 'cello & piano (**W182**). *See* **W182** for composer's note. Score and parts for sale.
First performance: 1990 (March 7) as *Sun Song II*. Adelaide (Elder Hall). Adelaide Festival of Arts. Synergy: Askill, Cleworth, Lagos, Piper (as in **Sun Song, W196**). Introduction by the composer. *Lit. & reviews:*

B1028-1029. *Also performed* (as *Sun Song I*): P90-10 (B1067), -11. *Recording:* D8 (to be released).

W204   String Quartet No. 11 (Jabiru Dreaming) (1990)
Dur.: 14:00. Commissioned by Musica Viva Australia for, and dedicated to, the Kronos Quartet. In two movements: I. *Deciso—meno mosso—deciso;* II. *Liberamente—poco amoroso—amoroso.* Score (23 p., c1990), and parts for sale.

> *Composer's note:* "The works inspired by the visit to Kakadu are all related, if not always thematically at least in their tempi, for they tend to be basically ritual-like and quick. **String Quartet No. 11** is one of these works. Both movements, although different in character, employ similar material. The second movement, however, is dominated by an Aboriginal melody [*chant,* as in **Sun Song, W196**]. The work takes its name after a rock formation near the East Alligator River in Kakadu. This rock is regarded as sacred, but there is nothing forbidding about it: on the contrary, in some ways it seems to beckon and welcome."

First performance: 1990 (March 10). Adelaide (Town Hall). Adelaide Festival. Kronos Quartet. *Reviews:* B1030, B1034.
Other performances: P90-3 (x33, Mar-Dec), -8, -11 (x3), P91-1 (x30, Jan-May), -6 (x2), -7 (& Aug, x5), -9 (x3), -10 (x2, +5 in Nov, +4 in Dec), -11 (dance, also 1992), P92-1 (& Feb), -4, -7 (& Sept). *Reviews:* B1032-1033, B1035-1036, B1038, B1049-1050, B1069, B1081-1083, B1087-1089, B1094-1095, B1107, B1119, B1123, B1130-1131, B1133, B1146-1147, B1158-1159, B1167-1169.
Recording: D61 (to be released).

W205   Haughty Sortie (1990)
For unison voices and piano. *Dur.:* 2:00. Text: Edna Sculthorpe. Written as part of a tributary garland for Vincent Plush, upon his fortieth birthday. Programme note devised by Kelly Trench. Score, 3 p.
First performance: 1990 (April 18). Colorado Springs, CO. Staff and students of the Department of Music, The Colorado College.

W206   Little Nourlangie (1990)
For organ and orchestra: 2.2.2.2., 0.2.0.0., timp, perc (2), strings. Composed for the Education Program of the Sydney Symphony Orchestra, for performance on the Sydney Town Hall's Hill & Son organ, the centenary of which was celebrated in 1990. The work uses the second musical idea of **Nourlangie (W201)**. *Lit.:* B1052, B1105.

> *Composer's note* (1990): "Little Nourlangie is a small rocky outcrop near the massive rock, Nourlangie, in Kakadu National Park. Nearby is Koongarra Saddle, a proposed uranium mining site. Under the base of Little Nourlangie are a number of Aboriginal rock paintings known as the Blue Paintings. These depict fish, boats and ancestral figures and they were at the back of my mind when I wrote the piece. The work itself consists of successive statements of a melody inspired by my visit. As in much of my recent music, a number of bird calls can be heard and there are references to Aboriginal music."

First performances: 1990 (June 6, 7). Sydney (Town Hall). SSO Education Program 1990. Schools concerts for years five to eight. David Rumsey, organ; SSO; John Hopkins, conductor. *Repeated:* three perfs. each day on July 17, 18 (Hopkins); four on July 20 (Summerbell).

W207 **Irkanda IV, arr. flute and string trio** (1990)
Dur. 11:00. Composer's arrangement of **Irkanda IV** (1961) for members
of the Australia Ensemble. Score (10p.) and parts for sale, c1990.
First performance: 1990 (August 30). Brisbane (QPAC). Australia En-
semble: Geoffrey Collins, flute; Dene Olding, violin; Irena Morozov,
viola; David Pereira, 'cello.
Official first performance: 1990 (September 3). Sydney (Opera House).
Musica Viva concert. Australia Ensemble. Recorded for broadcast by
2MBS-FM.
Other performances: **P90-9.** Reviews: **B1063-1064, B1066.**

W208 **Nangaloar** (1991)
For orchestra: 2.2.2.2(cbn)., 4.4.3.1., timp., perc (3—tam tam, Chinese
cymbal, bass drum, congas, tom toms, bongos, rain stick [or maracas]),
strings. Dur.: 10:00. Written especially for the Symphony Orchestra of
Ljubljana Radio-Television, Yugoslavia, **Nangaloar** was commissioned as part of a composer-exchange programme organized by the
Australian Music Centre with financial assistance from the Australia
Council. Inscribed at the end "Sydney, April 1991." (First announced
as "Nourlangie Dreaming".) Study score (56 p.) for sale; full score and
parts for hire.
Composer's note: "**Nangaloar** is among the works inspired by my visit to Kakadu
National Park early in 1989. It takes its name from a rocky escarpment that houses a
number of important aboriginal rock paintings. A powerful place, and a sanctuary for
birds, it is clearly sacred to the indigenous people of the area. I am concerned that
there is the possibility of further uranium mining in the area, the possibility of the
destruction of an ancient, sacred place."
First performance of revised version: 1991 (July 14). Aspen, CO (Music
Festival Tent). Aspen Festival Orchestra; Murry Sidlin, conductor.
Other performances: **P91-1** (x2), **-8.** Review: **B1085.**

W209 **Irkanda IV, arr. string quartet** (1991)
Dur.: 11:00. Composer's arrangement of **Irkanda IV** (1961). Score (10
p.) and parts for sale.
First performance: 1991 (September 14). Perth (Concert Hall). Kronos
Quartet. Review: **B1118.**
Also performed: **P91-9** (17, 20). Reviews: **B1119-1120, B1122.**

W210 **A Sun Song for Eric** (1991)
For alto recorder, violin and 'cello. Dur.: 2:30. Written as part of a trib-
utory garland for Eric Gross, upon his retirement from the Depart-
ment of Music, the University of Sydney, it uses material from **Little
Nourlangie (W206).** Score, 2 p.
First performance: 1991 (August 8), as A Sunny Song for Eric. Sydney
(Seymour Centre). Farewell concert for Eric Gross. Ian Shanahan, alto
recorder; Dominique Guerbois, violin; Susan Blake, 'cello. Review:
B1114. Recording: **D69.**

W211 **Lament** (1991)
For solo 'cello and strings. Dur.: 10:00. A version of **Lament for**

Strings (W135) extending the writing for solo cello that exists in the original. In one movement, three sections. Score (10 p.), c1991, for sale; parts for hire.

Composer's note: "In one movement, the music is in three clearly-defined sections: the first is desolate, with the melodic line shared between solo 'cello and first violins; the second is somewhat impassioned; and following the climax, the last, dominated by solo cello, is again desolate." [*See* note to W135 for background.]

First performance: 1991 (September 22). Sydney (Opera House Concert Hall). Raphael Wallfisch, 'cello; Australian Chamber Orchestra; Richard Tognetti, director. *Reviews:* B1121, B1124.

Also performed: P91-9, P92-10.

W212 **Tailitnama Song, arr. violin and piano** (1991)
Dur.: 6:00. An arrangement by the composer of **Tailitnama Song** (W163). Inscribed "To Kirsty Beilharz." Score (11 p.) and part for sale.
First performance: 1991 (October 27). Sydney (Australian Music Centre). Kirsty Beilharz, violin; Ross Hamilton, piano.

W213 **Second Impromptu** (1991)
For piano solo. An edition by Simon Docking and Peter Sculthorpe of *Second Impromptu* by M. Hauser (Sydney: Clarke, 1857).

W214 **Kooee** (1991)
For string quartet. An edition & arrangement by Peter Sculthorpe of *Kooee* for voice and piano by Isaac Nathan (Sydney: Whittaker, 1849).

W215 **National Country Dances** (1991)
For piano solo. An edition by Peter Sculthorpe of *National Country Dances*, vol. 4, by F. Ellard (Sydney: Ellard, 1854).

W216 **From Uluru** (1991)
For orchestra: 2.2.2.2., 4.2.3.1., perc (3—tam tam, susp. Chinese cymbal, susp. cymbal, whip, bongos, 3 tom toms), strings. *Dur.:* 3:30. Commissioned by the ABC especially for the Education Program of the Sydney Symphony Orchestra. For the most part, the music is a reworking of the fourth movement of **Landscape II (W145)**. Score, 19 p., and parts for hire.

Composer's note: The road between the two massive landmarks in Uluru National Park, Ayers Rock and the Olgas, was once as bumpy a road as could be imagined. When I first drove to the Olgas, I felt like turning back even before I was half-way there. I kept driving, though, and when I finally arrived, hot and shaken and dusty, I felt I had truly earned the right to visit this powerful place. Today, sadly, the road is sealed. **From Uluru**, then, was inspired by that rough road. The work is mono-thematic. The melodic line, unlike melodic lines in many of my recent works, is not based on Aboriginal material. My intention was to suggest the landscape and also the road itself. Although a short work, **From Uluru** clearly demonstrates my present compositional ideas, especially the idea that once a piece really begins it maintains its momentum until its conclusion.

First performance = recording: 1991 (December 11). Sydney (Eugene Goossens Hall). SSO; Peter Grunberg, conductor.

First performance of revised version: 1992 (February 25, 26). Sydney

(Town Hall). SSO Education Program; Colin Piper, conductor. *Educational materials:* **B1151**.
Also performed: March 25, 26, 27, Penrith, Gosford, Wollongong, schools concerts; May 12, Baulkham Hills, schools; Piper, conductor. June 24, 25, 26, Sydney schools (OH); Henryk Pisarek, conductor. November 3, Castle Hill; Piper, conductor.

W217   Threnody (1991-92)
For solo 'cello. *Dur.:* 7:00. Commissioned by the ABC as a tribute to the conductor Stuart Challender. Score is inscribed at the end "Sydney, Dec. '91/June '92." Score 51412-X, 1993; 5 p.

Composer's note: In one movement, **Threnody** is made up of four sections: *Cantando; Con malinconia; Risoluto; Con rassegnazione.* I chose to base the work upon the main theme of my orchestral piece **Kakadu**, this theme being a free adaptation of an Aboriginal lament from Elcho Island, in the Arafura Sea. **Threnody** is dedicated to the memory of the conductor Stuart Challender, who died of AIDS in December 1991. Considering that he conducted **Kakadu** on many occasions, it seems fitting that this lament should be sung for him.

First public performance: 1991 (December 20), as "Stuart Challender In Memoriam." Sydney (Town Hall). Memorial service for Stuart Challender. David Pereira, 'cello. *Lit.:* **B1137**.
Other performances: **P92-8, -11**.
Recording: **D73**.

W218   Hill-Song No. 1 (1992)
For string quartet. *Dur.:* 2:30. Written as a late wedding present for the composer's brother, Roger, and his second wife, Patricia, and performed at the wedding of the composer's niece, Anne, to Malcolm Wilson. Inscribed "To Pat and Roger." Score, 4 p.
First performance: 1992 (March 7). Longford, TAS (Jessen Lodge). Matthews Tyson String Quartet. This was followed by a performance of **Little Serenade (W141)**. *Lit.:* **B1157**.

W219   Irkanda IV, arr. flute and string quartet (1992)
Dur.: 11:00. Composer's arrangement of **Irkanda IV (W80)** for members of the Australia Ensemble. Score, 13 p.
First performance: 1992 (February 1). Brussels, Belgium. Australia Ensemble: Geoffrey Collins, flute; Dene Olding and Dimity Hall, violins; Irena Morozov, viola; Julian Smiles, 'cello.
Other performances: **P92-2** (tour). *Reviews:* **B1148-1149**.

W220   Jabiru Dreaming for percussion (1992)
For percussion ensemble of 4 players (vibraphone, 2 marimbas, tam tam, thunder sheet, 2 rain sticks, flexatone). *Dur.:* 14:00. This consists of an arrangement by the composer of the first movement of **String Quartet No. 11 (Jabiru Dreaming) (W204)**, followed by, as second movement, the percussion work formerly known as **Sun Song (W196)**. Score, 21 p.
First performance = recording: **D8** (to be released). 1992 (December). Sydney (ABC Recording Studio). Synergy.

W221 Dream Tracks (1992)
For violin, clarinet, and piano. *Dur.*: 14:00. Commissioned by the
Verdehr Trio of the University of Michigan, and inscribed "To the
Verdehr Trio." Uses **Djilile (W183)**, the cor anglais theme from
Kakadu (W192) and an elaboration of Djilile as in **Nangaloar (W208)**.
Score, 22 p.

Composer's note: "Since 1988 I have written a series of works inspired by Kakadu National Park, in the north of Australia. Some of these works have melodic material in
common, the contours of each line usually being transformed in some way, both within
pieces and in successive pieces. I have come to regard these melodies as *songlines* or
dreaming tracks. These are names used to describe the labyrinth of invisible pathways that, according to Aboriginal belief, are created by the totemic ancestors of all
species as they sing the world into existence. **Dream Tracks**, then, sets out to summon
up the spirit of a northern Australian landscape. The work is in four sections: *Lontano;*
Molto sostenuto; Lontano; Estatico. The first section takes as its point of departure the
contours of a Torres Strait Island children's song. This serves as an introduction to the
second section, which is based upon an Arnhem Land chant, *Djilile,* or 'whistling-
duck on a billabong.' The third section is an extension of the first, its melodic contours
also appearing in the fourth section. In this final section, however, *Djilile* is ever-
present, both in a much-transformed guise and in its original form."

First performance: 1992 (October 31). San Diego, CA. College Music
Society annual meeting. Verdehr Trio: Walter Verdehr, violin; Elsa
Ludewig-Verdehr, clarinet; Gary Kirkpatrick, piano.
Official first performance: 1993 (January 31). New York City (Merkin
Concert Hall). Verdehr Trio.

W222 Tropic (1992)
For clarinet, violin, 2 guitars, double bass and percussion. *Dur.*: 14:00.
Composer's arrangement of **Dream Tracks**, made especially for the
group Attacca. Score, 32 p.
First performance: 1992 (May 23). Brighton UK (Hove Town Hall).
Attacca: Nigel Westlake, clarinet; Rita Manning, violin; John
Williams and Timothy Kain, guitars; Chris Laurence, double bass;
Michael Askill, percussion.
Other performances: **P92-5** (& June), **-9**. *Review:* **B1181**.

W223 Awake, Glad Heart, arr. two trumpets and strings (1992)
Dur.: 3:00. Composer's arrangement of his Christmas carol **The
Birthday of Thy King (W193)**. Written upon a request from the
Australian Youth Orchestra. Score, 7 p.
First performance = recording: **D1**. 1992 (July). Sydney (Eugene
Goossens Hall). AYO; Graham Abbott, conductor.

W224 Simori (1992)
For solo 'cello. *Dur.*: 8:00. Inscribed "To David Pereira." Contents: *Yu*
(a war cry); *Wani* (a song of welcome); *Kamu* (a song to drive away
illness); *Pota* (an incantation); *Yu*. The music is based upon material
cited by Jaap Kunst in *The Native Music of Western New Guinea*
(Leiden, 1950). Score, 5 p.

Discography

This list is alphabetical by title of work or recording, and includes all commercially-produced recordings through early 1993. Included are 33 1/3-rpm twelve-inch discs (stereo, unless otherwise stated), cassette tapes (cass), and compact discs (CD). Cross-references with a **W** refer to the "Works" catalog, with a **D** to the "Discography," and with a **B** to the "Bibliography."

Awake, Glad Heart, arr. Sculthorpe for two trumpets and strings (W223)
   D1   Tall Poppies CD TP016. AYO; Graham Abbott, conductor. *Christmas Under Capricorn: Christmas Carols by Australian Composers.* Recorded 1992, Sydney (ABC's Goossens Hall, Ultimo).

Beautiful Fresh Flower, from Two Grainger Arrangements (W200)
   D2   ABC/PolyGram 426 989-2 (CD); -4 (cass). 1990. *Percy Grainger Orchestral Works.* Melbourne Symphony Orchestra; Geoffrey Simon, conductor. Notes: Steven Lloyd. *Reviews:* **B1059, B1073.** Work re-issued on ABC 510 799-1 (disc), -2 (CD), -4 (cass), *Percy's Country Gardens: The Best of Percy Grainger.*

Birthday of Thy King, The (W193)
   D3   CD SPC 1002. 1991. *Until I Saw: Contemporary Australian Choral Music.* St. Peter's Chorale; Graeme Morton, conductor. *Review:* **B1153.**

Boat Rise, arr. Hannan (W157)
   D4   Larrikin LRF 153 (disc); TC LRF 153 (cass). 1985. *Australian Songs and Ballads.* Gregory Martin, baritone; Norma Williams, piano.

Burke and Wills (W173)
   D5   American Gramaphone [sic] Records AGCD 900 (CD); AGC 900 (cass). 1987. Sydney Studio Musicians; Australian Chamber Orchestra; Phoenix String Quartet; Vanessa Fallon, soprano; folk musicians led by Doug Kelly; Louise Johnson, harp; Aboriginal music by Gapuwiyak community musicians; Bill Motzing, conductor. Contents: (1) *King of the Faeries;* (2) *Sand Dunes;* (3) *Wills' Variations:*

The Croquet Waltz, The Grail, The Cricket Quadrille, Wills's Death;
(4) *The Dream;* (5) *Dream Sequence: Premonition, Wire Music, Dreamtime* (Aboriginal), *I Dreamt I Dwelt in Marble Halls;* (6) *Dawn Travelling;* (7) *Burke & Wills March;* (8) *The Search;* (9) *Julia;* (10) *The Gulf;* (11) *The Coolibah Tree;* (12) *Stars;* (3) *Burke's Death;* (14) *Julia* reprise.

Callabonna (W197): D39

Child of Australia (W198)
D6   Philips ABC 834 740-1 (disc); -2 (CD); -4 (cass). 1988. *Music for Australia Day.* John Howard, speaker; Joan Carden, soprano; Australian Youth Orchestra; Sydney Philharmonia Choir; Carlo Felice Cillario, conductor.

Djilile (W183): D37; D39; and
D7   Tall Poppies CD (forthcoming). Lisa Moore, piano.

Djilile, arr. percussion (W203)
D8   Synergy. For future release (ABC PolyGram), with: **Jabiru Dreaming for percussion ensemble**

Earth Cry (W181): D36

Fifth Continent, The (W87)
D9   ABC recording O/N 40493 (disc, mono). 1963. Frederick Parslow, speaker; MSO; Thomas Matthews, conductor.

Four Little Pieces for Piano Duet (W149): D37; D39; and
D10   AVM Classics 1022 (disc, cass, CD). 1989. *The Duets Album.* Rhondda Gillespie and Robert Weatherburn, piano duet.

From Tabuh Tabuhan (W108)
D11   ABC RRC 72 (disc). 1968. Tasmanian Orchestra; Patrick Thomas, conductor. With: works of Ahern, Brumby, Cugley, Edwards, Fowler, Gifford, Hughes, Kay, Penberthy, Sitsky, Werder.

How the Stars Were Made (W121)
D12   Double Drummer DD001C (cass). 1987. *Australian Percussion.* Michael Askill, percussion (multi-track). Publication assisted by the Music Board of the Australia Council. With: works of N. Westlake, Wesley-Smith, Edwards.

D13   Great Island Records GIRLP 003 (disc); GIRLPC 003 (cass). 1987. *Australian Percussion.* Michael Askill (multi-track). *Review:* **B869.**

D14   Southern Cross SC CD 1021. 1989. *Australian Percussion Music, vol. I.* Michael Askill (multi-track). Re-issue of **D13.** Notes: the composer. *Review:* **B950.**

Irkanda I (W62)
D15   MBS 10 (disc). 1984. *The First Ten Years: Highlights from Ten Years of Music.* Jack Glatzer, violin.

D16   Tall Poppies CD TP018. 1992. *Australian Violin Music.* Elizabeth Holowell, violin.

Irkanda IV (W80): D31; D35; D36. The last re-issued on ABC 512 894-2 (CD), -4 (cass), 1993, *Bush Symphony.*

It'll Rise Again, from Love 200 (W112), arr. Michael Carlos
D17   EMI EMC 2505 (disc, quad). 1973. *Free Fall Through Featherless Flight.* Jeannie Lewis, singer, with instrumental ensemble; Michael Carlos, director. *Review:* B465. Re-issued on CD, 1992.

Jabiru Dreaming for percussion ensemble (W220): D8

Kakadu (W192): D36. Re-issued on ABC 434 712-2 (CD), *Symphony: An ABC 60th Anniversary Celebration.*

Koto Music I (W127)
D18   RCA VRLI 0083 (disc). 1974. Roger Woodward, piano. *Music Rostrum Australia—Vol. I: Contemporary Australian Piano Music.* Notes: the composer. *Review:* B527.

Koto Music I-II (W127, W133): D38, D39

Lament for Strings (W135): D35; and
D19   MBS 2 (disc). Australian Chamber Orchestra. *Reviews:* B614.

Landscape (W119): D38; D39; D43; and
D20   Festival L 42015 (SFC-80022) (disc). c1974. *Australian Festival of Music, vol. five.* David Bollard, piano. Notes: James Murdoch. With: works of Farr, Hollier, Sitsky. *Reviews:* B492-492n.

Landscape II (W145): D37

Left Bank Waltz (W70): D38; D39 (as #1 of Two Easy Pieces W104); and
D21   W & G SB 5589 (disc). 1972. *A Recital of 33 Modern Piano Pieces.* Max Cooke, piano. With: *Stars* from **Night Pieces.**

Little Serenade (W141)
D22   Cherry Pie CPF 1034 (disc); CPC 1034 (cass). 1978. *Serenades.* Also on CD: Cherry Pie VPCD 6776. Sydney String Quartet. With: works of Beethoven, Boccherini, Borodin, Dvorak, Haydn, Mozart, Tchaikovsky. *Review:* B582.

Love 200 (W112)
D23   ABC RRCS 1466 (disc). 1970. *Australian Composers and Artists at the Sydney Proms.* Jeannie Lewis, singer; Tully rock band; Sydney

Symphony Orchestra; John Hopkins, conductor.

Mangrove (W152): D36; and
    D24   ABC TS AC 1053 B (disc). 1979. *Australian Composers.* Sydney
         Symphony Orchestra; Louis Fremaux, conductor. Notes by Sue
         Tronser include biography and composer's note to the score. With:
         works of Howard, Edwards, Meale.

Morning Song, arr. Sculthorpe for string quartet (W115)
    D25   EMI (HMV) OASD 7563 (disc). 1970. Austral String Quartet. Notes:
         Michael Hannan. With: **String Quartet No. 7; String Quartet No. 8;**
         Werder, *String Quartet No. 4. Reviews:* **B429, B492.**

Morning Song for the Christ Child (W98)
    D26   ABC RRC 65 (disc, mono). Adelaide Singers; Patrick Thomas,
         conductor.

    D27   SAR 1. 1977 (disc). *The Corinthians at Christmas: Carols from St.
         Peters Cathedral, Adelaide.* Corinthian Singers; Dean Patterson,
         director.

    D28   Abel 3. 1988 (disc). *An Australian Christmas.* Canberra Grammar
         School Chapel Choir; Charles Colman, conductor.

    D29   (arr. Nore) EMI (HMV) HQS 1308 (disc, quad). The King's Singers.

Mountains (W162): D37; D39

Music for Japan (W113)
    D30   HMV (EMI Australia) SOELP 9721 (disc). 1970. *Australian Youth
         Orchestra.* John Hopkins, conductor. With: works of Grainger.
         Reviews: **B383-384, B390.**

Music of Our Time: New Music From Australia
    D31   World Record Club R 00028 (disc). 1966. A Special Presentation of
         the Foundation for the Recording of Australian Music, S/FRAM 1.
         MSO; John Hopkins, conductor. Notes: Roger Covell. Contents:
         Irkanda IV (with Leonard Dommett, solo violin); **Sun Music I;** Le
         Gallienne, *Sinfonietta. Reviews:* **B181-181n.** Used in exhibit: **B252.**
         Re-issued on Odyssey 32 16 0149 (stereo), 32 16 0150 (mono).

Night Pieces (W118): D21 (*Stars* only); **D38; D39; D43** (without *Stars*); and
    D32   **Snow, Moon and Flowers.** Move MCP 029 (disc); MCC 029C (cass);
         MCD 129 (CD). 1988. *Australian Pianists of Excellence,* by members
         of the Team of Pianists. Robert Chamberlain, piano.

Nocturnal (W198): D39

Nourlangie (W201)
    D33   John Williams, guitar; Michael Askill, percussion; Australian

Chamber Orchestra; Richard Hickox, conductor (for future release, Sony)

Orchestral Music of Peter Sculthorpe
D34 EMI Australia OASD 7604 (disc); TC OASD 7604 (cass). Melbourne Symphony Orchestra; John Hopkins, conductor. Recorded 1976 and 1977 in the Melbourne Music Studios of the ABC. Notes: Hannan. Contents: **Small Town; Sun Music I, Sun Music II; Sun Music III; Sun Music IV.** *Reviews:* **B619, B624.**

Peter Sculthorpe: Chamber Music from Australia
D35 Southern Cross SCCD 1016. (In US: Fifth Continent 1016.) 1987. Australian Chamber Orchestra; Carl Pini, conductor. Recorded in the Sydney Opera House Recording Hall, December 1983. Notes: the composer; biographical note: Hannan. Contents: **Irkanda IV** (with Carl Pini, solo violin); **Lament for Strings; Port Essington; Sonata for Strings.** *Reviews:* **B895, B941.**

Peter Sculthorpe: Earth Cry; Kakadu; Mangrove
D36 ABC PolyGram 426 481-1 (disc); -2 (CD); -4 (cass). 1990. Sydney Symphony Orchestra; Stuart Challender, conductor. Notes: Graeme Skinner. Also includes **Irkanda IV** (with Donald Hazelwood, solo violin); and **Small Town** (with Guy Henderson, oboe). *Lit. and reviews:* **B1037, B1042-1043, B1051, B1057, B1061.** *Award:* **B1102**

Peter Sculthorpe: Landscapes: Music for Piano and Strings
D37 MBS 16 CD. 1989. Introductory essay: Jonathan Mills; notes: the composer. "This recording has been made by 2 MBS-FM as a celebration of Peter Sculthorpe's 60th Birthday in 1989." Cover: Judy Cassab, *Portrait of Peter Sculthorpe* (1988). Contents: **Djilile** (Geoffrey Tozer), **Four Little Pieces for Piano Duet** (Sculthorpe, Tozer); **Landscape II** (Seymour Group—Leigh Middenway, violin; Dittany Morgan, viola; Catherine Hewgill, 'cello; Anthony Fogg, piano; recorded 1987 at the Broadwalk, Sydney Opera House); **Mountains** (David Bollard); **Requiem** (David Pereira); **Tailitnama Song** (Pereira, Tozer). *Reviews:* **B995-996.**

Peter Sculthorpe: Piano Music (1981)
D38 Move MS 3031 (disc). Notes: Hannan. Contents: **Koto Music I-II, Landscape** (Hannan); **Night Pieces, Sonatina** (Sculthorpe); **Two Easy Pieces: Left Bank Waltz** (Sculthorpe), **Sea Chant** (Hannan). Caricature by Spooner on cover.

Peter Sculthorpe: Piano Music (1990)
D39 Move MD 3031 CD. Team of Pianists; Hannan; Sculthorpe. Notes: Graeme Skinner, from original material by the composer and Hannan, and notes supplied by the performers. Contents: **Callabonna** (Linda Kouvaras); **Four Little Pieces for Piano Duet** (Max Cooke, Darryl Coote); **Djilile; Sonatina W59** (Alexander Furman);

Mountains; **The Rose Bay Quadrilles** (Gudrun Beilharz); **Night Pieces; Nocturnal** (Chamberlain); **Koto Music I, II** and **Landscape** (Hannan); **Two Easy Pieces** (Sculthorpe). *Reviews:* **B1092-1093, B1126, B1152.**

Piano Concerto (W167)
  D40 ABC TS AC 1074 A (disc). 1985. Anthony Fogg, piano; Melbourne Symphony Orchestra; Myer Fredman, conductor. Recorded March 1983. Notes: the composer. With: Edwards. *Lit.:* **B736.**

  D41 ABC PolyGram 426 483-2 (CD); -4 (cass). 1990. *Australian Piano Concertos.* Fogg; MSO; Fredman. Re-issue of **D40**. Notes: Dennis Hennig. With: Edwards, Williamson. *Lit.:* **B1051**. *Review:* **B1062.**

Port Essington (W143): D35

Requiem (W153): D37

Rites of Passage (W125): The Chorales and **Rebirth.**
  D42 World Record Club R 03074 (disc). 1976. Melbourne Chorale; Orchestra from Victorian College of the Arts; John Hopkins, conductor. Notes: composer. Photo of the composer, over a portion of the score, on cover. *Review:* **B568.**

Roger Woodward, Piano
  D43 EMI Australia (HMV) OASD 7567 (disc). 1972. Notes: Hannan. *Contents:* **Landscape**; *Snow, Moon and Flowers* and *Night* from **Night Pieces** (played on the piano strings); **Sonatina**. With: works of Meale and Edwards. *Review:* **B492.**

Rose Bay Quadrilles, The (W199): D39

Sea Chant, as #1 of **Two Easy Pieces (W104): D38; D39**

Small Town (W136): D34; D36. The latter re-issued on ABC 434 719-2 CD.

Sonata for Strings (W170): D35

Sonata for Viola and Percussion (W77)
  D44 ABC PRX 559 (disc, mono); 5599 (stereo). 1975. *Australian Composers.* John Glickman, viola; Glen Davies, percussion. With: works of Dreyfus, Werder.

  D45 Halcyon Records (Price Milburn Music) PM 102 (disc). Glynne Adams, viola; Wayne Laird, percussion. Notes: Murdoch. Cover photo of Sculthorpe and New Zealand composer Jonathan Ladd by Murdoch. With: works of Shostakovich and Ladd.

Sonatina (W59): D38; D39; D43; and
  D46 Electric Records ELEC 4334 (disc). 1977. Trevor Barnard, piano. Also

listed as World Record Club R-04969: *An Introduction to Piano Music*, p1977.

D47   Discourses ABM 30 (disc). 1980. *Australian Piano Music*. Penelope Thwaites, piano. Notes by the performer identify the composer and describe the three movements. With: works of Benjamin, Grainger, Le Gallienne, Sutherland, Williamson. *Reviews:* **B633, B698, B731**.

Song of Tailitnama, The (W129)
D48   ABC TS AC 1062 (disc). 1986. *Australian Composers*. Rita Baldacchino, soprano; Algimantas Motiekaitis, Gregory Elmaloglou, Robert Miller, Juris Muiznieks, Joyce Murphy, Maureen O'Carroll, 'cellos; Michael Askill, Colin Piper, percussion; Patrick Thomas, conductor. Notes: the composer.

D49   MBS CD (forthcoming). Jeannie Marsh, with 'cellos and percussion.

Song of Tailitnama, The, arr. medium voice and piano (W171)
D50   Canberra School of Music CSM 15. 1989. Disc No. 15 of *Anthology of Australian Music on Disc*. Elizabeth Campbell, mezzo-soprano; Anthony Fogg, piano. "Handbook" contains composer's programme note and Hannan's commentary and analysis, with musical examples. *Review:* **B1046**. Re-issued on CD in 1990.

D51   MBS CD 19. 1991. *Anthology of Australian Song, vol. 1: 'Banquo's Buried'*. Elizabeth Campbell, mezzo-soprano; Anthony Fogg, piano. Re-issue of **D50**.

Songs of Sea and Sky (W185)
D52   Tall Poppies TP004 (CD). 1991. Nigel Westlake, clarinet; David Bollard, piano. *Reviews:* **B1162-1163**.

Songs of Sea and Sky, arr. flute and piano (W186)
D53   MBS 13 CD. *Flute Australia, vol. two*. 1988. Geoffrey Collins, flute; David Miller, piano. Notes: the composer. *Reviews:* **B992, B995**. (Sometimes listed as MBS CD 2 [1987].)

String Quartet No. 6 (W91)
D54   World Record Club S 2473 (disc, A-601 mono, SA-601 stereo). 1965. *Australian Music Today, vol. one*. Austral String Quartet. Notes: Covell. Insert: Murdoch, "Notes on Music Today." *Lit.:* **B105-106, B225**. *Reviews:* **B116, B123, B143-143n, B151, 170, B174, B212, B220**.

D55   RCA Victor VX 79 (disc). *Contemporary Music of Japan #13*. Mari Iwamoto String Quartet. Recorded in 1971. Notes in Japanese; cover in English. *Review:* **B428**.

String Quartet No. 7 (W99): D25 (as Red Landscape)

String Quartet No. 8 (W111): D25; and

D56 ABC RRCS 1468 (disc). *Australian Composers*. Austral String Quartet. Recorded as **String Quartet Music**. With: quartets of Conyngham, A. Hill.

D57 Argo disc ZRG 672 (disc). 1970. *Radcliffe Quartets 1969*. Allegri String Quartet. Notes: Peter Evans. *Reviews:* **B398, B419**.

D58 Sounds Wonderful Cassette SWC 8201. 1984. Kronos Quartet. Rev. 1975 version of the work. With: quartets of Benshoof and Webern.

D59 Nonesuch 79111-1 (disc); 79111-2 (CD); 79111-4 (cass). 1985. *Kronos Quartet*. Notes: Gregory Sandow. With: quartets by Glass, Hendrix, Nancarrow, Sallinen. *Reviews:* **B819-820, B836, B843, B851**.

String Quartet No. 9 (W132)
D60 Cherry Pie CPF 1031 (disc). 1978. *The Sydney String Quartet*. Notes: the composer. *Review:* **B582**.

String Quartet No. 11 (Jabiru Dreaming) (W204)
D61 Kronos Quartet. For future release (Nonesuch).

Sun Music I (W94): D31; D34

Sun Music II (W110): D34; and
D62 ABC RRCS 134 (disc). 1969. Sydney Symphony Orchestra; John Hopkins, conductor. Recorded as *Ketjak*.
With: **Sun Music for Voices and Percussion**. Lyric Singers; percussionists from the West Australian Symphony Orchestra; Verdon Williams, conductor. Recorded as "Sun Music II." Disc includes works of Conyngham and Meale.

D63 ABC L 60023-4 (disc). 1985. *The Ambassadors Symphony*. Australian Youth Orchestra; Charles Mackerras, conductor. Recorded live at the BBC Proms, Albert Hall, London, 1984 [P84-8].

Sun Music III (W100): D34; and
D64 HMV (EMI Australia) OASD 7547 (disc). 1969. Sydney Symphony Orchestra; Bernard Heinze, conductor. Recorded February 1969. Notes: Covell. With: works of Cugley, Dreyfus. *Reviews:* **B297-298**.

D65 ABC A 07011 (disc). SSO; Heinze. *Lit.:* **B221**.

D66 World Record Club R O3242 (disc). 197-. *Sir Bernard Heinze: The Golden Years* (2 discs). SSO; Heinze. With: A. Hill, Lovelock.

D67 Louisville First Edition LS 735 (disc). "119th Release." Louisville Orchestra; Jorge Mester, conductor. Recorded Oct. 2, 1973. Notes: Robert McMahan.

Sun Music IV (W101): D34; and

D68   ABC RRC 401 (disc, mono). 1975. *Australian Composers*. Australian Youth Orchestra; John Hopkins, conductor. Notes: Covell.

Sun Music for Voices and Percussion (W96): D62

Sun Song for Eric, A (W210)
  D69   Evasound JAD CD1031. 1992. *Where No Shadows Fall*. Ian Shanahan, alto recorder; Dominique Guerbois, violin; Susan Blake, 'cello.

Tabuh Tabuhan (W106)
  D70   ABC RRCS 378 (disc). 1968. *Australian Composers*. University of Adelaide Wind Quintet; Richard Smith, Bevan Bird, percussion. Notes: the composer.

  D71   Philips 6508 001 (disc). New Sydney Woodwind Quintet; Barry Heywood, Albert Setty, percussion. Notes: Covell. *Review:* **B415**.

Tailitnama Song, arr. cello and piano (W194): D37

They Found a Cave (W82): Theme and Journey's End, arr. Hal Evans
  D72   Columbia (EMI Australia) 7 MA 997 (mono), 7XAA 994. 7" disc. 1962. Larry Adler, harmonica; instrumental ensemble. *Lit.:* **B55-56**.

Threnody (W217)
  D73   Tall Poppies CD TP017. 1992. *Evocations Volume Two: Only Cello*. David Pereira, 'cello. Notes: Skinner.

Two Easy Pieces (W104): D38; D39

Performances

This is a chronological listing of performances excluding first performances (first performances are listed by work in the "Works" or **W** catalog). The **P** numbers denote the year, then month (**P79-4** is April 1979). Cross-references to **W** numbers refer to the "Works" catalog, **D** numbers to the "Discography," and **B** numbers to the "Bibliography." Performers' full names are included in the Subject Index.

P45-5   May 19: *Piano Solo* [Frank Hutchens, *Weeping Mist*]. Launceston Competitions Association Grand Concert by Juvenile Prize Winners (National Theatre). #51, "Piano Solo, Aust. Composer 15-18: Peter Sculthorpe."

P45-8   Aug 31: **Winter Woodland [Winter Landscape], Puppet Show, Nocturne.** "Tasmanian Youth Clubs Calling." PS, 16-year-old composer-pianist, at 8:30 E.S.T., on 2BL, 2NC, 3LO, 4QR, 5CL, 7ZR (ABC radio stations in Sydney, Newcastle, Melbourne, Brisbane, Adelaide, and Hobart).

P45-9   Sept 11: **Piano works.** PS, pf. *Lit.*: **B1**. Other announcements, undated, in PS files include: **Winter Woodland; Falling Leaves, Nocturne,** "The North Entertains," 7:30, ABC radio broadcast of Australian compositions (Alfred Hill, Hutchens, PS); and **Piano works,** Launceston (TH), Mayoress's Soirée to benefit Newstead Child Welfare Centre.

P46-8   Aug 27 (7:30): **Two Evocations; Sonatina no. 1; Two Short Pieces.** ABC radio, 7ZR and 7NT. PS, pf. *Lit.*: "Launceston composer plays own work," *ABC Weekly*, 24 Aug.

P46   **Aboriginal Legend.** Melbourne. Heidelberg Eisteddfod, Australian composers' section. M. Olding. Awarded first prize.

P47-5   May 21 (Wed.): **Piano works.** Launceston (TH). Soirée to aid Food for Britain appeal (British Relief Fund). PS, pf. *Lit.*: *Examiner*, 22 May.

P47-10 Oct 6: **To Meadows** for three voices, unaccompanied (Ekins, Luijk, Clarke); **Six Sketches; Aboriginal Legend** (PS, pf); **Take, O take those lips away; Elegy for a Clown; Jack and Joan; Parting** (Cowper); **Aspatia's Song; Gardener Janus Catches a Naiad; Two Songs** to words by Housman (Cameron); **Suite for two violins and cello—Sarabande, Intermezzo, Chorale-Prelude, Puppet-Dance** (W. Lehmann, Dommett, Mahon). Melbourne (Con.). "Concert Practice."

Oct 15: program (in PS files) lists PS, double bass, in Mornington Peninsula SO concert at Mechanics Institute, Frankston VIC.

P47-12 Dec 6: **Aboriginal Legend; Five Scherzos.** Melbourne. Australian Literature Society concert. PS, pf.

P48-4 April: **Trio** for 3 unaccompanied solo voices. Melbourne Conservatorium Chamber Music Concert.

P48-5 May 10: **Reverie.** Melbourne (Con.). "Concert Practice." Cowper.

P48-8 Aug 3: **String Quartet [no. 2]** (W. Lehmann, Fegent, Barber, Maxwell); **Take, O Take Those Lips Away; Aspatia's Song; Jack and Joan; Parting; Elegy for a Clown; Reverie** (Cowper); **Two Preludes** (W4, W5); **Seascape; Nocturne; Falling Leaves;** and sketch for a **Concerto** movement (PS, pf). Melbourne. Fine Arts Society concert. *Review:* **B4.**

P48-12 Dec 4: **Nocturne; Reverie,** arr. pf; **Three songs: Mushrooms, Sleep, The Children's Minuet.** Melbourne. Australian Literature Society Rooms. PS, pf.

P49-5 May: **To Meadows** for string orchestra. Melbourne Conservatorium.

P49-6 June 22: **Two Nocturnes** (1945, 1949 [first perf]). Melbourne (Assembly Hall). Arts Council of Australia (Victorian Division). "An Evening Series of Recitals." Nemenoff. *Reviews:* **B6.**

June 28: **Three Preludes;** variations on a theme from a **Piano Concerto; Two Nocturnes; Sonatina no. 1: I, II; Dance [Aboriginal Legend]; Seascape; Siesta; Falling Leaves.** Melbourne. Fine Arts Society recital. PS, pf. *Review:* **B7.**

P49-9 Sept 12: **Piano works.** Melbourne (British Music Society's rooms). Austral Salon At Home. PS, pf.

P49-12 Dec 1: **Two Nocturnes.** Melbourne (Assembly Hall). Victorian Jewish Competitions Society Concert, farewell recital. Nemenoff.

P50-1 Jan 16 (7.20-7.30): **Piano works.** ABC radio (7NT). PS, pf.

P50-4 April: Recital of the composer's works for the Fine Arts Society. Melbourne (Union Theatre). PS, pf.

P50-6 June: **The White Bird**. Hobart. Gwennyth Dixon (mentioned in **B9**).

June 28: **SQ 4**. Melbourne (British Music Society's Rooms). Programme arranged by "Younger Circle," Society of Women Musicians of Australia. Cullity, Young, Kerr, Thoms.

P50-10 Oct 11: **SQ 4**. Melbourne (British Music Society's Rooms). Guild of Australian Composers (Victorian Branch). Recital of Australian compositions. Bull, M. Scott, Stooke, Horwitz. *Review:* **B10**.

P50-11 Nov: **Two Preludes; Seascape; Nocturne** (1949); **Aboriginal Legend**. Melbourne (New Theatre). Peace Congress Concert. PS, pf.

P51-7 July 31: **Concerto** and **Two Nocturnes** (nos. 1 & 5"). Devonport TAS (TH). Devonport Choral Society Subscription Concert. PS, pf. *Review:* "Successful Concert" (PS "was greatly appreciated in his finished rendition of his own pianoforte compositions").

P51-12 Dec 4: **Nocturne** (1949) and **Seascape**. Launceston (National Theatre). Launceston Male Choir Invitation Concert. PS, pf.

P52-4 Apr: **The White Bird; Reverie**. Radio Australia.

P52-6 June 20 (Sat.), 9:30: **A programme of piano works**. ABC radio (7NT). PS, pf. *Announcement:* includes photo and brief biography.

P53-5 May: **Aboriginal Legend**. Melbourne (National Theatre). Contemporary Dance Recital. PS, pf.

P53-8 Aug: **Two Nocturnes**. ABC radio. PS, pf.

P55-4 Apr 18: *We Were Dancing*, by Noel Coward, presented by Launceston Players. Launceston (National Theatre). Ninth Tasmanian Drama Festival (April 18-23). PS, pf.

P55-12 Nov 23-Dec 3: *1066 and all that*. Hobart Repertory Theatre. Wakefield and PS, pf.

P56-1 Jan 28: **Sonatina** (W59). ABC radio. PS, pf.

P56-2 Feb 25: **Irkanda** [I]. Lisbon Mozart Festival. I salão dos artistas de hoje, organizado com a colaborção da Juventude Musical Portuguesa. W. Lehmann. *Lit.:* **B17**.

P56-3 Mar: **Sonatina**. Festival of Contemporary Music. South African Radio. *Ref.:* **B17**.

P56-4 Apr 28: **Sonata for Violin Alone** ("Sonata for Unaccompanied Violin"). Melbourne. British Music Society concert. W. Lehmann.

P57-2 Feb: **A program of piano works**. ABC radio. PS, pf.

P57-3 Mar 2: **Sonatina**. Perth (Art Gallery). Australian Music Festival. Donald Thornton, pf. *Review:* **B22**. *Ref.:* **B53**.

P57-9 Sept (long run): *The Willow Pattern Plate*. Sydney. Children's matinee with **Cross Section**. Mendoza and PS, pf. Both produced by Orr.

P57-11 Nov: **Irkanda [I]**. Poznan (Concert Hall).

P58-4 Apr: **Irkanda [I]**. Moscow (Conservatorium H). W. Lehmann. **B24-25**.

P58-6 June 25-28: **Dear Charles**, comedy in three acts. Launceston (National Theatre). Launceston Players. Incidental music by PS. Barry Scott, pf.

P59-2 Feb 9-13: **L'Avare (The Miser)**. Birmingham, England. Univ. of Birmingham Cercle Français. PS, pf.

P61-1 Jan 22? (scheduled for May 14): **The Loneliness of Bunjil**. Birmingham, UK (Art Gallery). Sunday Chamber Music Concerts. Haydn Trio. *Lit.:* **B33**. *Reviews:* **B39**, **B41**.

P61-2 Feb 4: **Irkanda I**. Birmingham (Art Gallery). Broadcast Feb 16. W. Lehmann. *Review:* **B38**.

P62-3 Mar 23: **Sonata for Viola and Percussion**, first Australian perf. Hobart (Union Building, Univ. of TAS). Lunch-hour concert. Komlos. *Lit.:* Thespian, "Tasmanian's sonata for city concert," *Mercury*, 13 March; and "Wrote sonata" (unident. pubn.) with photo of PS.

P63-7 July 30: **Irkanda IV**, first Sydney perf. (Great Hall, Univ. of Sydney) A. Hoffmann; Pro Musica Society of Sydney Univ.; Peart. *Review:* **B61**.

P63-9 Sept 23: **Irkanda IV**. Hobart. Tasmanian Orchestra youth concert; T. Matthews. *Review:* **B65**.

P63-10 Oct 16 (Wed.): **Sonata for Piano, 1st movt**. TAS TV channel 2 & 3. Ralph. *Lit.:* **B66**.

P63-11 Nov 10: **Irkanda IV**. Melbourne (Nicholas Hall). J. Lehmann; Astra Chamber Orchestra; Logie-Smith. *Review:* **B68**.

P64-8 Aug 14: **Sonata for Viola and Percussion**, first Sydney perf. (Cell Block Theatre). ISCM concert. Ashley; van Hove. With: "A Talk on Alban Berg's *Lyric Suite*, with illustrations, by PS." *Reviews:* **B82-86**.

P65-2 Feb: **Irkanda III**. Barcelona. London Czech Trio. *Reviews:* **B93**.

P65-4 Apr 16 (2.00): **SQ 6**. Mittagong Festival (Frensham Hall). Austral SQ. **B102**. (11.00 am:) "Composers and Their Music" chaired by Covell.

Apr 26: **SQ 6**. Melbourne (Wilson Hall). Austral SQ. The composer was present. *Reviews:* **B104**.

P65-6   June 8-10: **Irkanda IV**. Sydney (TH). SSO youth concert; Post. **B112-113**.

June 24: **SQ 6**, introduced by the composer. Sydney. Paddington Arts Festival concert to raise money to build Paddington Arts Centre. *Lit.:* "Week of Arts Festival, *SMH*, 15 June.

P65-9   Sept 23: **SQ 6**. Liverpool. Austral SQ. Recorded by the BBC; broadcast Sydney, Oct 7. *Review:* **B120**. *Also performed:* Sept 28, London, John Lewis Partnership Music Society concert, Commonwealth Arts Festival. *Reviews:* **B122, B128**.

Sept 27: **Irkanda IV**. Brisbane (Albert Hall). QLD Con. Orchestra; cond. J. Sedivka. *Review:* **B121**.

P65-10   Oct 21: **Sonata for Viola and Percussion**. Melbourne (Assembly Hall). ISCM, Melbourne. Glickman; Davies. *Reviews:* **B137-138**.

P65-11   Nov 12: **SQ 6**. Sydney (Cell Block Theatre). ISCM subscription series concert. Austral SQ. *Review:* **B141-142, B144**.

Nov 18: **Irkanda I**. Sydney (Cell Block Theatre). Bartok Society recital. Jaggard. *Reviews:* **B145-147**.

Nov 24: **Sun Music [I]**, first Australian perf. Hobart (City Hall). ABC's Festival for Two Orchestras. Victorian SO (MSO); Heinze. **B148-149**.

P66-1   Jan: **Sun Music I**. National Music Camp rehearsal piece. *Lit.:* **B182**.

P66-2   Feb 11: **Sun Music I**, first Sydney perf. SSO Prom concert; Hopkins. *Reviews:* **B156-160**. Recorded for broadcast by ABC. *Lit.:* "Foundations of an original Australian music," *Mercury*, 19 Feb (announces broadcast next Saturday, with composer's program notes).

P66-4   April: **Three Haiku**. New Haven CT (School of Music, Yale University). PS, pf.

P66-5   May 10: **Irkanda I** (Jaggard); **Sun Music ("II") for Voices and Percussion**, first Sydney perf. (Pro Musica Society; Peart). Sydney (Cell Block Theatre). ISCM, Sydney, Tenth Season, First Concert. **B165-B169**.

May 27-28: **Sun Music [I]**. Perth celebrity concert. WASO subs; Heinze.

P66-10   Oct: **Sun Music I** in Czechoslavakia, cond. Hopkins (tour). *Lit.:* **B175**. Also Moscow, etc., in Soviet Union.

P67-2   Feb 16: **Irkanda IV**. Sydney (TH). SSO Proms. Hazelwood; SSO; Hopkins. *Reviews:* **B188-190**.

P67-3   Mar 1: **Irkanda IV**. Perth Festival, cond. Hopkins.

Mar 14: **Irkanda IV**, British premiere. London (Commonwealth

Institute). Mason; Salomon Orch; Braithwaite. *Reviews:* **B193-193n.**

P67-5   May 12: **SQ 7**. Zagreb Biennale (held May 11-21). Zagrebacki Kvartet.

P67-6   June 6, 7: **Anniversary Music**, Adelaide premiere (TH). SASO youth concert; Heinze. *Reviews:* **B201.** *Lit.:* **B202.**

June 17: **Anniversary Music**. Brisbane. QSO; Heinze.

P67-7   July 14: **Anniversary Music**, Tasmanian premiere. Hobart (City Hall). TSO youth concert; Heinze. *Publicity:* "Music and Drama" by "Pleiades," *Mercury*, 11 July, p. 14.

July 29 (Sat.): **Sonata for Viola and Percussion** (Powell; Smith); **SQ 6** (Dorian SQ). Adelaide (Teachers College Theatre). With a talk by Mr. Sculthorpe on recent developments in his own music; recordings of **Sun, Sun Music I, IV.** Presented by ISCM, Adelaide. **B208.**

July 30: **SQ 6**, one movt, used in *The Tree* excerpt, Australian Dance Theatre; choreog. Dalman. Adelaide (Dalman Studios). PS the official guest of the company at this premiere workshop perf. in his honour. *Lit.:* Tidemann, "Birth of a ballet," *Advertiser*, 31 July.

P67-8   Aug 21-22: **Anniversary Music**, Melbourne premiere. MSO; Heinze. *Reviews:* **B209-211.**

P67-9   Sept 5: **Sun Music IV** recording in "Audio-Visual Concert," illustrated with Dallwitz's photography; dir. Jolly. Adelaide (TH). *Lit.:* *The News* (Adelaide), 6 Sept; & Horner, "Sights and Sounds," *Advertiser.*

Sept 30: **SQ 6**. Canberra (Playhouse). Canberra Spring Festival. Austral SQ. Notes: Covell. PS also spoke at a morning seminar. *Reviews:* **B214-215.**

P67-10   Oct 24: **Anniversary Music**, Sydney premiere. SSO; Heinze. *Reviews:* **B218-219, B222.** Also: recording session in Sydney. SSO; Heinze. **B221.**

P67-11   Nov 8-9: **Irkanda IV**. Newcastle. SSO subs, schools; Hopkins.

Nov 20: **Sun Music IV**. Launceston (Albert Hall). SSO concert for school-children; cond. Hopkins, who explained the work beforehand. *Also:* Nov 21 (aft), Hobart (City Hall). *Lit.:* "Orchestra pleased children at L'ton, *Mercury*, 21 Nov.

P68-1   Jan 28: **Sun Music III**. Melbourne. Free concert. MSO; Heinze.

P68-2   Feb 8: **Sun Music IV**, first Sydney perf. (TH). SSO Prom concert; Hopkins. *Reviews:* **B230-B234, B255.**

Feb 28: **Irkanda IV**. Sydney Univ. A. Bonds; NTO; Miller. *Also:* Mar 1, Macquarie Univ.; Mar 5, Univ. of NSW (Science Hall), **B235.**

Feb 29: **Sun Music IV**. Perth (Basil Kirke Studio). Festival of Perth, composers workshop. WASO; Hopkins.

P68-3   Mar 21-22: **Sun Music IV**. Adelaide Festival youth concerts (TH). AYO; Hopkins. *Reviews:* **B240**. *Also performed at the festival,* Mar 21: **Morning Song; Autumn Song**. The Augmented Adelaide Singers; P. Thomas.

P68-4   Apr 14 (Easter Sun.): SQ 7 (Austral SQ); **Tabuh Tabuhan** on tape; **Music for Mittagong** (1968), first perf. Mittagong Festival. Also: **Sonata for Viola** (Glickman; Davies). *Reviews:* **B244-245, B255**.

P68-5   May 8-9: **Sun Music I**, second Sydney perf. (TH). SSO subs (red); Krips. *Reviews:* **B248-251, B253-254**.

May 14 (opening): **Sun Music I** [D31] is played in Cylinder no. 10 at "The First 200 Years," Sydney (Australia Square) exhibition by Robin Boyd. *Reviews:* **B252**.

P68-6   June: **SQ 6** used in play *Burke's Company*. Melbourne (Russell St. Theatre). *Lit.:* **B258, B627**.

June 1, 3: **Sun Music IV**. Melbourne. MSO subs (red); van Otterloo.

June 11: **SQ 6**. Aldeburgh UK (Jubilee H). Faber Music concert, Twenty-First Aldeburgh Festival of Music and the Arts. Cremona SQ.

June 11, 13: **Sun Music IV**. Sydney. SSO youth concert; Atzmon. *Reviews:* **B259, B261**. Photo in **B287** (PS and Atzmon taking a bow).

June 18, 22: **Sun Music IV**. Wangaratta; Canberra II subs. SSO; van Otterloo.

P68-8   Aug 12: **Sun Music IV**. London (Royal Festival Hall). BBC Northern SO; Thomson. *Review:* **B272**.

Aug 18: **Irkanda IV**. Sydney. Free Univ. concert. A. Bonds; NTO; Miller.

P68-9   Sept 11: **SQ 6**. Venice. (Salle Apollinée del Teatro La Fenice). Italian premiere. 31 Festival Internationale di Musica Contemporanea. La Biennale di Venezia. Quartetto della Società Camaristica Italiana.

Sept 14: **The Fifth Continent**. Hobart. ABC youth concert. Chris Waterhouse, narr.; Tasmanian Orch. *Lit.: Mercury,* 3 Sept.

Sept 23, 25: **Sun Music III**. SSO schools concerts; Heinze.

P68-10   Oct: **SQ 7** and [?]. Sydney. Arts Vietnam concert. *Review:* **B274**.

P68-11   Nov 1: **Tabuh Tabuhan**, first public perf. in Sydney (Cell Block

Theatre). New Sydney Ww Qnt; Miller; Heywood. Preliminary talk by PS. *Reviews:* **B275-277, B279.**

P69-2   Feb 13: **Sun Music for Voices and Percussion,** first perf. in WA (WASO; Lyric Singers; Williams); and **Sun Music III** (WASO; Mayer). Perth (ABC's Basil Kirke Studio). Seventeenth Annual Festival of Perth, Four Australian Composers' Workshops, presented by the ABC. PS was present. *Review:* **B291.**

P69-3   Mar 3: **Sun Music III.** Moomba Festival. MSO; Heinze.

Mar 8: "Morning Song for the Nativity" [**Morning Song for the Christ Child**]. Melbourne (Great Hall, Victorian Arts Centre). Moomba Festival. Australian Universities Festival Choir of Melbourne; Pyers. Programme also performed at the second international universities choral festival in Washington, D C, and New York, Mar 13-31. *Lit.: Music Now* 1, no. 4 (April 1971): 19.

Mar 10: **Tabuh Tabuhan,** British premiere. London (Purcell Room). Adelaide Wind Qnt, with substitute oboist Sutcliffe, +2 perc. *Reviews:* **B302-303.**

Mar 29: **Sun Music IV.** Sydney (TH). ABC and ISCM (Australian branch) Festival concert of new symphonic music. SSO; Atzmon. *Reviews:* **B305-306.** *Also:* Apr 1, Wollongong schools concerts.

P69-4   Apr 11: **Sun Music for Voices and Percussion** and **Night Piece.** Sydney (Great Hall, Univ. of Sydney). ISCM (Sydney) "New Bloom" concert. Fort Street Boys' HS students; Condon. *Lit.: Music Now* 1/4 (1971): 19. *Reviews:* Covell, "Delights in milk bottles," *SMH,* 12 April; Oakes, "Youngsters music a hit," *Daily Telegraph,* 12 April.

Apr 28: **Sun Music III.** Hamilton. MSO; Heinze. Apr 29, Horsham.

P69-5   May: **Sun Music IV.** Paris. Orchestre de la Radio-Television-diffusion Française (ORTF); Hopkins. *Lit.: Music Now* 1, no. 2 (1969): 34.

P69-6   June 28: **Sun Music III.** Hobart. TSO (subs); Krips.

P69-7   July 27: **Tabuh Tabuhan.** Sydney (Neutral Bay Music Hall Licensed Restaurant). Sunday Evening concert series. New Sydney Ww Qnt; Miller; Heywood. *Lit.:* **B315.** *Reviews:* **B316-317.**

P69-8   Aug 22: **Irkanda IV.** Melbourne. ISCM Melbourne concert. Astra CO. *Lit.: Music Now* 1, no. 2 (1969): 46.

P69-9   Sept 5: **SQ 6.** Sydney (Cell Block Theatre). ISCM Sydney concert. Austral SQ. *Reviews:* **B318-320.**

Sept 11, 12, 13: **Sun Music I.** Adelaide. SASO subs; Krips.

P69-10 Oct: **SQ 6** used in *The Tree*, Australian Dance Theatre; choreog. Dalman. *Lit*: Peter Ward, "Dancing on hope and dedication," *Bulletin*.

Oct 7: **Sun Music II**. Hobart. TSO youth concert; Hopkins.

P69-11 Nov 1: **SQ 8**. Univ. of Sussex, UK. Allegri SQ. *Review*: **B328**.

Nov 3, 4, 5: **Sun Music III** excerpt. Brisbane. QSO schools concerts; Boughen.

P70 **Sun Music II** used for *The Oldest Continent: Time Riders*, a Sound and Image 1970 production. Australian Dance Theatre. Several perfs.

P70-1 Jan 15: **Sun Music IV**, deutsche Erstaufführung. Düsseldorf (Robert-Schumann-Saal). Düsseldorfer Symphoniker; Schönzler.

Jan 25: **Sun Music II**. Hobart. Free (Capt. Cook). TSO; Williams.

P70-2 Feb 28: **Sun Music II**. Melbourne. MSO Proms; Hopkins. **B347-348**

P70-3 Mar 23?: **Irkanda IV**. London (QEH). Pauk; Bournemouth Sinfonietta; Braithwaite. *Review*: **B349**.

Mar: **Sun Music IV** used for *Sun and Moon* (created 1968 for Holland's Scapino Ballet), Australian Dance Theatre, choreog. Dalman. Adelaide Festival. *Also*: Devonport, Launceston, Hobart. *Lit.*: **B1074**.

P70-4 Apr 1: **Sun Music IV**. Newcastle. SSO country tour; Atzmon.

Apr 10: **Sun Music I**. Brisbane. QSO youth concert; Matteucci.

P70-5 May: **Twelfth Night** music. Lima, Peru. "Good Companions" foreign theatrical group; Petty. *Review*: El Comercio (Lima), 4 May (trans.).

May 8-21: **Sun Music ballet**. Sydney (Her Majesty's Theatre). Australian Ballet; Rosen (opening); Ringland; Nicolls. *Reviews*: **B350**. *Also*: perfs. in Melbourne in July, in other Australian centres to December.

P70-6 June 29-30: **Sun Music III**. Melbourne schools. MSO; Dommett.

P70-7 July 1: **Sun Music III**. MSO, country schools concerts; Dommett. *Also*: July 8, Horsham; July 9, Hamilton; July 10, Warrnambool.

July 14: **Music for Japan**. Canberra (Canberra Theatre). Farewell concert before Japan. AYO; Hopkins. *Reviews*: **B359**.

July 18: **Music for Japan**. Osaka (Festival Plaza, Expo '70). AYO; Hopkins. Other perfs. July 16-26 during Asian tour, in Manila, Hong Kong, etc. *Publicity*: **B359n**. In Japan, NHK television taped the concert for the ABC for broadcast in Australia. *Examiner* announcement of Apr 4, 1971 (Sun.) broadcast quotes from PS's programme notes.

July 20: **Love 200** is featured in film "Who Needs Art?," ABC-TV broadcast.

July 27, 28: **Sun Music II**. Perth schools concerts. WASO; Williams.

July 30, 31, Aug 1: **Sun Music III**. Adelaide. SASO subs; Heinze.

P70-8   Aug 11: **Sun Music III**. Melbourne. MSO youth; van Otterloo. *Also:* Aug 15, 17, subs (red). *Review:* **B361** mentions shortened version Aug 20, etc.

Aug 24: **SQ Music** ("Music for SQ" [translated to Japanese then back to English, says the composer, who was present]). Tokyo (Space Theatre). "Music Today 6," Expo '70. *Also:* PS in panel discussion, Aug 22.

P70-9   Sept 6: **SQ Music**. First Australian perf. Surfers Paradise QLD (Chevron Hotel). Austral SQ. On Sat. Sept 5 PS presented a talk about "his music and his experiences." *Review:* **B362**.

Sept 9, 10, 11: **Love 200**. Sydney (TH; 2nd night at Capitol Theatre because of strike). SSO youth concert; Lewis; Tully; Atzmon. **B363**.

Sept 24: **Sea Chant**. Sydney (Cheltenham). Beecroft District School Combined Choirs.

P70-10   Oct 13: **Tabuh Tabuhan**. Sydney (TH). Musica Viva 25th Anniversary Year concert. New Sydney Ww Qnt (Amadio; Henderson; D. Westlake; Cran; Mellor); Heywood; Piper. *Reviews:* **B366, B373**.

Oct 24: **Sun Music III**. Ann Arbor MI. MSO tour; van Otterloo. *Also:* Nov 10, New York (Carnegie Hall), International Festival of Visiting Orchestras. *Review:* **B376**. *Lit.:* **B701**.

P70-11   Nov 6: **Sonata for Viola and Percussion**. Tokyo. Okada; Yoshie

Nov 8: **Dream**. Sydney (Elizabethan Theatre, Newtown). Tully; the Extradition (folk group); the Renaissance Players; cond. PS. With Irish harp, krummhorn, shawm, and Rag Dun (Tibetan horn). *Lit.:* **B375**.

Nov 10: **Sun Music IV**. Hobart. TSO subs; Paul. Nov 11, Launceston.

P71-1   Jan 2: **Sun Music ballet**. Los Angeles. Australian Ballet. *Also performed* in New York City between Jan 26 and Feb 7.

Jan 31: **Irkanda IV** Sydney. Free concert (Aust. Day). Elliott; SSO; Llewellyn.

P71-2   Feb 11: **Music for Japan**, first Sydney perf. (TH). Opening Prom concert. SSO; Hopkins. *Reviews:* **B392-396**.

Feb 12: **Sun Music II**. Hobart. TSO Prom; Krips.

Feb 18: **The Stars Turn, arr. high voice and pf.** Festival of Perth (Basil Kirke Studio). Australian Composers' Workshop. McGurk; Dorman.

Feb 23, 25, 26: **Sun Music III.** Sydney. NTO; Miller.

P71-3   Mar 6: **Love 200.** Melbourne (TH). MSO Proms. Lewis; Jeff St. John and the Copperwine; Hopkins. *Reviews:* **B399.**

Mar 10 and 11: **Irkanda IV,** first Canberra perf. (Canberra Theatre), intro. by PS. Canberra Day celebration concerts opening the orch season. Edwards; Canberra SO; Llewellyn. *Reviews:* **B400-401.** Mar 11, 12.40-1.20 pm: Lecture "Pop Music: from Mozart to the Present Day." **B402.**

Mar 13: **SQ 8,** first Sydney perf. (Science Theatre, Univ. of NSW). Students' Union's Summer Arts Festival. Austral SQ. *Review:* **B403.**

Mar 24: **Love 200.** Sydney (Great Hall). Elizabethan Trust Orch; Syrius; Lewis; Rainbow lighting.

P71-4   April 7: **Irkanda IV.** Sydney (Great Hall). Kelly; Pro Musica Orchestra; Gross. *Review:* **B406.**

Apr 16, 17: **Sun Music III.** Brisbane. QSO subs; Rachlin.

P71-5   May 10: **Sun Music III.** Sydney (TH). NSW Public Schools' Concert Orchestra; Hunt.

May: ballets **Love 201** (Bach recording; Syrius), and *Duo* (to **Tabuh Tabuhan** recording). Sydney (Wallace Theatre). The Dance Company (NSW); choreog. Welch. *Review:* **B409.**

P71-6   June 5: **Tabuh Tabuhan.** London (QEH). ISCM concert. Members of the Atlantic Sinfonietta. *Reviews:* **B411-B414.**

June 15: **Sun Music III.** Bathurst. SSO country tour; Post. *Also:* June 16, Dubbo; June 17, Orange; June 21, Goulburn; June 22, Albury; June 23, Wagga.

June 19: **Irkanda IV.** London (Main Hall, Australia House). Collins; Chelsea Opera Group Orch; P. Thomas.

June 29: **Sun Music I.** Melbourne. MSO youth concert; Rieger. *Also:* July 1, Geelong, country subs.

P71-7   July 20: **Sun Music IV.** Perth. WASO youth concert; Paul.

July 30: **Morning Song.** Sydney (Great Hall). Pro Musica Choir.

July 31: **SQ Music.** Niagara-on-the-Lake, ONT, Canada (St. Mark's Church). "Music Today '71" concert, as part of the Shaw Festival. Orford Qt. *Reviews:* **B416-417.**

P71-9   Sept: **Landscape**. Hannan, Bollard, PS, on tape prep. by John Taylor of EMI (Australia) Ltd. In sculpture by Jack Meyer, in exhibition "Rooms on View '71." Sydney (Farmer's Blaxland Gallery). *Lit.:* **B420**.

Sept 27, 28, 29: **Sun Music II**. Sydney. SSO youth concerts; Post.

P71-10   Oct 3: **Sonata for Viola and Percussion**. Dunedin, NZ (Marama Hall, Univ. of Otago). Saunders; Brain.

Oct 3: **Sun Music II**. Sydney. Waratah Festival (free). SSO; Heinze.

Oct 5: **How the Stars were Made**, Sydney premiere (TH). Waratah Festival Prom concert. Les Percussions de Strasbourg. *Reviews:* **B423-425**. *Lit.:* **B426**. Also performed Oct 10 and Oct 23.

P71-11   Nov 24 (Wed.): **SQ Music**. Heslington UK (Lyons CH, Univ. of York). Allegri SQ. *Also:* Nov. 26, "Work" [**Dream**]. New Music Ensemble.

P71-12   Dec 5: **Music for Japan** used for *Rondel*, Australian Dance Theatre Workshop; choreog. Dalman. Adelaide. *Review:* "Brilliant new ballet to music by Sculthorpe," *Advertiser*, 6 Dec. *Repeated:* Mar 2, 1972, Adelaide Festival.

P72-1   **Tabuh Tabuhan** programmed on QANTAS airline in-flight entertainment. (**Small Town, Piano Concerto**, and other works also programmed in later years.)

P72-3   Mar 16: **Love 200**. Adelaide. SASO Prom; Jeannie Lewis and the Fraternity; Hopkins.

Mar 22, 23: **Sun Music II**. Adelaide. SASO youth concert; Hopkins.

P72-4   Apr 14: **Music for Japan**, British premiere. London (QEH). Polyphonia Orch; Fairfax. Program notes: Hannan. *Reviews:* **B434-B436**.

Apr 18: **Sun Music II**. Melbourne. MSO youth concert; Rieger.

Apr 18, 20, 21: **Sun Music III**. Wollongong, Tamworth, Armidale. SSO subs and schools; Post.

P72-5   May 15: **SQ 6; Sonata for Viola and Percussion; Tabuh Tabuhan**, movts I and V. Aberystwyth (Univ. College of Wales, Dept. of Music). "Music by PS in the presence of the composer. The 1,193rd Weekly College Concert."

May 20: **SQ Music**. Sydney (Cell Block Theatre). Austral SQ.

May 31: **Sun Music II**. Hobart. TSO youth concert; Quach.

P72-6   June 2: **SQ Music**. Falmer UK (Gardner Centre for the Arts). Allegri SQ.

June 5-July 17: *Premises 7* by Ballet Victoria, on tour, to music by PS.

June 17: **Sun Music III.** Brisbane. QSO youth concert; Heinze.

P72-8 Aug 2, 3: **Sun Music III.** Sydney. SSO subs (red); van Otterloo. *Also:* Aug 5, 7 (blue); Aug 8 (white); Aug 9, 10, Canberra subs.

P72-12 Dec 1: **Red Landscape (SQ 7).** Falmer (Univ. of Sussex Debating Chamber). Lunch-time, open rehearsal with PS; concert that evening. University SQ. *Lit.: Univ. of Sussex Music,* issue no. 1 (Dec 1972).

Dec 1 (7:30 pm): **SQ Music.** London (Purcell Room). Park Lane Group, "Music Today" series. Austral SQ. PS was present. *Reviews:* **B444-445.**

Dec 17: **Sun Music III** recorded at the first concert in the Sydney Opera House Concert Hall. Free, invitational. SSO; Heinze. *Lit.:* **B726.**

P73 date? " Nocturne" (= *Second Chorale*) from **Rites of Passage.** Pro Musica Society of Sydney University; Peart.

P73-2 Feb 25: **Night Pieces.** London (Wigmore Hall). Petter.

Feb 28: **Irkanda IV.** Sydney. Youth Prom (free). NTO; Miller.

P73-3 Mar 16: **Irkanda I.** Univ. of Sussex Mtg House. Woodcock. *Lit.:* **B449.**

Mar 30: **Tabuh Tabuhan.** Sydney (Post Aud.). New Sydney Ww Qnt; 2 perc. *Review:* Costantino, "All-Australian program from a wind quintet," *SMH,* 31 Mar, ("couldn't stay to hear it").

Mar 31: **Irkanda IV.** Newcastle Prom. G. Bonds; NTO; Miller.

P73-4 Apr 1 (2:30): **SQ Music**—*Con dolore/Ketungan.* Sydney (OHCH). "Trial Concert" to demonstrate acoustics. Austral SQ.

Apr 13 (Friday): **Irkanda IV.** London (QEH). Polyphonia Orch; Fairfax.

P73-8 Aug 7: **Sun Music III.** Adelaide. SASO youth concert; Krips.

P73-10 Oct 1: **Sun Music IV.** Horsham. MSO subs; Slovak. *Also:* Oct 2, Hamilton; Oct 3, Warrnambool.

Oct 2-10: **Sun Music ballet.** London (Coliseum). Australian Ballet (one of three programs). *Review:* John Percival, *Times,* 9 Oct: 23.

Oct 13, 15, 16: **Sun Music III.** Melbourne. MSO subs; Heinze

Oct 23: **Tabuh Tabuhan.** Sydney (OHMR). New Sydney Ww Qnt; 2 perc.

Oct 25: **Landscape; Night Pieces** without *Stars.* Sydney (OHMR). Opera

House opening season (*lit.*: **B460**). Woodward.

P73-11 Nov 1: **SQ 6**. Sydney (OH). Opera House opening season (*lit.*: **B460**). Fellowship of Australian Composers presents An Evening of Australian Music. Carl Pini Qt. *Review:* **B459**.

Nov 10-11: **Sonata for Viola and Percussion**. Melbourne (Werribee Park). "Music in the Round" 1973 festival. Glickman; Davies. *Lit.*: Hince, "In the round," *Australian*, Sat. 27 Oct: 17.

P74-2 Feb 9: **Sun Music II**. Hong Kong. SSO children's concert; Hopkins.

Feb 28: **Music for Japan**. Brisbane. Modern Music Forum. QSO; P. Thomas. *Review:* **B464**.

P74-3 Mar 5, 6, 7, 12: **Sun Music III**. Sydney. NTO youth concert (free); Miller. *Also:* Mar 23, Newcastle Univ., youth promo.

P74-5 May 24, 25: **Sun Music III**. Perth. WASO subs; Heinze.

P74-6 June 19 (Wed.): **Irkanda IV**. Brisbane. QSO gold; W. Lehmann; Krug.

June 19: **SQ 6**. Sydney (Great Hall). *Review:* **B468**.

June 28 (Fri): **Irkanda IV** for string sextet and perc, first perf. in this form. Sydney (OHMR). Australian Composers Retrospective, chosen, directed and documented by Roger Covell. A. Bonetti; chamber group; cond. Covell. *Reviews:* **B470-471**.

P74-8 Aug 27: **Sun Music IV**. Sydney. SSO subs (white); van Otterloo.

P74-9 Sept: **Sun Music IV**. Edinburgh (recorded for replay in Australia); Lincoln (Cathedral); Glasgow. SSO British tour; van Otterloo. *Reviews:* **B474, B476**. *Lit.*: **B701**.

Sept 7: **Sun Music I**. Brisbane. QSO youth concert; Krips.

P74-10 Oct 11: **Sun Music III**. Melbourne. MSO (free); Heinze (50th anniversary).

P74-11 Nov 10: **Sun Music III**. Sydney. NTO (free); Miller.

P74-12 Dec 6: **Landscape**. All-Australian recital dedicated to, and attended by, Sir Bernard Heinze. Sydney (Con.). Woodward. *Review:* **B502**.

P75-1 Jan 26: **Sun Music II**. Sydney. NTO (free, Aust. Day); Miller.

P75-3 Mar 13: **Sun Music III**. Canberra (free). NTO; Miller.

Mar 28: **SQ 6**. Musica Viva concert. Sydney SQ.

P75-4   Apr 9: **Sun Music III**. Scottsdale TAS. NTO country tour; Heinze. *Also:* Apr 10, Devonport.

P75-5   May 27: **SQ 8**. Sydney (OHMR). Musica Viva concert. Austral SQ.

P75-7   July 11-13, 15-17: **Irkanda IV** used for ballet *Shafts of Longing*. Adelaide Festival. Australian Dance Theatre 10th anniv.; choreog. Hall.

P75-9   Sept. 5: **SQ 6**. Sydney (OHRH). Sydney SQ.

         Sept 12: Chorales from **Rites of Passage**, world premiere of this version—*Chorales I-V, Rebirth, Chorale VI*. Melbourne (Dallas Brooks H). Music Rostrum Australia '75 concert. Melbourne Chorale; Orch of Victorian College of the Arts; Hopkins. *Reviews:* **B512-513**.

P75-10   Oct 10: **Irkanda IV**. Brisbane. QSO youth concert; Hopkins.

P75-11   Nov 12: **SQ 8**. San Francisco (Century Club). Concert presented by the English Speaking Union, Australian American Association, Southern Cross Chapter of B. A. C., and Australian Consulate-General. Austral SQ.

         Nov 30: **Sun Music IV**. Sydney (TH). ABC and APRA 50th anniversary concert. SSO; P. Thomas. *Review:* **B518-518n**.

P75-12   Dec 1: **SQ 9**, first European perf. London (Australia House). Australian Music Association concert. Austral SQ (international tour). *Reviews:* **B519-520**.

P76-1   January 2-17: **Music for Japan** (as ballet, choreog. Kerr); **Sonata for Viola and Percussion; SQ 7; Tabuh Tabuhan; Sun Music for Voices and Percussion**. Kerikeri NZ (Kerkeri Memorial H). Performing Arts Festival. Composers' workshop under the guidance of PS. Works rehearsed, and those to be performed selected from these. *Lit.:* **B525**.

         Jan 11: **Koto Music**. Berlin (Akademie der Künste). Australia Felix: Studio Neue Musik. Herscovitch, vibraphone; Conolan, vn. **B526**.

P76-2   Feb 20: **SQ 9**. Sydney (Post Aud.). Opening concert, NSW Conservatorium Sixtieth Anniversary series. Sydney SQ. *Reviews:* **B528-529**.

P76-3   Mar 5: **SQ 9**. Sydney (opening of Australia Music Centre on George Street). Free Carpet Concerts. Sydney SQ.

P76-4   April 6: **Sonatina; Night Pieces** (B. Sedivka); **Irkanda I; Sonata for Viola and Percussion; SQ 9**. Hobart (ABC Odeon Theatre). "Meet the Composer: PS." Continued Apr 8: **Overture for a Happy Occasion; Lament [for Strings]** (first perf.); **From Tabuh Tabuhan; Small Town; The Stars Turn**, arr. str orch (first perf.); **Sun Music IV; Irkanda IV** (J. Sedivka; TSO; Krug). *Lit.:* **B530**.

P76-5 May: **Sun Music I.** Melbourne (Robert Blackwood Hall). AYO. *Review:* **B531**. Followed by US tour (*ref.:* **B751**, Epstein).

May 26-June 9: **Lament [for Strings]** and **The Stars Turn**, arr. **string orchestra.** ACO tour of NSW. May 26, Wollongong (City Hall).

P76-6 June 1: ACO tour, cont.—Bathurst. June 2: Orange (Amoco Hall). Orange Pro Musica Society concert; with a lecture by PS. *Also:* June 9, Newcastle; Armidale (TH); Penrith (Springwood Civic Centre). **B532**.

P76-7 July 21: **Sun Music I.** Horsham subs. MSO; Iwaki. July 22, Hamilton subs.

July 23: **Sun Music II.** Hobart schools. TSO; Roberts.

P76-8 Aug 14, 16, 17: **Music for Japan.** Sydney. SSO subs (blu/wht); Iwaki.

Aug 28 (Sat.): **SQ 9.** Sydney (OHRH). Music Rostrum '76. Sydney SQ (Curby; Tincu; Todicescu; Waks). *Review:* **B533**.

P76-9 Sept 13: **Music for Japan.** Melbourne subs (gold). MSO; Iwaki.

Sept 28 (lunch hour): **SQ 9.** Sydney (Main Hall, NSW Con.). Petra SQ.

P76-10 Oct: **SQ 9.** Sydney SQ tour of the Americas, sponsored by the Australian government. Oct 6, San Francisco (Century Club); *reviews:* **B536-537**. Oct 8, Mexico City (Pinacoteca Virreinal). Oct 14-16, Venezuela. Oct 18, Rio di Janeiro; *review:* **B538**.

P76-11 Nov 28: **SQ 6.** Taipei (City Hall). An Evening of Contemporary Asian Music for Orchestra and Chamber Ensemble. Also, *SMH*, 23 Nov, announces **Sun Music** in Taipei.

P77-4 Apr 8: **SQ 9.** Mittagong Festival. New England Ensemble.

P77-5 May 2, 3: **Music for Japan.** Sydney schools. SSO; Pascoe.

May 24: **Night Pieces.** London (Wigmore H). Thwaites. *Review:* **B543**.

P77-6 June 20, 21: **Sun Music IV.** Sydney schools. SSO; Krug.

P77-7 July 11: **Sun Music I** excerpt. Hobart schools. TSO; Roberts.

July 24: **SQ 9** (Petra SQ); an interview with PS by Barry Conyngham; **Tabuh Tabuhan** (Pro Arte Wind Qnt of Switzerland). Melbourne (Melba Hall). New Audience final concert. *Review:* **B548**.

July 29: **Lament [for Strings]**, first Sydney perf. (Everest Theatre). Pro Musica Society; Platt. *Review:* **B549**.

P77-8 Aug 3: **SQ 8** (Petra SQ) and **Tabuh Tabuhan** (Pro Arte Wind Qnt).

Hobart (Univ. Centre). Lecture-recital by PS presented by Tasmanian Con. and Musica Viva Younger Group.

Aug 15: **Tabuh Tabuhan**. Sydney (Con.). Wind Qnt of NSW.

Aug 18: **Port Essington** (following Aug 16 premiere, Brisbane). Adelaide (TH). ACO. *Review:* **B552**. Aug 19, Melbourne (Robert Blackwood Hall); **B554-B555**. Aug 25, Sydney (OHCH). Musica Viva subs; **B556-B559**. Aug 26, Springwood. Aug 30, Wollongong.

Aug 24: **SQ 9**. Sydney. Sydney SQ. Also in Lismore in July or August. With **Little Serenade** as encore.

P77-9   Sept 13: **Irkanda IV** and **Lament for Strings**. Hobart. Univ. of TAS String Orch.

Sept 21: **Sun Music I**. Southport. QSO; P. Thomas. *Also:* Sept 22, Lismore.

P77-10   Oct 5: **SQ 9**. Smetana Hall (Czechoslovakia). Ostrava Qt.

Oct 12: **Sun Music III**, first London perf. (QEH). Australian Sinfonia (London-based Australian orchestra); Simon.

Oct 13: **SQ 8**. Newcastle (Univ. of Newcastle). Petra SQ. *Also:* Oct 23.

Oct 20: **SQ 9**. Wollongong NSW (Wollongong Branch of the NSW Con.). Petra SQ.

P77-11   Nov 7 (1.05 pm): **Night Pieces**. London (St. Martin-in-the-Fields). Thwaites.

Nov [14?]: **SQ 8**. San Francisco (Unitarian Center). Kronos Qt (group's local debut). *Review:* **B560**. *Also:* Nov 27 (Sun., 4 pm), San Francisco (Old First Church). *Review:* **B561**.

P78-1   Jan 29: **Night Pieces**. Cumbria UK (Theatre in the Forest). Thwaites.

P78-4   Apr 2: **SQ 8; Tabuh Tabuhan**. Melbourne (Melba H). New Audience '78 final concert. Petra SQ. Music introduced by Larry Sitsky.

Apr 2: **The Song of Tailitnama**. Auckland NZ (Maclaurin Chapel). "Sonic Circus" concert. Nieckarz; chamber ensemble; dir. de Saram. *Also:* **Sun Song** for recorder quartet. Auckland (Clock Tower, Univ. of Auckland), at 1:50 and 3:50 pm before clock chimes. College Consort; dir. Buckton.

Apr 8: **Music for Japan**. Dunedin NZ (TH). Dunedin Civic Orchestra; Platt.

Apr 17: **Sun Music III** excerpt. Launceston schools. TSO; Mills.

P78-5   May 13 (opening): **Koto Music** tape played for sculpture *Gambol* by
          Pamela Boden: "7 Sculptures/Compositions." Sydney (Australian
          Music Center). *Also:* June, in Melbourne. *Lit.:* **B576**.

          May 14: **Night Pieces** [probably]. Sydney (Australian Music Centre). D.
          Miller. *Review:* **B577**.

P78-7   July 8?: **Koto Music.** Sydney (Great H, Univ. of Sydney). Dept. of
          Music Lunchtime Concert. Grunstein. *Also performed:* c1980-1981,
          Grunstein's farewell concert. *Reviews:* **B580**.

          July 27 (Wed): **Sun Music III.** Melbourne (Melba H). NTO with strings
          from TAS Con. and members of Univ. of Melbourne Music Faculty
          Orch; Miller. *Review:* **B583**.

P78-8   Aug 7: **Night Pieces.** Broadcast ABC Melbourne. Thwaites. *Also:* Aug
          20, Canberra (Arts Council's rooms, Wales Centre). *Review:* **B584**.

          Aug 18: **Sun Music I** excerpt. Hobart schools. TSO; Mills.

          Aug 24: **Sun Music II.** Launceston schools. "Orchestra in 20th
          century." TSO; Mills.

P78-9   Sept 8: **Night Pieces.** Sydney (Post Aud.). Thwaites. *Review:* **B586**.
          Also: Sept 14, All India Radio broadcast; Sept 16, India International
          Centre; Sept 18, Bombay (National Centre of Performing Arts).

P78-11   Nov 8, 9: **Music for Japan.** Canberra (CSM). Canberra SO.

P78-12   Dec 3: **Snow, Moon, and Flowers; Stars.** Annapolis MD (St. John's
          College). Epstein.

P79-2   Feb 20: **How the Stars Were Made,** arr. Askill. Sydney (OHRH).
          Synergy (Askill, Bloxsom, Miller, Piper). With *Creations,* presented by
          Univ. of Sydney Theatre Workshop and Busy Bodies, Theatre of
          Dance; dir. & choreog. Hall. *Review:* **B590**.

          cFeb 28: **The Song of Tailitnama.** Sydney (TH). ABC Mozart Plus
          concert. SSO; Wyss. *Review:* **B591**.

P79-3   Mar 18: **SQ 8.** Singapore (DBS Auditorium). Petra SQ.

P79-4   Apr 10: **SQ 8.** Berlin (Amerika Haus). Kronos Qt. *Also:* Apr 12,
          Bologna, Italy (Sala Chopin); Apr 13, Lodi, Italy

          Apr 13 (aft): **Landscape II.** Mittagong Festival (Clubbe Hall). New Eng-
          land Ensemble; intro. by the composer. (eve:) **The Stars Turn, arr.
          Matthews,** first perf.; **Autumn Song.** Leonine Consort. Apr 14: **La-
          ment for Strings; Port Essington** (ACO); **Requiem,** first perf. (Waks).
          Apr 15: **SQ 6, 9.** Sydney SQ. *Reviews:* **B593-595, B607**.

Apr 24: **Sun Music I.** Brisbane schools. QSO; Cavdarski.

Apr 28: **Requiem; Four Little Pieces for Piano Duet** (first perfs.); "Tabuh Tabuhan" = **Snow, Moon and Flowers** (Woodward) and surprise birthday garland—works by Boyd, Conyngham, Cugley, Edwards, Gross, Hannan, Platt, Plush, Whitehead [*see* Appendix III]. *Also:* Trevor Pearce (PS student), *Digressions.* Sydney (OHRH). A Concert for PS's 50th Birthday. Seymour Group; dir. Plush. *Reviews:* **B600-601**

Apr 29: **Irkanda I** (C. Williams); **Sonata for Viola and Percussion** (P. Clark; Laird); **Tabuh Tabuhan.** Auckland (Maidment Arts Centre, Univ. of Auckland). Karlheinz Company of the Con., honoring PS's 50th birthday. *Review:* L.C.M. Saunders, "Performance tribute to composer," *NZ Herald,* 30 April.

P79-5   May 6: **Sonatina.** London (Wigmore Hall). Thwaites. **B605-606.**

P79-6   June 1: **SQ 8.** Stanford, CA (Spangenberg Auditorium). Kronos Qt. *Review:* **B608.** *Also:* June 3, Redwood City CA (Cañada College).

June 13-16: **Port Essington** ballet. Hobart (Theatre Royal). Tasmanian Ballet; choreog. Gillespie. *Also:* June 19-20, Burnie (Civic Theatre); June 22-23, Launceston (Princess Theatre).

June 21: **Tabuh Tabuhan.** Sydney (Old Darlington School). Seymour Group Ensemble; cond. Plush. *Review:* **B610.**

June 23: **Sun Music III.** Brisbane. QSO subs (red); Cavdarski.

P79-7   July 5: **Sun Music IV,** 5' excerpt. Launceston primary schools. TSO; Conolan. *Also:* July 10, Hobart secondary schools.

P79-9   Sept 17, 18: **Sun Music I** excerpt. Hobart schools. TSO; Roberts.

Sept 23: **Mangrove.** Perth. Indian Ocean Arts Festival workshop. WASO; Measham.

Sept 24: **Sun Music I.** Adelaide. ASO youth Plus; Hopkins.

P79-10   Oct 4: **Koto Music I** (Hannan); **SQ 9** (Sydney SQ). Sydney International Music Congress (OHRH.). *Also:* Oct 5, **Requiem** (OHRH), Waks; Oct 6, **Tabuh Tabuhan** (York Theatre); *review:* **B618.**

P79-11   Nov 1: **Sonatina.** London (British Music Information Centre). Thwaites. *Also:* Nov 20, London (St. Martin-in-the-Fields).

P79-12   Dec 3: **How The Stars Were Made,** first public perf. in Britain. Manchester (CH, Royal Northern College of Music). Percussion ensemble: Allen; Kitchen; Daniel; Waite; Malabar; Malpass.

P80film   Music by PS for "Arthur Boyd: A Man in Two Worlds." Australia:

ABC production company; BBC production company, 1980. Video-
tape (in NLA). Script, John Read; narrator, John Read.

P80-1   Jan 9-Feb 9: **Lament** and **Port Essington**. ACO Asian tour. Jan 11,
Singapore (Foyer of Australian Chancery). Jan 12, Singapore (P. U. B.
Aud.); **B634-636, B639**. Jan 23, Hong Kong (City Hall); **B640-641**. Feb 9,
Port Essington excerpts, Sydney (Arrival Hall, International Airport),
on return.

Jan 29: **Night; Snow, Moon and Flowers** (Bollard); **The Stars Turn,
arr.** Matthews; **Morning-Song for the Christ Child** (Leonine Consort,
soloists SSAATTBB; cond. Colman). Sydney (OHRH). *Review:* **B642.**

P80-2   Feb 1: **SQ 8, 2nd movt,** as encore. San Francisco (Palace of the Legion
of Honor). Kronos Qt. *Review:* **B644.**

Feb 11: **SQ 6.** Aberystwyth (Old Hall, Univ. College of Wales). 1,357th
Weekly College Concert. String Quartet: Robert Jacoby; Leonard
James; Peter Kingswood; Geraint John.

Feb 28 (Th.): **SQ 9.** San Francisco (Palace of the Legion of Honor).
Kronos Qt. *Reviews:* Shere, Tircuit **B647-648.** *Also:* Mar 1 (Sat.),
Oakland CA (Mills College).

P80-3   Mar 22: **Sonata for Viola and Percussion** (Crellin; Lagos); **Irkanda IV**
(Jan Sedivka [Con. dir.], vn; strings of the Tasmanian Con. Orch;
Lagos); **Night Pieces** (Lancaster); **The Stars Turn; Boat Rise,** first perf.;
SQ 9; Small Town, arr. SQ, first perf. Hobart (Univ. Centre, Univ. of
TAS). "The Composer Speaks." Printed program includes biography
of PS by Hannan. *Lit.:* **B649, B651.**

P80-4   Apr 16-17: **Mangrove.** Sydney (OHCH). SSO; Fremaux. *Reviews:* **B656-
657.**

P80-6   June 15 (Sun.): **Port Essington.** Sydney (Art Gallery of NSW). National Ensemble (young string orchestra resident at the NSW Con.).

P80-7   July 8 or 9: **SQ 6.** Petra SQ tour. Warsaw. XIVth World ISME Congress.
Also: **SQ 8** in Switzerland, and in London.

July 15: **Sonatina.** Beijing (Aud., Central Conservatory). Thwaites.

July 18: **SQ 8.** San Francisco (Great American Music Hall). Kronos Qt.

P80-8   Aug 9: **Sonatina.** Broadcast on Chinese National Radio. Thwaites.
Other 1980 broadcasts on Aug 14 and Oct 5.

P80-9   Sept 12: **Sonatina.** Sydney (Conservatorium). Thwaites.

Sept 27: **Mangrove.** Melbourne. MSO subs (red); Iwaki.

P80-10   Oct 1: **Sonatina.** Hong Kong (City Hall). Thwaites.

Oct 10: **Sun Music II,** "Monkey Dance." Perth. WASO family concert; Measham.

Oct 12: **Requiem** (Waks); **Sonata for Unaccompanied Cello** (1959), first perf. (Garner). Sydney (Old Darlington School). Seymour Group program "Direction 1980's." *Review:* **B677.**

Oct 13, 14: **Sun Music II,** "Monkey Dance"; **Sun Music III** excerpt. Brisbane. QSO schools concerts; Boughen.

Oct 31: **Port Essington.** Bathurst. National Ensemble workshop: local school music students learned several sections of the work during the day and played them in a concert that night.

P81-2   Feb 26: **Landscape II.** Sydney. Univ. of Sydney's Thursday at 5:15 series. Seymour Group Ensemble: Fogg; Middenway; Newsome; Garner. *Review:* **B685.**

P81-3   Mar (before 29th): **Requiem.** Waks, introduced by PS. Sydney (Macquarie Theatre, Macquarie Univ.). *Lit.:* **B688.**

Mar 27: **Irkanda I** (Segal) and **Requiem** (Pereira). Univ. of Wollongong, Heritage Week. "An Evening of Music and Song": Music of PS introduced by the composer.

P81-4   Apr 8: **Sun Music II.** Broken Hill. ASO schools; Cooper. *Also:* Apr 10, Barmera.

P81-5   May 17: **Landscape II.** Detmold (Nordwestdeutsche Musikakademie). Ensemble Australia Felix.

May 19: **Koto Music; Landscape I.** Sydney (Paddington TH). Concert in support of Aboriginal Land Rights. Didjeridu prelude played by Colin Bright (as in **W163,** first perf.). *Review:* **B689.**

May 28: **Eliza Fraser Sings,** Uraufführung der Neufassung. Musik= hochschule Saarbrücken. Australia Felix, tour of Germany; many other perfs. *Lit.: Age,* 22 April.

P81-6   June 2, 3: **Sun Music II,** *Ketjak.* Adelaide. ASO schools concerts; Hopkins. *Also:* June 4, 5, cond. Cooper, and June 22, 23, in Elizabeth.

June 7: **Eliza Fraser Sings** (Mildenhall; Linstead; Stegemann); **Koto Music I, II** (Tuck); **Mountains; Nocturnal** (McGuiness); **Requiem** (Waks). Canberra School of Art Gallery). Australian Contemporary Composers Series. Works introduced by the composer.

June 8 (Mon.), 11:30 a.m.: **Koto Music I** (Hannan) and **Landscape II** (student musicians). Sydney (Old Darlington School). Apollo and Pan: Third Annual Music Festival of the Dept. of Music. *Review:* **B692**. (aft.:) discussion of **Port Essington** and other works, led by PS. (eve.:) **Autumn Song**. Univ. of Sydney (Wool Room, International House). Sydney Univ. Chamber Choir; Routley.

June 13, 15, 16: **Mangrove**. Melbourne. MSO subs (red); Fremaux. *Also:* June 17, Geelong subs.

June 18: **SQ 7**. San Francisco (Palace of the Legion of Honor). West Coast US premiere. Kronos Quartet. *Review:* **B693**.

June 21: **Irkanda I**. Sydney (Ervin Gallery). Rantos. *Review:* **B694**.

June 27: **Autumn Song**. Sydney (Great Hall). Sydney Univ. Chamber Choir; Routley.

P81-7　July 8: "In memoriam Tass Drysdale" for cello alone (**Requiem** excerpts). Woollahra. Memorial service. Waks.

July 27: **Left Bank Waltz; Sea Chant; Mountains; Nocturnal** (1981), first Sydney perf.; **Snow, Moon; Sonatina**. Sydney (Old Darlington School). United Music Teachers of NSW presents PS; Australian Composers workshop. Rosalie Campbell, pf. *Lit.: SMH*, 18 July.

P81-8　Aug 2: **How the Stars Were Made**, arr. Askill for four players. Sydney (Ervin Gallery). Seymour Group concert. Synergy. *Review:* **B697**.

Aug 25: **Sun Music II**. Adelaide. ASO schools concerts; Williams.

P81-10　Oct 9, 10: **Mangrove**. Perth. WASO subs; Measham.

P81-11　Nov 5: **Sun Music II**. Angaston schools/country tour. *Also:* Nov 11, Narracoorte; 12, Millicent; 13, Bordertown. ASO; cond. Langbein.

Nov 6 (Fri.): **SQ 8**. Los Angeles CA (Schoenberg Institute, USC). Los Angeles debut of Kronos Qt. *Review:* **B699**.

P81-12　Dec 7: **Sonata for Viola and Percussion**. NYC (Borden Aud., Manhattan School of Music). Manhattan Contemporary Music Ensemble concert. Pitcher; Grossman.

Dec 15: **Lament**. Sydney (Clancy Aud.). ACO. *Review:* **B700**.

P82-1　Jan 10-Feb 8: **Lament for Strings**. ACO tour of Europe and the UK: Jan 10, L'Aquila, Italy; Jan 12, Rome; Feb 4, London (Wigmore); Feb 8, Brussels.

Jan 30: **Mangrove**. Melbourne. MSO (free, Aust. Day); Franks.

P82-2　Feb 19: **Koto Music** (1973). New York City (Lincoln Center). Juilliard

School recital. Grunstein (candidate for M.M. degree).

P82-4   Apr 28: **Mangrove**. Brisbane. QSO South Bank series; Wyss.

P82-6   June 24: **Requiem**. Sydney (Old Darlington School). Garner.

P82-9   Sept 5: **SQ 8**. Seattle (Seattle Center Playhouse). Bumbershoot Festival. Kronos Qt.

P82-11   Nov 8: **Nocturne (W1), Sonatina, Landscape, Night Pieces, Koto Music**, and **Pieces for Prepared Piano**. Sydney (OHRH). Lecture-recital by PS for the ABC and ISCM "Recital Series." Hannan & PS, pf. *Review:* **B723**.

         Nov 14 (Sun.): **Irkanda I**. Sydney (Old Darlington School). Seymour Group Direction 80s Champagne Brunch Recital Series. Middenway.

         Nov 20: **How the Stars Were Made**. Sydney (OHRH). NSW State Conservatorium of Music, School of Composition sixth and final concert in Contemporary Concert Series. Synergy.

P83   **Little Serenade**. Adelaide (TH). "An Evening with Marryatville High," student SQ.

P83-1   Jan 9 (Sun.): **Lament for Strings**. Sydney (Great Hall). Pre-American-tour farewell concert, during Festival of Sydney. Sydney Youth CO; Painter. *Review:* Blanks, "Our ambassadors leave in style," *SMH*, 11 Jan (gives name of work only).

         Jan 23 (Sun.): **Sun Music III**, New York premiere. NYC (Juilliard Theater). Juilliard Philharmonia; Mester. *Reviews:* **B732-733**.

P83-2   Feb 3: **Requiem**, UK premiere. London (Purcell Room). Hugh. Listed in *British Music Yearbook 1984*, ed. Marianne Benton (London: Classical Music): 34, in "first concert performances."

P83-3   Mar 10: **Irkanda IV**. La Jolla CA (Recital Hall, UCSD). Univ. of California at San Diego Chamber Orchestra; dir. Négyesy.

         Mar 27, 28: **Lament for Strings**. Hong Kong (Shouson Theatre of the Arts Centre). ACO Asian tour. *Review:* **B735**. Also on tour: **Port Essington**.

P83-4   Apr 28: **Irkanda I**. Sydney (Old Darlington School). Seymour Group concert of "Recent Australian Music." Middenway.

P83-5   May 17: **Mangrove**. Melbourne (CH). 13th Melbourne International Festival of Organ and Harpsichord. MSO; Hopkins. *Review:* **B740**.

         May 24, 25: **Small Town**, introduced by PS. Sydney (OHCH). SSO; Hopkins. ABC Series 6.30 concert intended for audiences under 25.

Lit.: Blanks, "The big three dominate ABC festival," *SMH*, 18 Dec 1982: 14. *Review*: Sykes, *Sun-Herald*, 29 May (the work's cheeky references to familiar musical motifs).

P83-6   June 17, 18: **Mangrove**. ASO subs; Gamba. *Review*: **B741**. *Also*: July 14, 9′ excerpts, schools concerts.

P83-8   Aug 20 (Sat.): **Piano Concerto**, first public perf. Canberra (Llewellyn H). Winther; Canberra YO; McIntyre. *Review*: **B742**. *Repeated*: Aug 27, Wollongong (TH); and Aug 28, Sydney (Verbrugghen H); **B743**

P83-9   Sept 16 (Fri.), 6.15 pm: **Landscape II**. Sydney (Art Gallery of NSW). Asian Interface concert; works introduced by PS. Seymour Group: Fogg; Ingram; Pfuhl; Woolley. *Review*: **B744**

Sept 28: **SQ 8**. Sydney (Macquarie Theatre, Macquarie Univ.). Petra SQ.

P83-10 Oct 16: **Night Pieces, Sonatina, Boat Rise, The Stars Turn**, and Hiscocks, *Toccata*, performed by student pianists and soprano. "PS Workshop," part of master class, Oct 15-16, presented by The Sydney Schumann Society. *Lit.*: "Sculthorpe explains Sculthorpe," *SMH*, 14 Oct.

Oct 23: **SQ 8**. Paddington (TH Mtg Rm). Petra SQ. *Review*: **B746**.

P83-11 Nov 9: **Small Town**. Newcastle schools. SSO; Gill.

Nov 30: **Requiem**: *Qui Mariam, Lux Aeterna*. Memorial service for Donald Peart. Sydney (Great Hall). Waks. With an address by PS.

P84-2   Feb 15: **Piano Concerto**. Adelaide. Prom series II. Fogg; ASO; Hopkins.

P84-3   Mar 7, 8, 27, 28: **Sun Music I**. Melbourne schools. MSO; Humble.

Mar 8: **SQ 8, 2nd movt**. Valencia, CA (Modular Theatre). California Institute of the Arts new-music festival. Kronos Qt. *Review*: **B755**.

P84-4   Apr 4: **Sun Music I** excerpt. Geelong schools. MSO; Humble.

Apr 17: **Piano Concerto**. Brisbane (ABC Music Centre, Ferry Road, West End). 1984 South Bank series. Fogg; QSO; Mills. *Review*: **B756**.

P84-5   May 14: **Sonatina**. Sydney (Martin Place lunchtime concert). McAdam. *Lit.*: **B758**.

May 16: **SQ 6**. Moscow USSR (Conservatoire). Soviet SQ. (Then perfs. on tour.) PS the guest of the Union of Soviet Composers at their Second International Music Festival (10 days beginning May 15). Then to London, New York, Los Angeles—five-week overseas tour, beginning May 12. *Lit.*: **B765, B767, B769**. *Review*: **B759**.

May 30: **Requiem**. La Jolla CA (Mandeville Auditorium, UCSD).

"Sonor" concert. Farrell.

P84-6 June 8 (Fri.): **Mangrove,** US premiere. NYC (Avery Fisher Hall). "Horizons '84, Program X." NY Philharmonic; Newland. Program notes by PS. "Meet the Composer" pre-concert talk by PS at 6:45. *Reviews:* **B761-763, B766-766n.**

June 16: **Requiem.** Sydney (Everest Theatre). "Napoleon & Franken-stein!! concert." Blake. *Review:* **B764.**

P84-7 July 9, 10: **Small Town.** Sydney schools. SSO; P. Thomas.

July 10: **Sun Music III,** 10' excerpt. Adelaide schools. ASO; Gamba.

July 12: **Port Essington.** Melbourne (Monash). MSO; Fredman.

July 28: **SQ 6.** Wollongong (Music Aud., School of Creative Arts). Petra SQ, in residence at the Univ. of Wollongong.

P84-8 Aug 6: **Requiem.** Sydney (Post Aud.). Hugh. *Review:* **B771.** *Also:* Aug 13, Canberra (CSM).

Aug 10: **Sonatina** (1954). Hobart (St. Michael's Collegiate). "A Musical Evening." C. Teniswood.

Aug 12, 7:45 pm: **Sun Music II,** *Ketjak.* London (QEH). South Bank Summer Music. AYO European tour; Zollman. *Reviews:* **B772-B774.** *Also:* Aug 25, Edinburgh International Festival (Usher Hall); cond. Mackerras; **B775-B777.** Apr 29: London (Albert Hall); BBC Promenade series (**D63**). *Publicity:* Susan Hely, *SMH,* 16 July: 10.

Aug 15: **SQ 8.** Wollongong (City Art Gallery). Petra SQ.

P84-9 Sept 22: **Mangrove.** Sydney (OH). SSO Sat. afternoon; Fremaux. *Reviews:* **B778-779.**

P84-10 Oct 24 (Wed.): **SQ 8.** NYC (Carnegie Recital Hall). Kronos Qt. **B782.**

P84-12 Dec 6: **Mangrove.** Brisbane. New Music. QSO subs (white); P. Thomas.

Dec 6: **Requiem.** Wellington, NZ (Memorial Hall). Pan-Pacific Conference. Bognuda. The composer was present. *Review:* **B785.**

Dec 7: **Mangrove.** Wellington, NZ (Opera House). NZ SO; Feliciano. The composer was present. *Reviews:* **B786-787, B792.** (Feliciano has also conducted the work in the Philippines.)

Dec 15: **Boat Rise; Night Pieces; Sonatina.** Sydney (Old Darlington School). "The Morning Star: A concert of contemporary Australian music without the pain" presented by the Music Dept., Univ. of Sydney. Lamkin; Scarlett.

Dec 15: **Sun Music III.** Sydney (TH). Sydney Youth SO; Challender.

P85film **Piano Concerto** used in film *Messengers of the Gods: A Study of Cranes in Human Culture.* Written by Ken Taylor. 50 min. Natural History Series instituted by the Queensland Film Corp. and the Australian Film Cmsn. Cmsd by QLD Nat'l Parks and Wildlife Service and Tsurukame Pty Ltd. *Lit.:* **B745.**

P85-1 Jan 26: **Small Town.** Perth. WASO (free); Measham

P85-3 Mar 13: **Requiem.** Armidale NSW (Univ. of NE, Univ. Hall). Earle Page College Foundation for the Promotion of Contemporary Classical Music concert by Australian Piano Trio. Laurs.

Mar 30: **Requiem.** Sydney (Verbruggen Aud.). A Special Benefit Memorial Concert for Stephen Semler. Blake.

P85-4 Apr 11: **Small Town,** 3' excerpt. Armidale schools. SSO; Pascoe. With **Mangrove,** cond. Hopkins. *Also:* Apr 12, Tamworth.

Apr 12: **Requiem.** London (QEH). "Pacific Connection I: Australia" concert by Lontano. Margaret Powell, vc. *Reviews:* **B793-794.**

Apr 15: **Requiem.** London (Purcell Room). Hugh. *Reviews:* **B795.**

Apr 25: **Sun Music III.** Beverly Hills, CA (Beverly Hills HS). Sydney Con. SO; cond. Smart. 1985 US tour. *Also:* Apr 27, Idylwild, CA; Apr 29, Paso Robles, CA (Flamson Middle School); May 5 New Jersey (Somerset County College); May 7, NYC (Trinity Church, Wall Street).

P85-6 June 16: **Requiem.** Rome. Gruppo Octandre di Bologna.

June 18: **SQ 6.** Sydney (Post Aud.). Sydney SQ (Michaels; Abe; Todicescu, Pedersen). *Review:* **B796.**

P85-8 Aug 11: **Requiem.** Armidale NSW (Univ. Hall, Univ. of NE). Laurs.

P85-9 Sept 17: **Port Essington.** Hobart (Odeon Theatre). ABC Major Series. TSO; Kamirski. *Review:* **B798.**

P86-1 Jan 16: **The Song of Tailitnama, arr. med. voice and piano.** "Summer Perspectives" series of Melbourne Summer Music (CH). Eureka Ensemble: Marsh; Hammond. *Review:* **B808.** *Also:* Jan 23, **The Stars Turn, arr. string orchestra.** *Review:* **B809.**

P86-3 Mar 11 (Tu): **SQ 8.** NYC (Symphony Space). Terra Australis Incognita concert. Kronos Qt. *Reviews:* **B811, B813.**

Mar 19: **Irkanda I.** Adelaide (Elder Hall).

Mar 20: **Sonata for Viola and Percussion.** Adelaide (The Space, Space

Theatre, Festival Centre). Adelaide Festival. Crellin; Pusz.

Mar 25, 26: **Small Town**. Goulburn subs, Wollongong subs. SSO; De Almeida.

P86-4 Apr 5: **Piano Concerto**. Melbourne (Robert Blackwood H, Monash U). Fogg; MSO; Iwaki. Direct broadcast ABC-FM. *Lit.: 24 Hours*, April.

P86-5 May 28, 29, 30, June 2: **Sun Music III**. Rockhampton, Mackay, Townsville, Cairns. QSO subs; Albert. *Also:* schools concerts, May 27-30, June 2, 4, 5, Bundaberg, Rockhampton, Mackay, Townsville, Cairns, Gladstone, Maryborough.

P86-6 June 1: **The Song of Tailitnama, arr. med. voice and piano**. Sydney (Broadwalk Studio). ISCM/ABC recital. Eureka Ensemble: Marsh; Hammond. **B814**. *Repeated:* June 2, Canberra (Recital Room, CSM).

June 5: **Mountains**. Perth (Callaway Aud.). Howat. *Review:* **B815**.

June 24: **Irkanda IV**. Melbourne (Great Hall, National Gallery of Victoria). Rantos Collegium; Rantos. *Review:* **B816-817**.

June 24: **SQ 6**. Sydney (Art Gallery of NSW). Australian SQ (Hennessy, Welland, Crellin, Laurs). *Review:* **B818**.

P86-7 July 11: **Small Town**. Hobart. Music for Pleasure. TSO; Braithwaite.

July 31: **Tailitnama Chant** [Song, arr. chamber ensemble]. Sydney (Old Darlington School). Magpie Musicians.

P86-8 Aug 12: **Mangrove**. Sydney (Verbrugghen Hall). Conservatorium SO; Hopkins. *Review:* **B822**.

Aug 14: **Small Town**. Toowoomba (QLD). QSO; Kamirsky.

Aug 17: **How the Stars Were Made**, arr. Askill. Sydney (OHRH). Synergy (Askill, Leak, Miller, Piper). *Review:* **B823**.

Aug 29: **Small Town**. Melbourne. MSO family concert; Measham.

P86-9 Sept 6, 8, 9: **Mangrove**. MSO subs (red); Iwaki. *Also:* Sept 10, Geelong subs.

Sept 10: **Burke and Wills** film music (recording) played at champagne reception, Sydney (NSW State Theatrette, State Office Block, Phillip Street), according to "City highlights," *Manly Daily*, 5 Sept.

Sept 22: **SQ 8**. Chicago premiere (Civic Theatre). Kronos Qt. *Review:* **B825**. *Also:* Nov 21, Washington, DC (LC?).

P86-10 Oct 5: **Djilile** (for *Hexaméron 1986*). Sydney (Post Aud.). Hanke. **B826**.

Oct 7: **SQ 6**. Adelaide (TH). Australian SQ. *Review:* **B827**.

Oct 28: **Sonata for Strings**. Sydney (Seymour Centre). Musica Viva concert. Franz Liszt CO from Budapest (16 players). *Reviews:* **B828-829**. *Repeated:* Nov 6, Melbourne (CH).

Oct 30: **Small Town**. Sydney (TH). A Festival of Australian Music.

P86-11 Nov 2: **Sonata for Viola and Percussion**. Perth (Conservatorium). Nova Ensemble concert. Tuckey; Pye. *Review:* **B830**.

Nov 5, 6: **Earth Cry**, first Sydney perf. (OHCH). SSO; Handley. Pre-concert speaker: PS. *Reviews:* **B831-B833**. B'cast nationally ABC-TV, Wed., Dec 17. *Also:* Nov 13, Newcastle subs (Master, red).

Nov 14: **SQ 8, 2nd movt** (as encore). New York (Lepercq Space, Brooklyn Academy of Music). Kronos Qt. *Review:* **B834**.

P86-12 Dec 5 (Fri.): **SQ 8**. San Francisco (Herbst Theatre). Kronos Qt. *Reviews:* **B837-838**. *Also:* Dec 12, Los Angeles; *review:* **B839**.

P87-1 Jan 17 (Sat): **SQ 8, 2nd movt**, Ann Arbor (Michigan Theatre). Kronos Qt. *Review:* **B848**.

Jan 22: **Cantares**. Sydney (St. Stephens Church, Macquarie Street). Calvo; Isaacs; White; Sydney School of Guitar Players (9 players); 3 electric guitars; bass guitar; and SQ—Saffir; Molnar; Quinn; Ayling.

Jan 27: **Cantares**. Melbourne (CH). Taped. Peña; J. Williams; Golla; Isaacs, etc.

P87-2 Feb 4: **SQ 8**. Denver (George Washington HS, for Friends of Chamber Music). Kronos Qt. *Also:* Feb 19, Kansas City (Folly Theatre). Feb 14, **2nd movt**, St. Louis (Edison Theatre, Washington Univ.). Feb 24, Purdue (Loeb Playhouse). Feb 27?, Cincinnati (Memorial H). *Reviews:* **B849**.

Feb: **Irkanda IV**. Brisbane (CH). Mainly Mozart Festival. QTO; Rantos. *Review:* **B850**.

Feb 21: **The Song of Tailitnama, arr. med. voice and pf**. Berlin (Kam=mermusiksaal, Shauspielhaus). Concert for the 11th Musik-Biennale Berlin (first perf. by an Australian ensemble in this new music festival). Eureka Ensemble, Eastern European tour. Marsh; Hammond. *Also:* Feb 23, Györ, Hungary (People's Cultural Centre). Feb 24, Budapest (Fészek Artists' Club), Jeunesses Musicales/Australian Embassy/Fészek Artists' Club concert. Mar 2 (Belgrade (Students' Cultural Center), Young Composers' society/Australian Embassy concert. Mar 4, Sofia, Bulgaria (Chamber Music Hall, Philharmonic Centre), Composers' Union/Cultural Committee concert.

P87-3   Mar 3, 4: **Sun Music III** excerpt. Brisbane schools. QSO; Boughen.

Mar 13: **SQ 8** used for *Ancestral Memories,* choreog. Rosen. Washington, DC (Publick Playhouse); *review:* Alan M. Kriegsman, "Curious collaboration," *Washington Post,* Sat. 14 March: G10 (& mentions a 1986 premiere). *Also perf.:* Feb 8, 1989, Kennedy Center; *review:* Kriegsman, "Layers of local artistry," ibid., Fri. 10 Feb: D2.

Mar 15: **SQ 8.** Cambridge MA (Sanders Theatre, Harvard Univ.) Fromm Music Foundation concert. Kronos Qt. *Review:* **B852.**

Mar 27: **Sun Music II.** Renmark schools. ASO; Braithwaite.

P87-4   Apr 2-11: **SQ 8, Sonata for Strings,** and **Mangrove** used for *Savage Earth,* Queensland Ballet, choreog. Buckman (40 min). Brisbane (Lyric Theatre). QTO; Flottman. "Both man and animal stalk the Savage Earth and ritualistic rhythms of life . . . parallel their journey. With music by foremost Australian composer PS." *Reviews:* Anna Zantiotis, *Australian,* Mon. 6 April; Mary Nemeth, "The savagery in humans," *AFR,* 10 April, "Weekend": 11-12.

Apr 14: **Earth Cry.** Brisbane. QSO (blue series); Albert.

Apr 30: **SQ 8** (5' excerpt, perf. live by members of the Paul Taylor Dance Company orch) used for solo *The Edge,* choreog. and perf. David Parsons. NYC (City Center Theatre). Repeated May 5 and May 10. *Lit.:* Jennifer Dunning, "4 Taylor dancers create works for the troupe," *NY Times,* 21 April. *Review:* Anna Kisselgoff, "Parsons' *Edge* on Taylor program," ibid., 1 May: C28.

P87-5   May 9: **Landscape II.** Sydney (Broadwalk Studio). Seymour Group subscription recital. *Review:* **B853.**

May 26: **Port Essington.** Maryborough (QLD). QSO; Kamirsky. *Also:* June 4, Bundaberg.

P87-6   June 12: **Lament.** Sydney (Holy Trinity [Garrison] Church, The Rocks). ACO; Pini. *Review:* Blanks **B858.**

June 13: **Sun Music I.** Sydney (OHCH). "Great Classics" series concert. SSO; Pido. Program notes: Covell. *Reviews:* **B856-857.**

June 14: **SQ 9.** Bendigo (VIC). Victorian SQ.

June 16, 17: **Piano Concerto.** Sydney. "Meet the Music." Fogg; SSO; Challender. *Lit.:* **B859.** *Review:* **B860.**

June 21: **The Song of Tailitnama, arr. mezzo-sop. & pf.** "The Twentieth-Century voice," 3rd programme, "Anything but love," ABC-FM radio. Jeannie Marsh; Len Vorster.

P87-7   July 1: **Lament for Strings**. Cloncurry QLD. QTO; Rorke. *Also:* July 3, Mount Isa; July 8, Brisbane.

July 9: **Mangrove**. Brisbane. QSO (ABC studio series); Measham.

July 12: **SQ 8**. Chicago. Kronos Qt. *Review:* **B863**.

July 16: **Mountains**. Sydney (Old Darlington School). "Homage to Igor Hmelnitsky." Howat. *Review:* **B864**. *Also:* July 20, Canberra.

July 18: **Sun Music III**. Adelaide (Elder Con.)

July 19: **Earth Cry**. Sydney (Opera House CH). "Tribute to Peter Seymour." Sydney YO; Challender. *Reviews:* **B865**.

July 25: **Sea Chant** (voices and orch). Bendigo VIC. Bendigo YO.

P87-8   August 15: **Songs of Sea and Sky**, first Australian performance. Sydney (Campbell Street Presbyterian Church, Balmain). Campbell Street Concert for the Nordoff-Robbins Music Therapy Centre.

P87-9   Sept 4: **Sun Music III** excerpt. Penrith schools. SSO; Pisarek.

Sept 30: **Piano Concerto**. Hobart. Houstoun; TSO; Bamert.

P87-10 Oct 9-10: **Piano Concerto**. Adelaide. Houstoun; ASO; Seaman. *Reviews:* **B867-868**.

Oct 16, 17: **Piano Concerto**. Perth. Houstoun; WASO; Seaman.

P87-11 Nov 18: **Sun Music III** excerpt. Newcastle schools. SSO; Pisarek.

Nov 24: **Sonatina**. London (Purcell Room). Thwaites.

Nov 28: **Sea Chant**. Sydney (Cranbrook School), cond. Armitage.

P87-12 Dec 13: **Burke and Wills Suite** for brass band. Sydney (Turner Hall, NSW Institute of Technology). Waverley Bondi Beach Band; Goodchild. Program notes by PS.

P88-1   Jan 1: **Irkanda IV**. TSO.

Jan 15: **Songs of Sea and Sky**, arr. fl & pf. Australia Ensemble.

Jan 23: **Earth Cry**. Geelong VIC (Geelong PAC). Australian Composers' Bicentennial Concert. Deakin Univ. Geelong Orch; Tony Hughes. (Cassette tape listed in ABN.)

Jan 31: **Sonatina**. London (Melling Arts Association). Thwaites.

P88-2   Feb: **Port Essington** (3 perfs.) and **Second Sonata for Strings** (4 perfs.).

ACO tour of US; Pini. Feb 4, Greenwich CT; Feb 5, NYC (Metropolitan Museum of Art); *review:* B879; Feb 7, Washington, DC (Kennedy Center); B880; San Francisco (Herbst Theatre); Feb 9, Berea College, KY; Feb 11, Nashville, TN (Vanderbilt Univ.); Feb 17, New Orleans LA; Feb 22, San Diego CA (East County Performing Arts Center).

Feb 10: **Sonatina**. London (West Bank). Thwaites. *Also:* Feb 24, Colchester Institute.

Feb 10: **Song of Tailitnama** (1979/84). Sydney (Vestibule, TH). "Virtuosi in the Vestibule" concert of "Songs by Australian Composers" for the Bicentennial Festival of Sydney. Campbell; Fogg. *Review:* B881.

Feb 14: **Port Essington**. Warsaw. Chopin Academy Orch.

Feb 15-16: **Earth Cry**. Perth. WASO; Braithwaite.

Feb 25: **SQ 8** (Everest Theatre). Kronos Qt, tour of Australia. B882. *Also:* Feb 26, Newcastle (B883); Mar 1, Melbourne; Mar 2, Tasmania.

Feb 29: **Tabuh Tabuhan**. Norfolk VA (Chrysler Museum). Norfolk Chamber Consort + 4 members of Toho Koto Society. *Review:* B884.

P88-3   Mar 7: **SQ 10**. Adelaide Festival. Sydney SQ. *Also at Festival:* Mar 7, 10: **SQ 8** (Edmund Wright House, Mar 7; TH, Mar 10); Kronos Qt. Mar 11, **Requiem**; Seymour Group concert. Mar 12, **Sun Music II**; ASO; cond. Tuckwell. Mar 18: **Alone** (Edmund Wright House); Woodcock. Mar 25: **Sonata for Strings**; Soloists of Australia; P. Thomas.

Mar 11: **Mountains**. Mississauga ONT (Huron Park Recreation Centre). Benefit Concert for Royal Conservatory of Music, Mississauga Branch. Skarecky.

Mar 11: **SQ 8** used for *Secret Rooms*, Claudia Murphey Dance Company. Mount Vernon College, VA, Spring Moves festival (Hand Chapel). *Review:* Kriegsman, "Murphey's well-trod steps," *Washington Post*, 12 Mar: C7.

Mar 16: **Irkanda IV**. London (Australia House). London College of Music Chamber Orchestra.

Mar 16: **SQ 8**. London (QEH). Kronos Qt. *Lit.* (for both Mar 16 concerts): *Times*, 16 March. *Review:* Paul Griffiths, ibid., 18 March: 20.

P88-4   Apr 3: **Mangrove**. Blandford UK. Hants City YO, UK tour; cond. Holmes. *Also:* Apr 16, Winchester; Apr 23, Waterloo; May 6, Farnham.

Apr 8, 10: **Port Essington**. Sydney (CH). ACO "Showcase to Europe" concert. B887. *Also:* Canberra; Apr 12: **Second Sonata for Strings**.

Apr 10: **Songs of Sea and Sky**. First QLD perf. Brisbane (Basil Jones Theatre). Univ. of QLD Australian Music Concert. F. Williams; Dickson. *Review:* **B889**.

Apr 15, 16: **Earth Cry**. Perth. WASO Master series; Braithwaite.

Apr 19: **Small Town**. Brisbane. QSO subs; Fredman.

Apr 20: **Child of Australia**. Sydney (Willoughby Civic Centre). NSW Dept. of Education: Metropolitan North Region Secondary Schools' Music Festival, 13th Annual Concert. Combined Workshop Choir and Orch. Program acknowledges "Mr. PS for his generous assistance and interest."

Apr 30: **SQ 8** (recording) for *I Do* duet by ISO (I'm So Optimistic) Dance Theater. Los Angeles (Royce Hall, UCLA). *Review:* Cathy Curtis, "ISO and the Bobs add voice to movement at Royce Hall," *LA Times*, 2 May. *Also:* May 1990, NYC (Joyce Theatre). *Lit.:* Phyllis Goldman, "ISO Dance Theatre," *Back Stage*, 1 June.

P88-5   May 1: **Sun Music IV**. Brighton, UK. Brighton Festival Orch.

May 3: **SQ 8**. Adelaide (Mtg H, Pirie St.). Arioso SQ. *Review:* **B891**.

May 4: **Alone**. Brisbane (Concert Studio BCAE Kevin Grove). Woodcock. *Review:* **B892**.

May 9: **Small Town**. Canberra. Opening of Australia's Parliament House by Her Majesty the Queen.

May 15: **Mountains**. Toronto (Royal Conservatory of Music, Runnymede Branch). Etobicoke Branch Spring Festival Concert by Faculty and Students. Skarecky.

May 17: **Irkanda IV**. Adelaide (TH). Newman; Adelaide CO; Kram. *Review:* Cary, "Confusion of motives mars smorgasbord," *Australian*, 19 May: 14 (only names the work).

May 20: **Port Essington**. Brighton Festival, UK (The Dome). ACO tour of the UK; Pini. *Also:* May 23, Perth, Scotland; May 28, St. Truiden. With: **Second Sonata for Strings** (*see* **W191**).

May 21: **SQ 10**. Sydney (Everest Theatre). Sydney SQ: Ronald Thomas; W. Lehmann; Todicescu; Pederson. Musica Viva subscription recital. *Reviews:* **B894, B905**.

May 21: **Songs of Sea and Sky**. Brighton Festival, UK. Damaris Wollen. *Also:* July 17, Cheltenham Festival.

May 22: **Autumn Song**. Canberra (NLA). Canberra Chamber Singers.

P88-6   June 4: **Small Town**. Canberra (CSM Aud.). Canberra YO. **B896**.

June 8: **Sonatina**. Doncaster Museum. Thwaites. *Review:* **B897**

June 16: **Second Sonata for Strings**. QTO; Kushar.

June 19: **Burke and Wills Suite** for brass band. Sydney (Macquarie Theatre, Macquarie Univ.).

June 24: **Sonata for Strings**, US premiere. Aspen CO (Music Festival Tent). Aspen Music Festival Chamber Orch; Mester. *Review:* **B898**.

June 27: **Sonata for Viola and Percussion**. Aspen CO (Music Festival Tent). Graham; Haas.

P88-7   July 7-16: **Piano Concerto** for *Once Around the Sun*, Queensland Ballet. Brisbane (Lyric Theatre, QPAC). Greg Roberts; QTO; Flottman. *Also:* July 27-30, Adelaide (Festival Theatre). *Reviews:* **B903**.

July 13: **Sun Music III**. Aspen CO (Music Festival Tent). Aspen Concert Orch; student cond. ("student of Paul Vermel").

July 13, 14, 16, 18: **Mangrove**. SSO (Epson Master); Challender.

July 17: **Mangrove**. Canberra. CSM Orchestra; Painter.

July 20: **Sun Music I**. London (QEH). Pegasus; Richard Crossland, director. *Lit.: Times*, "Songs from down under," 13 July: 22 ("the most interesting living Australian composer is PS," with photo).

July 25: **Irkanda IV**. Adelaide CO; Kram.

July 30?: **Songs of Sea and Sky**, first Sydney perf. of rev. version (Clancy Aud.). Australia Ensemble: Westlake; Bollard. *Reviews:* **B906-907**.

P88-8   Aug 9: **SQ 8**. Boulder CO (Chautauqua Aud.). Colorado Music Festival. Kronos Qt. *Review:* **B909**. *Also:* Aug 10, Aspen CO (Music Festival Tent), "An Evening with the Kronos Quartet."

Aug 12: **Sonata for Viola and Perc.** Perth (Her Majesty's Theatre). Aust. Contemporary Music concert. Migdal; Leek. *Reviews:* **B910**.

Aug 12: **Port Essington**. Aspen CO (Music Festival Tent). Aspen Chamber Symphony; Foster.

Aug 16: **How the Stars Were Made**. Aspen, CO. Wheeler Opera Percussion Ensemble.

Aug 20: **Songs of Sea and Sky**. Australia Ensemble.

P88-9   Sept 8: **Djilile**. Sydney. "State of Play," 12-concert conspectus of

Australian piano music, for New Directions Festival of Contemporary Music. Mays (London-based Australian expatriate). *Lit.* Carmody, "State of play from the past," *AFR, c* 9 Sept.

Sept 17: **Lament for Strings**. Brisbane (Nickson Room). QTO.

Sept 17: **Port Essington**. MSO; Kamirski. From the New Worlds. Broadcast live, ABC. *Lit.:* **B915**.

Sept 21, 24: **Eliza Fraser Sings**. Sydney. The Seymour Group in association with the Dept. of Music, Univ. of Sydney: "Opera and Music Theatre Triple Bill." Blyth; Draeger; Fogg; Stanhope. *Review:* **B916**.

Sept 25: **Sonata for Viola and Percussion**. Dublin (Hugh Lang Gallery, Park Square). O'Grady; O'Donnell.

P88-10 Oct 16 (Sun.): **Sonatina**. Sydney (Verbrugghen Hall). Hyde.

Oct 16: **Lament for Strings**. Brisbane. "UniMusic." University Orch; cond. G. Roberts. *Review:* **B918**.

Oct 23: **Mangrove**. Amherst, MA (Fine Arts Center, Univ. of MA). SSO 1988 bicentennial US tour; cond. Challender. *Also:* Oct 25, Hartford CT (Bushnell Theatre), with pre-concert talk by PS. Oct 27, Worcester MA. Oct 28, Storrs CT (Jorgensen Aud.). Oct 30, NYC (Carnegie Hall). *Lit.:* **B919**, **B935**. *Reviews:* **B920-B924**, **B926-930**, **B938**, **B949**.

Oct. 27: **SQ 8**. Wentworth Falls NSW (Blue Mts. Grammar). Blue Mountain Arts Festival. Binneas SQ. Repeated Nov 6. *Also* Oct 29: 'String Trio' from **Port Essington**. Leura (Anglican Church).

Oct 27: **Sonata for Viola and Percussion**. St. Lucia QLD (Nickson Rm). Perihelion Ensemble. Pollet; Hanusiak (guest). *Review:* **B925**.

P88-11 Nov 3, 5: **Kakadu**, first perf. of revised score. Rochester NY (Eastman Theatre). Rochester PO; Mester. *Also:* interview of PS by Alan Brunin, WXXI, pre-recorded, broadcast on Nov 2. *Reviews:* **B931-932**.

Nov 4, 5: **Sun Music III**. Cincinnati OH (Music Hall). Cincinnati SO; Loebel. (PS visiting composer at Univ. of Cin. College-Con. of Music, Nov 2-5.) *Review:* **B933-934**. *Also:* radio interview by Ann Santen.

Nov 7: **Child of Australia**. Sydney (OHCH). "Music of Time and the Sea." Illing, sop.; Enright, narr.; Sydney Philharmonia Choir; ACO; Grundy. Notes: Gordon Kerry. The composer added words, to be spoken and shouted, followed by a repeat of the motet. *Reviews:* **B936**.

Nov 18: **Small Town**. Gold Coast Centre. QSO; Kamirski.

Nov 19: **Sonatina**. Frinton Arts Society. Thwaites.

Nov 22, 23: **Earth Cry** excerpt. Brisbane schools. QSO; Flottman.

Nov 26: **SQ 8** NYC (Alice Tully Hall). Kronos Qt. *Review:* **B937.**

P89-1   Jan 21: **Dream.** Jan 22: **Mountains** and **Night Pieces** (Savage). Jan 29:
         SQ 10 (Festival Qt). Sunshine Coast QLD (Montville Hall). Montville
         "Mainly Mozart" Summer Music 1989.

P89-2   Feb 6: **SQ 10** (Festival Qt—Michelle Walsh; Margaret Connolly;
         Robert Harris; Rosemary Quinn); **Night Pieces; Mountains** (Savage);
         Songs of Sea and Sky (F. Williams; Dickson). "PS's 60th Birthday
         concert." Brisbane (Museum of Contemporary Art). *Review:* **B951.**

         Feb 21: **Night Pieces.** Brisbane (Hilton International). Savage. **B953.**

         Feb 24: **Sun Music I.** Troy, NY (Troy Savings Bank Music Hall); re-
         peated Feb 25, Albany, NY (Palace Theater). Australian Bicentenary
         commemoration. Albany SO; Mills. *Reviews:* **B954-955.**

P89-3   Mar 1: **Sun Music III.** Brisbane (Ferry Road Studio). QSO Studio
         Series; Pisarek. *Review:* **B956.**

         Mar 12 (Sun.): **Piano Concerto.** London (St. John's, Smith Square).
         Troup; City Univ. SO; Kess. *Reviews:* **B957-B960.**

         Mar 24-26: PS is guest composer at Mittagong Festival (Frensham
         School). Mar 24 (3 pm): **SQ 6.** Australia Ensemble: Olding, Zhao Qian,
         Morozov, Pereira. (8:15 pm:) **Lament for Strings** (ACO). Mar 25 (11
         am): **Night [Four Little?] Pieces.** Lee; Dillon, pf 4 hands (NSW Con.
         students). (2 pm:) Kim Williams in conversation with PS (Old School
         H). *Lit.:* Small photo, "KW interviewing PS," *2MBS-FM Programme
         Guide* 15 (Nov 1989): 39. (eve.:) **The Song of Tailitnama** (6 vc, dir. Pe-
         reira; Cowley; Askill); and **Requiem** (Waks). "The Great Cello Event."
         Mar 26 (11 am): **Songs of Sea and Sky, arr. flute & piano.** Collins; Bol-
         lard. (3 pm:) **Tabuh Tabuhan** and **How the Stars Were Made.** Synergy
         (Askill; Cleworth; Lagos; Piper); Canberra Wind Soloists (Hill; Nut-
         tall; Vivian; Johnson; McIntyre. *Lit., reviews:* **B962, B966.**

         Mar 31: **Kakadu.** Oakland CA (Paramount Theatre). West Coast US
         premiere. PS was present. Oakland East Bay Symphony; Mester. **B967.**

P89-4   Apr 2 (Sun.): **SQ 6.** Adelaide (Mtg Hall). Arioso SQ. *Review:* **B968.**

         Apr 3: **SQ 9.** Brisbane (Museum of Contemporary Art). PS 60th
         Birthday concert. Brisbane Festival Qt. With: **Djilile** (W182, first perf.).

         Apr 5: **SQ 9.** Adelaide (St. Peter's College Memorial Hall). Australian
         SQ. *Review:* **B969.** *Also:* Apr 11, Melbourne (CH); *reviews:* **B975-975n.**

         Apr 7 (12.30-2.45): **Kakadu.** 20th Century Orchestra Open Rehearsal for

Years 11 & 12. Sydney (TH). SSO; Challender. 12.30: students meet PS and Challender; 1.30, students observe rehearsal. *Lit.*: **B970**.

Apr 8: **Kakadu,** Australian premiere; Irkanda IV (Hazelwood); **Faeroe Island Song, arr.** Sydney (TH). "A Concert for PS's 60th Birthday." SSO; Challender. Pre-concert interview: Andrew Ford with PS. Concert broadcast direct on ABC FM. *Reviews:* **B973–974, B983, B1005.**

Apr 10: **SQ 8.** Chicago (Civic Theatre). Kronos Qt. *Review:* von Rhein, "Kronos sparkles with visual cool," *Chicago Tribune,* Wed. 12 Apr: Tempo sect, p. 3 (the work replaced a cancelled work).

Apr 18: **Mountains; Songs of Sea and Sky** (Westlake, Bollard); and **SQ 6** (D. Olding; Chiao; Morozov; Pereira). Sydney (Clancy Aud.). Second Free Lunch Hour Concert 1989: Tribute to PS. Australia Ensemble. Notes: Covell, quoting PS. *Review:* **B976**

Apr 23 (11:30 a.m.): **Sonatina, Night Pieces, Koto Music I, Mountains, Djilile, Nocturnal** (1981), **Four Little Pieces for Piano Duet.** Sydney (Broadwalk Studio). "Anthony Fogg Plays Sculthorpe." Broadwalk Concert for PS's 60th Birthday. Fogg and PS, pf. Broadcast on ABC-FM.

Apr 24: **SQ 6.** Perth (CH). Birthday concert. Arioso SQ. *Review:* **B977.**

Apr 27: **Overture** (1980). Sydney (St. Andrew's Cathedral). Thursday Organ Recitals. Bartlett.

Apr 28: **Kakadu** (shortened to 8', cut from reh. nos. 13 to 28). Austin TX. Austin Symphony HS Concert (three concerts); Welcher.

Apr 29: **Kakadu,** first Melbourne perf. (CH). "From the New Worlds" concert series. MSO; Iwaki. "This performance is in the presence of PS, who is celebrating his 60th birthday today." (Wilderness Society demonstration brought thousands, and banners "Save Kakadu.") Post-concert reception. *Reviews:* **B985–986.**

Apr 30: **How the Stars Were Made.** Sydney (Broadwalk Studio). Synergy. Broadcast ABC FM stereo "On the Broadwalk."

P89-5   May 5: **Mountains; Night Pieces.** QLD Con. Emmerson, pf. *Review:* Noble, "Singers show winning style," *Courier Mail,* 8 May: 19 (tastefully played).

May 6: *Chorales* from **Rites of Passage; It's You,** first perf.; **Morning Song; The Birthday of Thy King.** Sydney Philharmonia presents PS's 60th Birthday Concert. Sydney (OHCH). Sydney Philharmonia Motet Choir; Ritual Singers; Synergy (Askill; Lagos; Cleworth); Hewgill, Morse, vc; Herskovits, Woods, db; David Miller, pf; cond. Grundy. Pre-concert talk (7.15): PS speaks about writing choral music. *Review:* **B987.**

May 7 (2 concerts) and May 8: **How the Stars Were Made.** Sydney (Marionette Theatre, The Rocks). "Synergy—Australia's gift to the French bicentennial celebrations. See Them Before They Go!" **B988.**

May 12: **Four Little Pieces for Piano Duet** (Deng; Chinnappa); **Songs of Sea and Sky** (F. Williams; Dickson); **SQ 9** (Gardens Point SQ—Graeme Jennings; Elizabeth Jones; Katherine Lockwood; Craig Young); **The Stars Turn, W122** (Gormley; Savage); **Djilile, W183,** "first public perf." (Savage); **Irkanda IV** (Jennings; Con. CO strings and perc; cond. Savage); and **Mangrove** (Con. CO; cond. Savage). Brisbane (Basil Jones Theatre). PS's 60th Birthday Concert in the presence of the composer. Part of Owen Fletcher Master Teacher Program, two days of open rehearsals and discussions. *Review:* **B989.**

May 13: **SQ 8.** NYC (Alice Tully Hall). Kronos Qt. *Review:* **B990.**

May 20: **Songs of Sea and Sky, arr. fl & pf.** Adelaide (Pilgrim Church). Collins; Lockett. *Review:* **B991.**

P89-6   June 1: **Sun Song** for percussion, *création mondiale,* and **How the Stars Were Made.** Paris (Ravel-Debussy Aud., Neuilly-sur-Seine). Synergy. The composer introduced the work.

June 9 (Fri.): **Requiem.** St. Lucia (Nickson Rm.) Roberts. *Review:* Hebden, "A polished Perihelion," *Courier-Mail,* 12 June: 17 (Sculthorpe combines plainchant with his own more emotional passages).

June 18: **Requiem.** Orange NSW (Orange Regional Gallery). "Brunch with Bonetti." Marc Bonetti, vc.

P89-7   July: **SQ 10.** Sydney SQ. *Lit.:* **B998**

July 7: **Irkanda IV.** Hong Kong (HK Academy). HK Academy Orch.

July 9: **Requiem.** Sydney (OHCH). "Beginnings and Endings." Waks. *Review:* Blanks, "Adventures in music, old and new." *SMH,* 12 July: 14 ("sincere performance").

July 9: **Sun Music II.** Adelaide (Elder Hall). ASO (free); Abbott. **B999.**

July 9: **Snow, Moon and Flowers.** Melbourne (Ripponlea). Chamberlain. *Review:* **B1000.**

July 16: **Requiem.** Harnoy. *Lit.: Sun-Herald,* 16 July.

July 19: **Requiem.** Devonport TAS (TH). Recital of Baroque to 20th Century Music. Daniel Holloway, vc. *Repeated:* July 20, Launceston (Chalmers, Princess Square); July 21, Hobart (TH).

July 19: **SQ 9.** Sydney (Seymour Centre). Musica Viva concert.

Australian SQ. *Review:* **B1001**.

July 30 "Sculthorpe: A Celebration." Melbourne (Melba H). Max
Cooke's Team of Pianists. **Sonatina** and **Djilile** (Furman); **Night
Pieces** (Chamberlain); **Mountains; The Rose Bay Quadrilles** (G.
Beilharz); **Four Little Pieces for Piano Duet** (Coote; Cooke); "**Sonata**"
[**Callabonna**], first perf.; **Piano Concerto** (Chamberlain; Univ. of
Melbourne Faculty of Music Orch; Martin). Also: Broadstock, *In the
Silence of the Night. Review:* **B1003**. (4:15 pm): PS a member of a
panel discussing the use of video in music teaching generally.

July 31: **Tailitnama Song**. Melbourne (Flinders Street School of
Music). Urizen Ensemble. *Award:* **B1040**.

P89-8   Aug 6: **Port Essington**. Sydney. Armidale YO; Pulley.

Aug 15, 16, 17: **Kakadu** (excerpt). Sydney schools. SSO; Pisarek. *Also:*
Aug 30, Canberra schools.

Aug 18 (Fri.): **Snow, Moon and Flowers**. Wollongong (School of
Creative Arts, Univ. of Wollongong). Simon.

P89-9   Sept 1: **Requiem**. Melbourne. Green.

Sept: **The Birthday of Thy King**. Choir of Kings College, Cambridge.
Australian tour. *Lit.:* Healey, "The aural halo is missing," *AFR*, Fri. 8
Sept.

Sept 8: **SQ 8**, movts 1, 2, 3, 5, for "Eurythmeum" (Stuttgart dance company) on Australian tour (and world tour); Else Klink, artistic dir.
Carl Pini Qt.

Sept 10: **Sun Song** [II] for perc., Australian premiere. Sydney (L'Atelier
Art Studio, Glebe Point Road). Synergy. *Review:* **B1008**. *Awards:*
B1040n.

Sept 17: **Port Essington**. Christchurch NZ (James Hay Theatre). NZCO
tour of NZ (6 perfs.). *Also:* Sept 18, Nelson School of Music; Sept 19,
Wellington (State Opera House); Oct 1, Hamilton NZ (Founders
Theatre); Oct 2, Auckland (TH); Oct 3, Wanganui (Concert Chamber).
Lit.: Elizabeth Kerr, "Bush and Settlement."

Sept 28: **Kakadu**. London (BBC Maida Vale). Invitation Concert. BBC
SO; Holden.

Sept 28: **Sun Music I**. Tokyo (Suntory Hall). Shinsei Nihon SO's 20th
anniversary concert; Toyama.

Sept 30: **Tabuh Tabuhan**. Great Barrington MA. Atlantic Sinfonietta;
Virtuosi Qnt. *Repeated:* Oct 1, Williamstown MA.

P89-10 Oct 1: **How The Stars Were Made**. Sydney (TH). Synergy.

Oct 1: **Sonata for Viola and Percussion**. Austin TX (First Unitarian Church). ISIS concert. Kalisch; Bissell.

Oct 4-8: **Second Sonata for Strings**. ACO. Victoria Regional Tour: The Hills Centre, Bendigo, Nhill, Portland, Ararat, Melbourne (Oct 10). With Swedish colleagues of the Drottningholm Baroque Ensemble.

Oct 5: **Sonata for Viola and Percussion**. Dortmund, Germany. Hornung; Pusz. *Also:* Oct 16, Stuttgart (Silchersaal der Liederhalle). Australia Felix.

Oct 13, 15: **Second Sonata for Strings**. Sydney (OHCH). ACO subs concert; Tognetti. (With the Drottningholm Baroque Ensemble.) *Review:* **B1010**. *Also:* Oct 17, Newcastle *(review:* **B1011**); Oct 18, Canberra.

Oct 19: **Earth Cry**. Sydney (Great Hall, Univ. of Sydney). "The Peter Platt Farewell Concert." Pro Musica Orch; cond. Platt.

Oct 19: **Irkanda I**. Colorado Springs (Colorado College). Holowell.

Oct 22: **How the Stars Were Made**. Sydney (TH). "Music for Spring." Synergy. *Review:* **B1012**.

Oct 23: **Second Sonata for Strings**. Brisbane (CH, QPAC). ACO; Sparf. *Review:* **B1013**.

Oct 26: **Nourlangie** (after first perf. in Brisbane). Newcastle. Williams; ACO; Hickox. *Reviews:* **B1015**. *Also:* Oct 29, Melbourne; Oct 30, Sydney (OHCH); *reviews:* **B1017-1018**.

Oct 26: **Lament for Strings** and **Port Essington**. Grenoble, France. Ensemble de Grenoble.

Oct 27: **SQ 8**. Providence RI. Kronos Qt. *Also:* Oct 28, Boston MA.

Oct 29: **Sun Music III**. Armidale NSW (Lazenby Hall, Univ. of NE). Armidale SO; Irik.

Oct 30-31: **SQ 8** for Geulah Abrahams' Danceworks. NYC (Merce Cunningham Dance Studio, 2 perfs.); Princeton NJ. *Also:* Apr 7, 1991, Princeton (Arts Council); Apr 13, NYC (Dancespace). *Lit.:* Barbara Gilford, "Dance," *NY Times*, Sun. 24 Mar.

Oct 31: **Songs of Sea and Sky**. New Haven CT (Yale Univ. Music Society).

P89-11 Nov 1, 3, 7, 8: **Kakadu** excerpt. Grafton, Armidale, Orange, Griffith schools. SSO; D. Olding. *Also:* Nov 14, 15, Sydney schools, cond. Hopkins.

Nov 2: **Sun Music IV.** Goteborg, Sweden. Goteborgs Ungdomssymfoni Orkester; Neumann.

Nov 3, 23: **Port Essington.** Melbourne. Rantos Collegium.

Nov 29: **Second Sonata for Strings.** Mudgee (Huntington Winery). Huntington Festival. ACO.

P90-1   Jan 17: **Irkanda IV.** Vienna (Rotunda of the International Centre). William Larsen, vn; Chamber Strings of Melbourne; Rantos. *Also:* Jan 18, Vienna (House of Industry); Jan 22, Budapest (TH); Jan 26, Prague (Eden Concert Hall).

P90-2   Feb 2: **Mangrove.** London (Maida Vale [BBC complex]). Invitation Concert. BBC SO; Joly.

Feb 7: **Dua Chant.** New Haven (Yale Center for British Art). Trio called Not Your Average Recorder Ensemble. *Lit.:* Robert Sherman, "Music," *NY Times*, Sun. 4 Feb.

Feb 24, 25: **Small Town.** Glenorchy, Launceston. TSO (free); Franks.

P90-3   Mar 22: **Kakadu** (8'). Austin (TX). Austin Symphony HS Concert (three concerts); Melone.

Mar 24: **Jabiru Dreaming, SQ 11,** US premiere. Stanford CA (Dinkelspiel Aud.). Kronos Qt. *Reviews:* B1032-1033. *Also:* 32 more perfs. in 1990: Mar 30, Stonybrook NY; B1035. Mar 31, NYC (Alice Tully H), US premiere; B1036. Apr 3, Glassboro NJ. Apr 7, Iowa City, IA (Hancher Aud.). Apr 8, Minneapolis MN (World Theatre). Apr 19, Seattle WA (Meany Hall); B1038. May 10, NYC (Francesco Clemente Studio). June 15, Tubingen, Germany (Mensa Wilhelmstrasse). June 16, Hamburg, Germany (St. Johanniskirche). June 17, Berlin (HDK). June 23, Goslar, Germany (Kaiserpfalz). June 24, Ueizen, Germany (Theater an der Limenau). June 25 (Mon.), London (Royal Festival H); B1049-1050. July 3, Barcelona. July 4, Zaragoza. Aug 5, East Hampton NY (John Drew Theatre). Aug 6, Vienna, VA (Filene Center, Wolftrap). Aug 17, Salzburg Festival (Mozarteum). Aug 18, Willisau, Switzerland. Aug 24, Helsinki Festival, Finland (Savoy Theatre). Sept 14, Boston MA (Blackman Aud.). Sept 15, Atlanta GA (Music Stage), Arts Festival of Atlanta. Sept 16, Asheville NC (Lipinsky Aud.). Oct 16, Milan, Italy (Teatro Smeraldo); B1069. Oct 17, Graz, Austria (Haus der Jugend). Oct 19, Vienna, Austria (Konzerthaus), Vienna Festival. Oct 23, Seville, Spain (Teatro Lope de Vega). Oct 28, Aarhus, Denmark (CH). Nov 6, Vancouver BC, Canada (Centennial Theatre Centre). Nov 30, Columbus, OH (Weigel Hall). Dec 7, Anchorage, AK (Atwood CH). Dec 8, Juneau (Juneau Douglas HS Aud.).

P90-4   Apr 18: **How the Stars Were Made.** Austin TX. Univ. of Texas Percussion Ensemble; Frock.

Apr 26: **Irkanda IV** and **Small Town**. Birmingham Festival, UK (Birmingham Museum of Art). T. Jones; Red Mountain CO; Fillmer.

P90-5 May 2: **Small Town**. London (Australia House, The Strand, WC2). Australis Ensemble; Wheeler.

May 4-13: **SQ 8**, **Earth Cry**, and **Port Essington** used in *My name is Edward Kelly*, Australian Ballet; choreog. Gordon; design, Rowell. *Repeated:* June 15-26, Melbourne (State Theatre). *Reviews:* **B1041**.

May 14: **SQ 8** (Bennelong SQ) and **Djilile** (Young). West Berlin (British Council, Hardenbergstrasse). Antipodes Festival. *Review:* **B1044**.

May 25: **Sun Music II**. Adelaide. ASO family concert; Bandy.

May 27: **Little Serenade**. Launceston vicinity (Midlands sheep property). TSO Players, picnic concert. *Review:* **B1045**.

May 30: **Earth Cry** used in short film *Tasmanian by Design* by Tasmanian Development Authority

P90-6 June 1: Partsongs. Canberra (Greg Hall, Univ. House). ANU Choral Society; cond. Young. *Lit.:* Legge-Wilkinson, "20th-century harmonies," *Canberra Times*, 6 June.

June 17: **Sonata for Strings**. Melbourne. The Mozart Collection; Kelly.

June 21: **Dream**. Sydney. AustraLYSIS. *Review:* **B1047**.

June 22: **Second Sonata for Strings**. Sydney (TH). St. Andrew's Music Festival. ACO. *Review:* **B1048**.

June 29: **Sonatina**. Brunei Music Society (Teachers Abroad Association, Jalan Kota Batu). Lockett.

P90-7 July 7: **Sun Songs** for percussion (I= **Djilile**, II = **Sun Song**). Sapporo, Japan (Art Hall, Sapporo Art Park). Pacific Composers Conference concert at Pacific Music Festival. Aruga Makoto Percussion Group. PS a guest teacher at the Conference.

July 15: **Kakadu**. Sydney (OH). AYO; Shallon. *Lit.:* **B1053**. *Reviews:* **B1054-1055**. Followed by Australian tour to all State and Territory capital cities, Alice Springs and Shepperton. July 16, Canberra (Llewellyn Hall). July 17, Shepparton (TH). July 18, Melbourne (TH). July 19, Perth (CH). July 21, Adelaide (TH), & broadcast live across Australia on ABC-FM stereo. July 22, Alice Springs (Araluen Arts Center). July 25, Darwin (Performing Arts Centre); the composer was present; *lit.:* **B1056, B1058**. July 27, Brisbane (CH, QPAC).

July 19: **Requiem**. Devonport (TH). Holloway. *Repeated:* July 20,

Launceston (Chalmers, Princess Square); July 27, Hobart (TH).

July 20: **Four Little Pieces for Piano Duet** (Peelman; Fogg); **Autumn Song; Night Piece**. Sydney (NSW Con.). The Song Company concert.

July 23: **Irkanda IV**. Seoul, South Korea (Se-Jong Cultural Center). TSO's 1990 International Tour to Korea and Indonesia. Gilby, vn; Franks. *Also:* July 26, Ulsan, South Korea (Ulsan KBS Hall); July 29, Jakarta, Indonesia (Gedung Kesenian).

July 31: **Four Little Pieces for Piano Duet**. Jakarta (Taman Ismail Marzuki—Performing Arts Centre). In connection with TSO tour. Simbolon; Laban. Broadcast on TV in Australia, June 1991 (etc.).

P90-8 Aug 10-18: **Second Sonata for Strings**. ACO tour of Chile; Tognetti (leader). Aug 10, Santiago (Teatro Oriente); 12, Mendoza (Teatro Independencia); 16, Jujuy (Teatro Mitre); 18, Ignazu (Salón Alvar Nuñez).

Aug 14: **Four Little Pieces for Piano Duet**. Brisbane (Cremorne Theatre, QPAC). Musica Nova Festival. Page; M. Olding.

Aug 21: **Djilile**. Sydney (Everest Theatre). Selby.

Aug 22: **SQ 11, Jabiru Dreaming**. Brisbane (Cremorne Theatre). Musica Nova Festival 1990. Brisbane's Festival Qt.

Aug 22: **The Song of Tailitnama, arr. mezzo-sop & pf**. Devon UK. (Great Hall). Dartington International Summer School of Music late-night concert. Jeannie Marsh; Helen English.

P90-9 Sept 4: **Irkanda IV, arr. flute and string trio**. Canberra (Llewellyn H). Australia Ensemble; *review:* **B1063**. *Also:* Sept 8, Melbourne; **B1064**. Sept 22, Sydney (Clancy Aud.), 2 perfs., lunchtime and eve; **B1066**.

Sept 15: **Sonata for Viola and Percussion**. McWilliams; McClaren. NYC (Weill Recital H). *Review:* James R. Oestreich, "A violist in a short recital bill," *NY Times*, 19 Sept (only names the work).

Sept 19 (Wed.): **Irkanda I** (Holowell); **Night Pieces** (Wan); and **Sonata for Viola and Percussion** (Robson; Morton). Newcastle (Newcastle Con. of Music). "Composing for Today" with PS, intro. by Plush.

Sept 19: **Tailitnama Song, arr. 'cello and piano**. Sydney Spring International Festival (Everest Theatre). Pereira; Selby. *Review:* **B1065**.

Sept 19: **Kakadu**. Adelaide (TH). Meet the Music. ASO; Mester.

Sept 22 (etc.): **SQ 8, 2nd movt**, as "Rice Pounding Music." Kronos Qt. This music was also used in a 1990 video/film about the Kronos Qt produced by KQED Channel 9 in San Francisco.

Sept 23: **Irkanda IV**. Dunedin (Otago Univ.). Dunedin Symphonia.

Sept 27: **Dream**, for contrabass and tape. Sydney (Post Aud.). "Twilight Concert." Turetsky.

P90-10 Oct 5: **Small Town**. Canberra (Great Hall, Parliament House). "Australia Live." Canberra SO; Dommett. (*Lit.: Canberra Times*, 1 Oct.)

Oct 6: **Lament for Strings**. Bathurst NSW. Bathurst CO.

Oct 12: **Sun Songs** "Sunsong 1990" for percussion. Sydney (The Rocks Theatre). Synergy. *Review:* **B1067**. *Repeated:* Oct 14.

Oct 13 (Sat.): **Sun Music for Voices and Percussion**. Adelaide (Elder Hall). Adelaide Chorus; Abbott. *Review:* **B1068**.

Oct 18-27: **Second Sonata for Strings**. ACO tour of NSW—Springwood, Gosford, Goulburn, Wagga, Bega, Kiama.

Oct 26: **Kakadu**. Pasadena CA (Civic Aud.) Pasadena SO; Mester. *Review:* **B1070**.

Oct 27: **Kakadu**. Melbourne. MSO; Iwaki.

Oct 31: **SQ 9** used in *Silent Voice*, student dance production of National Aboriginal Islander Skills Development Association. Sydney (Belvoir Theatre). Preview on Oct 31; perfs. Nov 1-11.

P90-11 Nov 2: **SQ 11, Jabiru Dreaming**. Brisbane. Festival Qt. *Also:* Nov 10, Brisbane; Nov 11-27, in Gold Coast, Buderim, Toowoomba (QLD). Five perfs. for American Music Week (work written for Kronos Qt, an American group), to honour PS's "affiliation with America."

Nov 23-24: **Kakadu**. Hong Kong (HK Cultural Centre). HK PO.

Nov 29: **Sun Songs** for percussion. Huddersfield (UK). Huddersfield Contemporary Music Festival. Synergy. *Reviews:* Malcolm Cruise, *Huddersfield Examiner*, 3 Dec, and Simon Cargill, *Yorkshire Post*.

Nov 30: **Requiem**. Huddersfield Festival. Rohan de Saram.

P90-12 Dec 4: **Nourlangie**, European premiere. London (QEH). Williams; Askill; ACO; Hickox. Broadcast live, BBC, Radio 3. *Review:* Stephen Johnson, "Music," *The Listener* 124 (13 Dec): 37 ("entertaining").

Dec 4: **Second Sonata for Strings**. Hobart. TSO; Franks.

Dec 15: **The Birthday of thy King**. First perf. by Australian choir. Sydney (Great Hall). Sydney Chamber Choir Christmas Concert; Walker.

P91-1 Jan 11: **Jabiru Dreaming, SQ 11**. Scottsdale AZ (Center for the Arts).

Kronos Qt. *Also:* Jan 12, Los Angeles (Wadsworth Theatre); **B1081**. Jan 18, Cleveland OH (Severance H); **B1082**. Jan 19, Chicago (Park West); **B1083**. Feb 2, Berkeley CA (Hertz H); **B1087-1089**. Feb 10, Roanoke VA (Mill Mountain Theatre). Feb 12, Oberlin OH (Finney Chapel). Feb 16, Lincoln NE (Kimball Recital H). Mar 2, San Antonio TX (Carver Center Theatre). Mar 4, Tucson AZ (Leo Rich Theatre), Festival in the Sun; 2 perfs., lunchtime and eve.; PS was present; **B1094-1095**. Mar 12, Kumamoto, Japan. Mar 17, Kanagawa. Mar 18, Osaka. Mar 19, Nagoya. Mar 22, Tokyo (Orchard H). Apr 5, Milwaukee WI (Pabst Theatre). Apr 6, Madison WI (Civic Center). Apr 7, Beloit WI (Eaton Chapel). Apr 8, Princeton NJ (McCarter Theatre). Apr 9, Rochester NY (Kilbourn H). Apr 11, Brattleboro VT (River Valley PAC). Apr 13, San Rafael CA (Angelico H). Apr 17, East Lansing MI (Wharton Center). Apr 19, Detroit MI (Orch Hall). May 6, Santander, Spain. May 9, Palermo, Italy. May 14, London (BBC Lime Grove), taping **Part One** of the work, for BBC Special, b'cast May 31. May 22, Wels, Austria. May 23, Geneva.

P91-1 Jan 19: **Nangaloar**, pre-premiere perf. Parramatta NSW (Futter Hall,
(cont.) Kings School). National Music Camp. Bishop Orch; Hopkins.

Jan 22: **Port Essington**. Penrith NSW (Joan Sutherland PAC). AYO.

Jan 26: **Nangaloar**, official first perf. of first version. Sydney (The Domain [outdoors]). AYO; Hopkins. The composer, introduced by Dame Edna Everage (Barry Humphries), spoke before the perf. An estimated 40,000 people attended the concert. *Review:* **B1085**.

P91-2 Feb 2: **Earth Cry**. Sydney (The Domain). Festival of Sydney, free concert. SSO; Franks. The composer, introduced by Andrew Denton, spoke before the performance. Again, many thousands of people attended. *Review:* **B1086**.

Feb 10 (Sun.): **Songs of Sea and Sky**. San Diego CA (Smith Recital Hall, SDSU). "Music Down Under." The Capricorn Connection—Liebowitz; Ward-Steinman. **B1090**. *Also:* Feb 13, **Djilile**; Feb 15, **Night Pieces**; Richard Carr, pf. *Lit.:* Herman, "The new sounds from Down Under," *LA Times*, 7 Feb (interviews Ward-Steinman and Kerry).

Feb 16: **Overture for a Happy Occasion**. Launceston (Princess Theatre). TSO; Franks. *Lit.:* **B1091**.

Feb 23-24 (Sat.-Sun.): **Lament for Strings** used in *Always*, choreog. Hall. Sydney (Sydney Dance Company Studios).

P91-3 Mar 12: **Kakadu** (8'). Honolulu HI. "Music and Nature" series concerts for schoolchildren grades 4-6. Honolulu Symphony; Welcher. *Repeated:* Mar 13, 14, 19, 20, 21, Honolulu; Apr 18, 19, Hilo HI (2 perfs. each day).

Mar 16: **Earth Cry**. Pymble NSW (Ku-ring-gai TH). Twentieth

Anniversary Gala Concert. Ku-ring-gai PO; Flottman.

Mar 16-Apr 12: **Port Essington.** Camerata of the AYO; Hopkins. Tour of eastern US (9 concerts) and Venezuela and Brazil (6 concerts). (Small group because of Gulf War, fear of travelling.) *Lit.:* Pamela Payne, "You can get there from here," *Bulletin,* 19 Mar, p. 98. Mar 16, Kingsborough Community College, NY. Mar 18, Richlands VA (Tazwell HS). Mar 19, Covington VA (Allegheny State HS). Mar 20, Steubenville OH (Steubenville HS). Mar 21, Huntingdon PA (Oller Hall). Mar 23, New York City (Carnegie H); PS was present; *review:* **B1098.** Mar 25, Troy NY (Troy Savings Bank Music Hall). Mar 27, Miami FL (Lincoln Theatre). Apr 1, Sarasota FL (Van Wezel Hall). Apr 3, Maracay, Venezuela (Teatro de la Opera). Apr 4, Barquisimento, Venezuela (Teatro Juares). Apr 6, Caracas (Teatro Teresa Carreña); Apr 8, Rio di Janeiro [?] (*lit.: Jornal do Brazil,* 8 April: 2). Apr 9, Brasilia, Brazil (Teatro Nacional). Apr 10, 12, Sao Paulo, Brazil (Teatro Municipal).

Mar 19: **Requiem.** Colorado Springs CO (Packard Hall). Smith. Perf. to illustrate PS's lecture, "Kakadu Songlines." (*Lit.:* **B1096.**) Also (aft.): open rehearsal of **Tabuh Tabuhan** with the composer; performed Apr 22 (below).

Mar 20: **Small Town.** Colorado Springs, CO (Packard Hall). Colorado College Chamber Orchestra. The composer was present.

Mar 22: **Sun Song II** (announced as "Jabiru Dreaming"). Canberra (Llewellyn Hall). Synergy Percussion.

Mar 24: **Requiem.** Islington N1, UK (Almeida Theatre, Almeida St.). Shiva Nova Ensemble concert. Neil Heyde, vc. *Review:* **B1097.**

Mar 29: **Irkanda I.** Seattle WA premiere (Nippon Kan Theater). Pacific Rim Mini-Festival.

P91-4 Apr 9: **Songs of Sea and Sky.** Toronto (Roy Thompson H). Stoltzman; Vallecillo. *Review:* **B1099.**

April 11: **Sea Chant.** Launceston TAS (Launceston Church Grammar School Assembly Hall). The composer was present, to dedicate the school's new music building. *Lit.:* **B1100-1101.**

Apr 12: **Lament for Strings.** Cygnet (orchestral series). TSO; Abbott.

Apr 18: **The Song of Tailitnama, arr. mezzo-sop. & pf.** Melbourne (Melba Hall). Marsh; Hammond. Recorded by 3MBS-FM.

April 22: **Tabuh Tabuhan.** Colorado Springs (Packard Hall). "A Concert: Reminiscences of Albert Seay." Colorado College Faculty Ww Qnt (Muhonen; Dutra-Silveira; Stevens; Kroth; Murray); Nelsen; Cooper.

Apr 26: **Small Town**. Perth. Fantastic Friday. QSO; Bignell.

P91-5   May 3, 4: **Irkanda IV**. Hanoi, Vietnam. Ta Bon, solo vn; National SO of Vietnam; M. Olding.

May 8: **Songs of Sea and Sky, arr. fl & pf**. Pymble NSW. Linstead; Tapscott. *Repeated:* May 9, Canberra (Univ. House, ANU); **B1103**.

May 10-25: **Sun Music I**. Perth. Western Australian YO (on tour).

May 12: **Songs of Sea and Sky, arr. fl & pf**. Orange NSW (Orange Regional Gallery). Barker; Stevens.

May 12: **Sun Music IV**. Brisbane. Brisbane Biennial Festival. Univ. College of Southern QLD SO; Rorke.

May 26 (Sun. eve.): **Small Town**. Played during TV screening of Manning Clark's last interview.

May 29: **Port Essington**. Sydney. Trinity Grammar SO; Peter Dart, cond. *Repeated:* June 17, Mudgee; June 18, Orange; June 19, Bathurst.

May 30: **Sonatina**. BBC Radio 3, "Australian Connections." Thwaites.

May 30: **Sun Music I**. Melbourne (CH). Symphony at 7. MSO; Hopkins. *Review:* **B1104**.

May?: **Irkanda IV; Small Town**. MSO; Franks. Rehearsal and discussion for *c*200 students, in response to new Victorian Certificate of Education Music syllabus. *Lit.: Sounds Australian*, June 1991.

P91-6   June 3: **Lament for Strings**. Adelaide. Adelaide CO; Abbott. *Review:* **B1106**. *Also:* perfs. of **Small Town** with drawings by Rolf Harris.

June 8: **Jabiru Dreaming, SQ 11**. Baltimore MD (Shriver Hall). Kronos Qt. *Also:* June 16 (aft.): **Jabiru Dreaming, Part One**, and *Rice-Pounding Music* (**SQ 8, movt II**). SF (Stern Grove). *Review:* **B1107**.

June 19: **Sun Song** for orchestra. Vision Valley NSW. North Sydney Girls' School music camp. *Lit.:* "Girls head to the bush for music," *Hornsby Advocate*, 20 June. *Also performed* in Sydney a week later.

June 19-20: **Small Town**. Shyalla, Port Pirie (orch series). ASO; Taplin.

June 20, 21, 22: **Earth Cry**. MSO (Master series); Iwaki. *Also:* June 24, Meet the Music.

June 24: **SQ 9**. Sydney (Government House). Vice-regal command perf. Sydney Conservatorium SQ. *Lit.:* **B1108**.

P91-7   July: **Sonata for Viola and Percussion**. Bydgoszcz, Poland.

International Percussion Festival, July 1-15. Pusz.

July 6-7, 13-14: **Mangrove,** by Freelance Dance Company. Sydney (Sydney Dance Company Studios).

July 13: **Requiem.** Sydney (St. James' Church, King Street). Blake.

July 16: **Mangrove.** Sapporo, Japan (TH). Pacific Festival; M. Thomas. *Lit.:* **B1116.**

July 16: **Second Sonata for Strings.** Adelaide (Elder Hall). Adelaide CO; Summerbell. *Reviews:* **B1110-1111.**

July 22: **Jabiru Dreaming, SQ 11.** Oakland CA (Mills College Recital Hall). Kronos Qt. *Also:* Aug 1, Interlochen MI (Interlochen Center for the Arts). Aug 17, Emkendorf, Germany (Schleswig-Holstein Music Festival). Aug 22, Athens Festival (Lycabettus). Aug 25, Saalfelden, Austria (Jazz Festival Tent). Aug 26, Brussels, Belgium (Ancienne Belgique), Bruzzle Festival concert.

P91-8   Aug 3: **Irkanda I.** Sydney (Post Aud.). Australian Musician's Academy. Clohessy. *Also:* perfs. in Dubbo, Canberra, Mittagong.

Aug 5: **Night Pieces.** Canberra (Rehearsal Rm 3). Jacob. *Review:* **B1113.**

Aug 14: **Nangaloar.** Sydney (Great Hall). Sydney Univ. SO; Gross.

Aug 14: **Sun Music III.** Adelaide (TH). Meet the Music. ASO; Braithwaite. *Review:* **B1115.**

Aug 23: **Morning Song; The Birthday of Thy King.** Sydney (Post Aud.). Horizons concert. Sydney Philharmonia Choir; Sydney Con. Chorale; cond. Allan; Vine (pf).

Aug 24: **Piano Concerto.** Newcastle NSW (Conservatorium). Spiers; Newcastle Con. SO; Constable.

Aug 28: **Lament for Strings.** Melbourne (Melba Hall). Rantos Collegium. *Repeated:* Sept 1, Melbourne (Alexander Theatre, Monash Univ.).

P91-9   Sept 11 (opening): **Earth Cry, Small Town,** and **Kakadu** used in *Jedda* by AIDT (Aboriginal/Islander Dance Theatre)—The Company, choreog. Saliba and Blanco. Sydney (State Theatre). *Review:* Sykes, "Exciting fusion of two cultural traditions," *SMH,* Fri. 13 Sept (no mention of the music). *Also:* North and South American tours.

Sept 15: **The Birthday of Thy King.** Lismore NSW (Summerland Christian Life Centre). St. Peter's Chorale. *Also:* Sept 16, Newcastle (Waratah Primary School); Sept 18, Sydney (St. James Anglican Church, King Street); Sept 19, Canberra (Canberra Girls Grammar

Chapel); Sept 20, Canberra (Great Hall, Parliament House); Sept 23, North Melbourne (St. Mary's Anglican Church); Sept 26, Mt. Gambier SA (St Paul's Catholic Church); Sept 27, Adelaide (Immanuel College); Sept 29, Adelaide (St. Peter's Cathedral).

Sept 17: **Irkanda IV, arr. SQ,** and **Jabiru Dreaming, SQ 11,** Sydney premiere (OH). Kronos Qt. *Review:* **B1119.** *Also:* Sept 18, **Jabiru Dreaming,** Brisbane (CH); *review:* Hebden, "A delightful musical journey with Kronos," *Courier-Mail,* 19 Sept. *Repeated:* Sept 22, Melboune (CH), Melbourne International Festival, & broadcast Thurs. Oct 3; **B1123.** Sept 20, **Irkanda IV, arr. SQ,** Adelaide (Festival Theatre); **B1120.** Sept 21, Canberra (Llewelyn Hall); **B1122.**

Sept 23: **SQ 6.** Sydney (Clancy Aud.). Australia Ensemble.

Sept 24: **Lament for 'Cello and Strings** (1991). Canberra (Llewellyn Hall). ACO tour. *Review:* **B1125.** *Also:* Sept 26, Melbourne (Victorian Art Centre Concert Hall).

Sept 26: **SQ 8** used for *Precipice* duo, choreog. Carr. Washington, DC (Dance Place). Island Moving Company. *Review:* George Jackson, "Dance," *Washington Post,* Mon. 30 Sept: C12.

P91-10   Oct 1: **Requiem.** Tel Aviv, Israel. *Also:* Oct 1, Geneva, Switzerland.

Oct 24: **Jabiru Dreaming.** Tuscaloosa AL (CH, Univ. of AL). Kronos Qt. *Also:* Oct 25, Lexington KY (Memorial Hall, Univ. of KY). Nov 2, Carmel CA (Sunset Center). Nov 4, Columbia MO (Jesse Aud.). Nov 6, Storrs CT (Jorgensen Aud.). Nov 7, Amherst MA (Bowker H); Nov 11, Pittsburgh PA (Fulton Theatre); **B1130-1131.** Dec 1, Huddersfield (TH), Huddersfield Contemporary Music Festival concert; *review:* **B1159.** Dec 14, Munster, Germany (Horsaal H1). Dec 16, Messina, Sicily (Teatro in Fiera). Dec 17, Catania, Italy (Teatro Metropolitano).

Oct 27: **Kakadu.** Canberra. Canberra YO.

P91-11   Nov 3: **Night Pieces.** Canberra (Australian National Gallery Theatre). Legge-Wilkinson. *Review:* **B1129.**

Nov 6-11: **Dream.** AustraLYSIS. Wellington (Radio NZ); Christchurch (Arts Centre); Dunedin (Bagdad Cafe).

Nov 8: **Djilile.** London (Downer Room, Australia House). Association of Australian Artists. D. Lewis.

Nov 10: **Requiem.** Tucson AZ (School of Music Annex, Univ. of AZ). DMA recital. Dubé.

Nov 15, 16, 17: **Jabiru Dreaming, SQ 11** (Kronos Qt, live) used for *Sightings,* choreog. Jenkins. Oakland Ballet. Oakland CA (Paramount

Theater). (Program and reviews refer to 'SQ 8'.) *Reviews:* **B1133**. *Also:* May-June 1992 (to a Kronos Qt recording), SF (Theater Artaud) and Bay Area tour; Jenkins Company. *Lit.:* Marilyn Tucker, "It's home sweet home for Jenkins troupe," *SF Chronicle*, 3 May. Nov 13-15, 1992 (Kronos Qt recording), Berkeley (Zellerbach H), Oakland Ballet.

Nov 17: **Songs of Sea and Sky**. Boston (Jordon Hall, NE Conservatory). Stoltzman; Vallecillo. *Review:* **B1132**.

Nov 23: **Little Suite for Strings**. Richmond (NSW) Regional String Ensemble; cond. Raymond Hill.

Nov 28, 29, 30, Dec 4, 5, 6: **Earth Cry, Mangrove** excerpts for *Invisible Barrier*, Dance North, choreog. Phuong. Townsville (Arts Centre).

Nov 30: **Earth Cry**. Alice Springs NT (Simpson's Gap). Darwin SO; Jarvis. *Lit. & reviews:* **B1134**.

P91-12   Dec 7: **Night Pieces** (in Junior sect.); **Mountains** (in Open sect.). Townsville QLD (Perc Tucker Regional Gallery). Barrier Reef Piano Competition. PS an adjudicator. *Lit.:* **B1135**.

Dec 8: **Burke & Wills Suite; Little Suite for Strings; Earth Cry; Mangrove; Night Pieces; Two Grainger Arrangements; Songs of Sea and Sky**. Townsville QLD (Civic Theatre). A Grand Peter Sculthorpe Concert. Pimlico HS Brass Band; Pimlico Strings; Dance North; Barrier Reef Piano Competition winners.

Dec 16: **Requiem**. Canberra (Recital Room, CSM). Pereira.

P92-1   Jan 15: **Jabiru Dreaming**. Dayton OH. Kronos Qt. Also: Jan 24, Houston TX; Jan 25, Costa Mesa CA (*review:* **B1146**); Jan 30, San Diego CA (**B1147**); Feb 9, NYC; Feb 11, Indianapolis IN; Feb 12, Greencastle IN.

P92-2   Feb: **Irkanda IV, arr. fl & SQ**. Vienna. Australia Ensemble. *Review:* **B1148**. *Also:* Feb 5, La Spezia, Italy (TH). Feb 7, Paris (Australian Embassy). Feb 10, Bonn, Germany (Beethoven Halle); *review:* **B1149**.

Feb 19: **Sun Music II**. Pittsburgh PA (Heinz H). Pittsburgh SO; Maazel.

P92-2   Feb 28: **Songs of Sea and Sky**. Chicago IL (Mandel H). Stoltzman; Vallecillo. *Also:* Mar 1, NYC (Avery Fisher H).

P92-3   Mar 11-14 (Wed.-Sat.): *Questionnaire Song* from **Ulterior Motifs** (1956). Acton ACT (Theatre 3, Ellery Crescent). Canberra Repertory "Showcase 60"—a pot-pourri from 60 years of entertaining Canberra.

Mar 22: **Landscape II**. Sydney (Con.) Novalis Quartet.

P92-4   Apr 1: **SQ 8**. Melbourne (Prince Philip Theatre). Southern SQ.

Apr 2: **Small Town.** Melbourne (CH). Symphony at 7. MSO; Thomas.

Apr 5: **Sonatina.** Canberra (CSM). Hyde. *Review:* **B1156**.

Apr 5: **Songs of Sea and Sky.** Montreal (Pollack H). Stoltzman; Valle-cillo. *Review:* Ilse Zadrozny, *Gazette*, 6 Apr.

Apr 23: **Jabiru Dreaming.** Hartford CT. Kronos Qt. *Review:* **B1158**.

Apr 25: **Small Town.** Melbourne. AYO.

P92-5 May 8: **SQ 8.** Los Angeles (UCLA Center for the Arts). Kronos Qt. *Review:* **B1160**.

May 9: **Sun Music III.** Melbourne VIC (Toorak Uniting Church). Victoria YSO; Bailey.

May 13: **Piano Concerto.** Hobart (ABC Odeon). Cislowski; TSO (subs); Braithwaite. *Review:* **B1161**. May 14, Launceston (Princess Theatre).

May 16: **Small Town.** Brisbane. QSO family concert; Mills.

May 17: **Mountains.** Penrith NSW (Joan Sutherland PAC). Howat. *Also:* July 28, London (BBC Radio 3).

May 23: **Tropic.** Brighton Festival UK (Hove TH). Attacca. UK tour. *Also:* May 30, Swindon (Wyvern Theatre); May 31, Reading (Hexagon); June 3, Birmingham (Symphony H); June 6, Cambridge (Corn Exchange); June 7, Cheltenham (TH); June 11, Northampton (Derngate); June 13, London (Barbican).

May 29: **Small Town.** Adelaide. ASO family concert; Abbott.

P92-6 June 1: **Songs of Sea and Sky.** London (QEH). Stoltzman; Martineau. *Reviews:* Christopher Grier, *Evening Standard*, 2 June ("*dernier cri*"); Edward Greenfield, *Guardian*, 3 June ("warmth and lyricism").

June 3 (Wed. noon): **Sonatina.** Chicago (Chicago Cultural Center). Dame Myra Hess Memorial Concerts. Sangiorgio. *Review:* **B1164**.

June 7: Works. Adelaide. "Sunday Live" radio broadcast.

June 8: **Burke and Wills Suite, arr. brass band,** 2 movts, US premiere, and **Tabuh Tabuhan.** Boulder CO (Grusin Hall). Univ. of CO Summer School Ensembles; Aldrich.

June 17, 24, July 1: Works. Newcastle NSW. Newcastle Univ. Faculty.

June 20: **Autumn Song.** Sydney (Great Hall). Sydney Chamber Choir.

June 29: **Tabuh Tabuhan.** Montreal. Kulgarni Wind Qnt; Cossom.

P92-7   July 16: **Second Sonata for Strings**. Adelaide (Elder Hall). New Perspectives. Adelaide CO; Summerbell.

July 30: **Jabiru Dreaming**. Tanglewood Music Center (Theatre-Concert Hall). Festival of Contemporary Music. Kronos Qt. *Reviews:* **B1167-1169**. *Also:* Sept 26, Poland (Warsaw Festival, Academy of Music).

P92-8   Aug 7: **Threnody**. Canberra (Tilley's Bar, Lyneham). Pereira.

Aug 12 (Wed.): **Lament for Strings**, UK premiere. London (Royal Albert H). BBC late-night Prom; live radio broadcast. ACO; Hickox. *Reviews:* **B1170-1174**. *Also:* two-week European tour: England (Harrogate International Festival); Austria (St. Florian Monastery); Amsterdam (Concertgebouw); Slovenia (Ljulbljana Festival).

Aug 15: *Jabiru Dreaming* [**Sun Song**] for perc. Sydney (Seymour Centre). Synergy. *Review:* **B1175**. *Also:* Aug 17, Melbourne (CH); Aug 20, Brisbane (QPAC). *Reviews:* **B1176-1177**.

Aug 20: **Songs of Sea and Sky**. Sydney (Old Darlington School). Playoust; Docking. *Also performed* Aug 25, St. Lucia (Nickson Rm). Perihelion Ensemble: Sabin; Flemming.

Aug 23: **Sonatina**. Wollongong (Hope Theatre). Hyde.

P92-9   Sept 2, 4: **Kakadu**. Melbourne. MSO; P. Thomas.

Sept 12: **SQ 8**. Sydney (Clancy Aud.). Australia Ensemble: D. Olding; D. Hall; Morozov; Smiles. *Review:* **B1179**.

Sept 13: **Port Essington**. Melbourne (Toorak Uniting Church). Chamber Strings of Melbourne; Rantos. *Repeated:* Sept 14 (Melba H).

Sept 16: **Requiem**. Melbourne. Waks.

Sept 20: **Autumn Song**. Sydney (Goossens Hall). Horizons Festival. Sydney Chamber Choir; Kempster.

Sept 21: **Tropic**. Melbourne (CH). Attacca. *Also:* Sept 26, Sydney (OH). *Review:* **B1181**.

Sept 25: **Irkanda IV, arr. fl & SQ**. Rosario (Auditoria Fundación). Australia Ensemble tour to Argentina and Chile. Sept 30, Buenos Aires (Theatre Opera). Oct 3, Nuequen (Sala 2, Casa de la Cultura). Oct 5, Santiago (Oriente). Oct 7, Bahía Blanca (Theatre Municipal).

P92-10   Oct 2: **Second Sonata for Strings**. Bangkok (Thailand Cultural Center). ACO tour. *Also:* Oct 5, Singapore (Victoria Hall). Oct 7, Gedung Kesenian, Indonesia. Oct 9-10, Medan, Indonesia.

Oct 7: **Overture for a Happy Occasion**. Light Pass SA (Immanuel

Church). Barossa Music Festival. Kinsela.

Oct 8: **Earth Cry**. Kiev. Kiev Philharmonic Orchestra; Kuchar.

Oct 9: **Djilile**. Univ. of Birmingham, UK. Perihelion tour. Flemming. *Also:* Oct 12, Univ. of Southampton; Oct 13, London (Australia House); Oct 15, Univ. of Glasgow.

Oct 14, 15: **Earth Cry**. Sydney. Meet the Music. SSO; Shallon. **B1182**. With pre-concert talk by PS. *Also:* Oct 16, "Tea and Symphony." Oct 21, Adelaide, ASO; Shallon.

Oct 24: **Kakadu**. South Africa. NAPAC. (*Lit.: Sounds Australian.*)

Oct 24: **Port Essington**. Montevideo, Uruguay. Sodre Difusion Radiotelevision y Espectaculos; Fredman. *Also:* **Mangrove**, Oct 25.

Oct 25: **Lament**. Sydney. International Spring Festival of New Music.

Oct 27, 28: **Kakadu**. Ft. Lauderdale FL (Broward Center). Florida PO; cond. Judd. *Also:* Oct 29, Miami (Gusman Center); Oct 30, Boca Raton (Florida Atlantic Univ. Aud.); Nov 2, West Palm Beach (Kravis Center). Pre-concert lectures by PS. *Reviews:* **B1184**.

Oct 28: **How the Stars Were Made**. Sydney (Conservatorium).

Oct 30: **Kakadu** excerpt for The Langshaw Dance Company. Sydney (OH) SSO family concerts; Buggy. *Also:* Oct 31, Castle Hill (Hills Centre; Nov 1, Parramatta (Picnic in the Park).

P92-11 Nov 1: **Threnody**. Canberra (Aust. National Gallery Theatre). Pereira.

Nov 7, 8: **Port Essington**. Perth. Camerata of West Australia; Smalley.

Nov 13: **Songs of Sea and Sky, arr. fl & pf**. Melbourne (Music School, Victorian College of the Arts). Nicholson; Gilsionan.

Nov 20: **Requiem**. Mudgee. Huntington Festival (H, Estate Winery).

P92-12 Dec 3: **Port Essington**. Adelaide (Elder Hall). Adelaide YO; Hennessy.

Dec 3, 4: **Mangrove**. Newcastle. Hunter Orch; Peelman.

Dec 5: **Irkanda IV**. Melbourne (Melba H). Australian Heidelberg Youth Sinfonia; Clinch.

Dec 13: **Irkanda IV**. Melbourne. Chambers; Geminiani CO; van Pagee.

Dec 13: **Kakadu**. Sydney. Sydney YO; Pisarek.

Bibliography

This bibliography lists writings by and about Sculthorpe, in chronological order from 1945 through 1992. Cross-references with a **W** refer to "Works," with a **D** to the "Discography," and with a **P** to "Performances."

B1   "Schoolboy composer writes opera." *ABC Weekly*, September 1945.
Peter Sculthorpe, 16-year-old pianist who has already written a Chinese opera, "The Golden Fisherman," will include three of his compositions in a piano recital of Australian music on 7ZR-NT Tuesday September 11 at 7:30.

B2   [Prize announcement.] Launceston *Examiner*, 1946.
PS's **Chamber Suite** has been awarded the J. A. Steele Composition Prize for best musical composition of the year at the Melbourne Conservatorium of Music.

B3   [Scholarship award.] *Examiner*, 1947.
PS is one of three people awarded 1947 scholarships by the Examination Board of Melbourne Conservatorium.

B4   "Fine Arts Society." *Farrago* (University of Melbourne), 10 August 1948.
Mr. PS's music (Aug 3) gave strong promise of even better things to come. The brief SQ [2] showed a considerable ability in the more extended forms of musical expression.

B5   "Composer's success." *Examiner*, [early] 1948.
Mr. and Mrs. J. T. Sculthorpe's 18-year-old son, Peter, was a runner up in the Victorian School Music Association's Australian-wide song competition.
Also announced in: "Youth runner-up in song contest," *Examiner*.

B6   John Sinclair. "Arts Council music recitals 'anaemic'." *Herald*, 23 June 1949.
The playing of two pieces [**Nocturnes**] by a young Melbourne student Peter Sculthorpe had a warmth and fluidity that seemed inherent in the music itself.
Also reviewed in: "Recital by young artists," 23 June ("smooth and vigorous" playing).

B7   "Fine Arts." [Melbourne newspaper, 29 June 1949]
The recital by PS, composer-pianist, showed that he has eventually singled out as his most comfortable style that exemplified in the second of the two **Nocturnes**.

B8   Linda Phillips. "Recital of music by Australians." *Sun*, 27 October 1949.

PS's **SQ 3** showed definite creative promise, but lacked thematic development.
Also: "Australian compositions" (unidentified review) finds the work "youthful in construction with too much interest directed to the voice of the first violin."

B9   "Launceston composer's success. *Examiner,* June 1950.
PS, 21-year-old St. Leonards composer, has had much success in Melbourne recently with his latest composition, a **fourth string quartet.**

B10   Linda Phillips. "Australian composers show sincere work." *Sun,* 12 October 1950.
PS's **SQ 4** was rather thin in texture but showed promise and some original ideas. A large audience attended yesterday's concert.

B11   John Sinclair. "Plenty to listen to this week." *Herald,* 2 December 1954.
PS's **Sonatina** and five other Australian works will be submitted later this month to an international jury for the ISCM Festival in Baden-Baden next year.
Other announcements: "L'ton composer's work to be sent overseas," [*Examiner?*]; "Distinction for L'ton pianist," *Mercury?*; and "Success for composer," December.

B12   "Weltmusikfest der IGNM 1955." *Melos* 22 (February 1955): 47.
IGNM (= ISCM) festival program lists the **Sonatina** on Sunday 19 June at "1600 Uhr".

B13   E. M. W. "Brother and sister give recital." [Melbourne newspaper, 30?] March 1955.
A very modern **Sonata for Violin Alone** gave the impression that the composer's aim was musical "stunting" rather than musical expression.
Also: Phillips, "Talented, pleasing violinist," *Sun* (sonata was "also heard").

B14   Dorian Le Gallienne. "Mozart sonata a delight." *Age,* 30 March 1955.
PS's **Sonata for Violin Alone** has many attractive and unexpected sounds, and holds the listener's attention throughout, despite a certain monotony in the melodic lines (or rather their harmonic implications) and the frequent use of repeated figures.

B15   John Sinclair. "Handled Bach skilfully." *Herald,* [30?] March 1955.
Sonata for Violin Alone is written with more facility than musical impulse. It might want less tricks and more substance. (Sinclair's pre-recital announcement repeats the information about Baden-Baden.)

B16   H. H. Stuckenschmidt. "Unity of aim, dispersion of styles mark 1955 ISCM Festival." *Musical America* 75 (August 1955): 6, 24.
Almost touching in its naive programmatic character and its folkloristic jargon reminiscent of Grieg and MacDowell was the **Sonatina** by the Australian PS. Maria Bergmann was a fine pianist.

B17   [Shirley Hawker.] "Carena's column." *Examiner,* February 1956.
With an amazing range of sounds, PS [in **Irkanda I**] has painted a vivid picture of sunburnt country and native mysticism.
Later, "Carena's column" reports that **Irkanda** took the Lisbon audience of 1500 by storm. Another Launceston press cutting, about the Outdoor Sports Supplies shop, mentions European performances of the "uncannily out-of-this-world" solo.

B18   Franz Holford (ed.). "Australian musicians: Peter Sculthorpe." *Canon: Australian Music Journal* 9 (March 1956): 227-8.
PS (shown in small photo) estimates his **Irkanda** for unaccompanied violin to be his

finest composition to date; it is, he states, "truly Australian."

B19 "Repertory performance exuberant." *Canberra Times*, 30 June 1956.
Background music for **Twelfth Night** was composed by Peter Sculthorpe.
News-'n-Views (Launceston Players newsletter), August, also reports on the Canberra production; "Congratulations to PS."

B20 J. M. G. "Sundry shows. **Ulterior Motifs**." *Bulletin*, 21 Nov 1956: 19.
PS's music for **Ulterior Motifs** is always apt and pleasant, though his skill doesn't seem to lie in the field of catchy tunes.
Other press coverage: "Repertory's enjoyable musical skit"; "Repertory composer and pianist," *Canberra Times*, c11 Nov (photo of pianists); other photos. *Cue* (Canberra Repertory Theatre newsletter), Nov, describes "delightfully catchy and clever tunes."

B21 Sir Bernard Heinze. "Music in Australia." *Vogue Australia*, Midsummer [February] 1957: 66-68.
PS (shown in photo) is among the promising young stars on the musical horizon here, a composer with a highly experimental, atonal style, stemming from Schoenberg.

B22 Fidelio. "Composer has fresh ideas." [*West Australian?* March 1957.]
Sonatina was much the most interesting instrumental item at the Art Gallery concert. PS, its young Victorian composer, shows freshness of idea and of idiom.

B23 "Sundry Shows. **Cross Section**." *Bulletin*, 18 September 1957: 24.
"Bright, smart, topical stuff" is the reason **Cross Section** is sold out. The whole ensemble brings the house down in *Manic espresso*—"you can't keep a good cup down".
Other reviews: Elizabeth Riddell, "**Cross Section** bright" (songs and sketches are up to standard); *Truth*, 15 Sept; review with photo, *Pictorial-Show*, 16 Sept: 37.

B24 "Tchaikovsky Violin and Piano Competition: American wins Piano Section—Russian the Violin." *Australian Musical News*, May 1958.
A Diploma of Distinction was awarded Australian violinist Wilfred Lehmann, who played Tasmanian PS's **Irkanda [I]** in Moscow's Tchaikovsky competition.

B25 "L'ton man impresses Oistrakh." *Examiner*, 1958.
Wilfred Lehmann performed **Irkanda [I]** in Moscow; David Oistrakh obtained a copy from PS during his Australian tour and will put it in the Moscow Conservatoire library.

B26 "Music award to L'ton man." *Mercury*, [mid-] 1958.
PS was among three finalists for the Lizette Bentwich award, and today was notified that he is the winner. (Award is also announced in the *Examiner*.)

B27 "About Launceston," *Tasmanian Truth*, Saturday 19 July 1958: 9.
A round of farewell parties begins this week for popular PS who is to sail August 5 in the Neptunia for Europe. Headquartered at Oxford, he will be away three years.

B28 "Music award to L'ton man." *Examiner*, 11 June 1959: 14
PS's **string quartet [no. 5, Irkanda II]** won a prize for a chamber work for 2-4 performers.
Other coverage: "Tasmanian Wins Composers Award," *Australian News*, 18 June.

B29 "Performance of a new work." *Oxford Mail*, c2 March 1960.
A new **string quartet [no. 5, Irkanda II]** by PS, a young Australian, attempts to express Australian life in the "outback." It has an often effective austerity of expression and a generous degree of sharp rhythmic contrasts.

B30   [Robin Drummond-Hay. Concert review.] *Oxford Magazine* 78 (3 March 1960), inside back cover.
On the evidence of **Irkanda [II]** (scrub country), PS has a remarkable gift for evoking the atmosphere of his own country in music which exploits string technique to the full.

B31   Frank Dibb. "Italians in Oxford." *Music and Musicians* 8 (April 1960): 37.
PS's **string quartet [5]**—a picture in sound of life in the Australian "outback"—revealed a writer with vitality if without, as yet, strong structural discipline.

B32   "High award for young Launceston composer." *Examiner*, June 1960.
One of Australia's outstanding young musicians, PS, has won the Composers' Prize at Oxford for the second successive year, for **Sonata for Viola and Percussion**.
Also announced: "Tasmanian wins composers' contest," *Australian News*, June.

B33   J. F. Waterhouse. "Chamber music." *Birmingham Post*, [mid-] 1960.
For the 1960-61 season, the Birmingham Chamber Music Society has commisioned a new work from the very interesting young Australian composer PS, a **Piano Trio [Irkanda III]**, for the London Czech Trio. Also this season the Haydn Trio will present the first Birmingham performance of his **String Trio [The Loneliness of Bunjil]**.

B34   Don Chapman. "King Lear with all the obstacles." Oxford newspaper, October 1960.
Director of **King Lear** is to blame for allowing "such music." (*Other reviews:* PB, "A powerful 'King Lear'," finds the musique concrète battles an apt and satisfying innovation; and O. R. F. D., "Lear," mentions "concrètish dissonances".)

B35   Peter Sculthorpe. "Music: Miss Lutyens." *Oxford Magazine*, [Oct?] 1960.
Elizabeth Lutyens, distinguished composer and pioneer of dodecaphony in England, visited the Contemporary Music Club. We were very fortunate in being able to hear a recording of her String Quartet No. 6. She talked about her work (many quotes follow).

B36   "Composer has overseas commissions." Sydney, November 1960.
The 31-yr-old Australian composer PS arrived by BOAC comet in Sydney yesterday. There are more opportunities overseas, he said.
Also reported: "Back from U. K. studies," *Examiner*, 10 Nov.

B37   Franz Holford (ed.) "Peter Sculthorpe." *Canon* 14, nos. 6-7 (Jan-Feb 1961): 106.
PS recently returned to Australia from England where he became well known as composer (**The Loneliness of Bunjil, Sun, King Lear**), lecturer, and author.
"London Czech Trio impresses," *Times* [? Dec 1960] reviews **The Loneliness of Bunjil**.

B38   J. F. Waterhouse. "Four strings only." *Birmingham Post*, 10 Feb 1961.
PS's **Irkanda [I]** is well worth your hopeful attention. It might, I suppose, be generally described as "impressionistic," for its evocation of wilderness and solitude includes more than a hint of bird-calls and perhaps some echoes of festive *corroboree*.

B39   J. F. Waterhouse, "London Czech Trio: Mr. Sculthorpe again." *Birmingham Post*, 20 February 1961.
Like **The Loneliness of Bunjil**, introduced to Birmingham less than a month ago, and like the remarkable **Irkanda [I]**, the new Pianoforte Trio [**Irkanda III**] shows PS paralleling certain Australian painters in his evocation of aboriginal landscape; though in this case the primitive appears to be viewed remotely across a busy city foreground.

Waterhouse, ibid. [n.d.], also reviewed **The Loneliness of Bunjil.**

B40 "In Hobart this week. Local composer's success." *Mercury,* March 1961.
PS will make his first television appearance in Tasmania on March 14 at 3:45 as he fills the "In Hobart this Week chair in "Telewives' Time." He will play his latest composition and talk of his recent stay at Oxford University. (*Also announced* in the *Examiner* [n.d.]; and *mentioned* later in "Telewives Time is a year old" [n.d.].)

B41 E. E. Doherty. "Birmingham." *Musical Times* 102 (April 1961): 244.
A young Australian composer, PS, has shown solid achievement as well as promise in two works heard here recently—a striking one-movement work called **The Loneliness of Bunjil,** using quarter-tones, and a rather less compelling Piano Trio [Irkanda III].

B42 B. M. "Melbourne." *Canon* 14 (May/June/July 1961): 182.
One of the surprises of the present concert season was a first performance of PS's Irkanda IV. It is a fine work possessing remarkable strength and imagination.

B43 "News of the day." *Age,* 2 August 1961.
PS (shown in photo) wrote **Irkanda IV** in memory of his father who died two months ago. Aboriginal themes intrigue the composer, who is in Melbourne from Tasmania.
Other announcements: "Astra orchestra to play new work," *Listener-In,* 29 July; Sinclair, "All Australian music," *Herald,* 3 August.

B44 John Sinclair. "Surprise of the concert season." *Herald,* 7 August 1961.
Irkanda IV was the most exciting surprise. This first-rate work creates emotional intensity with great economy of means and the strictest discipline of technique.
Linda Phillips, "Crowded music," *Sun,* 7 August, does not mention **Irkanda IV.**

B45 Felix Werder. "First performance of Australian work." *Age,* 7 Aug 1961.
PS's new **Irkanda IV** is a truly Australian work with haunting writing and a warm melodic line. This young Australian composer, with his unconventional and intensely imaginative handling of basic ideas, and passionate and inspired musicianship, has an undoubted touch of genius. (Reviews by Sinclair and Werder are reported in Launceston in "Praise for musical work," *Examiner,* 10 August.)

B46 John Gilfedder. "Significant Tasmanian composer." *Advocate* (Melbourne), 10 August 1961.
Irkanda IV *sounds* Australian, yet personal and highly original. The solo line, with its striking "snap" interjections grows organically from germ-implications.

B47 Max Oldaker. "This music evokes Australia's loneliness." *Examiner,* 2 September 1961.
At Oxford, PS (pictured in a drawing signed McIntyre) was able to rationalize the chief source of his stimulus, that is, Australia, and to bring to his work a universal quality. Here in the quiet of Tasmania, he has time to evaluate modern European trends. **Irkanda IV,** acclaimed by Melbourne critics, shows the growth and extension of his vision.

B48 Gilbert Price. "New work in Melbourne." *Music and Musicians* 10 (October 1961): 32.
Irkanda IV revealed a new Australian composer of outstanding talent. The work is of a fine lyrical intensity achieved by purely musical means and without gimmicks.

B49 "Composer shows how he works." *Saturday Evening Mercury,* 7 October 1961.

Television program "Composer at Work" will follow the progress of an original work by Launceston composer PS (shown in photo) from the first stages of composition to its completion and public performance [**Irkanda IV**, arr. fl, viola, 'cello, and percussion]. (*Also announced:* a photo captioned "Launceston composer PS, whose work will be discussed in 'Spectrum,' October 12, at 9," *Examiner.*)

B50   David Simon. "Music in Melbourne . . . 1961." *Music and Dance* 52 (January 1962): 7-9.
Of the five new Australian works performed this season, pride of place might be justly given to PS's **Irkanda IV**, a first-rate piece, thoroughly contemporary in its language but timeless in the sincerity, directness and gravity of its feeling.

B51   Max Oldaker. "Two Australian composers." *The London Magazine* 2 (September 1962), "Australia" issue: 75-8.
Some of "the essential Australia" in modern music is found in the music of Margaret Sutherland (b. 1897) and PS. While critics have hailed **Irkanda IV** as "a truly Australian work," it has a greater universality.

B52   "Three Tasmanian composers." *Examiner*, September 1962.
Photo shows "Three Tasmanian composers who will be featured in performances of their own works in 'Music Room' from ABT2 on Friday night, September 7, at 9:30"— Felix Gethen, Ian Harris and PS, all looking at a large score on a piano.

B53   James Penberthy. "Rejected music praised." *Canberra Sunday Times*, 1962.
Tasmania's most interesting composer is young Launceston "bicycle shop [gun shop] proprietor" PS. He told me he has the usual difficulty in peddling his compositions in Australia; three that were rejected by the ABC were highly praised in London.

B54   "Prominent Australian composers." *Canon* 16 (Sept-Oct 1962): 42.
Under this heading appear photos of Sculthorpe (captioned, simply, "Peter Sculthorpe") and Dorian Le Gallienne.

B55   "News of the day." *Age*, 22 November 1962.
The theme for **They Found a Cave** [D72] is a waltz, a flexible little tune. From the way Mr. Sculthorpe whistled it across our desk yesterday, we think it should have a good chance of getting high up on the hit parade.
   Also: "Young stars in new fim," *Australian Women's Weekly*, 24 Oct,"Teenagers' Weekly" supplement (color photo on the cover shows the five Tasmanian teenagers who are the stars of the film; story mentions the film's music); and coverage of a party held in Launceston to celebrate the completion of filming.

B56   Max Oldaker. "Personal approach." *Examiner*, December 1962.
Three principals of the film **They Found a Cave** are Tasmanians—PS, author Nan Chauncy, and director Andrew Steane (of Hobart). Familiarity increases the haunting quality of the happy little waltz tune, available on disc [D72] and as sheet music.

B57   "Light relief from Bergmann's Hell." *Age*, 24 December 1962.
The lilting theme by PS for **They Found a Cave** is played by Larry Adler.
   Of the many other film reviews, only a few mention the music. " 'Cave' film makes Northern debut," *Examiner*, says that Sculthorpe attended the premiere last night.

B58   C. M. Prerauer. "Praise for Sculthorpe." *Nation*, 23 March 1963: 19-20.
Having written about Dreyfus and Meale [in "At the local," 20 Oct 1962], it is only fair to confess that at the time I was unaware of Launceston's PS. His **Irkanda IV** produces

the elation which overcomes one when one is face to face with a great work of art.
C.M. Prerauer, "Killing Time," ibid., 10 Aug: 21, refers to the new "modern" era of
Sculthorpe and Meale and others.

B59   "Music composers' fund requested." *Mercury,* 22 April 1963.
The first Australian composers' seminar yesterday made several recommendations to
bring Australian music into the sixties. Prof. D. R. Peart of Sydney said the majority of
Australian composers were out of touch with the rest of the world.
Covell, "Composers' 'exciting' seminar," *SMH,* 20 April, reports that the three most
interesting younger composers are Sitsky, Meale, and PS of Tasmania. (Oldaker, "High
cost of printing music handicaps our composers," *Examiner,* 27 March, had earlier
discussed some of the seminar's concerns.)

B60   John Sinclair. "Australian composer in contemporary society." *Music
and Dance* 53 (May/June 1963): 12-13.
Among the younger composers at the Hobart seminar, PS of Tasmania is by far the most
promising and accomplished.
Other coverage: Penberthy, "Composers' Seminar," ibid.: 13, 15; and "Composers'
Seminar," Report of the Adult Education Board, Hobart, Tasmania, 1963.

B61   Roger Covell. "New work in Great Hall." *SMH,* 31 July 1963: 10.
Irkanda IV last night momentously introduced to Sydney one of the major talents of
Australian composition in a work of passionate certainty of expression. Its throbbing
emotionalism speaks directly and immediately to any listener.

B62   "Award in memory of Alfred Hill." By the *Herald* music and drama
critics. *SMH,* 7 August 1963.
The Musica Viva committee's first commission went out last week to PS of Launceston
[for SQ 6].
Also announced in: Martin Long, "Two cheers for little orchestra," *Telegraph,* 7 Aug;
and "L'ton composer wins top award," *Examiner,* November 1963. The latter adds that
PS, recently appointed to Sydney University, has sent to Italy **The Fifth Continent.**
The Sydney University appointment is also mentioned in: "Oldaker's 'Prospero'
praised," *The Express* (Tasmania), 9 Nov: 12; and "Dixon's success in Hamburg," *SMH.*

B63   Max Oldaker. "Writing a symphony is arduous work." Launceston
Examiner, 17 August 1963.
The Fifth Continent, PS's most important orchestral work to date, is now taped and on
its way to Italy. Oldaker describes each of the five movements in some detail.

B64   [Roger Covell.] "Music in Australia." *Current Affairs Bulletin* 32, no. 8
(2 September 1963). P. 126.
PS of Tasmania, recently appointed to the Univ. of Sydney staff, has emerged from
experiments in total serialisation to write music of a personal intensity and lyricism
recalling Bloch or Bartok.

B65   Pleiades. "Tasmanian music at concert." *Mercury,* 24 September 1963.
PS's **Irkanda IV,** which represents the composer's feelings on the death of his father,
had a place in a programme which featured contemporary music.
Other performances: "Tasmanian composers in the 'spot'," *Examiner* (n.d.), refers to a
first perf of **Irkanda IV** by the Tasmanian Orch, conducted by Gethen, broadcast from
7ZR; and "Musicians will play together after 20 years," *Mercury* (n.d.), mentions that
violinist William Komlos visited Hobart and will take the **Irkanda IV** score to Europe.

B66   "Peter says farewell." *Women's Weekly,* 6 October 1963.

Before leaving for Sydney, PS will make his final appearance on Tasmanian television in "Women's World." Eileen Ralph will play a movement from his [**Sonata for Piano**].

B67   Fred R. Blanks. "Concert at Cell Block." *SMH*, 4 November 1963.
PS's **Piano Sonata** is pervaded by a sense of lonesomeness, and its chief virtue is a complete lack of anything superfluous.
    Wolfgang Wagner, "Top performance," *Sun*, 4 November, calls it an "interesting contribution." Pre-concert announcement appears in *SMH*, 30 October.

B68   Felix Werder. "Balanced playing by string group." *Age*, 11 Nov 1963.
The hauntingly beautiful **Irkanda IV** by the brilliant PS, is, in spite of its aboriginal title, a post-expressionist piece with elements of full-blooded romanticism.

B69   Pleiades. "Music and drama." *Mercury*, 14 December 1963.
The Fifth Continent possibly can be regarded as the nucleus of a full symphony as yet to be written. The third movement, *Small Town*, is first-class music, full of colour, warmth and originality, but is so short that the listener obtains only a superficial impression.
    Publicity: "Launceston composer's new work."

B70   [Art exhibition.] *Examiner*, 1964.
An exhibition of paintings by Geoffrey Stocks inspired by the music of **The Fifth Continent** [he heard it on tape in 1963] is opening in Launceston.

B71   C. M. Prerauer. "Words by D. H. Lawrence." *Nation*, 8 February 1964: 20.
The Fifth Continent is vigorous if somewhat lightweight. We are waiting for a really major work of PS, with large architectural dimensions.

B72   [Opera announcement.] *Telegraph*, 19 February 1964.
Two of Australia's brightest young composers are at the moment writing or preparing to write operas—Sculthorpe (if all goes well), to a libretto by Patrick White, and Meale.
    Ray Castle's column, ibid., 16 March, also discusses the opera plans.

B73   "Film music seminar." *Advertiser*, 8 March 1964.
PS will explain his film music **El Alamein Fountain** at the Australian Unesco Seminar on Music for Film this week. Seminar participants will compare three soundtracks.

B74   Peter Sculthorpe. "New and freer use of music." Australian Unesco Seminar: Music for Film [*Proceedings*]. Adelaide, 9-13 March 1964: 54-56.
Sculthorpe discusses, with illustrations, the use of *musique concrète* in commercial films, and in his own music—background music for a radio play in 1956, and the sound track for a short animated film *Man from Outer Space* (heard on tape).

B75   Robert Hughes. [Adelaide Festival.] *Sunday Mirror*, 15 March 1964.
I had to listen to a tape of PS's **The Fifth Continent** because the Adelaide Festival organizers have not scheduled a live performance. And Australian writers do no better.

B76   John Horner. "Work of 5 composers." *Advertiser*, 21 March 1964.
All five composers represented at the final ISCM concert at the Adelaide Festival were residents of Australasia. (*Other announcements* of **Irkanda IV**: "New compositions at the festival," *SMH*, 25 March; Long, "Off the beaten track," *Telegraph*, 26 Feb.)

B77   Joss Davies, ed. "Culture in Australia: Adelaide's Festival." *Current Affairs Bulletin* 33, no. 12 (27 April 1964): 190.
When PS submitted **The Fifth Continent** to the Adelaide Festival organizers, at the

BIBLIOGRAPHY 157

ABC's suggestion, there was no response. This kind of story explains the dearth of Australian works at the Festival.

B78 [Seminar announcement.] *Daily Telegraph,* Wednesday 20 May 1964.
A seminar "The Composer Speaks" will be presented by the University of Sydney. Four composers will address "Problems the Composer Faces": Dulcie Holland (traditional); PS and Eric Gross (middle-of-the-road); and Richard Meale (avant-garde).

B79 John Small. "Patrick White's opera: The advent of Peter Sculthorpe." *Bulletin,* 13 June 1964
Update on the opera commission includes a substantial interview of PS.
   Other news items about the opera include: "New works," ibid., 11 July; and "Australian opera commissioned, *SMH,* 4? July.

B80 Roger Covell, the "Herald" music critic. "New stature in creating." *SMH,* Monday 13 July 1964, "Australia Unlimited 1964" section.
Irkanda IV is among the new works that promise distinctive developments in Australian music. (Editorial: "How sophisticated are our audiences?" ibid., 4 July: 2, finds Sydney audiences sophisticated, and Meale and Sculthorpe distinctive composers.)

B81 Curt Prerauer. "Music—The conservatism of tomorrow." *Quadrant* 8 (August-September 1964): 56-60.
Now comes a breakthrough in Australian music history: two *resident* Australian composers have been heard at ISCM Festivals—Sculthorpe in 1955 and Meale in 1963.

B82 Roger Covell. "Recital at Cell Block." *SMH,* 15 August 1964.
PS's **Sonata for Viola and Percussion** is a rigorously static work. The sonata, the dry gongs and desert glare of its percussion encircling the lonely human agony of the viola, exists in a climate in which emotion is all the fiercer for being half-stifled and haltingly articulate. (*Publicity:* "Major work by Richard Meale," ibid., c10 Aug.)

B83 Martin Long. "Emotional depth in modernity." *Telegraph,* 15 Aug 1964.
The **Sonata for Viola and Percussion** suggests spacious loneliness. The impressionistic background of percussive sounds is effective until the climax when bass drum and cymbal overwhelm the viola. (*Publicity:* Long, "Opera House lesson," ibid., 5 Aug.)

B84 Kenneth Hince. "New music at the Cell Block." *Australian,* 17 Aug 1964.
Sonata for Viola and Percussion springs from a strong positive feeling for Australia.

B85 C. M. Prerauer. "A terse sonata." *Sun,* 17 August 1964.
The terse **Sonata for Viola and Percussion,** between two works of the Schoenberg style, proved the strong promise and conspicuous talent of the composer. The seemingly absurd combination of one viola and one percussion player achieves new tensions, with only a bit of purely conventional padding—about two bars each.

B86 "Composers search for an Australian music: Kenneth Hince interviews Peter Sculthorpe." *Australian,* Saturday 22 August 1964.
PS's **Sonata for Viola and Percussion** was performed last week between two serial works, where it shone like a good deed in a naughty world. He is in touch with the new image of Australia as an Asian continent.

B87 "Local composers need practical help." *SMH,* November 1964.
Irkanda IV score is the first of the long-heralded publications by the Australian Music

Fund. (*Also:* "L'ton composer gets music fund grant" [Hobart, early 1964].)

B88   "More Australian music published." By the "Herald" music and drama critics [Covell]. *SMH*, 28 December 1964.
The series entitled University of Sydney Music Publications has distinguished itself by producing an outstanding edition of PS's 1954 piano **Sonatina**.

B89   [Roger Covell.] "Australian composers, 1964: Emergence from a cult of musical cobwebs." By our music critic. *SMH*, 30 December 1964.
This was a year in which PS collected his thoughts for possible new departures rather than a time of significant achievement. (Another announcement, "Improvement seen in school music," *SMH* [n.d.], lists the subjects he will teach at Sydney University.)

B90   "Seven Australians receive awards to study in US." *Herald*, 30 December 1964.
Sculthorpe and six others have won Harkness Fellowships worth about £3,125-£3,500 a year for up to 21 months' study and travel in the US.
Other announcements: "Fellowships for two lecturers," *Telegraph*, 30 Dec; "7 fellowships for study in the US," *Australian*, 30 Dec; and "US Award for L'ton composer," *Examiner*, Jan 1965.

B91   C. M. Prerauer. "Scores in print." *Nation*, 23 January 1965.
In the newly-published score of PS's **Sonatina** a strong sense of sound-colour is evident, with characteristic percussive rhythm. After ten years it has lost nothing of its freshness and originality.
Another review: "Cugley faces the music," *Honi Soit*, 9 March 1965.

B92   Martin Long. "Society is going national." *Telegraph*, 27 Jan 1965.
The Australian section of the ISCM submitted **The Loneliness of Bunjil** for Madrid in May. Sculthorpe handed over the music for his new **string quartet [no. 6]** to Musica Viva at a small ceremony at the society's George St. headquarters last night.

B93   [**Irkanda III** review.] *La Prensa* (Barcelona, trans.), 10 February 1965.
In this work we find combined a primeval ruggedness, the grandeur of the forces of nature, and a rough, strong poetry which does not exclude delicacy and tenderness.
Other Barcelona reviews: *Vanguardia*, 10 Feb (an acute and cleverly developed composition); and *Diario de Barcelona*, 11 Feb (this short piece tortured us).

B94   "Sculthorpe quartet for Musica Viva." By the "Herald" music and drama critics. *SMH*, 24 March 1965.
SQ 6 is written in a directly communicative and passionately lyrical style.
Long, "April begins well for Australian composers," *Telegraph*, 3 March, also announces the premiere.

B95   Franz Holford (ed.) "Musica Viva." *Canon* 17, no. 2 (April 1965): 2.
PS's elegaic **SQ 6** had a notable first performance full of expressive intensity.
The *Musica Viva* newsletter, 1 April, also includes a long article on the work.

B96   Roger Covell. "Quartet plays Sculthorpe." *SMH*, 2 April 1965.
SQ 6 speaks its mind and heart with rare immediacy and eloquence. PS has constructed the three movements out of motives bearing an ancient weight of human reference.

B97   Frank Harris. "It's music for the export list." *Daily Mirror*, 2 April 1965.
Musica Viva, which has been importing the best quartets for years, offered music worth

exporting at the Town Hall last night. The highlight was PS's new SQ 6.

B98   Martin Long. "Premiere of new work." *Telegraph*, 2 April 1965.
PS's SQ 6 uses an original and untraditional language, yet is lucid and direct enough to communicate to an audience accustomed to traditional fare.

B99   Julian Russell. "A lucid, eloquent quartet." *Sun*, 2 April 1965.
PS's moving SQ 6 is at once lucid and eloquent in its part writing. Although free use was made of atonal licence, the work was always firmly in a tonal climate.

B100 Kenneth Hince. "New quartet has warmth and melodic line." *Australian*, 3 April 1965.
PS calls his new SQ 6 "freely atonal" but it is far from forbidding. "Freely tonal" might be a better tag. The warm and intense score was open-heartedly applauded.

B101 David Salter. "Sculthorpe's Quartet." *Honi Soit*, 14 April 1965.
SQ 6 can be enjoyed as well as "appreciated." The work's movements are in a slow-quick-slow form, dominated by brooding melody over a very sparse harmonic structure.
   "LP record to aid world refugees." *SMH*, 14 April, notes that Musica Viva is flying Sculthorpe to Melbourne at the end of next week for its performance there.

B102 Kenneth Hince. "Melodic Easter in a girls' school." *Australian*, Saturday 24 April 1965.
PS's moving SQ 6 was received with spontaneous warmth at Mittagong. Covell's "Composers and their music," with Sculthorpe, Butterley, Meale, and Eric Gross, aimed at closer relations between Australian audiences and Australian music.
   Long, "A singalong with Bach," *Telegraph*, 14 April, announces the concert and panel discussion.

B103 Jack Kunst. "Sculthorpe's busy schedule." *Bulletin*, 24 April 1965: 48-9.
Very few knowledgeable observers of the international music scene have failed to recognise 35-year-old bachelor PS as one of the most important of our composers. He says that he himself cannot quite fathom his music's intangible "Australian idiom."

B104 Felix Werder. "Quartet gets big ovation." *Age*, 27 April 1965.
SQ 6 is a tense work, ruthlessly overpowering in its emotional arguments and reflecting a strongly romantic approach—a Jeremiah-like strength—to the problems of the lost individual in a world facing desolation.
   Linda Phillips, "Musica Viva begins subscription series," *Sun*, notes that the composer was present to receive the "ovation he rightly deserved." *Pre-concert announcements:* Sinclair, "String quartet by society"; Werder, "Chamber music season."

B105 "Australian works on record." By "Herald" critics. *SMH*, 5 May 1965.
Rehearsals start this morning at the ABC Studio in Chatswood for the recording of SQ 6 [D54]. South by Five will be performed at the UNESCO seminar.

B106 Martin Long. "The staff of music." *Daily Telegraph*, 12 May 1965.
PS's music is included in three UNESCO projects which should give valuable aid and encouragement to Australian composers: the seminar on school music; the International Rostrum of Composers; and the Foundation for Recording Australian Music [D54].

B107 Roger Covell. "New music for young people." *SMH*, 22 May 1965.
South by Five has unabashedly traditional melodic shapes, and a softly glimmering atmosphere.
   Also mentioned in: Covell, "Demand for a better system of teaching in schools,"

ibid., 15 June; and pre-seminar publicity, such as "Fame of a former music teacher."

B108 Martin Long. "Conservatorium: School music. Tempo too slow for young fry." *Daily Telegraph*, 22 May 1965.
South by Five used a relatively traditional idiom in a fresh and appealing way.

B109 C. M. Prerauer. "Brilliant Bartok." *Sun*, 24 May 1965.
South by Five was charmingly persuasive and beautifully sung.

B110 "Composers 'well received.' " *SMH*, 2 June 1965.
Richard Meale reports (through A. A. P.-Reuter) that works by Sculthorpe, Dreyfus, Butterley, and Meale are doing well at the tenth International Rostrum of composers in Paris. (Editorial, "Australian music abroad," ibid., applauds the news.)
Another report: Long, "Opera's hard times," *Telegraph*, 2 June.

B111 Martin Collins. "Martin Collins turns up an Opera House problem." *Australian*, Saturday 5 June 1965.
PS wants a simple libretto and Patrick White's first drafts are said to be nothing like that. White has been replaced by historian Alan Moorehead and critic Roger Covell.
(*Other reports on the opera in progress:* "Mrs. Fraser for the opera house?" [*Age*?]; Long, "Australian works for London concert," *Telegraph*, 9 June.)

B112 Roger Covell. "Sculthorpe's **Irkanda IV**." *SMH*, 9 June 1965.
The performance made many listeners wonder at the neglect of the passionately accented elegy, one of the few totally satisfying achievements in Australian music.

B113 Martin Long. "Deputy fills in at concert." *Telegraph*, 9 June 1965.
Irkanda IV was a little tentative at first, then increased in intensity.

B114 Roger Covell. "Meale brings good news." *SMH*, 17 June 1965.
PS's SQ 6 won enough votes at the Paris Rostrum to be "on the list."

B115 Felix Gethen. "Arcadia Australis: A survey of the Tasmanian musical scene." *Canon* 17, no. 5 (1965): 4-8.
I am proud to have been helpful in promoting performances of PS's works in Tasmania. His move to Sydney was a gain for NSW, a loss for Tasmania.

B116 Franz Holford. "Gramophone Records. Australian Music Today, on record." *Canon* 17, no. 6 (1965): 21-3.
The personalized emotions and lonely quality of PS's SQ 6 [D54] give it an unconscious completeness. There is a strength and simple truthfulness about it.

B117 Roger Covell. "Festival overture ready." *SMH*, 19 August 1965.
PS finished his overture **Sun Music** and delivered the full score this week to conductor Sir Bernard Heinze. The several sections of unusual scoring are intended to produce sounds related to electronic music and musique concrète.
  Commonwealth Festival plans are also reported in: Covell, "Music appointment in London," *SMH*, 10 June 1965; and Long, "A two-way test," *Telegraph*, 14 July.

B118 Wilfrid Mellers. "Antipodal." *New Statesman*, 4 September 1965: 458.
Australia has become a creative "presence." At the Univ. of Sydney, Mellers and Maxwell Davies found PS's composition class enthusiastically writing and performing remarkable serial compositions, and the oriental music class creating their own Japanese music. Australia's future must lie with an acceptance of Asia and a partial rejection of

Europe, or at least the moribund British tradition—as will be heard in **Sun Music.**

B119   Larry Sitsky. "Reports. Australia. Emergence of the new music in Australia." *Perspectives of New Music* 4 (1965): 176-9.
PS, coming to the US next year, has a large body of work. But there is very little "American" influence heard or admitted in our music.

B120   Gerald Larner. "Austral String Quartet at the Town Hall, Liverpool." Manchester *Guardian*, 24 September 1965.
In SQ 6 (Sept 23) PS is impressive in slow movements when he is himself.
    In Sydney, "Quartet to perform in Britain," *SMH*, 29 May, announced the concerts; "Chamber quartets praised" quotes UK reviews.

B121   Dr. W. Lovelock. "Big variation in concert's quality." *Courier-Mail*, 28 September 1965.
Irkanda IV was "way out" and effective, despite its unrelieved gloom. A better performance would have made it more convincing.

B122   "Two intriguing quartets by Australians." London *Times*, 29 Sept 1965.
SQ 6 has a lucid structural logic and an attractive clarity of sound. The outer scherzando sections of the central movement seem to contain the strongest invention.
    "Australian opera commissioned," ibid., 28 Sept: 13, announces PS's year-end visit.

B123   Roger Covell. "Australian music goes on record." *SMH*, 30 Sept 1965.
The issue of *Australian Music Today* [D54] is one of the most important events in the history of Australian music—and this is only a moderate estimate.

B124   "Wide range of Australian music." London *Times*, 1 October 1965.
As a study in atmospheric sonority, **Sun Music** is a strikingly imaginative aural achievement.

B125   David Cairns. "Sydney Symphony Orchestra." *Financial Times*, 1 October 1965.
Sun Music is a powerfully evocative piece—a coherent and fascinating and sometimes beautiful piece of music. A string quartet by Sculthorpe was performed earlier this week and very well spoken of. He is clearly a talent.

B126   Neville Cardus. "Australian music at the Festival Hall." *Guardian*, 1 October 1965.
Sun Music is calculated to convey impressions of sub-tropical sun, all changed into tonal effects which stimulate the visual almost as much as the aural senses. Maybe, after Sculthorpe has shed one or two acquired sophistications, or truly drawn them into his instinctive way of feeling and thinking in music, he will lay the foundations of an original and characteristic Australian music. (Quoted in the *SMH*, 2 Oct.)

B127   Noël Goodwin. "Sun Music has 'ear appeal.' " *Daily Express* (London), 1 October 1965.
PS seems to me to be a new musical name decidedly worth remembering. His **Sun Music** possesses a distinctive character and, what is more, ear-appeal.

B128   Arthur Jacobs. "A delicate bit of fist." [*Sunday Times*?], October 1965.
Mr. Sculthorpe, still under 40, is no mere cultivator of freakish effects. His **Sun Music** has shape and delicacy. Sculthorpe's **SQ 6** was even better than **Sun Music.** (Another Jacobs review is "Successful Festival," 8 October.)

B129 Colin Mason. "Influence of electronic music." *Daily Telegraph* (London), 1 October 1965.
Sun Music has considerable interest as a sequence of experimental orchestral sounds. It reveals an orchestral and musical imagination of which it is worth taking account.

B130 Eric Mason. "A gong throbs with quiet menace." *Daily Mail* (London), 1 October 1965.
In Sun Music a gong throbbed with quiet menace, violins were bowed unconventionally, and electronic-type noises were ingeniously extracted from the horns. Effective, I thought, and not least because it stopped before monotony could set in.

B131 Roger Covell. "Orchestra assertive." *SMH*, 1 October 1965.
Concertgoers struggled through a traffic jam and heavy rain. Sun Music received the most encouraging and unanimous reception of a new work during the whole festival.
Covell reports the next day ("Our orchestra in vigorous mood," *SMH*, 2 Oct) that Sun Music provided the program with genuine distinction.

B132 Peter Grose. "Flop for festival finale." *Australian*, 2 October 1965.
Sun Music was a flop; the hall was two-thirds full and the piece drew only a polite response.

B133 Martin Long. "Sun Music was real scorcher." *Daily Telegraph* (Sydney), 2 October 1965.
Long reports that the audience was "baffled" and he quotes from the London press. (He also prints an interview with conductor John Hopkins.)

B134 Meirion Bowen. "Light from Nigeria." *Observer*, 3 October 1965.
Sun Music had lots of far-out sounds which just didn't *tell*, for all their ingenuity. And the sixth SQ (on Tuesday) sounded also like etiolated Bartok or Schoenberg.
Sun Music is also reviewed by: Felix Aprahamian, "Acclaim for Ozawa"; Judith Eddie, Launceston *Examiner*, 30 Sept; the *Sun* and other Sydney papers (A.A.P. reports with headlines like "Orchestra acclaimed" and "Crowd wild with delight"); John Warrack, "Truly national opera," 3 Oct; Julian Exner, "Das Commonwealth tanzt, singt und spielt," *Der Tagespiegel*, 9 October (mentions the "höchst modernen Sonnenmusik); and "Orchestra a big hit," *Sun Telegraph* (interviews Hopkins upon his return).

B135 "Australian composer wins UK contract." *Daily Telegraph* (Sydney), Monday 4 October 1965.
The London house of Faber and Faber has contracted to publish Sculthorpe's works.
Other announcements: "Publisher for music in London," *Age*, 4 Oct; "Contract for composer," *SMH*, 7 Oct; "Australian Composer Signs New Contract," *Canon* 17, no. 6 (1965): 28 (with photo); and "Composer's top contract," *Canberra Times*, 1 Feb 1966: 15, quoting from a "recent" *APRA Journal*.

B136 C. M. Prerauer. "The SSO on trial." *Nation*, 16 October 1965: 20.
In Sun Music (heard on radio broadcast) PS does not fulfill his great promise. When he writes his first great work after his excellent Sixth Quartet, I shall be ready to cheer.

B137 John Sinclair. "Creative songs fresh, vital." *Herald*, 22 October 1965.
Last night's important concert included a fine Sonata for Viola and Percussion by PS.

B138 Felix Werder. "20th century concert." *Age*, 22 October 1965.
Sonata for Viola and Percussion finds PS in a sober, meditative mood. Like a true romantic he builds organic bridges out of passionate sound blocks.

B139 "Editorial Notes." *The Strad* 76 (November 1965): 253.
Sun Music surprised us with the authentic flavour of that country. If gimmickry, it was gimmickry in the service of an individual talent of what we hope developing powers.

B140 George Montagu. "Commonwealth Arts Festival." *Musical Opinion* 89 (November 1965): 85.
PS's Sun Music is certainly an extremely original and intriguing piece of writing, containing some striking sonorities and unusual qualities of tone.

B141 F. R. Blanks. "Quartet recital." *SMH*, 13 November 1965.
Further hearings of PS's SQ 6 have familiarised its very beautiful and distinctive tonal palette. The prominent use of lower strings and long-held notes makes this a weighty, sombre, reflective work, emotionally sincere and unified. (*Pre-concert publicity*: "Chamber music recital," *SMH*, 9 Nov.)

B142 David Salter. "Polished work of players." *Telegraph*, 13 Nov 1965.
Beneath its apparently conventional atonal surface, SQ 6 is a rawly emotional record of desolation, loneliness and intense personal experience.

B143 Jack Kunst. "Catching the world's ear." *Bulletin*, 13 Nov 1965: 48.
One of the most significant events in Australian music for many years is the two-volume *Australian Music Today* [D54]; contents include PS's SQ 6.
Also: Kenneth Robins, "Musical landmark"(SQ 6 "is a beautiful work and may well be a great work"); and "Australian National Music Committee: Report 1965-66," *World of Music* (International Music Council, UNESCO) 8 (Jan-Feb 1966): 38 (describes for its international readers the recording's production and distribution).

B144 C. M. Prerauer. "Exciting." *Sun*, Monday 15 November 1965.
SQ 6 (Nov 12), which was magnificently performed, remains in my view Sculthorpe's best work to date.

B145 Romola Costantino. "Recital at Cell Block." *SMH*, 19 November 1965.
To hear a work for the first time and to be immediately convinced of its outstanding qualities is an astonishing sensation; this was the effect of PS's 1955 Irkanda I.

B146 C. M. Prerauer. "Sensitive violin." *Sun* 19 November 1965.
The main novelty on Betty Jaggard's atrociously difficult program was a fine and deeply expressive solo for unaccompanied violin—PS's Irkanda I.

B147 David Salter. "A violinist of youth, energy." *Telegraph*, 19 Nov 1965.
In Irkanda I the unmistakable "Australian loneliness" of PS's compositions is much in evidence. Miss Jaggard was at her best in this demanding piece.

B148 Frank Harris. "Sun Music rising." *Mirror*, Tuesday 23 November 1965.
Sculthorpe, interviewed in his Woollahra studio before this week's Hobart performance of Sun Music by the MSO, says, "I have always been a sun worshipper. The sun is my god. Sun-baking is just the physical expression of something deeper."

B149 Pleiades."Exciting stage of festival." *Mercury*, 25 November 1965.
Sun Music last night impressed by its esoteric approach to contemporary music, and technically was of great interest. (Pleiades, "Hobart performance first in Australia," ibid., 23 Nov, announces the concert.)

B150 "A party goes on camera." *Sun*, 25 November 1965.

Farewell party for "Sydney music man" PS (shown in photo) was held at Sydney's
Darlinghurst Gallery and filmed for inclusion in a portrait study.

B151   C. M. Prerauer. "On the record." *Nation*, 27 November 1965: 18.
To hear PS's **SQ 6** straight after Meale, on *Australian Music Today* [**D54**], points up the
diametrical contrast of their musical aims.

B152   [Henry Raynor.] "Australian composer with something new to say."
London *Times*, 29 December 1965.
A little conversation with Mr. PS is enough completely to explode the myth of the
New World's (the Commonwealth people's) artistic dependence on the Old. The com-
poser of **Sun Music**, briefly in London on the way to the US, said that his intention is to
compose music which is definitely Australian because his experience is all Australian.
   Raynor's interview is widely quoted, as in: "Sculthorpe's new world," *Canberra
Times*, 30 Dec; "All their own work," *Bulletin*, 8 Jan 1966; "Peter Sculthorpe: Australian Composer," *Faber Music News*, Autumn 1966: 29-32; and **B326** in 1970.

B153   Craig McGregor. *Profile of Australia* (1966). Harmondsworth, England:
Penguin Books, 1968.
(P. 250:) PS is in the younger, avant-garde generation of composers well known to
critics, musicians, and enthusiasts, but now reaching a wider audience.

B154   Robert B. Goodman (photographer) and George Johnston (writer). *The
Australians*. Adelaide: Rigby, 1966.
Chapter "The Arts" speaks of a cultural revolution in Australia (p. 211), with a photo
of PS (p. 234), who is planning to write an original all-Australian opera-ballet.

B155   Felix Gethen. "Profile of Peter Sculthorpe." *Tasmanian Architect*, February 1966: 42-3.
I know that at heart Sculthorpe wants to do something big for Australian music, for
the great continent itself which he loves passionately and intensely.

B156   Roger Covell. " 'Sun Music' shines on first Prom." *SMH*, 12 Feb 1966.
Sun Music [I] is still a fascinating collage of sounds. The audience, predominantly young
and casually dressed, was attentive and enthusiastic.

B157   Martin Long. "New work for Proms." *Telegraph*, 12 February 1966.
Sun Music is a fascinating but only three-quarters successful, exploration of orchestral
atmospherics.

B158   Julian Russell. "No lustre at the Proms." *Sun*, 14 February 1966.
The Prom audience was predominantly youthful and generously responsive. Despite
the handicap of a hall full of dead, wet February air, **Sun Music** glared and brooded.

B159   C. M. Prerauer. "Nights at the Prom." *Nation*, 19 February 1966: 21-22.
Sun Music sounded like a more modern version of what Sculthorpe had already stated
in his **Fifth Continent**.

B160   Paul Frolich. "As good as a feast." *Bulletin*, 26 February 1966.
Sun Music improves with every hearing. From the first three Sydney Promenade concerts, only **Sun Music** emerged as wholly satisfactory.

B161   Donald Peart. "Asian music in an Australian university." *Hemisphere* 10 (March 1966): 13-17.

Australia is a meeting place of Eastern and Western cultures because of its central geographical position. PS's University of Sydney classes in composition are closely related to his classes in Asian and Polynesian music.

B162 Donald R. Peart. "Some recent developments in Australian composition." *Composer* (London), no. 19 (Spring 1966): 73, 75, 77-8.
The most important development during the past five years has been the sudden appearance of an *avant-garde* of Meale, Sculthorpe (SQ 6 is described), and Dreyfus.
Frank Callaway, "Some aspects of music in Australia," ibid.: 81, mentions the opera commission.

B163 John Wesley Barker. "Contemporary NSW 'firsts.' " *Advertiser*, 14 March 1966.
Sun Music for Voices and Percussion is a study in pure sound without any definite implications of pitch. It was pleasing to have a repeat performance to end the programme.
Craig McGregor, "Our best festival, but ... Adelaide needs more of the Australian arts," *SMH*, 11 Dec 1965, previewed the 1966 festival.

B164 Roger Covell. "Sculthorpe quartet gets prompt printing." *SMH*, 30 April 1966.
Printed copies of PS's SQ 6 arrived from London by air this week. Now, with the score and the recording, students have as much first-hand equipment for exploring an Australian work as for an established European one.

B165 Frank Harris. "It's new, strange and true." *Mirror*, 11 May 1966.
Sun Music for Voices and Percussion was strange music, but it made instant communication with its scalp-prickling excitement. There was an absolute rightness about every sound which marks PS as a major composer. The same quality was evident in Irkanda I.

B166 Martin Long, "No compromise with tradition." *Telegraph*, 11 May 1966.
Sun Music for Voices and Percussion is about as uncompromising in its radicalism as any piece of music yet heard from an Australian composer. Irkanda I seemed somewhat uneven, some of it effective and some harshly provocative.

B167 Julian Russell. "Is this music?" *Sun*, 11 May 1966.
In Sun Music for Voices and Percussion PS, the gifted young Australian, foresook music to experiment with extra-musical sounds. Irkanda I is slightly more accessible.

B168 Roger Covell. "Sweet and sour." *SMH*, Thursday 12 May 1966: 11.
Betty Jaggard was relatively at ease in Irkanda I. Sun Music for Voices and Percussion is a striking instance of the composer's ear for the sweet-and-sour possibilities of sonority. It is also a new kind of musical theatre for the concert hall—and strongly emotional as well. (*Announcement*: "Sculthorpe works for concert," ibid., 9 May: 7.)

B169 C. M. Prerauer. "Joke in the sun." *Nation*, 28 May 1966: 20.
I think too much of PS's potentialities to take his Sun Music for Voices and Percussion as anything but a joke, reasonably clever, the old trick of noise in the manner of Antheil. On disappointingly mild applause, the joke was told all over again.

B170 Alexander Macdonald. "Hybrid monsters and the ABC." *Daily Mirror*, 27 May 1966.
PS's SQ6 [D54], broadcast last Saturday, sounded suspiciously like someone plucking a barbed wire fence with the tines of a pitchfork, and simultaneously striking an

upturned bucket with a crowbar—a long and oppressive experiment in abstract sound.

B171 Robert Henderson. "Peter Sculthorpe." *Musical Times* 107 (1966): 594-5.
A distinctive Australian character is most fully developed in the work of PS (shown in photo). **Night Piece** (this month's supplement), is his "atomic age nocturne."

B172 C. M. "Norfolk music." *Lakeville [CT] Journal*, 28 July 1966.
Teotihuacan is a tense, well-integrated piece with a clearly outlined form.

B173 George W. Stone. "Norfolk hosts Friday night music program." *Hartford [CT] Times*, 30 July 1966.
SQ 7 was full of glissandi effects that suggested an air-raid siren or the din of city traffic. And it provided a technical challenge that the players handled beautifully.

B174 Malcolm Macdonald. "Australian Music Today, Vols. 1 and 2." *Gramophone* 44 (September 1966): 182.
PS's SQ 6 (D54) is a mature, impassioned work by a composer who has been through various serial techniques and emerged unscathed on the other side.

B175 Roger Covell. "Australian's score printed with a Drysdale cover." *SMH*, 4 October 1966.
Faber Music have blessed **Sun Music I** with clean, spacious typography (four measures are reproduced here as illustration) and a magnificent cover (shown in photo) by Russell Drysdale—a burnt orange sun. This score is unusual and experimental; a separate page is needed to list these unusual symbols and their meanings.

B176 Alun Hoddinott. "Deep symphony." *Western Mail* (Wales).
Sun Music I relies entirely on sound-structure and so a mere reading of the score makes any assessment of the music an impossibility. SQ 6, beautifully written, shows musical gifts of a substantial nature, and a capricious and inventive creativity.

B177 Donald R. Peart. "The Australian Avant Garde." *Proceedings of the Royal Musical Association* 93 (16 November 1966): 1-9.
Sculthorpe, Meale, and Dreyfus from 1960 onwards may fairly be held to constitute an "avant-garde" among Australian composers. PS's music is essentially "world music."

B178 Felix Werder. "Brilliant work by Australian." *Age*, 19 November 1966.
"Sun Music III for string orchestra" is a new work by the brilliant Australian composer PS. A true romantic, he uses music not to express an emotion but to describe one.

B179 John Gilfedder. "Stimulating program by Astra." *Sun*, 19 November 1966.
The powerful modern "Sun Music III" contributed to a bracing second half.

B180 Eileen Geary. "Australian work was dazzling." *Advocate*, 24 Nov 1966.
"Sun Music for strings" flashed into the deep consciousness of listeners with the brilliance of a comet. It evokes the vast beyond of our country, the timeless dreamland.

B181 Kenneth Hince. "The sweet sound of a musical breakthrough." *Australian*, 19 November 1966.
FRAM it's called [D31], and the inclusion of PS's **Irkanda IV** and **Sun Music I** puts on record for the first time the major orchestral music of one of the young musicians effecting a rapprochement between Australian music and modern European music.
Other reviews: Sinclair, *Herald*; Leo Stevens, *Age*; "Stradivarius," *Sunday*

Telegraph; Tidemann, *Advertiser;* and the Brisbane *Telegraph* (all quoted in the publicity brochure).

B182 Roger Covell. "Orchestra tops the 1966 bill." *SMH,* 31 December 1966: 8.
Sun Music I was the piece with the most rewarding circulation of all.

B183 Helen Bainton. *Facing the Music: An orchestral player's notebook.* Sydney: Currawong, 1967.
Member of SSO recalls that at Sun Music premiere in London, instructions for the required new instrumental techniques were pinned to players' parts.

B184 Roger Covell. *Australia's Music: Themes of a new society.* Melbourne: Sun Books, 1967. P. 139, 187, 200-211, 229, 234, 266, 335-7.
Covell reviews PS's work to Sun Music IV, with seven musical illustrations. (*Book review:* Blanks, "New music with some cautious notes," *The Bridge,* June 1968: 17-20.)

B185 Ian Cugley. "Peter J. Sculthorpe: An analysis of his music." *Arna* (1967): 49-56.
PS's Sun Music series began perhaps a new period and style for him. Irkanda IV and SQ 6 prepared the way, with certain style characteristics (illustrated in 13 examples).

B186 Arthur Jacobs. *A New Dictionary of Music.* Penguin Reference Books. 2nd edn; Harmondsworth: Penguin, 1967. P. 342.
Entry identifies Peter Sculthorpe, b. 1929, as "Australian composer of Sun Music for orchestra, six string quartets, etc."

B187 C. M. Prerauer. "Before the Promenade." *Nation,* 28 January 1967.
A copy of the recent Faber publication of Morning Song for the Christ Child has reached me a little belatedly. The music has a pretty bell effect.

B188 Roger Covell. "The still centre of Mahler." *SMH,* 17 February 1967: 9.
Despite a lack of passion in the playing of Irkanda IV, the performance established, even if only fitfully, the memorable climate of this work. Ian Cugley's Pan, the Lake, which followed, irrigates the parched, lonely agony of Irkanda IV.

B189 Martin Long. "Music to make friends. *Telegraph,* 17 February 1967.
Hazelwood was a tensely effective soloist in PS's moving threnody Irkanda IV.

B190 Julian Russell. "A refusal to sparkle." *Sun,* 17 February 1967.
Irkanda IV's indebtedness to Bloch is even more marked the better one gets to know the piece. (Salter, "Missing the target," *Bulletin,* 4 March: 34-35, finds that Irkanda IV is still the finest Australian work of this decade.)

B191 "Reviews of new music. Peter Sculthorpe: **String Quartet No. 6.**" *Musical Opinion* 90 (March 1967): 327.
SQ 6 contains some concentrated musical thought, if little to charm or beguile. My impression is of a composer who is striving too hard for originality, and is determined to suppress a Romantic in him. (Review is unsigned; editor is Laurence Swinyard.)

B192 "Music seminar at Devonport." *Mercury,* March 1967.
PS, just returned from the US, spoke last night on "A new approach to aural training." Tonight he will lecture on "A new approach to music notation." (*Also announced:* "Composer gives music teachers new approach," *Examiner.*)
"Beethoven and Mozart regret" [n.d.], announces that PS will speak in Abbotsleigh

for the 40th anniversary of the Wahroonga Music Club.

B193   "Sculthorpe technique in **Irkanda**." By our London music critic. *Glasgow Herald,* 16 March 1967.
The short and funereal piece, **Irkanda IV**, like most of Sculthorpe's music that is known in this country, is strongly impressionistic. Blocks of sound are placed side by side in a manner that precludes organic growth.
Also reviewed: "Individual character in new work," London [*Times?*], 16 March (it showed an acute ear for orchestral sonority and a sure sense of formal requirements).

B194   Sally Trethowan. "Young musician again wins A.B.C. concert." *West Australian,* 17 May 1967: 15.
Anniversary Music is a skilfully contrived fabric of interesting sonorities, many of them percussive in origin.

B195   David Salter. "Sculthorpe's taste of money." *Bulletin,* 29 April 1967: 38.
PS has returned from the US a more widely recognised composer. While at Yale, he observed that money—"dough"—is the big thing in the American arts and academic climate. Now the relatively relaxed pace of Australian academic life allows him to do both teaching and composing. To him, Australia is the "last paradise."
Covell, "Commissions for composers," *SMH,* April, announces the APRA Music Foundation commission for **Sun Music IV**.

B196   Linda Phillips. "Orchestra gives farewell concert." *Sun,* 30 May 1967.
Sun Music IV captured much of the remoteness and loneliness of the Australian deep-heart country; many novel effects enhanced the eerie feeling of heat and stillness. The work was well received and the composer took the acknowledgement.

B197   John Sinclair. "An odd sound in our Expo music." *Herald,* 30 May 1967.
Sun Music IV is a brief and extremely clever essay in orchestral textures.

B198   Felix Werder. "Sober view of the score." *Age,* 30 May 1967.
Sun Music IV is a serious and thoroughly composed piece, an original voice creating an onomatopoetic music. Van Otterloo took a sober view of the score.
Other advance news about Montreal mentions PS: Werder, "Expo exports: Showing the world our mettle," ibid; and "Brilliance all the way," *Age* (n.d.).

B199   Kenenth Hince. "A smooth musical reshuffle on the eve of the grand tour." *Australian,* 2 June 1967.
Sun Music IV did resound with the sense of singing the composer wants. It is an essay in the physical face of Australia beaten, like brass under the hammer, by harshly concentrated light: music which is almost impossibly stark and flat. (*Announcement:* "A small slice of home," ibid., 27 May, deplores the small Australian content.)

B200   Roger Covell. "Australian composers win votes in Paris. *SMH,* 7 June 1967.
Because **Sun Music I** placed in last year's voting at the Paris Rostrum, it has had seven broadcasts in various European centres.

B201   John Horner. "Anniversary concert." *Advertiser,* 7 June 1967: 24.
Sir Bernard Heinze's musically illustrated chat about **Anniversary Music** had us all agog to hear it. Better yet, his enthusiasm turned out to be fully justified.
Publicity: "Founder honored," ibid., 6 June, includes a photo of Heinze being greeted

at the Adelaide airport; PS recalled his first "live" contact with orchestral music at a youth concert conducted by Heinze nearly 20 years ago.

B202 Stewart Cockburn. "Final flare from Mr. Sculthorpe." [Adelaide], *c*10 June 1967.
PS is still delighted and a little dazed by the ASO's performance of—and the ecstatic audience reaction to—**Anniversary Music**. "I would rather listen to the Beatles than to a large part of 19th-century European music," he says—a final flare of provocation.

B203 "Australians close visit." *The Gazette* (Montreal), 7 June 1967.
Sun Music IV is a brief evocation of the broiling sun on desert sands, of distorted light waves, of parched earth and man. The piece has intensity and inner heat.

B204 Jacques Theriault. "L'Orchestre de Melbourne se surpasse." *Le Devoir* (Montréal), 7 June 1967.
Sun Music IV demonstrated a manifest desire to create an original work, even if we have a reservation about the excessive use of prolonged sonorities.

B205 Howard Klein. "Music: 2d Australian night at EXPO 67." *New York Times*, Thursday 8 June 1967.
PS's Varèse-like **Sun Music IV** had tonal patches here and there, but most of its eight minutes contained the sound effects current among avant-garde composers.
Also: "At the end of a wonderful day." *SMH*, 8 June (**Sun Music IV** was a highlight of Australian events); and Don Riseborough, "Mixed feelings at debut." ibid., 9 June (quotes Klein).

B206 Edward Sheil. "Spectacular day for Australia at Expo 67." *Telegraph*, 9 June 1967.
The Canadian music critics all agreed in their praise of **Sun Music IV**. Eric McLean in the Montreal *Star* described it as "a real ear-opener."

B207 John Cargher. "Collier's return." *Bulletin*, 10 June 1967: 46.
PS seems the only genuinely original talent in Australian music. With **Sun Music IV** the question is whether he has not by now explored all that can be explored in his method of sound picture painting. (Small color photo of PS, ibid.: 12, is captioned "one of the few Australian academics internationally recognised for his work.")

B208 James Renfrey. [ISCM report.] *The News* (Adelaide), 31 July 1967.
PS's charming informality proved a very good method of letting us into the secret of some of his mental processes of composition. A recording of [**Sun**] was played, then **Sun Music I** and **Sun Music IV** against a golden lighted curtain, and live performances of the **Sonata for Viola and Percussion** and **SQ 6**. (*Announcements:* Barker, "Wes on the scene," *Advertiser*, 21 July; "Wes looks at . . . Peter Sculthorpe" [interview]; Dr. Enid Robertson "Wistful Beethoven," 29 July; and Daryl Warren, "Wildly new, different," 29 July. In "Composer issues Festival warning," PS warned that the Adelaide Festival will decline unless the city gets its own Festival Hall.)

B209 John Sinclair. "Concert was good, but ..." *Herald*, 22 August 1967.
Like so much of Mr. Sculthorpe's recent music, **Anniversary Music** is a brilliant essay in unconventional orchestral textures—with a few elements of Oriental music.

B210 Felix Werder. "Sprightly concert." *Age*, 22 August 1967: 6.
Anniversary Music is evocative tone-painting and displays all the usual mannerisms of the Sculthorpe individuality.

B211 Kenneth Hince. "Two decades of music for the youth of a nation." *Australian*, 26 August 1967: 10.

Anniversary Music, has clear associations with the now-celebrated Sun Music series but is a work of essentially different character. As an occasional piece it is brilliant.

B212 Donald Mintz. "Reviews of records. Australian music." *Musical Quarterly* 53 (1967): 596-603.

SQ 6 [D54] is an exceptionally impressive work, possibly a great or near-great one. The third movement uses thematic material from the first two in a manner both readily apparent and subtle. (Review occupies most of p. 599.)

B213 "Peter Sculthorpe." Interviewer: Hazel de Berg. From the Oral History Collection of the National Library of Australia. Tapes DeB 296-298. 1967 (12 October), c75 min. Transcript 36 p.

Sculthorpe speaks of his childhood in Launceston; studying and teaching music; his first musical success Irkanda IV; his method of work; his main difficulty in writing music; his fear of death; writing Sun Music. (Acknowledgement required by library.)

B214 W. L. Hoffmann. "Ensemble gives high-standard performances." *Canberra Times*, 2 October 1967.

The Austral Quartet gave an authoritative performance of PS's sixth SQ.

Other reviews: Hince, "Boost for our own music," *Australian*, 3 Oct (a performance of great eloquence); Covell, "Spring Festival," 2 Oct; and Salter, "Definite sense of event at music festival," *Telegraph*.

B215 Paul Frolich. "Notes on notes." *Bulletin*, 14 October 1967: 61.

At the Canberra Spring Festival's morning sessions, six composers—Butterley, Dreyfus, Sculthorpe, Sitsky, Werder, and Williamson—discussed their work and ideas before an intelligently participating audience. PS's SQ 6, interesting and well-made, was already known to many.

Tapes: "Musica Viva Spring Festival," sound recording, Sept 30-Oct 2, 1967, NLA Oral History Program TRC 1-499; five tape reels; 3-1/2 ips, mono; 7 in. *Further discussion:* "Festivities in Canberra," *Currency* 8 (Nov 1967): 4+; Salter, *Bulletin*, 18 Nov.

B216 "Bali & Djawa musics inspire Australian composer." *Djakarta Times*, 23 October 1967.

Information from the Australian Information Office here is that PS uses Western instruments in Anniversary Music in such a way that they give a similar emotional feeling and type of sound to that of a gamelan orchestra. His piece for the 1968 Adelaide Festival will also be Indonesian. (Information also appears in *Kompas*, Indonesia.)

B217 John Carmody. "Figures in Contemporary Australian Music: Peter Sculthorpe." *Tharunka* (Univ. of NSW) 13, no. 17 (24 October 1967): 17.

Article is the third of three about composers responsible for Australian music's recent rise to more than national competence: Meale, Butterley, Sculthorpe.

B218 Roger Covell. "A musical birthday." *SMH*, 25 October 1967.

Anniversary Music stirred and gleamed as though gently wakened from a dream, brought to life by the breezes of a green paradise. An unabashed tune was shaped in a way wholly personal to the composer. The work is one of his best.

B219 David Salter. "Nostalgic 20th anniversary." *Telegraph*, 25 October 1967.

Anniversary Music can be responded to in an openly emotional manner. With concertmaster Hazelwood and Sculthorpe, Heinze executed the ceremonial cut of the birthday cake and the orchestra played *Happy Birthday* in at least three keys at once. ("The music goes on and on," 25 Oct, also reports on the after-concert party.)

B220 Charles Osborne. "Australia: Three aspects." *London Magazine*, new series, vol. 7, no. 8 (November 1967): 49-50.
SQ 6 [D54] is fascinating and poetic. PS's engagingly baroque personality conceals a seriousness of purpose. Sculthorpe is a name to watch. He may well develop into being the first internationally important Australian composer.

B221 David Salter. "An event well worth recording." *Bulletin*, 4 Nov 1967: 74-5.
Recording session for **Anniversary Music** [D65] finds Sculthorpe crawling around on hands and knees in the ABC's Sydney studio, stringing a set of antique cymbals together before the percussion player's cue, and demonstrating how to play the instrument, then answering constant queries from the musicians. Score has been revised.

B222 Paul Frolich. "Happy anniversary." *Bulletin*, 4 November 1967: 75-6.
At a recent seminar, PS asserted that he wrote from the heart, every time, and the remarkable **Anniversary Music** seems to prove it: it is completely logical, thoroughly delightful, and certain to charm most listeners.

B223 Brian Buckley. "We'll meet again in Adelaide." *Bulletin*, 9 December 1967: 74.
Plans for the 1968 Festival (where Marlene Dietrich will be the star-quality name) include the first performance of a wind quintet by PS. (*Other publicity:* Kay Tyson, "World premiere for Tas. composer's work," *Examiner*.)

B224 Graham Bartle. *Music in Australian Schools*. Acer Research Series No. 83. Hawthorn, VIC: Australian Council for Educational Research, 1968.
In this survey of music performed at school concerts, **South by Five** was part of the repertoire performed by one school in the "sample" group (p. 194). (*Book review:* Meredith Oakes, "School music under fire," *Daily Telegraph*, 4 Dec 1968.)

B225 Harvey Blanks. *The Golden Road: A record collector's guide to music appreciation*. Adelaide: Rigby, 1968: 108-9, 331.
Discussed are Sun Music/Irkanda IV [D31] and SQ 6 [D54], with quotations from **B174**.

B226 *Entertainment Arts in Australia*. Editorial, John Allen; design, Roy Garwood; photographs, Robert Walker. Introduction by Dr. H. C. Coombs, Chairman, Australian Council for the Arts. Sydney: Paul Hamlyn, 1968.
Sculthorpe is quoted on the genesis of **Sun Music** ("I don't like overtures"), and the **Sun Music ballet** is shown in photos: p. 6, 112, 116, 119.

B227 James Glennon. "Peter Sculthorpe." *Australian Music and Musicians*. [Adelaide]: Rigby, [c1968].
Biographical sketch (p. 174-5) includes PS's teachers, awards, teaching (at Univ. of "NSW" [Sydney]), major works, commissions, and performances.
    Review: Oldaker, "When does a visitor become an Aussie?" *Examiner:* "our own PS" is vouchsafed 40 lines or so. Few composers have merited more space.

B228 Anne Boyd. "Peter Sculthorpe's **Sun Music I**." *Miscellanea Musicologica: Adelaide Studies in Musicology* 3 (1968): 3-20.

Analysis describes the sound materials, form, instrumental strata, and durational organization. It focuses on mm. 63-70, based on **Haiku** for piano, showing the pitch series and rhythmic series. (Copy of the original Univ. of Sydney paper is in the NLA.)

B229 Craig McGregor (text) and Helmut Gritscher (photography). *To Sydney with Love*. Sydney: Thomas Nelson (Australia), 1968.
(P. 130:) Sydney is the home of the nation's leading composers—Sculthorpe, Meale, Butterley—and writers Patrick White and Thomas Keneally.

B230 Roger Covell. "Oh, for a punkah!" *SMH*, 9 February 1968.
Town Hall under February conditions is too hot for disturbance by anything more aggressive than the sigh of a punka, but **Sun Music IV** came through the ordeal well—its gaunt-nerved, non-fleshy sound resists wilting.

B231 Frank Harris. "Great start for Proms." *Mirror*, 9 February 1968.
Sculthorpe was cheered like a hero for his **Sun Music IV**, which rounded off the Prom series handsomely, though it says nothing new.

B232 David Salter, "Enjoying the bare facts of the music," *Telegraph*, 9 February 1968.
Sun Music IV, in a revised score, was a new work to Sydney audiences. Hopkins narrowed the range of startling contrasts in underplaying the harsher moments.
(*Announcements:* Hince, *Australian*, 27 Jan; and Salter, "The ABC of 'good listening'," *Telegraph*, 24 Jan, followed by "Audience's views on ABC series," 7 Feb: 30.)

B233 Paul Frolich. "Well-hidden beauty." *Bulletin*, 17 February 1968: 65.
The only piece which could legitimately arouse enthusiasm at the first Proms concert was **Sun Music IV**. (Frolich, " 'Prom' rebel," ibid., 24 Feb: 63, praises the work again.)

B234 Maria Prerauer. "The Polish style." *Nation*, 17 February 1968.
The technique in **Sun Music IV** belongs to the Penderecki category. PS seems to be stretching flimsy musical material beyond its limits. (In "Packed at the Prom," *Sun*, 9 Feb, she finds the work superficially effective but without lasting musical substance.)

B235 Roger Covell. "Overall gain in standards." *SMH*, 6 March 1968: 18.
Irkanda IV yesterday was valuable new territory for the NTO players and made, I think, a deep impression on the mainly student audience.

B236 "Sculthorpe in Adelaide." *Advertiser*, 13 March 1968: 8.
Tabuh Tabuhan will have its world premiere next Wednesday. PS will conduct a series of seminars entitled "Asian music and the Australian composer" which will feature other leading Australian musicians, films, discussions, and recorded performances—on March 20 (Indonesian music), 21 (Japanese music), and 22 (Australian music). (*Another announcement:* "Governor at city service," *Mail*, Sat. 16 March.)

B237 Howard Palmer. "The Oriental sound of music." *Sun*, 18 March 1968: 23.
PS says Australia must look to Asia in music as in politics and trade. For his wind quintet—such a Germanic form—he added percussion and used Indonesian textures.

B238 "Uses Japanese mouth organ." *Advertiser*, 20 March 1968.
Photo shows PS holding a *sho* with 17 pipes, to be used at his seminars [*see* B236].
In "Composition commended," ibid., 19 March, the Festival's music adviser says **Tabuh Tabuhan** rehearsals show it to be "a real world-beater."

B239   John Horner. "Commissioned work wins applause." *Advertiser,* Thursday 21 March 1968.
Tabuh Tabuhan was an immediate success with the audience and tremendous applause greeted players and composer. Mr. Sculthorpe gave an interesting account of how he came to choose gamelan music of Indonesia as the basis for his composition. ("First Women's Page," ibid., includes a short history of the Bishop Memorial Award.)

B240   John Horner. "Youth players are 'trumps'." *Advertiser,* 22 March 1968.
The AYO performed **Sun Music IV** with discipline, creating a vivid sound picture of Australia panting with heat; the composer was present to give the performance his blessing. (*Other reviews:* Tidemann, "Impressive debut by orchestra," ibid., 20 March; and Renfrey, "Young players splendid," *The News,* 22 March. *Announcement:* Dr. Enid Robertson, "Sublime variations," *Advertiser,* 16 March.)

B241   James Renfrey. "Music grows better." *The News,* 22 March 1968.
PS explained **Tabuh Tabuhan**, with examples mirth-making out of context. **Tabuh Tabuhan** is an impressionistic work; I'd like to hear it again. The more I hear PS's compositions, the more I like them.

B242   James Glennon. "Commissioned work has premiere." *Sunday Mail,* 24 March 1968.
Fortunately, the composer was present to explain in a down-to-earth style what we should listen for in **Tabuh Tabuhan** by calling on members of the ensemble to illustrate the themes and sounds allotted them. At the end of the evocative performance applause recalled composer and performers to stage several times.

B243   Grahame Dudley. "John Bishop Memorial Award Concert." *Sound: The Music Magazine* 1 (April 1968): 12-14.
The Adelaide concert was "an event" because of the performance of a new PS work. In **Tabuh Tabuhan** as in **Anniversary Music,** he uses Indonesian sounds and materials.

B244   Roger Covell. "First principles at Mittagong." 16 April 1968.
PS introduced a session of his own music: **Teotihuacan,** and on tape, the tender and dream-hazed splendours of **Tabuh Tabuhan.** He also gallantly undertook to devise a piece for players and audience, organized in periods of specific activity between downbeats, under the title of **Music for Mittagong or Fun Music I.**

B245   Kenneth Hince. "Sound of our own music." *Australian,* April 1968.
Despite the ugliness of some of the sounds, **Teotihuacan** is a pleasant experience.

B246   Paul Frolich. "Straight furrows and fine Mozart." *Bulletin,* 27 April 1968: 65-6.
Tabuh Tabuhan (at Mittagong) was of great emotional impact. Photo of PS by Robert Walker illustrates the review.

B247   George Farwell. "The myths that they live by abroad." *Australian,* Saturday 4 May 1968.
Sun Music IV, which one prominent Canadian told me epitomised for him the Australian ethos, drew applause at Montreal, not Mozart or Dvorak. (Farwell is defending life in Australia, responding to expatriate art critic Robert Hughes who prefers the US.)

B248   F. R. Blanks. "A conductor with vitality." *SMH,* 10 May 1968.
Sun Music I quivers with elemental power.

B249   Frank Harris. "Sun Music gave warmth to concert." *Mirror*, 10 May 1968.
Sun Music I was one of the high spots in a year of otherwise dull programming.

B250   Julian Russell. "Music of the sun." *Sun*, 10 May 1968.
Sun Music I acquired a new poetry as Krips seemed to concentrate on the upper end of the spectrum to shed a radiance only Australians know.

B251   Wolfgang Wagner. "Krips' specialties in Sydney." *Australian*, 10 May 1968.
Whether this harsh, brutal, uncompromising Sun Music I has any appeal to you or not, nobody can deny its immediate impact and effective forcefulness

B252   "Duke opens design exhibit." *SMH*, 15 May 1968: 1.
Photos of Cylinder no. 10, "Music," in which Sun Music I [D31] is being played at the Industrial Design Council exhibit, show the trousered legs of PS, the Duke of Edinburgh, and others, standing inside, and the Duke exiting. Report on inside page is by Helen Frizell. (*Other reviews:* "Australia: the first 200 years," *Australian*, 21 May ["PS's music vibrates within this drum"]; and in *Nation*, 25 May.)

B253   David Salter. "Contrast lacking in subdued tone." *Bulletin*, 25 May 1968.
Sun Music I was an accurate account, but I missed the tightness and edge of ensemble and violence in the climaxes.

B254   Maria Prerauer. "Masters of the strings." *Nation*, 25 May 1968.
Sun Music I appeared more coherent, logical, and all of a piece than at its premiere.

B255   Fred R. Blanks. "Australia." *Musical Times* 109 (June 1968): 561-2.
This year's Mittagong festival (April) included two concerts of works by PS, in residence to explain and direct his music. Most impressive was Sonata for Viola and Percussion, splendidly played. The Sydney Proms (Feb) included the fierce Sun Music [IV].

B256   Penelope Rogers. "A Buddha in the living-room." *Australian Home Journal*, June 1968: 64-65, 67.
The first thing you notice about PS's tiny house (shown in photos) is the warmth of atmosphere. The decoration is basically simple, with elaborate touches of the East.

B257   [Ballet publicity.] *Examiner*, 6 June 1968.
The Sun Music ballet production will employ innovations such as stereo sound projected from several points around the theatre. Rehearsals will be in Melbourne.
   Other publicity: James Murdoch, "Penny Whistles," *Sound* 1 (March 1968): 4-8 (will be interesting); *Mercury* (quotes PS); "Sculthorpe composing new ballet Sun Music," *Mainichi Daily News* (Tokyo), 5 July; *Sun*, 19 July; and *Bulletin*, 27 July: 73.

B258   Gil Wahlquist. "Organised noise down south." *Sun-Herald*, 9 June 1968.
Here I was in Melbourne watching a group of actors dancing to PS's Sixth String Quartet in a play called *Burke's Company*, when I should have been at a disco called Sebastians listening to the pop group Procession—though I enjoyed *Burke's Company*.

B259   Romola Costantino. "A program to delight young ears." *SMH*, 12 June 1968: 18.
Sun Music IV, like Sun Music I, is abstract painting, but as if about to become a sunburnt

Sibelius. The composer was present to explain the piece, and then it was repeated.

B260 Roger Covell. "Birthday works good notion by ABC." *SMH*, 26 June 1968.
Short works in honour of Stravinsky's 86th birthday were broadcast in two half-hour radio programs. PS was ingenious: he simply extracted and arranged music from his **Tabuh Tabuhan** (not yet heard in Sydney) for **From Tabuh Tabuhan**. He also received his own sincere tribute in the string writing of Ross Edwards' *Little Orchestra Piece*.

B261 Kenneth Robins. "Distinction and value." *Bulletin*, 20 July 1968.
Sun Music IV was impressive, even memorable, and was certainly an extraordinary incentive to individual imaginative excursions.

B262 Fred Blanks. "Helpmann creation is total theatre." *SMH*, 3 Aug 1968.
Sun Music is a turbulent tour de force of total theatre. The five sections, not meant to have dramatic connection, form a vaguely ceremonial rite with atavistic undertones.

B263 Wolfgang Wagner. "A ballet that may be too allusive." *Australian*, 8 August 1968.
The entire **Sun Music** ballet score (described) was amplified from the proscenium.

B264 Katherine Brisbane. "Something new under the sun." Ibid.
Theatre critic reports that the applause went on almost as long as the **Sun Music** ballet itself, with bouquets and champagne and curtain calls. Its splendid theatricality is due to the designer as much as to the choreographer .

B265 Maria Prerauer. "Early sunrise." *Nation*, 17 August 1968.
There is no doubt that all those **Sun Musics** which until now have haunted concert programmes at a bit of a loose end have finally been exorcised in this ballet.
    Other reviews: Virginia Gerrett, *Canberra Times*, 3 Aug; Griffen Foley, *Telegraph*, 3 Aug; *Sun*, 5 Aug; Daniel Thomas (art critic), "Pleasure at the theatre," *Sunday Telegraph*, 11 Aug; Carolyn Symes (ballet critic), "Fence-sitting," *Bulletin*, 17 Aug; and an article in *Hemisphere*, Aug 1968. *Also*: (Brisbane performances) Constance Cummins, *Courier-Mail*, 9 Oct; (Melbourne) Geoffrey Hutton, *Age*, 25 Oct. Helpmann, in "Sir Robert Helpmann," *Sound* 1 (Sept 1968): 25, describes the ballet.

B266 Peter Sculthorpe. "Charles Ives (1874-1954)." *Sound* 1 (Sept 1968): 26-8.
The aspect of Ives' music that impresses most is its American flavour. Ives wrote that "if local colour, national colour, any colour is a true pigment of the universal colour, it is a divine quality. And it is part of substance in art, not of manner." (Article includes photos of Ives, an original Ives manuscript, and his piano and books at Yale.)

B267 "Composer to tackle four new operas." *Examiner*, 7 September 1968.
PS is on a short visit to his home state to be a guest at a Tasmania Week dinner in Hobart on Monday, and to attend the christening of his niece, Elizabeth Margaret Sculthorpe, in Launceston tomorrow. (*Other reports*: "Famous Tasmanians return for Tasmania Week" *Examiner*, 9 Sept; and notice in *Mercury*, 9 Sept.)

B268 "Australian composer in Japan." *Canberra Times*, 23 September 1968: 9.
From Tokyo, A.A.P.-Reuter reports that PS, 38-year-old composer and specialist in Japanese music, arrived today for an international Round Table Conference sponsored by UNESCO in Kyoto.

B269 Anne Boyd. "Asian music in Australian music education," Part I.

Australian Journal of Music Education, no. 3 (October 1968): 42.
PS is among the Australian composers with Asian interests, particularly *yokyoku,* or Japanese singing style (sounds used in the **Sun Music** series) and Bali's *gender wayang* (in **Sun Music III, Tabuh Tabuhan,** and the music for the film **Age of Consent**).

B270 Roger Covell. "Peter Sculthorpe: an introduction." Ibid.: 65-6.
The effortless tune of **Sea Chant** (this month's musical supplement) is a part of PS's natural musical manners. He offers us both unusual assemblages of sonority and some of the traditional pleasures of music.

B271 "People are talking about: The busy life of Peter Sculthorpe." *Vogue Australia* 12 (October 1968): 122-123.
A wider public is becoming aware of what the cognoscenti—here and overseas—already knew: that PS (shown in large photo) is a creative artist of international repute, probably the most important musical talent we Australians have ever produced.

B272 Gerald Larner. "Harrogate." *Musical Times* 109 (October 1968): 944.
Sun Music IV is an athematic colour piece, intended to evoke one particular aspect of the Australian scene, but by now, unfortunately, PS's *glissandi* and tone clusters tend to sound like all the others.

B273 Tony Morphett. "Composer back with a song of praise." *SMH,* 26 October 1968: 22.
PS (photographed in monk's robes and with Japanese flute) has just returned from Japan where he attended a UNESCO roundtable discussion, spent a week in a Zen Buddhist monastery (but couldn't give up his possessions and worries), and fell in love with an entire country. "It was finally going to the fountainhead of what has influenced me for so many years. I know that my music will be different."

B274 Kenneth Robins. "Savage division." *Bulletin,* 26 October 1968.
In SQ 7 the composer has found much joy in harmonics high up on the strings and keeping the viola's bow on the wrong side of the string. The quartet realises some fascinating sounds from Japanese Noh plays. The second S. contribution evoked a gentle Asia.

B275 Meredith Oakes. "Standard of music high." *Daily Telegraph,* 2 Nov 1968.
Tabuh Tabuhan is a beautiful piece of music. The best, longest and least ingratiating part is the third (middle) movement, where sounds heard in the song-play and Balinese shadow-play are put together in a more or less atonal, Western structure.

B276 Roger Covell. "Notable in any company." *SMH,* 4 November 1968: 9.
The five movements of **Tabuh Tabuhan** alternate the chiming, neo-Balinese grace of his **Anniversary Music** with two interludes that conjure up nocturnal expectancy and erotic excitement with **Sun Music** sonorities. The result is enchanting. (Photo shows PS.)
Covell, "Cell Block revival of ISCM," ibid., 2 Nov, promises the review.

B277 Julian Russell. "Bright evening of local work." *Sun,* 4 November 1968.
In **Tabuh Tabuhan,** the flautist Neville Amadio expressed what Sculthorpe described in a preliminary talk as—if I remember rightly—"a sigh of ecstasy."

B278 Meredith Oakes. "Music." *Telegraph,* 13 November 1968.
PS, previously a Senior Lecturer in Music at the Univ. of Sydney, will be promoted as of next year to the position of Reader, freed from most of his lecturing responsibilities.

B279 Maria Prerauer. "Praise to Nature." *Nation*, 23 November 1968.
Tabuh Tabuhan was the stuff of which light film music is usually made, or perhaps it
will end up in a ballet, like Sun Music.

B280 "$10,000 awards to composer, scientist and poet." *SMH*, 23 Nov 1968.
A 1968 Britannica Australia award for contributions of outstanding merit in the arts,
science and humanities has been presented to composer PS, 39.
  Other announcements (all 23 November): "3 awarded big grants," *Sun;* "The honour,
the glory ... and the cash," *Age;* "L'ton man's win," *Examiner;* and "Composer, scientist
and poet get $10,000 awards," *Australian*.

B281 Meredith Oakes. "Award gives boost to Aust. composers." *Telegraph*,
27 November 1968.
For the first time since its inauguration in 1964, the Australian Encyclopedia Britannica
award has been presented to a composer. For PS it's more than just a personal triumph.

B282 "I don't like overtures: interview with Peter Sculthorpe." *Masque*, no.
7 (December 1968): 33.
How did **Sun Music I** come about? Sir Bernard Heinze wanted an overture for the Commonwealth Festival. I said, "I don't like overtures." He said, "Well, a piece to start
the night with. If you want to write a piece without rhythm, melody or harmony, you
can do just that." (Section "Ballet Season 1968," also includes a photo from the **Sun
Music ballet**, a photo of PS, and an interview with designer Kenneth Rowell.)

B283 Roger Covell. "1968 advance in music." *SMH*, December 1968.
PS's **Sun Music IV** probably signified the end of a phase in his search for a richer
vocabulary. **Sun Music III** belonged in the series only by adoption; its neo-Balinese
sonorities and tense melodies seem to bear the promise of his next development.

B284 Andrew D. McCredie. *Catalogue of 46 Australian Composers and
Selected Works.* (Music by Australian Composers: Survey No. 1, ed.
Ian Spink. Published by the Advisory Board, CAAC.) Canberra, 1969.
Paragraph of biography is followed by a classified list of Sculthorpe's works, with
publishers, and a bibliography of eight items (p. 17).

B285 _____. *Musical Composition in Australia (Including Select
Bibliography and Discography).* (Music by Australian Composers:
Survey No. 1, ed. Ian Spink. Published by the Advisory Board, CAAC.)
Canberra, 1969.
(P. 20-21:) PS's music shows the composer's natural lyric gifts combined with a
sophisticated professionalism. Various approaches are evident from the early string
quartets and **Music I, II, III**, etc., through **Tabuh Tabuhan**. Discography (p. 30) lists
four recordings [**D31, D54, D64,** and **D73**].

B286 Peter Sculthorpe. "Peter Sculthorpe." *The Composers and Their Work.*
(Music by Australian Composers: Survey No. 1, ed. Ian Spink.
Published by the Advisory Board, CAAC.) Canberra, 1969: 17-18.
This volume contains published versions of talks from the "Australian Music Survey
No. 1: Composers introduce their music," recorded on three 12-inch 33 1/3 rpm discs,
Festival Custom Recording AMS 001-AMS 003.

B287 Craig McGregor (editor and author), David Beal (photographer), David
Moore (photographer), and Harry Williamson (book designer). *In the*

Making. Sydney: Thomas Nelson, 1969.
PS is one of the subjects of this beautifully-designed study of artists at work (p. 11, 64-7, 100-101). He is quoted, concerning his work [as in B226, B282], and shown in photos.
   Reviews: Jock Veitch, "How our major talents live, work and create their wares, *Sun-Herald,* 23 Nov (quotes the Sculthorpe pages); Daphne Guinness, "Out and about," *Bulletin,* 29 Nov (reports on book-launching party). Advance publicity: April 1969

B288   Kay Lucas [Dreyfus]. "Music discussion groups notes." Australia: Council of Adult Education, 1969.
       Volume includes notes on **Sonata for Viola and Percussion** and other Australian works.

B289   *Proceedings of the International Round Table on the Relations between Japanese and Western Arts, Tokyo and Kyoto, 23-30 September 1968.* Tokyo: Japanese National Commission for UNESCO, 1969.
       Sculthorpe's comments and introductions to taped examples appear in these transcripts in several sessions: in the "Group Session on Music (Tokyo)" (p. 160, 168); in the "Group Session on Music (Kyoto)" (p. 170); and in an "Afternoon Session" (p. 204).

B290   Peter Sculthorpe. "Peter Sculthorpe." (Article's heading is "Sculthorpe on Sculthorpe.") *Music Now* 1, no. 1 (February 1969): 7-13.
       Article (with photo of PS), is the edited transcript of a 1968 lecture for the ISCM, "Australian Music: A Revolution in the Making." Sculthorpe talks about his life and music. Cover is by Russell Drysdale: "The Ancient Maestro—Benefit Performance, Sydney Opera House A.D. 2025."

B291   Sally Trethowan. "Works by Aust. composers popular." *West Australian,* 14 February 1969.
       At the Australian composers workshop last night, PS proved to be affable, witty, modest and generous with his tributes to his colleagues. **Sun Music [for Voices and Percussion]** and **Sun Music III** received markedly enthusiastic audience response. (*Publicity:* "Composer praises Octagon," ibid., 13 Feb [Octagon Theatre, Univ. of WA].)

B292   Roger Covell. "John Hopkins gave us a big occasion." *SMH,* Monday 24 February 1969.
       Ketjak [Sun Music II] was designed to have a special appeal to a Prom audience, as the composer disarmingly indicated in his spoken introduction. The hard-edged rhythms gave us something new and welcome in Sculthorpe, neither choked nor anguished.

B293   Frank Harris. "Concert with a kick." *Daily Mirror,* 24 February 1969.
       For the world premiere of **Ketjak,** the double bass players wore army boots and stamped with parade-ground thunder—a comic touch amusingly exploited by the composer in his introductory speech. There was no loss of excitement at second hearing.

B294   Meredith Oakes. " 'Beatlemania' at final prom." *Daily Telegraph,* 24 February 1969.
       Ketjak, a virile, and at times grotesque, Balinese-inspired drum piece, sounds more cohesive, more at home with itself, than anything PS has written for quite a while.

B295   Maria Prerauer. "Prom fever runs high." *Sun,* 24 February 1969: 37.
       Ketjak, tuned exactly to the romping Prom spirit, was the big popular hit. PS took a bouncing Asian monkey-dance rhythm and re-scored it for assorted drums.

B296   Wolfgang Wagner. "Convention at the Proms." *Australian,* 24 Feb 1969.

In **Ketjak** the percussionists emerged with flying colors, and Sculthorpe scored a rousing success, so much so that the piece had to be repeated.

Blanks, "Australia," *Musical Times* 110 (April): 410, reports overseas that **Ketjak** was the most striking new Australian work on the Proms season concerts.

B297   Roger Covell. "Bold presentation of Aust. music." *SMH*, 25 Feb 1969.

Heinze's deep affection for **Sun Music III** is evident on the recording [D64]. The work is one of the most shapely and beautiful works to come out of this country. PS (shown in photo) never puts a foot wrong. One can admire his mirror-still control.

B298   Frank Harris. "New light on our music. *Daily Mirror*, 25 Feb 1969.

Sun Music III was a turning point, as PS admits in "Sculthorpe on Sculthorpe" in the new magazine *Music Now* launched at the weekend. The work is also a star offering on the new HMV disc [D64], and the best of all in sound quality.

B299   Peter Kyng. "Sculthorpe the scrutable." *SSO Newsletter* (issued by the orchestral committee), no. 8 (March 1969): 6-7.

PS is interviewed about **Tabuh Tabuhan** and the love poem on which it is based.

B300   Kenneth Hartney and Susan Morris. "Student's-eye view of Peter Sculthorpe." *Music Maker* 37 (March 1969): 14-15.

Two of PS's definitions are the basis of his style. First, a piece of music has a form which breathes freely, not confined in form or style. Second, music includes conforming rhythms, an ordered succession of sound.

B301   Maria Prerauer. "Lost for words." *Nation*, 8 March 1969: 17.

Four composers (including PS) were called upon to introduce their works at the Proms. Garrulousness is begining to look like an epidemic. Even the new serious quarterly *Music Now* contains popular lectures like "Sculthorpe on Sculthorpe" [B290].

Ketjak was the big, popular success of the Proms. It had to be repeated, and quite right. It was rollicking, lighthearted and incorporated some good unclean fun for the brass—straight out entertainment, a field in which the composer excels.

B302   Colin Mason. "Avant-garde sound facade." *Daily Telegraph* (London), 11 March 1969.

Basically conservative in thought and conception **Tabuh Tabuhan** uses the medium with great skill to assume a more avant-garde facade of sound. Such sounds are common enough in music today, but are rarely used with such sensitivity, precision, and beguiling, if otherwise unambitious, musical purpose.

B303   Stephen Walsh. "Polished modernity." *Times*, 11 March 1969: 7.

Unquestionably the most intriguing item on the program was PS's **Tabuh Tabuhan**. A fine, atmospheric performance intensified my anxiety to hear it again.

B304   Kenneth Robins. "Reactions riotous and aesthetic." *Bulletin*, 15 March 1969.

At the Proms the pounding rhythmic vitality of **Ketjak** involved the audience.

B305   Meredith Oakes. "Some beautiful sounds in a long, long night." *Telegraph*, Monday 31 March 1969.

PS in **Sun Music IV** came off the best of the Australian composers. He has a feeling for rhythmic shape and cadence.

B306   Julian Russell. "Avant garde mood at Town Hall." *Sun*, 31 March

1969.
I found the evocative orchestration in **Sun Music IV** much more interesting than the
melodic content.
   Other reviews: W. Wagner, "Amateurs with flare," *Australian;* Covell, "New
music at the Town Hall," *SMH*, 31 March (familiar but powerful); Harris, "Modern—
but too much," *Mirror;* Prerauer, "Atzmon goes now," *Nation*, 5 April (brief mention).

B307 Roger Covell. "New composers are in harmony." *Times*, 1 April 1969,
special suppl., "Australia," p. x.
PS is the best known of the composers who are following Asian styles and techniques.

B308 Margaret Clarke. "Peter Sculthorpe premiere." *ABC*, 1 April 1969.
In rehearsing **Ketjak**, to be broadcast on April 10, the orchestra didn't quite understand
what PS wanted, until he explained that the music was "sexy."

B309 Peter Thoeming (illustrations) and Michael Hannan (captions). "Peter
Sculthorpe: Sun Music III." *Music Now* 1, no. 2 (1969): 12-19.
Eight excerpts from the **Sun Music III** score (with illustrations) represent six elements
of the work: birdsong; gamelan textures; sun sounds (tone clusters in the strings); the
ecstatic tune; the wild timpani section at the work's climax; and the final tutti chord.

B310 Max Oldaker. "The performing arts." *Examiner*, May 1969.
I had no hand in Peter Sculthorpe's establishment in Britain, but I claim to have
written the first story about him in a London magazine in 1962 [**B51**]. Since then his
stride has taken him well beyond the future I envisaged.

B311 Fred R. Blanks. "Australia." *Musical Times* 110 (June 1969): 660.
The spectrum of the 9th Mittagong festival (at Easter) extended to the modern end
with two "Composer at Work" sessions—one for PS and his disciples Anne Boyd and
Barry Conyngham rather aimlessly ruminating into childhood motivations.

B312 "$25,000 for Australian operas." *Daily Telegraph*, 11 June 1969.
The Australian Elizabethan Theatre Trust has already commissioned PS and five
other Australian composers to write operas. (The same information also appears in
"Theatre, arts bodies closer—Trust head," *SMH*, 11 June.)

B313 Roger Covell. "Sculthorpe in a new score." *SMH*, 16 June 1969.
The new Faber edition of **Irkanda IV** is typographically handsome and easy to read.

B314 Kenneth Robins. "Australia, Hurrah!" *Bulletin*, 21 June 1969: 51-52.
Globally speaking, Australia is a long way from being admitted to the big league;
musically the situation is infinitely more tenuous—despite a few ephemeral successes
and some genuinely musical successes (including PS's **SQ 6**).

B315 Judy MacGregor-Smith. "Lover's poem inspired music." *SMH*, Saturday 26 July 1969: 18.
A Balinese boy's poem to his mistress (the poem is quoted in full) inspired PS to write
one of his finest works, **Tabuh Tabuhan**.

B316 Roger Covell. "A tidal wash of feeling at the music hall." *SMH*, 28
July 1969: 11. Also published as "Happy conformity at music hall."
The musical equivalent of (according to the composer) an amorous, Balinese daydream,
Tabuh Tabuhan asks to be experienced with passive absorption, moment by moment, as
a tidal wash of feeling rather than as a structure.

B317 Meredith Oakes. "Nastiness out of question."*Telegraph,* 28 July 1969.
The more often I hear **Tabuh Tabuhan,** the more complex becomes my attitude towards
it. This kind of sophistication is a most unexpected product for a culture as new as ours.

B318 Roger Covell. "New quartet climax of recital." *SMH,* 6 September 1969.
SQ 6, now a standard work, demonstrated how to make every note tell; its elemental
structure is part of its strength. ("New quartet" of the headline by Ross Edwards.)

B319 Meredith Oakes. "World premiere of challenging piece." *Telegraph,*
Saturday 6 September 1969: 40.
SQ 6 with its repetitions and ostinati sounded a bit old. It made one understand why
PS's Asian experiments are so important—to enable these techniques to become beauti-
ful in themselves, rather than jostling uncomfortably with the dynamic tendency of
the European idiom.

B320 Kenneth Robins. "Not that dead." *Bulletin,* 27 September 1969: 55-56.
SQ 6 (Sept 5), is the most evocative and moving piece of chamber music composed by an
Australian. It is tragic and deeply felt, terse, shattering in its impact.

B321 Clifford Tolchard. "Orpheus in the sun." *Walkabout* (Melbourne:
Australian National Travel Association, etc.), October 1969: 28-30.
PS's small terrace house reflects his personality, his profession and his interests.
Sculthorpe compares visual aspects and musical life in the US and Australia.

B322 *Australia, New Zealand and the South Pacific: A Handbook,* ed.
Charles Osborne. London: Anthony Blond, 1970.
(P. 323:) PS, the one contemporary Australian composer whose name is known abroad,
is conscious of the need to define, if not create, an Australian music.

B323 John Cargher. *Music for Pleasure, or How to Enjoy Music Without
Really Trying.* Sydney: Ure Smith, 1970. P. 127, 163, 165, 166.
In Australia the general public's interest in the Sun Music series rose substantially
after the music was used for a ballet. Photo between p. 86 and 87 is captioned "PS:
Australian-Australian Composer." (*Reviews:* Robert Drewe, *Australian,* 13 Feb 1971,
with a photo of PS; Hince [does not mention Sculthorpe].)

B324 Charmian Clift. *The World of Charmian Clift.* Introduction by George
Johnston. Sydney: Ure Smith, 1970.
Shouldn't we care about, thank the dear Lord for, the important Australians who came
back [from overseas]—Russell Drysdale, Patrick White, and Peter Sculthorpe?

B325 Rob Hillier. *A Place Called Paddington.* Sydney: Ure Smith, 1970.
A large photo of PS at the piano (Queen St. house) is captioned: "Composer PS whose
modern compositions have been played by leading SOs throughout the world."

B326 J. M. Thomson. "The role of the pioneer composer: some reflections
on Alfred Hill 1870-1960." *Studies in Music* (University of Western
Australia), no. 4 (1970): 56-7.
A decisive change in Australian music was forcibly conveyed to English audiences (and
is still remembered by many musicians and composers) through PS's 1965 interview in
The Times [**B152**] in which he declared that European music was dead. This view was
recapitulated by Covell [**B307**] (quoted).

B327 "Fusing the lights with pop at the proms." *Masque,* no. 13 (January

1970): 31-2.
Conductor John Hopkins says that **Love 200** will attempt a fusion of the arts—classical music, lightshows, and pop. Photos show PS and some of the performers.

B328 Michael Chanan. "Quartet Competition." *Music and Musicians* 18 (January 1970): 61-2.
String Quartet Music (November 1969) was the easiest to play and the easiest to listen to of the Radcliffe quartets, as well as being the strongest of the four works.

B329 William Mann. "Four winning quartets." *Times*, 16 Jan 1970: 13.
SQ Music was one of the two more striking quartets. It has two dance-like movements, sandwiched (double-decker) by three slow, rather incantatory movements. The effect of the whole work is most curious, for me greatly fascinating.

B330 Colin Mason. "4 quartets in Bartok's footsteps." *Daily Telegraph*, 16 Jan 1970.
String Quartet Music skilfully and attractively adapts traditional Balinese material to the medium, but is intellectually unambitious.

B331 Roger Covell. "Rhythmic winner for strings and chin rest." *SMH*, 17 Jan 1970: 11.
Dateline: London. PS's **String Quartet Music** is the best of the four Radcliffe winners, not only because it escapes from stereotypes of serious thoughtfulness, but because Sculthorpe has the rare gift of not trying to say too much at any one time.

B332 Desmond Shawe-Taylor. "Free-for-all." *Sunday Times*, 18 Jan 1970.
String Quartet Music is highly coloured and atmospheric. It includes Balinese elements in its unashamedly picturesque course.

B333 Stephen Walsh, "Magnetic Stockhausen," *The Observer*, 18 Jan 1970.
String Quartet Music, characteristically individual and somewhat attenuated in layout, suffered by being placed at the end of a difficult programme.

B334 "Editorial notes." *The Strad* 80 (February 1970): 443.
PS's works devoted to the newer exploitation of string sonorities have made the biggest mark with British audiences. **SQ Music** explores the inner qualities as well as the colour possibilities of Balinese music, resulting in a mystical atavistic quality.

B335 " 'Love 200': Prom and pop." *SMH*, c12 February 1970.
Love 200 is occupying all the time of its composer. PS describes the work.
Other publicity: Ray Castle's column, *Telegraph*, Th. 4 Dec., 1969; "Soon... the PROMS," *SMH*, Jan; "Tully beat it out—under a classical baton," *Australian*, 12 Feb (with a photo of Tully); Jane Perlez, "Love 200," ibid., 14 Feb: Weekend Review: 1 (with large photo); and a piece in *GO-SET*, 14 Feb.

B336 F. R. Blanks. "Ear-shattering end." *SMH*, 16 February 1970.
Love 200 can, at the very best, be regarded as a successful failure.
In "Australia," *Musical Times* 111 (April 1970): 413-14, Blanks reports that **Love 200** alternated serious music with pop amidst a delirium of coloured lights and puffs of fog.
"Prom concert encore," *Sunday Mirror*, 15 Feb, reports the enthusiastic reception.
Love 200 is listed in "First Performances," *World of Music* 12, no. 2 (1970): 80, and again (as "Love 2000") in vol. 13, no. 1 (1971): 74.

B337 Meredith Oakes. "**Love 200** did not say 'love'." *Daily Telegraph*, 16

February 1970.
Love 200 brought an uproarious end to the Proms. A group like Tully, though, has its own sound which cannot readily be put at the service of an outsider's musical conception. The love thing has been mauled out of recognition by public relations and human nastiness. PS's music, his own sound, is not about love.

B338 Maria Prerauer. "**Love**'s labours lost." *Sun*, 16 February 1970.
In **Love 200** PS didn't come to within shooting distance of that hot beat, that enormous vitality that launched mother *Hair* into zippy orbit. Instead of rising to a climax, it just fizzled out. (*Also:* Prerauer, "Night on a bald patch," *Nation*, 21 Feb: 18-19.)

B339 Eva Wagner. "**Love** 200: good fun, but not much more." *Australian*, 16 February 1970.
As so often before, PS's great gifts and pleasant personality won me over long before the walls stopped vibrating under the impact of sound. **Love 200** was most suitable for the occasion, excellent entertainment and noisy, uninhibited, good fun.

B340 Frank Harris. "**Love** show for Tokyo." *Daily Mirror*, 17 February 1970.
PS says that **Love 200** is built from elements of an opera on which he has been working for some time—"a sort of pull-apart opera. You can pop in numbers, or take them out."

B341 Marion Macdonald. "But where was the classical figure of the shy musician?" *Daily Telegraph*, 19 February 1970.
Though some of the critics were dubious, **Love 200** received a rare ovation. Sculthorpe is a surprising man to meet, if one expects the gaunt, shy figure of the working musician. Interviewer reviews his education, teaching, and compositions.

B342 Kenneth Robins. "God forgive my pleasure in Simon and Garfunkel." *Bulletin*, 28 February 1970.
[Headline quotes Leonard Bernstein.] **Love 200** was an unmitigated disaster. Performers, brutally amplified, almost obscured Mr. Sculthorpe's first class sophisticated pop tunes and a contrapuntal string passage of quite ravishing beauty.

B343 Dominic Gill. "Radcliffe quartets." *Musical Times* 111 (March 1970): 297.
SQ Music, heard in January, was very agreeably flavoured, freshly persuasive. (Review repeats Gill's "Wigmore Hall: New quartets," *Financial Times*, 16 Jan.)

B344 David Simmons. "London music." *Musical Opinion* 93 (March 1970): 295-6.
SQ Music (January) produced atavistic suggestions ... [review paraphrases **B334**].

B345 Donald Peart. "Editorial." *Music Now* 1, no. 3 (March 1970): 3.
Love 200 has had to atone for the warmth of its acceptance in the Town Hall by a cold and uncomprehending press reception.
Also: Mike Williams, "New discs: uneasy amalgam," *Australian*, 28 March, mentions **Love 200** as an example of pop-classical amalgam which is no longer interesting.)

B346 "People of Interest. Music of Asia." *Hemisphere* 14 (March 1970): [41].
PS (photographed with students) lectured on Japanese classical music and on contemporary Japanese music at the University of Sydney's summer school [January].

B347 Kenneth Hince. "Lessons for a critic from an old master." *Australian*, 7 March 1970.

Ketjak, alone of the works on the program, had an irresistible gusto that made me hustle up an aspiration for Sculthorpe's soul.

B348   Kay Lucas. "Flowerpot power hits Melbourne." *Bulletin*, 14 March 1970
In February the youth of Melbourne was given its first course of instruction [by conductor Hopkins] in that exciting new game of Australian Rules Concert—Going to the Proms. In **Ketjak** double bass players were asked to kick their instruments but the more conservative Melbourne musicians preferred to stamp loudly on the floor.

B349   Hugo Cole. "Today's music." *Financial Times* (London), 25 March 1970.
Irkanda IV is a long, meditative piece. The work has an aggressive simplicity: a slow melodic unwinding. PS's simply-textured backgrounds seem to be newly-conceived, never borrowed from the common stock of clever and up-to-date technical tricks.

B350   Frank Harris. "Helpmann was tops." *Mirror*, 11 May 1970.
Watching the Australian Ballet's revival of **Sun Music** reminded me of the overwhelming richness of this choreographer's imagination.
Other reviews: R. S., "Sun Music only partly survives," *Telegraph*, 11 May; Beth Dean, *SMH*, 11 May (fascinating Sculthorpe score); Pamela Saunders, "Ballet: Dancers who keep it cool," *Australian*, 16 May; and a review in *Nation*, 16 May.

B351   Linda Phillips. "A triumph for youth." *Sun*, 26 May 1970.
I felt nothing but admiration for the AYO. **Music for Japan** was mainly percussive, though highly interesting, very objective, and rhythmically vital.

B352   John Sinclair. "His dream a success." *Herald*, 26 May 1970.
Music for Japan began promisingly enough with mysterious veils of orchestral tone but disintegrated in a hail of percussion, all of which did not disguise a lack of rhythmic invention.

B353   Felix Werder. "They're a credit to Australia." *Age*, 26 May 1970.
Music for Japan in the "Sun-music" genre provided the thrill of the AYO concert.
Also reviewed: Advocate, 4 June [no head].

B354   David Ahern. "Clothes maketh a composer." *Daily Telegraph*, 28 May 1970.
Amid chortles of delight over recent additions to his wardrobe, PS talked about **Music for Japan**, "my best work so far." If compositions are the apparel of the composer, Sculthorpe is "well clothed" in both senses of the term.

B355   Suzanne Gartner. "Seven Men Igniting the New Opera." *Vogue Australia* 14 (June/July 1970): 88-9, 1006.
Seven composers have been commissioned to write one-act works for the new opera house. Sculthorpe calls his, tentatively, *Cook*.
(Almost all press coverage of the opera house construction-in-progress mentions Sculthorpe's opera plans, as, for example, *SMH*, 16 May 1970. Ahern, "Operatic goings-on," *Bulletin*, 24 June 1972: 43, mentions that in 1969 PS turned down the one-act commission; the contract gave the opera company the right to refuse performance.)

B356   "Leading members in the arts." *Daily Telegraph*, 13 June 1970.
Sculthorpe has been awarded the MBE for his services to music. Investiture ceremony at Government House three months later (25 Sept) is announced in "Lifesaver honoured

for 2,000 rescues," *SMH*, 26 Sept (Australia "is coming of age musically," says PS).

B357 Larry Sitsky. "Peter Sculthorpe." *Current Affairs Bulletin* 46, no. 3 (29 June 1970), "New Music" issue: 40-41.
Entry appears in section headed "Six Australian Composers" and includes a classified list of works. Sculthorpe is motivated by an intensity of emotion, usually one of loss, loneliness and grief; his music is strongly sensual, and generally hovers between extremes of static sounds and a sort of cultivated primitivism.

B358 "People of interest: composer for Tokyo." *Hemisphere* 14 (Aug 1970): [41].
PS (shown in photo with AYO member) will be a guest at a seminar at Orchestral Space in Tokyo this month. He believes "a successful blend of music from East and West would be the greatest music ever heard." (*Also:* Maslyn Williams, "Youth Orchestra's Success at Expo," *Hemisphere* 14 (October 1970): 30-35, interviews conductor Hopkins (shown in photo with PS, p. 32) after **Music for Japan** performance.)

B359 "Talented composer is inspired by Asia." *QV: Quarterly Journal for World Travellers* 3 (Aug/Sept 1970).
PS says that **Music for Japan** is "a putting together of the Australian elements which I see as the desert, bush and city."
Expo items include: "Australian Youth Orchestra to give concerts in Osaka," *Asahi Evening News*, 7 July; and two pieces by Hazel Reader, "The dream comes true," [unident. newspaper, 15 July], and a typescript "Review of the Canberra Concert given by the AYO on July 14th, 1970

B360 "Composer has won world acclaim." *Examiner*, 11 August 1970, Supplement: 11.
At 40, PS (shown in photo) is Australia's leading composer. This essay reviews his early musical experiences, education, teaching, and compositions, as in **B341**.

B361 Kenneth Hince. "Second-rate prelude to tour." *Australian*, 22 August 1970: 17.
It was disappointing that the short-winded **Sun Music III** will be played on the MSO's US tour. (Letter to the editor on 31 August says Hince heard a cut version.)

B362 Dr. W. Lovelock. "Musica 'Viva' style." *Courier-Mail*, 7? Sept 1970.
Festival performances in Brisbane (including SQ 8) left nothing to be desired. PS spoke on some of his experiences in Japan.

B363 Roger Covell. " 'Love 200' again at Town Hall." *SMH*, 10 Sept (late edns) & 11 Sept 1970: 10.
The popular acclaim for **Love 200** seemed to me entirely deserved. I was as glad as most other members of the audience to hear a repeat of the final section.
Other reviews: Eva Wagner, "All good fun, even when the lights failed" (at Capitol Theatre, second night), *Australian* ("PS, I am sure, can do much better"); and Ahern, "Definition of position needed," *Telegraph* (PS should define his position vis-à-vis avant-garde music).

B364 David Ahern. "Society's first two concerts." *Telegraph*, 23 Sept 1970.
Peter Kenny played a Beethoven piano sonata on a prepared piano, resulting in a wonderfully tinny, de-composed Beethoven. **Dream** contained interesting sounds.

B365 Roger Covell. "Music cocktail." *SMH*, 23 September 1970.

Dream was essentially a vocalise for Jeannie Lewis with various plinking, sighing, gonging sounds as background, rising to an amplified climax. As preparation, Sculthorpe heaped objects on the piano strings to distort a Beethoven sonata to a half choked jangle. It dispelled the rather earnest, slightly glum air of the proceedings.

B366 F. R. Blanks. "VIVA! This was electrifying." *SMH*, 14 October 1970.
Tabuh Tabuhan, given an electrifying performance last night, can lay fair claim to be considered the most beautiful piece of music (not, mind you, the best) written by a contemporary Australian. (*Brief mentions*: Ahern, "Life, music in Orient," *Telegraph*, 14 Oct; and Prerauer, "Never a dull moment," *Sun* [one of the best pieces ever written for wind quintet, with percussion added].)

B367 "Gongs but no cow bells for farmers." *SMH*, 14 October 1970.
The SSO began the world premiere of **Music of Rain** without announcement, after 20 minutes of speeches. When it ended, the dairymen applauded Sculthorpe all the way to the stage. (*Pre-concert publicity*: Ann Treweek, "Sculthorpe's rain theme," *SMH*, 9 Sept: 5; "Anthem for farmers," *West Australian*, 11 Sept: 7 [with photo of PS]; "XVIII International Dairy Congress," *SMH*, 12 Oct; and an *Examiner* item.)

B368 David Ahern. "Sunny outlook for this music." *Telegraph*, 15 Oct 1970.
Music of Rain discovers no new paths but I think it is his best work. It is hauntingly charming, ingenuous, and well constructed, giving me a very soft, warm-inside feeling.
   Also: Ahern, "Control, balance," *Telegraph*, 16 Oct (subscription audience accepted the work "hook, line and sinker").

B369 Roger Covell. " 'Rain' highly pleasing." *SMH*, 15 October 1970 (late edn). Also published as "Sculthorpe's rain image," 16 October: 32.
Music of Rain exists in that glinting, chiming, sighing climate which has reflected the composer's love of Indonesian gamelan sounds from his **Anniversary Music**.
   Covell, "Eloquence of Barry Tuckwell," ibid., 19 Oct, reports that the repeated performance confirms that **Rain** is extremely pleasant and well-calculated music.

B370 Frank Harris. "Stars didn't flash." *Mirror*, 15 October 1970.
In **Music of Rain** the dairymen certainly got their money's worth in an outwardly pleasing and beautiful composition.

B371 Maria Prerauer. "Alarm clock baton." *Sun*, 15 October 1970: 71.
Based on a Javanese melody but reorchestrated for our instruments, **Music of Rain** seemed about as Australian as a boomerang made in Japan. (In "Northern Opera," *Nation*, 31 Oct: 17, she calls it PS's latest contribution to light musical meteorology.)

B372 Kenneth Robins. "A confusion of values." *Bulletin*, 17 October 1970.
Dream is in the current Sculthorpe syndrome, a combination of delight, expediency and perversity. It was visually if not aurally entertaining.

B373 Eva Wagner. "Only the spark of excitement was missing." *Australian*, 19 October 1970.
Two pieces by Sculthorpe heard last week [**Tabuh Tabuhan, Music of Rain**] demonstrated his technical facility, amiability, and approachability; yet I feel that he has not really given us a sample of his total capabilities.
   Reporting overseas, Blanks, "Australia," *Musical Times* 111 (Dec 1970): 1249, names **Music For Rain** among new works recently performed.

B374 Anne Boyd. "Not for export: recent developments in Australian music." *Musical Times* 111 (November 1970): 1097-1100.

PS achieved recognition overseas before his importance was discovered in Australia. Australian government policy does not yet support overseas circulation of our music, so that much of it is "not for export."

B375 "Dream music." *Australian,* 7 November 1970.
Dream is an extension of chance music. PS will ring an ancient Tibetan temple bell to signal a move to the next section.

B376 Raymond Ericson. "Australians give 1st concert here." *NY Times,* Thursday 12 November 1970: 53.
Sun Music III is a tonally handsome blend of gamelan-like sounds, percussive effects (some by the strings) and bleating horns. It is longer on color than density of ideas.

B377 "Composer back for opening." *Mercury,* 12 November 1970: 6.
PS is at Launceston for the opening of the city's new "live" theatre, the Princess. He has written **Overture for a Happy Occasion** as opening music.
Other coverage: "A gala night for city's new theatre," *Examiner,* 13 November, "Women's World" sect.; and "Overture for birthplace," [*Examiner* ?].

B378 Tess Lawrence. "Only room for music." *Examiner,* 14 November 1970.
Asked why he was "still unmarried," PS replied that there was only room in his life for music. He was once voted one of the four most eligible bachelors in Sydney, and he is in constant demand for interviews at home and overseas.

B379 Max Oldaker. "Australian Ballet." *Examiner,* 17 November 1970.
Sculthorpe's **Overture** is the finest thing he's written.

B380 "Composer's gift to city." *Examiner,* 18 November 1970.
PS has given the city of Launceston the original manuscript of **Overture for a Happy Occasion**. Photo shows library assistant Barbara Bailey looking at the score.

B381 John Clare. "Peter Sculthorpe." *Music Maker* 38 (December 1970): 6-7.
PS discusses his music and his combining classical and rock musicians in **Love 200** and **Dream**. Interview includes a small photo of the composer at home and a large photo on the cover of this issue, and is illustrated with the beginning of the chart for **Dream**.

B382 Robina Rathbone. "Asia's influence on Australian music." *Hemisphere* 14 (December 1970): 26-30.
Large photo shows PS with Javanese *gamelan* instruments acquired for the University of Sydney (where Rathbone studies music).

B383 Frank Harris. "AYO makes a tour hit." *Daily Mirror,* 8 Dec 1970: 50.
Recording session before the tour went well, and **Music for Japan** was the "star piece" of the record [D30], which is out now.

B384 Bob Engisch. "Youth orchestra stole the show." *Examiner,* [Dec 1970].
Launceston-born PS has "pride of place" among the Australian composers on the AYO recording of **Music for Japan** [D30] which caps a good year for this group.

B385 Roger Covell. "Great music year for Sculthorpe." *SMH,* 30 Dec 1970.
Past year saw an unparalleled series of performances of his music.

B386 Ronald Conway. *The Great Australian Stupor: An interpretation of the Australian way of life.* Melbourne: Sun Books, 1971.

(P. 221:) PS and others are able to live in both the academic and creative worlds and thus avoid the "cultural cringe" that A. A. Philips describes.

B387   Ian Cugley. "The contemporary composer and education." *Music in Tertiary Education. Australian UNESCO Seminar* (University of Queensland, August 1969), ed. Gordon D. Spearritt. Canberra: Australian Government Publishing Service, 1971. P. 27-32. Repr. in *Music Now* 2, no. 1 (April 1972): 30-34.
PS's music is highly personal and empirical; he writes by inspiration rather than technique. His commitments are almost overwhelming.

B388   "Music in Australia." *Larousse Encyclopedia of Music*. London: Hamlyn, 1971. Based on "La Musique: les hommes, les instruments, les oeuvres," ed. Norbert Dufourcq.
The 1963 Hobart conference proclaimed the maturity of the new generation of composers such as PS (shown playing an Indonesian gong chime, p. 505).

B389   Ronald McCuaig. *Australia and the Arts*. Canberra: Australian News and Information Bureau, n. d. [c1971]. P. 35.
PS and other present-day Australians have composed for the AYO.

B390   Roger Covell. "Wand of youth for Sculthorpe." *SMH* 3 January 1971.
Music for Japan (D30) shows PS at the summit and summation of the **Sun Music** idiom.

B391   Art exhibition opening. *Sun-Herald*, 7 February 1971.
"Our own composer" PS opened the Modern Japanese Decorative Art exhibition at the Arts Council Gallery in the presence of the president and the Consul-General of Japan, Mr. Masuro Takashima; photo shows PS and Mr. and Mrs. Takashima. (Report by Di Arthur, "Hello there," *Sunday Mirror*, 7 Feb, also includes photo.)

B392   David Ahern. "Orchestra conductor 'brilliant.'" *Telegraph*, 12 Feb 1971.
At its best, **Music for Japan** was a lukewarm leftover from PS's **Sun Music** series.

B393   Roger Covell. "A more varied Sculthorpe." *SMH*, 12 February 1971.
Music for Japan is among Sculthorpe's most rewarding and shapely musical achievements. The strongly rhythmic central section reaches a real climax.

B394   Frank Harris. "Music goes naked for the Proms." *Daily Mirror*, 12 February 1971.
Introducing his **Music for Japan**, PS, in a blazing yellow open-neck shirt, touched lightly on its experimental sound textures, then added consolingly, "I've introduced two stark naked E major chords—and that's about as way out as one can get." Tremendous applause came from the "with it" crowd. The piece was bright.

B395   Maria Prerauer. "A pretty good start for Prom." *Sun*, 12 Feb 1971.
Music for Japan was bright, colourful and foot-tapping rhythmic "pop." It came off with a touch of brilliance especially in the percussion. (*Also:* in "Composers allsorts," *Nation*, 6 March: 17, she calls it "the best of Sculthorpe's Nipponese music.")

B396   Eva Wagner. "Power and the Proms." *Australian*, 15 February 1971.
Music for Japan seemed a great step forward in this composer's creative activity.

B397   "Musetta's column" [Ahern]. *Sunday Australian*, 28 February 1971.

The Percussionists of Strasbourg obviously have a puckish sense of humour. PS, scared that he wouldn't finish **How the Stars Were Made** in time for the March 31 deadline, asked for an extension. It was willingly given. The deadline is now April 1.

B398 William S. Mann. "Radcliffe Quartets." *Gramophone* 48 (March 1971): 1484.
SQ Music [D57] is unlike any music I know, and durably compulsive, fascinating and stimulating, a certain cure for lassitude.

B399 Linda Phillips. "Happening at a Prom." *Sun*, 8 March 1971.
Love 200 caused somewhat of a sensation. The young people responded with streamers, balloons, and cheers in what was indeed their cup of tea, if a bit too strong for me.
Other reviews mention the work briefly: Sinclair. "A good time was had by all." *Herald* (things have changed since Captain Cook); and Werder, "Should bleak normality follow Proms?" *Age* (it was an ungainly failure at musical alchemy).

B400 Sue Falk. "Sculthorpe work glowed." *Canberra News*, 11 March 1971: 4.
The presence of PS and the performance of his **Irkanda IV** were the undoubted highlights of last night's concert.

B401 W. L. Hoffmann. "An adventurous beginning." *Canberra Times*, 11 March 1971.
Irkanda IV is a dark-toned and obsessive threnody and a deeply personal utterance that remains one of the most important and enduring of this composer's output.

B402 W. L. Hoffmann. "Re-establishing contact." *Canberra Times*, 12 March 1971.
Sculthorpe's lunch-hour talk, "Pop music: from Mozart to the present day," was illustrated with a tape of **Love 200**. He pointed out that while "pop" music has always been able to communicate simply and directly with the people, since Mozart's time classical music has become gradually more sophisticated and so appealed to fewer listeners. ("Free lecture on pop," ibid., 11 March, announces the lecture.)

B403 Roger Covell. "Quartet's rapport." *SMH*, 15 March 1971.
The first Sydney performance of **SQ Music**, which neatly alternates songful rumination and sharply splintered cross-metres, was well prepared but lacked the extra edge of conviction of the London performance last year.

B404 Malcolm Williamson. "How Australian can Australian music become?" *Music Now* 1, no. 4 (April 1971): 13-15.
PS's intelligence, wisdom, and tranquility are unusual in a composer. In the **Sun Music** pieces he has invented a music. Head and heart collaborate in his compositional processes to produce a whole music of innate romanticism and cerebral brilliance.

B405 Larry Sitsky. "New music." *SMH*, 6 April 1971: 21.
Paragraph headed "Peter Sculthorpe" (with small photo) is part of an assessment of the "revolution" in Australian music and its move to international standing.

B406 Fred Blanks. "Better but not as good." *SMH*, 8 April 1971.
Irkanda IV (April 7) has the great elegaic beauty of this composer's Bloch-phase.

B407 "Pop with a Bachground." *SMH*, 13 May 1971: 10.
Publicity for **Love 201** includes a picture from the rehearsal. *Also:* Ursula O'Connor, "Sculthorpe writing rock for Uni arts festival," [Canberra, April].

B408   Roger Covell. "A Brandenburg ballet from Sculthorpe." *SMH, c*24 May 1971.
Love 201 is the musical equivalent of collage. Unfortunately, deficiencies in volume control allowed Bach to drown out Sculthorpe. Dancing was harmless and forgettable.
   Blanks "Australia," *Musical Times* 112 (Sept 1971): 885, reports that Love 201 combined, in dubious logic, Bach with "rock".

B409   Romola Costantino. "Doing their 'thing' to Bach." *SMH*, May[?] 1971.
Garth Welch's conventional ballet-dressed "Duo" was set, inappropriately, to seductive Balinese-style music by PS. Worst of all, musically and visually, was Love 201.

B410   "The art of seduction aided by the gastronomic arts: composer Peter Sculthorpe." *Vogue Australia* 15 (June 1971): 98.
Sculthorpe recommends oysters Kilpatrick, then cold lobster with lots of pepper, a little zabaglione, and a good champagne.

B411   Joan Chissell. "ISCM Festival. Queen Elizabeth Hall." *Times*, Monday 7 June 1971: 8.
PS was the most familiar name. Tabuh Tabuhan uses Indonesian materials.

B412   Robert L. Henderson. "Work's Pacific link." *Daily Telegraph*, 7 June 1971.
Tabuh Tabuhan created nothing vital, with oceanic sounds only sentimentalised.

B413   Andrew Porter. "Incredible Floridas." *Financial Times*, 7 June 1971.
PS has written better music than Tabuh Tabuhan, travelogue music which was lucky not to be laughed off the stage by the ISCM audience. (Bowen, "Goehr's Triptych," *Guardian*, 7 June, does not mention Sculthorpe's piece.)

B414   Harold Schonberg. "Avant-garde music irritating to critics in London." *New York Times*, Tuesday 8 June 1971: 33.
Tabuh Tabuhan was a curious choice for a festival of avant-garde music, and was greeted with a few boos. While out of place surrounded by stern atonalism, it was a rather pretty misfit.

B415   John Moses. "Living on a song." *Telegraph*, 4 July 1971.
One can imagine Tabuh Tabuhan (D71) as a very beautiful ballet, and as a magnificent aid to seduction. Article includes a photo of Sculthorpe.

B416   Theodore Price. " 'Music Today' returns for Shaw Festival." *Rochester Democrat and Chronicle*, 2 August 1971.
SQ 8 is extremely, and at times profoundly, communicative.

B417   William Littler. "Modern music workshop a stimulating experience." *Toronto Daily Star*, 2 August 1971.
SQ 8 captured the spotlight. (*Also mentioned by:* Peter Godard, ibid.)

B418   Peter Sculthorpe. "Take us to our leaders." *Sunday Australian*, 29 August 1971: 11.
"Does Australia have leaders to take it into the future? Six prominent people answer." Says Sculthorpe, Australia seems to have only a future; the heroes and myths of our own past are almost forgotten. When our children are educated about our heroes, and emulate them, an abundance of leaders will be found to help us to find our identity and

our direction. I am an optimist, but optimism is only a beginning.

B419 Hugh Ottaway. "Sebastian Forbes (etc.). Argo ZRG 672." *Musical Times* 112 (September 1971): 866.
SQ Music [D57] is by far the most encouraging piece on this record, for its personal impress and its independence from the usual post-Schoenberg, post-Bartók modernism. Asian (Balinese) elements contribute to the music's primitive vitality.

B420 "A room for Peter Sculthorpe, composer." *Australian Home Journal,* September 1971: 53, 56.
An electronic music sculpture plays PS's music [Landscape]; some of his way-out manuscripts will be on one wall. The room is one of several rooms for famous people to be in the exhibition "Rooms on View 1971" to commemorate the 20th anniversary of the Society of Interior Designers of Australia.
Other coverage: Diana Fisher, "Briefly over breakfast." *Sunday Australian,* 19 Sept, 1971: 27A; "A room—with a view" [unident. pub.]; Melanie Petrovic, "With a view to their rooms" (most popular room at opening was PS's); Ron Saw, "What I want for Christmas," *Telegraph* (would trim the "electronic music sculpture" with a shotgun); and "Peter Sculthorpe's magic music room." *Electronics Today* 1, no. 8 (Nov 1971), cover (color photo) and p. 6, "Room for Peter Sculthorpe."

B421 Roger Covell. "Sculthorpe's sounds suit ensemble." *SMH,* 6 Oct 1971.
How the Stars Were Made is a finely judged and idiomatic score. The eight brief sections have a strong sense of continuity between them.

B422 Frank Harris. "Sculthorpe scores in Musica Viva's concert." *Mirror,* 6 October 1971.
For the young people at least How the Stars Were Made, was the hit of the night. It was typical—and beautiful—Sculthorpe.

B423 Kenneth Hince. "Percussion and a zest for sound." *Australian,* 9 Oct 1971.
How the Stars Were Made is delightful music, with impressive and very heartwarming vigour. The performance was partially encored.
Hince, "The beat of a different drum," ibid., notes the group's use of theatre.

B424 Maria Prerauer. "Communing with chamber music gods." *Sun-Herald,* 10 October 1971.
In his brilliant How the Stars Were Made PS recreates an elemental atmosphere of earth, fire and water. At the well-built-up point of highest dramatic tension the music suddenly explodes magically into the silvery shimmer of shooting comets.

B425 Kenneth Robins. "With bells, drums and wobble-board." *Bulletin,* 16 October 1971: 39-40.
The performance of How the Stars Were Made by the spellbinding Percussions of Strasbourg (shown in photo) must have been a composer's dream.

B426 "Musetta's column." *Sunday Australian.* 17 October 1971.
The entrance foyer of an unnamed big city hotel at 2 a.m. was the site of some impromptu playing by PS and the Strasbourg percussionists.

B427 Diana Fisher. "Briefly over breakfast." *Sunday Australian,* 24 October 1971: 21A.
PS, a neighbour, leaves on Thursday for the University of Sussex. Peter told me that he

can't wait to get lost in the antique shops of Brighton again.

B428   [Recording review.] *Mainichi Daily News* (Tokyo), 3 December 1971.
PS's **SQ 6** is stunning, as is the new recording by the Mari Iwamoto Quartet [**D55**].

B429   Kenneth Hince. Standout in the local field of few-and-far-between."
Australian, 27 December 1971.
Recording of **SQ Music** [**D25**], one of PS's finest works, defines beautifully his move
towards a personal, convincing, and thoroughly self-consistent idiom. In **SQ 7** the
mannerisms are integrated directly into the fabric of the music.
   Other reviews: Wentworth Courier, 1 Dec; and T. H. Naisby, "Classics," *Newcastle
Morning Herald and Miner's Advocate,* 11 March 1972.

B430   Suzanne Gartner. "Vogue's eyeview: Music." *Vogue Australia* 15 (December 1971/January 1972): 26.
In **How the Stars Were Made** the crotali or antique English cymbals are especially
enchanting, and used for when the stars come out. "I got the web of sound from the
xylophones, also timpani," he explains.

B431   James Glennon. *Understanding Music.* Adelaide: Rigby, 1972.
Under "Peter Sculthorpe" is a brief biography and list of works (p. 211, 307). (Similar
coverage is in: *Australia, The Fifth Continent* [Sydney: Angus & Robertson, 1972]: 130.)

B432   James Murdoch. "Peter Sculthorpe." In *Australia's Contemporary
Composers.* South Melbourne: Macmillan, 1972. P. 163-73.
PS has emerged as Australia's representative composer, both in Australia and overseas. Included is a list of 73 works and a discography of 17 items. PS is also mentioned
in the introduction, and in the foreword by Peter Maxwell Davies. Photo: after p. 130.

B433   Fred R. Blanks. "Australia." *Musical Times* 113 (February 1972): 178.
The Fellowship of Australian Composers now has over 120 members. Its idiomatic
spectrum ranges from the experimental, via the advanced and standard (PS is in this
group) to various shades of the traditional and nostalgic.

B434   Robert Henderson. [Concert review.] *Daily Telegraph* (London), 15
April 1972.
Music for Japan seemed a model of reticence, creating a highly evocative atmosphere.

B435   Max Harrison. "Polyphonia Orchestra." *Times,* 15 April 1972.
In **Music for Japan** the influences of Tibetan chant and *gagaku* percussion are fully assi-
milated into an extremely personal idiom. This music grows without a sign of motion.

B436   Ronald Crichton. "Polyphonia." *Financial Times,* 18 April 1972.
Music for Japan is short, immediately apprehensible in form, but strange in detail. The
effect is not slight or simple: Sculthorpe evidently knows what he wants to do and
how to achieve it. (Essentially the same review appears in Crichton's "New Music:
Polyphonia," *Musical Times* 113 [June 1972]: 577.)

B437   David Gyger. "Opera House premiere by Sculthorpe." *Australian,* 6
June 1972: 3.
A highly experimental opera, provisionally titled **Rites of Passage**, is almost certain
to be the first opera staged at the Sydney Opera House when it opens late next year.

B438   Editorial: "Rite night at the opera." *Telegraph,* 10 June 1972: 6.

The first opera performed at the Sydney Opera House is going to be ritual ceremonies associated with man's life crises, accompanied by hymns. Life crises will be when people who have paid $5,000 for their seats want their money back.

B439   Buxton Orr. "Notes: First Performances and Commissions." *Composer*, no. 44 (Summer 1972): 39.
List includes **Ketjak** at the Cheltenham Festival. So does the list in "First Performances," *World of Music* 14 (1972), no. 4 : 87.

B440   Joan Chissell. "Commonwealth Music. Cheltenham Festival." *Times*, 10 July 1972.
Ketjak was the strongest reminder it's 1972. The sound effects were ingenious, and there was rhythm. The work can scarcely fail to make its mark as a virtuoso stunt, a comment on what Sculthorpe considers the world's increasing repetition.

B441   Martin Cooper. "Tape echoes make six into a crowd." London *Daily Telegraph*, 10 July 1972.
In **Ketjak** PS uses feedback to convert his six singers into what seems a huge gathering of men. These variations of density and rhythmic complexity are handled with imagination as well as virtuosity.

B442   Elizabeth Webster. "Cheltenham." *Music and Musicians* 21 (September 1972): 74, 76.
Ketjak produced only boredom.
      E. M. Webster, "Cheltenham Festival," *Musical Opinion* 95 (Sept 1972): 629, 631, 633, reports that the pretentious **Ketjak** produced tedium.

B443   "New opera 'breaks all rules' " (p. 1); "A rite at the Opera" (p. 7). *SMH*, 27 September 1972.
According to reports from London, **Rites of Passage** will enact Aboriginal tribal rites which are common to all mankind, he says. "If we need sex on stage, we must have it."
      Similar sensational reports, with photos of PS, appear the same day in: Robert Milliken (in London), "New opera may shock," *Advertiser*, 27 Sept: 5; "Nude start for Opera House" (from London), *Sun* (Melbourne), 27 Sept: 2; "Sculthorpe talks from London about his nude opera," *Sunday Examiner-Express*, 30 Sept: 5; and (brief notices) "Queen is 'welcome,' " *Mercury*, 27 Sept; and "Opera head will grin and bare it," *Examiner*, 28 Sept. "Today's Man Friday" in Sydney *Sun*, 29 Sept, is PS. "Sayings of the week," *SMH*, 29 Sept (quotes PS); Barry Wilson, "Opera work—composer confident," *Mercury*, 6 Oct: 10; "The lover of the opera," *West Australian*, 10 Oct: 8; Marion Macdonald, *Bulletin*, 11 Nov: 30. Earlier progress reports include: "Marietta's column," *Australian*, 21 March 1971: (PS will get the commission for the Opera House opening; that rules out Joan Sutherland); and "Musetta's column" [Ahern], *Sunday Australian*, 26 March 1972: 23 (PS is writing his own libretto).

B444   A. E. P. "Varied styles of Australian composers." London *Daily Telegraph*, 2 December 1972.
SQ Music has something of the broad dry stillness and ancient roots of Australia, and refers also to neighbouring cultures in its Balinese timbres. It seems a close cousin of Bartok's Fourth Quartet but is a less emphatic work, less tense.

B445   Stephen Walsh. "Austral Quartet, Purcell Room." *Times*, 2 Dec 1972.
PS is much less free of "the European heroic gesture" than he may like to imagine. I would say that his **SQ Music** is at least as successful in its Western, dynamic characteristics (however unintentional) as in its Polynesian, reflective ones.

B446 "The Times Diary. Gone under." *Times*, 13 Dec 1972: 14 (signed PHS).
Sculthorpe's opera will not be presented in the first season in the Sydney Opera House.
Elizabeth Riddell, "Writer denies row over opera," *Australian*, 15 Dec: 9, reports
that PS in London explained that a change of director caused the work to be postponed.

B447 Peter Sculthorpe. "The Walter and Eliza Hall Institute Lecture." Summary in *The Walter and Eliza Hall Institue of Medical Research* [annual report], 1972-73. Melbourne, 1973.
(P. [20-22]:) PS (shown in photo) illustrated his professional evolution by long excerpts
of his music. Instead of writing the lecture for publication, he has written a piece of
music, *Microscope Music* (score follows, from **Rites of Passage**, *Fourth Chorale*).

B448 Geoffrey Serle. *From Deserts the Prophets Come: The Creative Spirit in Australia 1788-1972.* Melbourne: Heinemann, 1973. (P. 205-6, 228.)
PS's career illustrates the comparative advantages open to his generation. Australian
artists will increasingly reach out to Asia as Sculthorpe and Meale have done.

B449 James Erber. "Peter Sculthorpe." *University of Sussex Music*, no. 4 (March 1973): 2.
Sculthorpe (shown in photo on cover), whose **Irkanda IV** will be performed on March
16, was visiting professor here from 1971 to 1972. No one has had a greater influence on
the way I write music than Peter.

B450 Lenore Nicklin. "Composer explains airport mixup: 'Why I became Mr. Scuthorse.' " *SMH*, 3 March 1973: 12.
Peter Sculthorpe, MBE, was surprised to hear would-be interviewers were claiming he
had sneaked back into Australia this week under an assumed name. But it was only a
mistake with the plane booking in Singapore. He is planning several projects.

B451 Fred Blanks. "Music seminar." *SMH*, Monday 26 March 1973.
Weekend seminar ended yesterday with a forum of four composers under the chairman-
ship of Professor Donald Peart: R. Murray Schafer of Canada; PS, just back from the
fleshpots of England and hankering after those of Bali; Ross Edwards; and Kim Williams. PS said that all publicity, good or bad, was in the long run good for a composer.

B452 Fred Blanks. "A gallery of talent." *SMH*, 1973.
Last night in the Great Hall, celebrating the 25th anniversary of the University of
Sydney Music Department, PS with lectern and microphone and tape-recorder set out
to deflect the limelight of composing successes from himself on to the numerous and
impressive echelons of composers nurtured by his and Professor Donald Peart's regime.
Covell, "University's role in music," ibid., reviews the department's achievements.

B453 James Murdoch. "Under Peter Sculthorpe, our music has at last grown up." *National Times*, 2-7 July 1973: 22.
Long article is essentially Murdoch's "Peter Sculthorpe" chapter from his 1972 book
Australia's Contemporary Composers (**B432**), with a new (not from the book) photo.

B454 "Six lyrics out of 2500 chosen in anthem quest." *Australian*, 5 July 1973.
In the second stage of the quest, which will close on August 31, four judges, PS among
them, will select which tunes should be considered for the anthem.

B455 "L'ton is Peter's haven from fame!" *Examiner*, Saturday 21 July 1973: 3.
"World famous composer Peter Sculthorpe" is at home in Launceston for two days

before flying to Bali to make a film. He has several other projects, and his phone is always ringing. (On same page, "On the spot" reporter "Mister Ex" reports that PS consented to become one of the National Anthem contest judges so that people entering the contest would stop phoning him.)

B456   Roger Covell. "Music in Australia: Are we a colony of Europe?" *Current Affairs Bulletin* 50, no. 3 (1 August 1973): 14-21, *infra*.
Among the sparse credentials of the Australian *avant-garde* of the early sixties were some early, mostly discarded works of Peter Sculthorpe.

B457   Fred Blanks. "Sculthorpe on Bali." *SMH*, Wednesday 19 Sept 1973: 24.
During his talk for the Australian Society for Music Education (Sept 17) PS revealed that until six weeks ago he had never visited Bali. Winnowing myth from reality, he found that in Bali music is not all-important, not specially creative, and just as elitist as elsewhere. He can hardly wait to go back.

B458   "Anthem quest judges stick to old tunes." *SMH*, 29 Sept 1973: 1.
Dateline: Canberra. After consideration of 1,300 tunes submitted, the judges (including PS, shown in photo) in the national anthem quest have recommended familiar and established songs. (Item appears next to coverage of last night's Opera House opening.)

B459   Fred Blanks. "Ingenuity in an unholy alliance." *SMH*, 3 Nov 1973.
Sculthorpe's **String Quartet No. 6** is still one of his finest non-oriental works.

B460   Fred R. Blanks. "Australia." *Musical Times* 114 (December 1973): 1262-3.
The opening of Sydney Opera House was celebrated in a succession of memorable concerts; composers included PS [**P73-10, -11**]. Also on p. 1263 is a news item: the Australian National Anthem Quest Committee has rejected all 1300 compositions submitted.

B461   W. J. Hudson. "1951-72." In *A New History of Australia*, ed. Frank Crowley. Melbourne: William Heinemann, 1974.
(P. 549:) Though there is perhaps less activity in music than literature, locally-based composers like Peter Sculthorpe are making their mark.

B462   "Peter (Joshua) Sculthorpe." *Dictionary of Contemporary Music*, ed. John Vinton. New York: E. P. Dutton and Co., 1974.
Brief biography notes the Asian influences on PS's music. Works are listed chronologically from **Sonatina** through **Music of Rain**.

B463   Ned Rorem. *The Final Diary, 1961-1972*. New York: Holt, Rinehart, and Winston, [1974]. Also published as *The Later Diaries of Ned Rorem, 1961-1972*, Northpoint Press. P. 194.
Yaddo, September 18, 1966: This evening we heard the tapes of one Peter Skullthorpe [*sic*], a mustachioed Tasmanian whose musical canvas is soaked in novel color.

B464   John Villaume. "It's a good idea, but . . . ." *Courier-Mail*, Monday 25 February 1974: 8
First of three ABC modern music forums chaired by PS (with Prof. Noel Nickson and John Gilfedder) at the Univ. of Queensland on Saturday night was rather elementary. Villaume reports on the second forum in "Music Forum 'off the ground,' " ibid., 27 Feb, and on the final one in "Modern Music a real success," ibid., 29 Feb (**Music for Japan** brought revealing comment from the composer and the orchestra excelled itself).

B465   Suzanne Gartner. "New recordings." *Vogue Australia*, April 1974.

One of the most exciting of the new releases is Jeannie Lewis's *Free Fall Through Featherless Flight* [D17]. Here is one of the best soprano voices in the country doing extraordinary things with a great collection of local songs, including *It'll rise again*.

B466 Wenzel de Neergaard and Peter Sculthorpe. "Rites of Passage—half a year before." *Opera Australia* no. 2 (April 1974): 30-31.
PS reviews his work in the theatre up to the composition of **Rites of Passage**.

B467 Elizabeth Auld. "Opera without heroes." *Australian*, Sat. 11 May 1974.
PS yesterday heard **Rites of Passage** for the first time, at a rehearsal (shown in photo) in Melbourne. The Victorian Police Pipe Band could be heard faintly. Sculthorpe was delighted and regretted there was no place for bagpipes in the **Rites**.

B468 Roger Covell. "An uncommitted quartet." *SMH*, Friday 21 June 1974.
PS's masterly **SQ 6** was performed Wednesday night with the Second Quartet of Anne Boyd (who is now in England). His quartet is similarly economical in its given material, and more economical in its use of it.

B469 Peter Sculthorpe. "Rites of Passage." *Opera Australia* no. 3 (July 1974), 31-3.
PS discusses the ideas on which **Rites of Passage** is based and plans for its production.

B470 Fred Blanks. "Australian music liberated." *SMH*, 1 July 1974.
Friday's concert included the profoundly elegiac **Irkanda IV** in a new version for string sextet and percussion. Unfortunately, there were few paying customers. Thursday evening in the well-filled Opera House Music Room, "PS the cunningly entertaining lecturer analyzed PS the patriotically versatile composer" of **Rites of Passage**.
(*Also:* Lindsey Browne, "Music of the spheres," *Sun-Herald*, 30 June, mentions "the Hardyesque grandeur of Sculthorpe's conception.")

B471 David Gyger. "New gem by Shostakovich." *Australian*, 1 July 1974: 10.
Irkanda IV for string sextet with percussion was thoroughly successful.

B472 "Composer to receive grant of $36,000." *SMH*, 7 August 1974: 8.
PS has been given a special three-year $36,000 grant by the Federal Government, awarded by the music board of the Australian Council for the Arts and announced by the Prime Minister, Mr. Whitlam, in recognition of his contribution to Australian music. It will enable him to work full-time on several projects. (*Other announcements: Australian*, 1 Aug: 1; and "A gentle knock for the rock," *Sunday Telegraph*, 11 Aug.)

B473 Dorian Wild. "$36,000 grant to fight music 'shame.'" *Australian*, 14 August 1974.
PS says that his grant will enable him to write books on how to make music so that future generations of Australian musicians and composers need feel no shame, or inferiority, at writing music the way it could be written in Australia.

B474 Roger Covell. "First-up tour triumph." *SMH*, 9 September 1974.
Sun Music IV in Edinburgh was taut and dramatic in its contrasts. [*See also* **B701**.]

B475 Romola Costantino. "Rites of stormy passage." *SMH*, 14 Sept 1974.
Rites of Passage has had a stormy passage, but now all seems to be under control. *Other publicity:* Leonard Lindon, "Who is this Flier character anyhow?" *Opera Australia* no. 4 (Sept 1974): 24-26; and "Four strike Rite notes," *Telegraph*, 19 Sept, a story, with photo, about the three drummers and pianist Michael Hannan.

B476 Roger Covell. "London audience takes orchestra to its heart." *SMH*, 16 September 1974.
The slow tides and pulsations of **Sun Music IV** were effective in Lincoln's cathedral, with its good acoustics. An audience of 1,700 to 2,000 gave a standing ovation.

B477 Maria Prerauer. "The sound and sight of music." *Sunday Telegraph*, 22 September 1974.
"Survey" on Channel 2 begins next week with *Sun Music For Film*, about PS's **Song of Tailitnama**. It is beautifully filmed, and Sculthorpe's Aboriginal-inspired rhythms are particularly effective. In the first part, he supervises student musicians playing the soundtrack and talks to conductor Hopkins about himself and his music.
(*Other publicity:* "Naked . . . and so discreet," *Sunday Telegraph*, 29 Sept; "Look for Sculthorpe on TV," *Mirror*, 25 Sept.)

B478 Geraldine Pascall. "New opera different and Australian." *Australian*, 28 September 1974.
Rites of Passage was finally in performance after four years, four [seven] abandoned librettists, and 18 hours putting the set on stage. (*Also:* Pleiades in Sydney [from Hobart] reports "New opera was great success," *Mercury*, 28 Sept. "**Rites** opens after a slow passage," *SMH*, Sat. 28 Sept: 19, is illustrated with photos.)

B479 Lindsey Browne. "Sculthorpe's Rites." *Sun-Herald*, 29 September 1974.
This is a work with no future: grotesque dancing, quasi-musical sounds of an electrifying nervous vitality.

B480 Romola Costantino. " 'Rites' striking—but opera?" *SMH*, 30 Sept 1974.
The Australian Opera was jolted into unfamiliar territory, by the often beautiful, striking and original dance-oratorio **Rites of Passage**. Jill Sykes writes (says Costantino), that the action comes in the form of exciting, imaginative dance.

B481 David Gyger. "Stunned by Sculthorpe." *Australian*, 30 Sept 1974.
Rites of Passage is an undoubted milestone for the Australian Opera, for Sculthorpe, and for Australian creativity, even, perhaps, world creativity. There is more in a work of art than can be absorbed fully on first contact.
Gyger reports in "Australia," *Opera Canada* 15, no. 4 (December 1974): 28, I am in the minority of Australian critics who found **Rites of Passage** appealing for the way it strives toward a new form of total musical theatre.

B482 Maria Prerauer. "The Rites of Sculthorpe were wrong." *Telegraph*, 30 September 1974.
Whatever else you might like to call **Rites of Passage** you could never call it an opera. Musically, it is rather a non-event. (In "Boring Rites guilty of all that is wrong." *Sunday Telegraph*, 6 Oct: 4, Prerauer judges it neither good music nor good theatre.)

B483 Frank Harris. "Rites is a pointer to new paths." *Daily Mirror*, 2 Oct 1974.
PS's music was beautifully melodic and expertly conducted. For those prepared to listen to something excitingly new in music theatre, **Rites** is a must.

B484 Nadine Amadio. "Sculthorpe disappoints." *AFR*, 4 Oct 1974.
Rites of Passage was not the compelling, eternal return life-cycle that one might have expected after Sculthorpe's highly articulate lectures, notes and explanations.

B485 Kenneth Hince. "Switching off the Western circuits." *Australian*, 5

October 1974.
Rites of Passage was a thing adequately tedious and overly pretentious.

B486 Brian Hoad. "An essence of Australia." *Bulletin* 96 (5 October 1974): 46.
Rites of Passage emerges as a seminal work of Australian art.

B487 Kevon Kemp. " 'Rites of Passage': a great vision for the future using elements of the past." *National Times*, 7-12 October 1974: 27.
I am quite inexplicably happy that the opening night audience showed a new taste for adventure in taking the work to its heart, albeit with much reserve and argument. Stage excitements included the dance, the music, the physical sight of players drumming away to an almost unbearable level of arousal, the cool, non-verbal singing.

B488 Graham Pont. "Opera's wasteland." *Nation Review*, 18-24 Oct 1974: 26.
Rites of Passage is a failure as an opera. Most people are being *very polite* about this work. People still feel the cultural cringe, especially at the embarrassing lack of an *Australian* opera, and Sculthorpe (shown in a photo) is a respected local musician.

B489 Peter Hellstrom. "Music." *West Australian*, 26 October 1974: 26.
Taxpayers should question some expenditures on new Australian music, including the Federal Government's $36,000 to PS, of whom prize-winning author Patrick White has said, "About ten years ago I felt him incapable of composing an opera. I withdrew."

B490 Julian Russell. "Mixed reception for 'Rites of Passage.' " *Sun*, 30 Oct 1974.
Rites of Passage proved as controversial as expected, engrossing, exciting sometimes.

B491 [Comments as **Rites of Passage** continued.] *SMH*, November 1974.
On 2 Nov: An usher courteously opened an exit door when she saw a man walking down the aisle just as the performance ended. But it was Mr. Sculthorpe himself coming forward to take a bow. [In the Opera House exit doors are in front of each section of seats.]
In "Column 8" (p. 1), 4 Nov: Can't the lights to be turned down outside the exit doors, so that when people walk out during **Rites of Passage** there is no distracting blaze?

B492 Klaus Stahmer. "Schallplatten." *Melos: Zeitschrift für neue Musik* 41, no. 6 (Nov-Dec 1974): 382-3.
Three recent Australian recordings [D20, D25, D43] include works of PS, who represents the Australian avant garde and makes virtuosic use of local color.
In Australia, Barry Jones, "All our own work." [*SMH*?, n.d.], finds the Festival recording [D20] to be unquestionably of export quality.

B493 William Shoubridge. " 'Rites' would not please everyone." *Advertiser*, Friday 8 November 1974: 11.
Rites of Passage was a gripping piece of dramatised philosophy on mortality, a song and dance of the earth.

B494 James Glennon. "Fast moving opera-ballet." *Sunday Mail*, 10 Nov 1974.
Rites of Passage is a striking study of the human life pattern, and a fine achievement by everyone concerned.

B495 "Bali changed his tunes." *SMH*, Monday 11 November 1974.
The film *Tabuh Tabuhan* on ABN 2 on Wednesday night, includes a full Balinese gamelan, a male dancer performing the *kebyar trompong*, and the *ketchak* with a

male chorus of 100. ("Sound of Bali" [unident. pub.] announces a screening on Dec 19.)

B496   Kevon Kemp. "Peter Sculthorpe looks for a writer he can level with." *National Times*, 11-16 November 1974: 23.
The composer of **Rites of Passage** has little in his mind but contriving a way through to his next opera. "What I need is a writer" with whom true rapport can be made.

B497   Fred R. Blanks "Australia." *Musical Times* 115 (December 1974): 1065-6.
In **Rites of Passage**, dark and percussive music acted as a motivating force for dance rites alternating with static choral sections. This earnest multi-media exercise in contemporary allegory lacked variety and any sense of inbuilt excitement.

B498   John Cargher. "Sydney." *Opera News* 39 (28 Dec 1974-4 Jan 1975): 46.
Rites of Passage is not an opera—there is no audible pattern of dramatic progress, only ninety minutes of unbroken music of an admittedly high standard.

B499   Michael Hannan and Peter Sculthorpe. "Rites of Passage." *Music Now* II, no. 22 (December 1974): 11-19.
Hannan interviews Sculthorpe about the work, quoting at length from *Opera Australia* no. 2 (**B465**). A photo from **Rites of Passage** is on the cover of this issue.

B500   Maria Prerauer. "Australia." *Opera* (London) 25 (Dec 1974): 1072, 1089.
Long-awaited **Rites of Passage** premiere proved a big disappointment. Though written for the theatre (it is a "modern ballet"), it is neither good music or good theatre.

B501   "Rites or Wrongs?" *Opera Australia* no. 5 (December 1974): 6-12.
Reactions, pro and con, to **Rites of Passage** come from audience and critics [**B478n, B481-483, B485-488, B490, B493**]. There are nine black-and-white and four color photos from the production and a color photo on the cover. Introduction is by John Winther, General Manager of The Australian Opera, Sydney (which publishes the magazine).

B502   David Gyger. "Classics and a toy piano." *Australian*, 10 December 1974.
Roger Woodward (shown in photo) played **Landscape** in almost total darkness with a rather overpowering dramatic effect.

B503   Peter Crowe. "The crisis of identification: why NZ composers should take an interest in Oceanic music." Auckland: Composers' Association of NZ, 1975. Typescript, mimeo; 12 p.
Crowe urges composers to question the authenticity of their idioms, lists Pacific music resources, and cites ten features identifying PS's music as distinctively Australian.

B504   Martin Johnston. "The Arts." *This is Australia*. Sydney: Hamlyn, 1975.
(P. 249-51:) PS is known for the **Sun Music** series and **Irkanda IV**, a work that demonstrates how some of our artists are learning from Aborigines. This appraisal of Sculthorpe is too short (says its author)—**Rites of Passage** deserves a chapter all to itself.

B505   *Junior Encyclopedia Yearbook 1975: The events of 1974/5*. Sydney: Bay Books, 1975.
(P. 47:) In 1974 **Rites of Passage** debuted at the Opera House. A small photo shows the composer at the piano, and another shows a scene from the production.

B506   Howard Risatti. *New Music Vocabulary: A guide to notational signs for contemporary music*. Urbana: University of Illinois Press, 1975.
Passage from **Irkanda IV** is used to illustrate notation of the direction of the notes of a

stringed instrument's arpeggiated pizzicato (p. [69]).

B507   "Peter Sculthorpe, composer." [Statement on music criticism in unidentified Australian magazine], 1975 (?): 85.
Although we have no tradition of composers or criticism, we do have a few very good critics, like Roger Covell who is internationally recognized. I really emerged as a known composer through criticism in Sydney in the early sixties.

B508   "Around the town." *Sunday Telegraph*, 13 July 1975: 80-81.
Photo shows PS handing over his score of **Rites of Passage** to a member of the ladies committee of the Opera House appeal fund for display in the exhibition hall. Diana Fisher, "Talkabout," reports.

B509   Hugh Ottaway. "Modern orchestral." *Musical Times* 116 (August 1975): 718-719.
Sun Music IV is 'sonic art' rather than music.

B510   Frank Dawes. "Modern piano: Sculthorpe, **Night Pieces**." Ibid., 719-720.
Night Pieces can be played directly on the strings if desired, a fact that probably accounts for their delicate, harplike textures. They are evocative little sketches of a distinctly impressionistic kind. This is music of quality.

B511   Harry Billington. "Planning a course in music for Form 1." *Creative Music Making/Teachers' Handbook*. Glebe NSW: Scoutline Publications, September 1975: 30.
Sun Music III is a work that uses chord clusters.

B512   Tony Gould. "Music's century of the fraud." *Sun*, 13 Sept 1975: 20.
The *Chorales* from **Rites of Passage** is a marvellous work by PS. The conducting was first class and the choir in top form.

B513   Felix Werder. "Composer's modern sound follows great traditions." *Age*, 13 September 1975: 2.
The *Chorales* from **Rites of Passage** were a fine demonstration of pure creativity in the great tradition of organic sound morphology.

B514   Roger Covell. "Of walls, quartets and electrical drones." *SMH*, 20 October 1975: 7.
SQ 9 provided listeners with confirmation of an established and distinguished musical personality. A photo of PS and Covell illustrates the review.

B515   Maria Prerauer. "As Aussie as kangaroo butter." *Australian*, 21 Oct 1975.
SQ 9 is another of PS's atmospheric Great Australian Loneliness works. Players' bows become tapping corroboree sticks, strings drone incantations.

B516   Peter Sculthorpe. "All Australia lacks is a new philosophy." *Australian*, 6 November 1975, "The Arts" supplement: 5.
We have produced few serious writers on our music and the society from which it stems. The composer here is forced to create his own view of himself as a composer and as an Australian.

B517   *Brief Biographical Notes of Some Australian Composers.* Compiled by

the Permanent Recording Section, ABC. Sydney, December 1975. P. 17.
PS composes in most musical forms, has won many prizes in Australia and England, and
has represented Australia at world exhibitions and festivals.

B518   Roger Covell. "Celebration in a vacuum." *SMH*, 2 December 1975.
Sun Music IV contains less of the essential Sculthorpe than a number of his other
works. (Prerauer, "A concert of their own music," *Australian*, 2 Dec, notes: Sun Music IV
came over most effectively in a flashing kaleidoscope of glittering color and lights.)

B519   William Mann. "Austral Quartet." *Times*, 3 December 1975: 11.
SQ 9 is characteristic in its suggestion of mystery and exoticism behind direct musical
language and form. PS went home, this reminds us, not only for Australia but for the
Asian countries nearer at hand and, to him, more stimulating than Europe. (Review is
quoted in "Austral Quartette performs in London," *SMH*, 5 Dec.)

B520   Desmond Shawe-Taylor. "Lyrical and elegant." *Sunday Times*, 7
December 1975: 37.
SQ 9 was true quartet-music, admirably conceived for the medium. I found it a most
vivid and compelling piece.

B521   David Ahern. "Our composers are set in old ways." *Sunday Telegraph*,
7 December 1975.
During the fifties and sixties, music of Meale and PS helped us close the gap from
about fifty years behind Europe or America to about ten years behind or almost equal.
PS has helped in the Sydney-based rejection of European complexity.

B522   John Bird. *Percy Grainger*. London: Elek Books, 1976; Melbourne:
Macmillan, 1977.
Sculthorpe is mentioned in the Acknowledgments, p. xiv.

B523   David Formby. *Australian Ballet*. Sydney: Ure Smith, 1976, P. 34-39.
Six full-page photos of the Sun Music ballet show the *Mirage* and *Growth* scenes.

B524   Peter Game. *The Music Sellers*. Melbourne: Hawthorne Press, 1976.
(P. 182:) Sculthorpe's music is in George Allan's catalogue.

B525   [Interview.] *New Zealand Herald*, 7 January 1976.
Sculthorpe is tutoring the composer group at the Kerikeri Arts Festival, and several of
his works are to be performed. He says, "All the countries around the Pacific share a
heritage and I would like to see this culture expressed in music in its own right."

B526   Ko. "Australia Felix—felix Australia." *Der Tagespiegel/Feuilleton*, No.
9219, Wednesday 14 January 1976: 4.
Koto [Music] was the most interesting. A piece of music of delicate suggestion, it is built
from a four-tone piano ostinato, with violin now and then breaking into its repetitions.

B527   David Ahern. "Keyboard romantics." *Sunday Telegraph*, 15 Feb 1976.
Koto Music [D18] sounds too Asian for the listener to find the composer's reference to
the Australian landscape believable.
Also reviewed: Covell, "The crystallography of the snowflake," *SMH* (date?):
while the plucking of the piano strings is derived from koto music, the result is evocative of the Australian landscape—its stringybark, tin-roof and gibber-plain elements.

B528   Fred Blanks. "Now a sexagenarian Con." *SMH*, 23 February 1976.

In SQ 9 PS's back-to-Bali and back-to-Bloch idioms merge naturally and beautifully. Prerauer, "Life, fire and the old prom spirit," *Australian*, notes that SQ 9 sounded still more devastatingly beautiful than when premiered last year [October 1975].

B529 Denby Richards. "The contemporary scene Down Under." *Musical Opinion* 99 (April 1976): 307-8.
English writer visiting Sydney finds SQ 9 to be a powerful, instensely personal work. Fortunately, many of PS's compositions are now being heard in England.

B530 "He's nervous." *Mercury*, Tuesday 6 April 1976: 3.
PS has accepted the invitation by the ABC and the Adult Education Board to be this year's subject for "Meet the Composer." How will he explain composing? No wonder he's nervous. Tonight and Thursday there will be performances of his music. (*Mercury*, 8 April, reports that he was also guest of honor at a reception on Monday.)

B531 Clive O'Connell. "American tour preview." *Australian*, 18 May 1976.
The AYO treated Sun Music [I] in a cautious manner.

B532 E.M.W. "Second concert." *Central Western Daily*, 2 June 1976.
Lament is a lovely work, wistful, yearning, elusive, and full of atmosphere. The Stars Turn too was a work of great atmosphere and sensual beauty, excellently performed.
    Other reviews of the ACO tour: Cor Anglais, "This is where the action is." *Western Advocate* (Bathurst), 3 June (the hauntingly beautiful Lament); *Penrith Press*, 7 June (two miniatures, both of them melodic, a little acid, and satisfying); T. H Naisby, "Lusty baby holds its audience," *Newcastle Morning Herald*, 10 June ("I was engaged with the Lament, in which linear strands ebbed and flowed over the deeps of grief"); Margaret Cominos, "Undaunted by weather" (Armidale).

B533 Fred Blanks. "Is it eventide for Music Rostrum?" *SMH*, 30 August 1976.
In SQ 9 PS reverts to his Bloch-in-Bali idiom, with long-drawn melodies attractively keening over a patter of ostinatos.

B534 Neil Sorrell. "Peter Sculthorpe: **Sun Music for Voices and Percussion.**" *Contact* (Dept. of Music, Univ. of London), issue 14 (Autumn 1976): 32.
Sun Music for Voices and Percussion is fairly sparse, atmospheric music, with a hint of Balinese interlocking patterns in the *con precisione* section. It is not a difficult piece and, now that it is readily available in score, deserves frequent performances.

B535 Arnold Whittall. "Recent Australian Music." *Music and Letters* 57 (Oct 1976): 450-451.
Sun Music for Voices and Percussion abounds in illustrative intent. The choice of forces ensures a highly atmospheric evocation of sizzling and scorching.

B536 Arthur Bloomfield. "Chamber music to hear again." *SF Examiner*, 8 October 1976
SQ 9 last night was music you could listen to. The piece is short, as the famous string quartets of the post-Haydn era go; however, brevity can be sweet. The slow section at the top of the arch is the heart of the matter. When the tempo picks up for the second time, the effect is like coming out of an interesting but dark tunnel and breezing along with cheering countryside outside your picture window.

B537 Heuwell Tircuit. "Marvelous departure for strings." *SF Chronicle*, 8 October 1976.

SQ 9 is an interesting blend of quasi-electronic noises and fairly traditional passages of tonality. Like Bartók, Sculthorpe has achieved a smooth blend of current avant garde techniques with folk music, and beautifully too.

B538 Edino Krieger. "Tradição e novidade em alto padrão de qualidad." *Jornal de Brazil,* 21 October 1976.
Without PS's SQ 9 the program [Oct 18] would certainly have been incomplete. The composer utilizes instruments in perfect harmony with avant-garde elements.
Also: Antonio Hernandez, "A primeira mensagem musical australiana" ("First musical message from Australia"), *O globo,* 19 Oct (the best part of the program was SQ 9, an airy work without avant-garde commitments); "Musetta's column," *Sunday Telegraph,* 31 Oct: 94 (reports to Sydney readers that SQ 9 on the Sydney SQ tour received a great deal of space and rave reviews).

B539 John Cargher. *Opera and Ballet in Australia.* Melbourne: Cassell Australia, 1977.
(P. 270, 273, 294, 298, 312:) The **Sun Music ballet** (shown in several photos) was another attempt at an all-Australian definitive work.

B540 Wenzel de Neergaard, ed. *Australian Opera: The first twenty years.* Sydney: The NSW Friends of the Australian Opera, 1977.
Rites of Passage was the first full-length Australian work presented by the company. Two pages in the section "1974" contain several photos of PS, performers, and others.

B541 Peter Sculthorpe. "Mirrie Hill: A personal note." *Stereo FM Radio,* March 1977: 7.
Half-page article is an introduction to an interview to be broadcast on 2MBS-FM (Sydney) on March 11. PS discusses the music of Mirrie Hill and of her husband Alfred Hill in connection with Henry Tate's 1924 book *Australian Musical Possibilities.*

B542 Peter Sculthorpe. "Mrs. Fraser Sings: Preliminary sketches." *Quadrant* 21 (April 1977): 38-9.
Series of musical examples from **Eliza Fraser Sings** with explanatory captions by the composer follows publication of full text of Barbara Blackman's "Eliza Surviver [sic]" with photographs of a diorama by Charles Blackman.

B543 "Penelope Thwaites, piano, Wigmore Hall, May 29." *Review of London Recitals,* May 1977.
Epigrammatic and evocative, and well-written for the piano, **Night Pieces** received persuasive advocacy.

B544 "Port Essington." *Quadrant* 21 (June 1977): 31-3.
The score of the third variation from sect. II, *Theme and Variations* (The Settlement) of **Port Essington,** is printed here with notes by PS (as in the printed score).

B545 Mirrie Hill. "Peter Sculthorpe: A personal observation." *Stereo FM Radio,* June 1977: 7.
PS is "Musician of the Month" (his photo is on the cover). At the 1963 Hobart seminar, asked what I thought of PS's music I replied: "If he were a racehorse, I'd back him." His work has a fine cultural approach. I feel he has vivid dreams that are disciplined by his scoring, and intellect or soundness of judgment.
(Five years later, on Hill's 90th birthday, Olive Lawson comments (24 *Hours,* Dec 1982: 9): "We now know that had Peter been a racehorse, Mrs. Hill certainly would not have been out-of-pocket.")

B546 "Queen's Silver Jubilee and B'day Honours." *SMH*, 11 June 1977: 6.
Peter Sculthorpe is listed as recipient of an OBE in the NSW State list.
Other announcements: Daily Telegraph, 11 Jun: 8 (with photo of PS); "Sydney painter receives OBE," *Advertiser*, 11 June; and "On the spot," *Examiner*, 30 June.

B547 David Marr. "Peter Sculthorpe: Australia's musical nationalist." *National Times*, 4-11 July 1977: 28-9.
Though Australian musicians can't begin to agree, the country's leading composer, as far as public reputation goes, is PS (shown in large photo). He thinks deeply about the pattern of his own life. This substantial essay analyzes his work and his career.
Prerauer, quoted in Patricia Rolfe, "Music '77: A whole new arts game" *Bulletin*, 15 Oct 1977: 49, protests Marr's statement that she and Curt championed Meale over PS.

B548 Tony Gould. "The new world of Peter Sculthorpe. *Sun*, 25 July 1977.
A large and enthusiastic audience heard **SQ 9** and **Tabuh Tabuhan** played superbly. The composer also gave a fascinating insight into his musical philosophy.

B549 Fred Blanks. "Elegance undermined." *SMH*, 30 July 1977.
The ensemble's anarchy of tuning made it difficult to determine which dissonances were authorized by the score. **Lament** is a basically tonal piece that wears its heart on its sleeve with a profound show of romanticism.

B550 Rodney M. Bennett. "Jubilee honours." *Music and Musicians* 25 (August 1977): 10, 12.
Queen's Jubilee-year birthday honours list includes almost a score of names with musical connections, and several Australians, including PS.
Other announcements: Australian, 1 Aug: 9; *SMH*, 1 Aug: 8; and "News in Brief. Queen's Silver Jubilee and Birthday Honours." *APRA Journal* 2/3 (1977): 24.

B551 Geoff Wyatt. "Listening to the landscape." *Pol*, Aug/Sept 1977: 87-90.
PS (shown in large, double-image photo) says that if his music is performed more than that of any other Australian composer, it is because "I'm always trying to tap this landscape thing." Still, I need to live in old houses to be able to explore in my mind, instead of out there in the landscape.

B552 Warren Bourne. "Delightful concert full of unexpected." *Advertiser*, 19 August 1977: 22.
In **Port Essington** I found the impossible attempt to discover some kind of common ground a fascinating aural exploration.

B553 Val Vallis. "Brightness and body of sound." *Australian*, Friday 19 August 1977.
Port Essington (Aug 16) has to be seen performed as the orchestra "stalks" the stalwart colonials. The hand of genius is on the composition.

B554 Tony Gould. "Viva Vivaldi—but go Peter." *Sun*, 20 August 1977: 26.
In **Port Essington** the orchestra, and PS's music, sound distinctly Australian.

B555 Felix Werder. "Bach played respectfully." *Age*, 22 August 1977.
In this return of the prodigal Sun Music, **Port Essington**, a colonial tune is baked into programmed variations that in the end serve no cause or master.
Sinclair, "An orchestra transformed," *Herald*, 22 Aug, does not mention the work.

B556 Roger Covell. "Musical parable of the early days." *SMH*, 26 August

1977: 8.
In **Port Essington** the beautiful epilogue features the sound of an understanding the settlers and the bush could and should have reached. Calling the work simple-minded is description, not abuse.

B557 Daniel Moody. "Encores and bumps." *Australian*, 29 August 1977.
Port Essington is another of Sculthorpe's forays into the irreconcilable. It is simple but effective and quite moving; the sounds of the nocturnal bushland are quite irresistible.

B558 H. R. Forst. "Great chamber group makes it all look so easy." *Sunday Telegraph*, 4 September 1977: 59.
Port Essington sets cloying, arty persistence against uncontrolled humming and chirping and weaving.

B559 W. and R. Travers. "Australian Chamber Orchestra—Opera House." *Wentworth Courier* (Sydney), 5 October 1977.
Port Essington has its moments when the string trio sings beautifully.

B560 Charles Shere. "Kronos: A sensational debut." *Oakland Tribune*, Friday 18 November 1977: EE35.
A good new quartet, the Kronos Quartet, recently introduced itself to a small but extremely significant audience. PS's SQ 8 contrasted Bartoky lamentation (mostly for solo cello) with quick ostinatos and drones taken from Balinese sources.

B561 Heuwell Tircuit. "Smooth balance from an impressive quartet." *San Francisco Chronicle*, 29 November 1977: 42.
PS's SQ 8 (an eleventh-hour substitute), which looks like it will be a classic, is a good audience piece, highly virtuoso, with all sorts of percussion effects glittering from the surface. Cellist Walter Gray had an especially sensitive time with his big solos.

B562 "Australian Music: Peter Sculthorpe. Set 1, Years 11-12," and "Set 2, Years 11-12: **String Quartet No. 8.**" Typescript. Sydney: NSW Correspondence School, n. d. [ca. 1978]
These two manuscripts are in the Sounds Australian library in Sydney.

B563 "Peter Sculthorpe." *Baker's Biographical Dictionary of Musicians*. 6th edn.; completely rev. by Nicolas Slonimsky. New York: Schirmer Books, 1978.
Entry (p. 1571) includes a paragraph of biography and a classified list of titles through 1974, and a short description of sources (Australian, Asian) and style.

B564 James Glennon. "Peter Sculthorpe." *1,000 Famous Australians*. Adelaide: Rigby, 1978.
(P. 330:) PS is an adventurous and busy composer whose work reveals an unmistakable Australian identity. His list of compositions is long and varied.

B565 "Peter Sculthorpe." In: Frank/Altmann *Kurzgefaßtes Tonkünstler-Lexikon, Part 2 (Ergänzungen u. Erweiterungen seit 1937)*, vol. 2. 15th edn. Wilhelmshaven: Heinrichshofen, 1978. P. 228.
(P. 228:) Brief entry (nine lines) presents birth date, education, titles of a few works, and a summary of genres ("orchestral works and compositions for chamber ensemble").

B566 Michael Hannan. "Peter Sculthorpe." In *Australian Composition in*

the Twentieth Century, edited by Frank Callaway and David Tunley. Melbourne: Oxford University Press, 1978.
PS was the first to establish for himself a concept of an Australian music and an appropriate response to Australian social sensibility. Chapter (p. 136-45) discusses individual works and includes a bibliography, list of works, and discography. PS is also mentioned in connection with other composers (p. 3, 4, 81, 201, 212-13, 214, 220, 234).
    Review: Prerauer, "Flawed guide to the sonic assault," *Weekend Australian Magazine,* 24-25 Feb 1979:11.

B567 Elizabeth Salter. *Helpmann: The Authorised Biography.* Brighton: Angus & Robertson, 1978.
(P. 224:) In 1966 Helpmann was working on a new ballet based on PS's **Sun Music.** Dancers are shown in a two-page photo, p. 220-1.

B568 Roger Covell. "Escape from tradition of the opera." *SMH,* 2 Jan 1978.
Whatever the fate of the complete **Rites of Passage** in the theatre, the *Chorales* on disc (**D42**) have a rare grandeur and sublimity.

B569 Dinah Dugteren. "Peter and the cave." *Australian,* 19 Jan 1978: 8.
PS describes his work on **They Found A Cave** sixteen years, and several films, later.

B570 "Peter Sculthorpe." *The Flautist* 8, no. 1 (February 1978): 12.
Journal of the Victorian Flute Guild presents a sketch of Sculthorpe's life and works.

B571 "Koto Music." *Quadrant* 22 (February 1978): 36-9.
Four pages contain **Koto Music I, II** scores and directions for performance.

B572 Jill Sykes. "Exchanges with Aaron Copland." *SMH,* Sat. 18 March 1978.
The exchange of views at PS's home revealed as much about Sculthorpe as it did about Copland—on revising works, using Italian terms, and film music (**They Found A Cave**).
    A later reference appears in Aaron Copland and Vincent Perlis, *Copland Since 1943* (New York, 1989): 395: "I arrived in March and enjoyed spending time with Vincent Plush and PS (both had promoted first performances of some of my works in Australia).

B573 Roger Covell. "Composer changes territory." *SMH,* 29 April 1978.
The airy, open intervals of a Shinto tune give **Landscape II** a special sort of melancholy bliss. As the three string players shared the melody, pianist Wendy Lorenz, poised like the priestess of an enigmatic cult over the piano, plucked deep throbbing notes to measure each phrase.
    (Review by H. R. Forst. "Slow birth for new chamber piece," *Sunday Telegraph,* 7 May. Forst, "Music," *Telegraph,* 24 April, explains that the first movt was intended for a concert before the King and Queen of Thailand [Harris, "Aussie work has won the royal touch," *Mirror,* 23 Nov 1977], but not performed because of political turmoil.)

B574 Lindsey Browne. "Sculthorpe's world premiere an oasis." *Sun-Herald,* 30 April 1978.
In **Landscape II** PS courageously pushes out to an orbit of distinctly avant-garde experimentation.

B575 Maria Prerauer. "Musical terrain." *Australian,* Monday 1 May 1978: 10.
In **Landscape II** PS seems to have gone back to his Japanese period, and the overall impression is still cherry-blossom picturesque.

B576 Nadine Amadio. "A sculpture music first to be staged at The Rocks."

Australian Financial Review, 12 May 1978: 8.
James Murdoch, Australia Music Centre director, says that PS's music, for Pamela Boden's spiky sculpture called *Gambol* that has a feeling of whirling movement, is a Japanese Koto piece, performed on a piano's strings.
  Other coverage: Margaret O'Sullivan, "Met as students in Paris—here for exhibition," *Sun-Herald,* 14 May: 157 (spotlight moves to a sculpture and its recorded music is played); Margaret Geddes "Sculpture and music and novel audio visual" *Age,* 10 June: 2 (Glanville-Hicks looked at *Gambol* and thought, "Well, obviously, PS must do this"); and Alan McCulloch, "Composers lend a hand," *Herald,* 15 June.

B577 Fred Blanks. "Music." *SMH,* 15 May 1978.
Snow, Moon and Flowers (May 14) are romantic vignettes of fleeting charm.

B578 Michael Hannan. "Eastern music and the Australian composer." *World of Music* 20 (1978), no. 2: 103-5.
The illustrated talk (summarized here in English, French, and German) at the 1975 "Musicultura II" conference in Breukelen, Holland, discussed the use of Asian materials by PS and others.

B579 Roger Covell. "Two Elizas associated in theatre." *SMH,* 3 July 1978: 4.
The performance of Blackman's "Eliza Surviver" [sic] lessened the impact of Eliza Fraser Sings, which was intended to be less dramatically immediate. Events of the narrative were distanced, fixed and cadenced so as to codify the experience instead of creating it as a living nightmare. PS's vocal line, as distinct from his half-sung or intoned sections, was deliberate and formal. It did not belie his personality.

B580 Fred Blanks. "East and West meet musically." *SMH,* 10 July 1978: 4.
Sarah Grunstein played a serenely hypnotic Koto Music inside a piano.
  A couple of years later, Blanks, "Signpost to success," reviews her farewell concert before Juilliard: her willingness to experiment found attractive scope in Koto Music I.

B581 Fred Blanks. "Music with exotic sounds." *Australian Jewish Times,* 13 July 1978.
This was a concert of exotic sounds. The improvisation to Blackman's text [*see* **B579**] was more effective than Eliza Fraser Sings in recreating a mood. PS's score was simpler, with an impressive singer.

B582 John Moses. "Fine double by local quartet." *Sunday Telegraph,* 23 July 1978: 110.
On the local Cherry Pie label Little Serenade [D22] is a small gem from PS. SQ 9 [D60] is a thoroughly contemporary piece, original and inventive, but not self-consciously experimental. Innovation here is used to stir the mind and the imagination.

B583 Clive O'Connell. "Mediaeval sounds abound." *Age,* 1 August 1978.
Sun Music III was given a generally fine airing (July 27), even if one could quibble with conductor Robert Miller's tight hand on the percussion for the sake of over-fullblooded brass chords.

B584 W. L. Hoffmann. "Music." *Canberra Times,* 22 August 1978.
On Penelope Thwaites' recital program the three short Night Pieces [Snow, Moon and Flowers] were suited to the intimate, almost drawing-room dimensions of the venue.

B585 Fred R. Blanks. "Australia." *Musical Times* 119 (Sept 1978): 784-5.
Eliza Fraser Sings was among the attractively piquant new Australian music supplied

this season by the Seymour Group, directed by Vincent Plush.

B586   Fred Blanks. "The arts." *SMH*, 9 Sept 1978.
Penelope Thwaites found the right staccato touch for the pin-points of tone in the
Night Pieces [Snow, Moon and Flowers].

B587   John Loughlin. "Australiens Komponisten auf eigenen neuen Weg-
en." *Instrumentenbau Musik International* 32 (October 1978): 664, 666.
Report from Melbourne to this Siegburg (W. Ger.) periodical notes that many Australian composers are influenced by Asian musics. PS's **Sun Music** pieces are influenced
by Australian geography. Says PS, if new music is to attain international value, it
must first speak its own national language.

B588   Andrew D. McCredie. "Peter Joshua Sculthorpe." *Die Musik in Ge-
schichte und Gegenwart*, vol. 16, Supplement. Kassel u. Basel: Bären-
reiter, 1979, cols. 1688-9.
A paragraph of biography is followed by a list of works, description of style, and
selected bibliography.

B589   George F. Loughlin. *Cities of Departure: An Autobiography*. West
Melbourne: Jenkin Buxton Printers, 1984.
Loughlin, Ormond Professor at the University of Melbourne, notes that the **Sun Music**
ballet helped show that original, first-rate dance settings could be made in this
country. He presents a brief biography of Sculthorpe (p. 129, 136-7).

B590   Roger Covell. "Percussion recital was a hit." *SMH*, 21 February 1979.
Synergy performance of **How the Stars Were Made** last night was perhaps better than
in 1971. The work seeemed far more exhilarating in metrical lob and volley.

B591   Roger Covell. "Borrowing with variable interest." *SMH*, 1 March 1979:
8.
In **Song of Tailitnama** Sculthorpe borrows a melody from Australian Aboriginal culture
and borrows a texture from Brazilian composer Villa-Lobos. The characteristic
percussion is his own, as is the vocal which frames the central section. The central
dance-like episode offers homage to a mood and a presence; he does not try to make it
his cultural property.

B592   Suzanne Gartner. "People are talking about ... Peter Sculthorpe: a year
of explosions." *Vogue Australia* 23 (April 1979): 97.
Celebrations for PS's 50th birthday on April 29 are exploding like firecrackers.

B593   Maria Prerauer. "Sculthorpe: The man and his music." *Weekend
Australian*, 14-15 April 1979.
PS's 50th birthday is the occasion of special works and concerts. Faber has recently
published his **SQ 9**. ("You called it as Australian as kangaroo butter in your review,"
he smiles, presenting an autographed copy.) A large photo of Sculthorpe in informal
pose illustrates this half-page feature essay which describes his renovated house.

B594   Roger Covell. "Requiem for cello a festival high point." *SMH*, Monday
16 April 1979: 8.
The emotional high point at Mittagong so far has been provided by the first performances of PS's **Requiem**. The *Libera Me* section has a mood of slithering outrage and
disquiet in contrast to the reflective intensity of most of the work. The composer is, he
assured us, a reasonably happy man despite his predilection for musical grief.

B595 Roger Covell. "Festival of chamber music a success." *SMH*, 17 April 1979: 8.
At Mittagong, PS let listeners and performers in on the origins of his SQ 6 and SQ 9. He shared more ideas, jokes and personal and professional information with his listeners under a spreading tree on the main school lawn.
Other coverage: Emily Booker, "Festival is a tribute to composer," *Berrima District Post*, Friday 20 April: 5; page includes three photos, one of them of PS and his mother.

B596 "Music world says: Happy Birthday Maestro." By a special correspondent. *Tasmanian Mail*, 25 April 1979: 1, 3.
A national magazine this month reported that PS (shown in large photo) has become, like Merle Oberon and Errol Flynn, one of the few to rise from the pastoral corners of Tasmania to international fame. In a telephone conversation, he was happy to talk about his Tasmanian past. (Article also quotes from B593, above.)

B597 Jill Sykes. "Sculthorpe at fifty." *SMH*, 28 April 1979, Good Weekend: 15-16.
Arriving at Sculthorpe's home for this interview, Sykes him preparing lunch for his housekeeper Dot [Hockley], who keeps the well-ordered house sparkling by a generous use of Mr. Sheen [furniture polish].

B598 Roger Covell. "Mangrove, the heart of being." *SMH*, 28 April 1979.
Mangrove takes us at once into the heart of the mystery. The opening bars croak and quiver, stir and murmur with the sound of contending energy, of a thousand invisible beings saying yes to the idea of being. **Mangrove** seems to end just as it has embarked on a summary of its ideas. I should like to hear more of it.

B599 Laurie Strachan. "Music." *Australian, c*30 April 1979.
In **Mangrove**, the composer is concerned with the mangrove as a symbol of life. It is a work of considerable beauty, similar to Sibelius's symbolic nature-painting.

B600 Roger Covell. "A birthday garland for a composer." *SMH*, 30? April 1979.
Tabuh Tabuhan listed on the printed program proved to be only a dummy entry for a series of birthday surprises [P79-4, April 28]. The concert must have provided the best kind of evidence for Sculthorpe of the respect and affection in which he is held.

B601 Maria Prerauer. "Many happy returns." *Australian*, 30 April 1979.
Only three of the fifteen works (April 28) were by PS, including the Sydney premiere of **Requiem** stunningly performed by Nathan Waks.

B602 Peter J. Pirie. "Modern quartets." *Musical Times* 120 (May 1979): 413.
Faber score of PS's **Eighth Quartet** is beautifully produced. The music, with just one or two patches of four-part texture, has no trace of the great tradition of quartet writing as an intellectual and complex medium.

B603 Diana Fisher. "Talkabout." *Sunday Telegraph*, 6 May 1979.
PS's wonderful 50th birthday party was a superb affair held in his garden courtyard beneath a bright yellow awning which reached out from his famous studio.

B604 H. R. Forst. "Sculthorpe fires a double salvo for his birthday." *Sunday Telegraph*, 6 May 1979: 62.
In **Requiem** the range of expression commands admiration and interest. In **Mangrove** instrumental color is the main virtue. The work is rather sketchy and static.

B605 Marie Ambrose. [Review.] *Hampstead Express and News*, 11 May 1979.
The basic Australian aboriginal theme of PS's **Sonatina** could have opened up greater imaginative possibilities.

B606 Margaret Reizenstein. "Penelope Thwaites, piano." *Review of London Recitals*, May 1979.
In PS's impressionistic, introvert **Sonatina** one senses the impact of vast open spaces and skies, and also the harsh reality of life lived close to nature.

B607 Fred R. Blanks "Australia." *Musical Times* 120 (June 1979): 512.
PS's music, which was the central theme of this year's Mittagong Festival, is idiomatically inviting, emotionally intense, technically full of ingenious competence.

B608 Angela Owens. "Kronos has no equal among popular chamber groups." *Peninsula Times Tribune* (Palo Alto, CA), 2 June 1979.
SQ 8 pushes string technique beyond traditional limits. Yet there also are gentler melodious sections that achieve a maximum of effect within a minimum range.

B609 "ABC success." *Australian*, 21 June 1979.
Mangrove, the ABC's entry at this year's Paris Rostrum of Composers, took fifth place and earned a commendation, the most an Australian entry has achieved at the event. *Tasmanian Mail*, 27 May, announces ABC-FM radio broadcast of **Mangrove** on June 1.

B610 Fred Blanks. "Sojourn among survivors." *SMH*, 23 June 1979.
The most substantial work, masterly both in its inventiveness and use of sonorities for woodwinds and percussion, was **Tabuh Tabuhan**.

B611 Roger Covell. "Stepping to musical maturity," *SMH*, 16 July 1979.
PS's work is mentioned in this survey of recent Australian music.

B612 Fred Blanks. "On the side of the angels." *SMH*, 6 August 1979: 8.
Koto Music exerted its hypnotic attraction as surely on the harp as inside a piano.

B613 Fred Blanks. "Missionary zeal for new music." *SMH*, 11 August 1979.
Night Pieces for harp sounded like tonal epigrams from a musical autograph album.

B614 Laurie Strachan. "Records." *Weekend Australian*, 15-16 Sept 1979.
Lament for Strings [D19] is a gently brooding work, trying to get down to a more primeval level of feeling than that expressed by song.

B615 Warren Burt. "Music in the 1980s." *24 Hours*, October 1979: 4; and Vincent Plush, "The Search for Musical Identity," p. 5-6.
Australian composers should use freedom to take materials that they want. PS (shown in photo) turned to music of Aztec civilization for his *Conquest of Mexico* **[Cantares]**.

B616 Roger Covell. "Contemporary music in Australia." *Quadrant* 23 (October 1979): 38-41.
Contemporary music "mood" is much quieter than in the sixties, when contemporary music flourished more strongly than at any other time.

B617 Donald Peart. "Letters to the editor. Quartets and intellectualism." *Musical Times* 120 (October 1979): 793, 812.
Letter takes issue with Pirie's review [B602 above]. SQ 8 shows PS concerned not with "the 'great' European tradition," but with a "world" tradition. An earlier *Musical*

Times critic (**B419**) heard in this work "European archetypes" transformed.

B618 Roger Covell. "Getting in touch with Eastern traditions." *SMH,* Monday 8 October 1979.
Tabuh Tabuhan performed on Saturday is beautifully composed, if slightly overlong.

B619 Roger Covell. "Sun Music in sequence." *Sun-Herald,* 14 October 1979
Sun Music seekers will find the definitive version of this well-known series of pieces by PS on a new recording made in Melbourne (**D34**), with the remarkable little piece called **Small Town** thrown in for good measure. (Photos show Hopkins and PS.)

B620 Jim Bradley. "A little journey into the home of Peter Sculthorpe, one of our great contemporary composers." *APRA Journal* 2, no. 6 (November 1979): 21-2, 24.
PS says, "I'm really excited about writing the music for **Manganinnie** because I have an entirely free hand." Favourite works just now? **Requiem** and **Mangrove**, just written. He also discusses commissions and other business matters, and artistic aspirations.

B621 "Sydney this week." *Sunday Telegraph,* 11 November 1979.
PS's Georgian-styled formal garden will be one of three gardens designed by Timothy Abrahams opened to visitors in "The Art of Landscape Gardening", Nov 13, for the Art Gallery Society of NSW. (*Also announced in:* "What's on show" [unident. pub.])

B622 "The shooting begins." *Examiner,* Thursday 15 November 1979: 3.
Filming has begun for "Darkening Flame" [**Manganinnie**]. In the film, "Anna" [Joanna] (shown in photo) chants an Aboriginal song.
  The *Sunday Examiner Express,* 17 Nov: 9, also covers the filming and mentions PS's preparations; later, the *Examiner* reports that shooting is completed.

B623 David Hush. "Interview with Peter Sculthorpe." *Quadrant* 23 (December 1979): 30-33.
PS discusses Australian music's maturity with Hush (a former student), and describes the kinds of Asian characteristics he has used in his music.

B624 Frank Harris. "Hopkins is right for Sun Music." *Mirror,* 12 Dec 1979.
New recording of entire **Sun Music** series [**D34**] is brilliant, a treasured piece.

B625 Roger Covell. "Music [year-end review]." *SMH,* 29 December 1979.
Sculthorpe demonstrated a capacity for development and renewal in his **Requiem**, an elegy for the passing of people and things, and in **Mangrove**, his no less important affirmation of the teeming variousness of life.

B626 Nevill Drury. *Music and Musicians.* Making Australian Society series. West Melbourne: Thomas Nelson Australia, 1980.
A three-paragraph biography of PS is in the chapter "Orchestral Music," p. 44-5.

B627 Donald Horne. *Time of Hope: Australia 1966-72.* Sydney: Angus & Robertson, 1980.
(P. 118, 146, 150:) The sixties saw the return of PS and other composers, and many opportunities. In 1968 came the **Sun Music ballet** and *Burke's Company* [used SQ 6].

B628 Michael Kennedy. "Peter Sculthorpe." *The Concise Oxford Dictionary of Music.* 3rd edn. Oxford: Oxford University Press, 1980. P. 582.
Entry includes biography, description of style, and classified list of works through

1974. Updated to 1978 in: Kennedy, *The Oxford Dictionary of Music* (1985): 649.

B629 Andrew D. McCredie. "Peter Sculthorpe." *The New Grove Dictionary of Music and Musicians.* 20 vols. London: Macmillan, 1980. Vol. 17, p. 90-2.
Entry includes biography, summary of style, classified list of works from the **Sonatina** through **Eliza Fraser Sings**, and a bibliography of six titles. (Australian review: Carmody, "The $1495 dictionary of music," *National Times*, 22-28 March 1981.)

B630 Craig McGregor. *The Australian People.* Sydney: Hodder and Stoughton, 1980. P. 270.
Composers like PS emerged during the post-war development of composition.

B631 Bernard Smith. *The Spectre of Truganini.* 1980 Boyer Lectures. Sydney: ABC, 1980.
Composers like Peter Sculthorpe have begun to draw on the corpus of Aboriginal music, a significant source for Australia's future music (p. 51).

B632 Fred Blanks. "Music." *SMH*, Good Weekend, Saturday 5 January 1980.
The most frequently performed Australian composer in 1979 was PS, and he also leads the long-term field—my 35 years of music diaries.

B633 Laurie Strachan. "Chauvinists of the keyboard." *Australian*, 1980.
Sonatina [D47] lacks characterisation. The use of legend is reminiscent of Sibelius.

B634 "Aussie composer's Bush sounds bring tears to expatriate eyes." *Straits Times* (Singapore), 14 January 1980.
Port Essington made expatriate Australians decidedly homesick.

B635 John Edwards. "Moving strains by Aussies." *New Nation* (Singapore), 15 January 1980.
In the **Lament for Strings** a barren atmosphere was sensitively evoked.

B636 Melissa Shuler. "Ensemble scored with its encores and colourful play." *Straits Times*, 15 January 1980.
Port Essington [Jan 12] was filled with beautiful tonal melodies, but the 20th-century techniques were too programmatic.

B637 Roger Covell. "Requiem for a culture." *SMH*, 18 January 1980: 8.
Despite the great talent of the performers, **Cantares** seemed lacking in intensity.
Publicity: Sykes, "Men of strings," ibid., 10 January.

B638 Peter Robinson. "Stringing a hit together." *Age*, 18 January 1980.
PS appears to have scored a palpable hit with **Cantares**.

B639 Nigel Beeson. "An illuminating and satisfying performance." *Business Times* (Singapore), 21 January 1980.
In **Port Essington** it was disconcerting to hear drawing-room music incessantly eaten away by the scratches and insect sounds of the orchestra.
Publicity: Australian News Bulletin 14, no. 47 (18 Dec 1979); *SMH*, 9 Jan 1980; *North Shore*, 16 Jan; *Business Times*, Jan 1: 7; *Manyang Siang Pau* (Singapore, in Chinese).

B640 Jane Ram. "Chamber orchestra's splendid performance." *South China*

Morning Post (Hong Kong), 25 January 1980.
Lament for Strings showed the poignant effect of single threads of melody, patiently spun and finally woven together.

B641 Harrison Ryker. "Chamber orchestra one of the finest." *Hong Kong Standard*, 25 January 1980.
PS's **Lament** does not have much personality of its own.

B642 Fred Blanks. "Brevity, beauty." *SMH*, 30 January 1980: 8.
At the Leonine Consort concert, tenderness and sensitivity were close to the surface in PS's serene carol **Morning Song for the Christ Child**, an arrangement of **The Stars Turn**, and a handful of very thin Sculthorpe mood pieces [**Night Pieces**].

B643 "Musica Viva Australia," *SMH*, Wednesday 30 January 1980: 13-14.
In the sixties Musica Viva began commissioning music from Australian composers, establishing a close relationship with PS.

B644 Charles Shere. "Kronos concert soars over heights of string quartet music." *Oakland Tribune*, 2 February 1980.
PS's **Eighth Quartet, 2nd movt**, played as encore, had absolute precision.

B645 Lou Klepac. *The Drawings of Russell Drysdale*. Exhibition catalog. Perth, Art Gallery of Western Australia, February 21-March 15, 1980.
In a letter to Lou Klepac of December 28, 1979, Lady Drysdale refers to the mail bringing music by PS and others—"associations which fill me with pride" (p. 32).

B646 Vicki Raymond. "Peter Sculthorpe." *University of Tasmania News*, no. 64 (29 February 1980): 1-2.
PS, in Hobart to work on the music for the film **Manganinnie**, discusses his work. "There's never been a great deal of interest among students in my particular ideals, that is, in trying to write an Australian music."

B647 Charles Shere. "Kronos Quartet presents record-perfect evening." *Oakland Tribune*, 1 March 1980.
SQ 9 is arid, insectlike, bleakly beautiful to match his country. It's a fine piece.

B648 Heuwell Tircuit. "An acrobatic violinist shows his stuff." *SF Chronicle*, 1 March 1980.
The terse SQ 9 is a major addition to the quartet repertory.

B649 Wendy Bowler. "Putting people in his music is the 'secret' of success." *Mercury*, 12 March 1980.
PS talks about the **Manganinnie** score. He says the emotive side of his music "wells up from my Tasmanian experience."

B650 "Guitarist here." *The Examiner* (Sydney), 18 March 1980: 2.
Guitarist John Williams taught guitar at a January symposium and will be back at the middle of the year to play a new work by Peter Sculthorpe for the ABC.

B651 Karl Hubert. "Composer kept his date with tradition." *Mercury*, 24 March 1980: 10.
Six pieces were performed. PS's remarks could have been more elaborate.
Other press coverage: "Sculthorpe will introduce concert of his works," ibid., 19

March: 31; and notices of the March 25 civic reception in Launceston to honour him.

B652 "Home town inspired him." *Examiner,* 24 March 1980.
PS believes it was his childhood years in Launceston that influenced his music.

B653 Jim Dickenson. "Sculthorpe: on a springboard." *Examiner,* Wednesday 26 March 1980: 20.
With more commissions in hand and in sight, PS enters this decade with his spring-board bouncing all the higher.

B654 "Honorary doctorate." *University of Tasmania News,* 28 March 1980: 5.
At the Conferring of Degrees Ceremony on March 21, the Univ. of Tasmania conferred the honorary degree of Doctor of Letters on PS (shown in photo), who delivered the address. Also presented was an Hon. D. Litt. oration, "Peter Sculthorpe," by David Caro. (Event is also reported in the *Univ. of Sydney News,* 22 April: 58 [with photo].)

B655 Meredith Oakes. "Music. From the Rostrum" *Listener* (London) 103 (27 March 1980): 412.
Of the music from last year's International Rostrum of Composers (broadcast March 18) I liked best PS's **Mangrove**.

B656 Roger Covell. "Pleasure from a violinist." *SMH,* 17 April 1980.
In **Mangrove,** Sculthorpe attains an orchestral songfulness of a grandeur previously rare or unknown in his music and an engaging variety in his representation of the whisper and nibble and murmur of minute and hidden life.

B657 Laurie Strachan. "Vaughan Williams, Chinese-style." *Australian,* 18 April 1980.
Mangrove is by no means "avant-garde" but the thinking is modern. The composer was on hand to receive well-earned applause.

B658 Larry Sitsky. "Contemporary Composers in Australia." *Canberra School of Music Educational Pamphlet No. 3.* 1980.
PS (p. 4) is one of the most frequently performed of Australian composers. His work is miniaturistic, avant-garde, and direct.

B659 Rita Erlich. "Orchestrating the past." *Age,* 13 June 1980.
Sculthorpe's new work **Visions of Captain Quiros** will have its premiere in Sydney next month, rather than in Melbourne later this month.

B660 Margaret Clarke. "Exploring for music." *24 Hours* 5 (July 1980): 2-3.
Interview examines the subject of **The Visions of Captain Quiros** and its musical content—like **Mangrove** and **Requiem** it is more melodic than the **Sun Music** style.

B661 Jill Sykes. "Direction 1980's," *2MBS-FM Radio,* July 1980: 9.
Vincent Plush says that Copland-Sculthorpe parallels are inappropriate: America in the 20s is not like Australia in the 80s, he says.

B662 Jill Sykes. "Orchestral work features guitar." *SMH,* 8 July 1980: 8.
Visions of Captain Quiros is a major work, breaking new ground for Sculthorpe (shown in caricature drawing) and for Australian composition.
Other coverage: Vema [Greek-language Sydney newspaper], 26 July.

B663 "Column 8" item. *SMH,* 9 July 1980: 1.

A colleague heard an immortal announcement on ABC radio Monday afternoon: "And now you will hear PS's SQ 9 of 1975. When it was written it was his latest."

B664 Andrew Horton. "Deserves cultural acclaim." *Mercury*, 10 July 1980: 1.
"Our very own premiere" of **Manganinnie** last night was also telecast in Hobart. Further information on p. 17, describes the bands that played, the arrival of official guests in a horse-drawn brougham, and what people wore.
Examiner, 10 July, has a front-page story with photos of the stars and the crowds, and a short review by Chris Copas on p. 2.

B665 Fred Blanks. "Superior work but slow." *SMH*, 11 July 1980.
Visions of Captain Quiros is superior music for a very slow-moving film. It is "becalmed somewhere between adagio and lento." (Blanks repeats this report in "Australia," *Musical Times* 121 [October 1980]: 649.)

B666 H. R. Forst. "John strums a storm." *Telegraph*, Monday 14 July 1980.
The **Guitar Concerto** had evocative, atmospheric effects at the beginning, but it all got becalmed and failed to recapture its initial air of inspiration.

B667 Laurie Strachan. "Williams, Sculthorpe provide puzzling mix." *Australian*, 14 July 1980.
PS's new **Guitar Concerto** had only moderate applause, indicating puzzlement. The guitar part is more an accompaniment to the orchestra than a concertante solo.

B668 Graham Bicknell. "Tragic tale of history. *Telegraph*, 14 July 1980, "Entertainments," p. 1.
The musical score for **Manganinnie** is dirge-like and did not help quicken the film's pace. (Article and three photos occupy almost the entire front page of this section.)

B669 Film *Notes on a Landscape*. Sydney: Australian Music Centre, 1980. (Premiere: 29 July, Sydney Opera House cinema.) William Fitzwater, director and co-producer; James Murdoch, co-producer.
Film features ten Australian composers from the early sixties; PS is represented by **Port Essington**. (Video recording is in NLA.)

B670 Fred Blanks. [Review.] *SMH*, 2 August 1980.
At the Sydney University Music Department concert, students presented a parody, "Stun Music V" for PS and his Balinese seagulls.

B671 Haruko Morita and Peter Robinson. "Avant garde music is dead! We're all too comfortable." *Australian Financial Times*, 15 Aug 1980.
Article's headline is an excerpt from PS's words (other composers are interviewed as well). If there were another Vietnam war, would we then have an active avant garde?

B672 Geraldine Pascall. "Dark deadly deeds." *Australian*, 16 August 1980.
The only discordant notes in **Manganinnie** came from PS's difficult music.
Other materials: Andrew Saw, "The film star with a mind like a razor," *Telegraph*, 11 August (about actress playing Manganinnie); announcement, *Examiner*, 20 August, that film won the Australian Trophy of the OCIC (Organisation Catholique du Cinéma) for the promotion of human values combined with artistic merit; and item from *Examiner*, 23 August (the Premier, Mr. Lowe, said Sydney critics praised the film).

B673 Christine Hogan. [Film award.] *SMH*, 18 September 1980.
An Australian Film Institute award for best original musical score was awarded to PS

for **Manganinnie.**
Other announcements: Australian Film Institute Newsletter, no. 16 (Oct/Nov 1980);
Australian, 18 Sept; and *Daily Mirror,* 18 Sept. One quotes PS ("This makes me a proud
Tasmanian"). The *Examiner* includes a photo of "Dr. Sculthorpe."
  On October 17, at the Australian Film and Television Awards ceremony in Sydney,
for the Variety Club of Australia, he received a "Gold Sammy" for best theme music.
Lit.: Hogan, "Most top Sammy winners out of town," *SMH,* 18 Oct: 5 (PS was present);
and "Awards for Bert and Caroline," [*Mercury? Telegraph?*], 18 Oct.

B674 Jim Bradley. "Profile: a man called Peter." *Sydney Calendar Magazine,*
Third Year, no. 27 (Aug-Sept 1980): 26.
Interview with PS presents essentially the same information as **B620** in 1979.

B675 Monica Danvers. "A stunning new movie of the past." *Sydney
Calendar Magazine,* Third Year, no. 28 (Sept 1980): 25.
PS's music plays an important and effective part in the film **Manganinnie,** although it
does tend to encroach at times on the silence of the bush.

B676 Dennis Tucker's column. *Tasmanian Mail,* 7 October 1980.
For nominations for the Launcestonian of the year, I suggest, from the Arts, PS.

B677 Fred Blanks. "Stimulating recital." *SMH,* 15 October 1980: 8.
PS's **Sonata for Cello Alone** of 1959, until now unperformed, was conspicuously clever
and outward-looking. The **Requiem,** by contrast, had heartfelt intensity.

B678 [**Overture** premiere.] *Examiner,* Saturday 22 November 1980: 1.
Half-page photo shows crowds in the Albert Hall at last night's opening ceremony.
(Coverage includes advance notices in "Northern Scene" and *Examiner.*)

B679 Brian Hoad. "A 133-year search may end in Voss." *Bulletin,* 2 Dec 1980:
76-84.
The long search for Australian opera has produced **Rites of Passage** (p. 78). **Eliza
Fraser Sings** is among the smaller works (p. 83).

B680 Jill Sykes. "Future of thriving film industry poses a dilemma."
London *Times,* Thursday 4 December 1980.
Film is dominating the Australian arts scene, even to its spin-offs in other areas such
as PS's award-winning score for **Manganinnie.**

B681 *The Oxford History of Australian Literature.* Ed. Leonie Kramer.
Melbourne: Oxford University Press, 1981. P. 424.
Composers Meale and Sculthorpe have found enrichment in Asian music, showing
something like the cross-cultivation in Australian writing.

B682 John Spooner. *Caricatures, Drawings and Prints.* Melbourne: Thomas
Nelson Australia, 1981. P. 126.
Included is "Peter Sculthorpe" (etching, aquatint and drypoint), p. 126. It is reproduc-
ed for the book review by John Douglas Pringle, "Lines of sight," *Age,* 10 October 1981.

B683 "Sun Music I by Peter Sculthorpe" and "A detailed study of **Sun Music
I.**" Sets 26 and 27 in *Twentieth Century Music Core—Year 12.* [Mel-
bourne: Victorian Department of Education,] 1981.
Materials include a review of PS's life and works, description of the work's sounds, and
some suggestions for writing exercises about the music.

B684 Ava Hubble. "Sculthorpe's music of anguish and passion." *24 Hours* 6 (February 1981).
"Music Australia," at 8.00 pm on February 11, will look at recent music by PS. "I often find program notes incomprehensible," I confessed to him. To my relief, he agreed.

B685 Fred Blanks. "Piano jerked like a yo-yo with hiccups." *SMH*, 27 February 1981.
Landscape II had contrast, originality, and above all aural appeal.

B686 Anne Carr-Boyd. "Australian Music 1950-1980." Report for the Asian Composers Conference-Festival, Hong Kong, March 4-12, 1981.
A historical survey is followed by a focus on the recent work of PS and others.

B687 The Borgia column: "Film on our composers a big success." *Sunday Telegraph*, 22 March 1981: 54.
At the recent Asian Composers Conference in Hong Kong, *Notes on a Landscape* had tremendous impact. Afterwards, everyone knew the faces of our five composers at the conference (PS, Boyd, Conyngham, Carr-Boyd, Gross) and knew the sound of their music.

B688 Leslie Walford's column. *Sun-Herald*, 29 March 1981.
At Macquarie University, a lecture was presented for the Rundle Foundation for Egyptian Archeology, the Governor and Lady Rowland being present. After opening speakers, PS introduced cellist Nathan Waks who played the **Requiem** as a divertissement. The scholarly slide lecture followed.

B689 Fred Blanks. "From out of limbo into alternative listening." *SMH*, Thursday 21 May 1981.
Koto Music (May 19) used two kinds of tape, pre-recorded and sticky (for taping down piano keys while dark doings went on inside). **Landscape I** was plain ghastly.
Publicity: "Sykes on Sunday," *Sun-Herald*, 10 May.

B690 "The Way In." *Vogue Living* 15 (June-July 1981): 109
Two photos show the "inner hall" or stairwell area of Sculthorpe's home.

B691 Peter Sculthorpe. "From Corroboree to *Corroboree*." *2MBS-FM Music Lectures* No. 4. 1981. (Broadcast June 4, 1981.)
PS discusses (with illustrations) Aboriginal music and the four periods of Australian music since white settlement: The Colonial Period (1788-1850); The Boom Period (1850-1901); The Period following Federation (1901-1945), and The Period following World War II (1945 to the present). (*Lit.:* "Tracing our traditions," *SMH*, Monday 1 June.)

B692 Fred Blanks. "Apollo and Pan set scene where anything goes." *SMH*, Tuesday 9 June 1981.
Hannan played **No. 1** of PS's two hypnotic **Koto Music** pieces, because someone had mislaid the No. 2 tape. The impressive **Landscape II** had a near-successful student reading which recalled Glazunov's dictum that amateurs would make the best musicians if they only knew how to play.

B693 Heuwell Tircuit. "The Kronos Quartet introduces enjoyable avant-garde music." *SF Chronicle*, Saturday 20 June 1981: 35.
PS's **SQ 7**, subtitled **Red Landscape**, turned out to be pure picture painting. In this mood piece of odd, static sonorities, one sees as much of Mars as of Northern Australia. But that's beside the point, when the piece so captures and holds one's attention.

B694   Fred Blanks. "Prickly program was a thorn in the side." *SMH*, 23 June 1981.
Sculthorpe's harsh but evocative **Irkanda I** had an untroubled performance (June 21).

B695   Fred Blanks. "The keyboard gladiators of the music competitions." *SMH*, 11 July 1981.
For Stage I of the Sydney International Piano Competition, 20 pianists selected PS's **Mountains**, a slow and sombre piece.

B696   "Peter Sculthorpe's exercise in symmetry." *Vogue Living* 15 (August-September 1981): 66-71.
The old Sydney cottage where composer PS lives expresses his strong feeling for symmetry. "I find ways to create a balance," he says, "then find another way to throw it out—as one does in writing music. Otherwise it would be boring." Photos show the interior of the house and studio.

B697   Fred Blanks. "Composers face the music." *SMH*, 4 August 1981: 28.
How the Stars Were Made devised some intriguing, mostly gentle sounds that told their Aboriginal legend concisely.

B698   Philip Sommerich. "The Australian desert blossoms." *Hampstead Express*, 14 August 1981.
The idiomatic pictorialism of PS's **Sonatina (D47)** is fascinating.
  Also: Lionel Salter on BBC Radio 3, 27 June 1981: the spare-textured **Sonatina** by PS "suggests the clear pungent light of the Australian scene."

B699   Mark Swed. "High-tech sound, style from Kronos Quartet." *Los Angeles Herald Examiner*, Monday 9 November 1981.
SQ 8 found the Kronos Quartet at home with rice-pounding rhythms from Bali.

B700   W. T[ravers]. "Australian Chamber Orchestra," *Wentworth Courier*, December 1981.
Lament [Dec 15] explores the softer, dark-hued tones of the strings.

B701   Charles Buttrose. *Playing for Australia: A Story about ABC Orchestras and Music in Australia*. Sydney: ABC and Macmillan, 1982. P. 141, 143, 149-150.
The MSO played **Sun Music III** in Ann Arbor on its 1970 American tour. In 1974 the SSO performed **Sun Music IV** in Glasgow (for "MR" of the *Glasgow Herald*, it conjured up a vision of an arid landscape), and in Edinburgh.

B702   Michael Hannan. *Peter Sculthorpe: His Music and Ideas 1929-1979*. St. Lucia: University of Queensland Press, 1982.
The first book about PS analyzes his creation of an Australian music, with extensive discussion of **Rites of Passage**. The book includes many score excerpts and twenty photographs. The cover uses an ink drawing of PS by Graham Bryce, 1979.
  Reviews: Sun-Herald, 25 April 1982; S. C. [**B709** below]; David Symons, *Australian Journal of Music Education* 31 (Oct 1982): 68-9; and Treborlang [**B752** below].

B703   "Peter Sculthorpe." *Dictionary of Music*, ed. Alan Isaacs and Elizabeth Martin. London: Chancellor Press, 1982.
PS rejected European techniques in the search for an authentically Australian nontonal style and his works (several are listed) show the influence of eastern music.

B704 "Peter Sculthorpe." In *Australian House and Garden's Celebrities at Home: 30 famous people talk about their lifestyles.* Special issue, edited by Beryl Clarke, [1982?]: 74-81.
PS's force patterned the avant garde movement of serious music in Australia, yet his Sydney home depicts a gentle 18th century influence. A full-page black-and-white photo of Sculthorpe precedes six pages of photographs of his home.

B705 Geoff Brown. "Tasmanian magic and mystery." London *Times*, Friday 29 January 1982.
Three Tasmanians contributed to the film **Manganinnie** now playing at the Paris Pullman cinema—composer PS, director John Honey, and author Beth Roberts.
Favorable London reviews are reported in Australia by A.A.P., as in "State film praised by UK critics," *Examiner*, 30 Jan.; and *SMH*, 31 Jan.)

B706 Richard Phillipps. "Special opera for 50th anniversary." *Scan*, 15 March-4 April 1982: 7.
PS has been commissioned to write **Quiros**, which will be going into production shortly.

B707 Laurie Strachan. "A high note on ABC television." *Australian*, Friday 14 May 1982: 10.
Executive producer Tony Hughes says that **Quiros** is a virtuoso piece of writing. "I wanted Sculthorpe to delve deeper into himself than he ever had before."

B708 Jill Sykes. "Quiros absorbing as a simulcast." *Sun-Herald*, 20 June 1982.
Quiros is absorbing television with a clear, musical unravelling of an extraordinary story. Quiros is presented as a man of faith and vision, surrounded by unpleasantness.

B709 S. C. "Spotlight on Peter Sculthorpe: New opera featured by ABC." *University of Sydney News*, 22 June 1982: 113. With companion piece, "Music and ideas analysed": 113, 115 [reviews Hannan **B702**].
According to PS, Quiros was the last of Spain's great explorers, a man of vision, and Australia's first patriot. Two of Sculthorpe's pupils at the University, Jim Franklin and Mark Bensted, have contributed to the compositional work.

B710 Frank Harris. "At last, Quiros finds success." *Mirror*, 23 June 1982.
Quiros is one of Sculthorpe's finest works and it also has a noble libretto by Brian Bell.

B711 Maria Prerauer. "Quiros—a triumph for Sculthorpe." *Weekend Australian Magazine*, 26-27 June 1982: 12.
The dramatic musical score is different from anything PS has done. Indeed, he could even emerge one day as the long-awaited heir to Benjamin Britten. The music is a combination of the known and the not so familiar, which should be accessible to most listeners. (Publicity in same issue: "Documentary, drama and a new opera".)

B712 Roger Covell. "Salute to ABC." *SMH*, ca. 26 June 1982.
Collaborators Sculthorpe and Bell have been successful in telling the story of the three voyages of **Quiros** and the reasons for their failure.

B713 John Carmody. "Voyages of hope and desperation." *National Times*, 27 June to 3 July 1982: 28.
"Much of my other music has been concerned with landscape," PS said at a recent preview of **Quiros**, "but this music is about people. Its horizons are those of the mind." Attractive tunes give full rein to his abilities as a songsmith.

B714 Margaret Clarke. "Sculthorpe's **Quiros**." *24 Hours*, July 1982: 2-4.
Sculthorpe is "thrilled" with the music of Quiros ("it's passionate") and with how well it goes on television. (In a companion article, "The theme of struggle," ibid.: 2-3, Anthony Hughes, Assistant Director of Music at the ABC, talks about the opera.)

B715 Fran Hernon. "Sculthorpe strikes a chord with obsession." *Australian*, 1 July 1982.
Quiros is a big, emotional piece. PS is a man in control of his emotions. The fires are there, they're just well-banked. Essay reviews his life and works. (*Other coverage: Australian*, 12, 16, 21, 23 July, published letters pro and con the Quiros production.)

B716 Jill Sykes. "To mark the occasion—an opera."*SMH*, 1 July 1982.
Sculthorpe says that Quiros has a lot of his best music in it.

B717 Nadine Amadio. "New era reached in ABC opera." *Sunday Telegraph*, 4 July 1982: 122.
Sculthorpe understands to some degree the obsession of Pedro de Quiros, as "I live an obsessed life as a composer." Opera Quiros received an outstanding performance.

B718 Peter Sculthorpe. "Sir Bernard Heinze—a tribute." *Radio Guide* (ABC), 17-23 July 1982.
Sir Bernard Heinze was one of the most special people in my life. Without his support I may never have succeeded as a composer. I have lost a father and a friend; so, too, has Australian music, and indeed the whole world of music.

B719 Nadine Amadio. "About music." *24 Hours* 7 (August 1982): 17.
Quiros focused a spotlight on a man who is a model composer for this country in terms of creativity, commitment, and generosity to his students and former students.
   Also in this issue "John Williams: a string of successes," p. 9, mentions the July 1981 performance of The Visions of Captain Quiros.

B720 Fred R. Blanks. "Australia." *Musical Times* 123 (September 1982): 631.
PS's opera Quiros was well received, both for its music and its performance.

B721 "That's entertainment: garden tour." *Sun*, 24 September 1982.
The garden of PS (a photo shows him in his garden) will be open for Garden Day on Sunday, Sept 26, organized by Cranbrook School—with three other gardens. (Tour is also announced in the *Wentworth Courier*, 22 Sept.)

B722 Laurie Strachan. "The composer's clef stick: art versus bums on seats." *Weekend Australian Magazine*, 16-17 October 1982: 5.
PS (one of several composers interviewed) agrees that the rate of pay for composing is ludicrously low—about $1 an hour for Quiros. He finds it "irrelevant" that classical music does not command a mass audience.

B723 Fred Blanks. "Sculthorpe tweaks the emotions." *SMH*, 10 Nov 1982.
Sculthorpe's autobiographical lecture-recital showed that he is not immured in an ivory tower; his music tweaks the emotions. PS and Michael Hannan charted the development of the piano music from a childhood Nocturne (1945) to **Mountains**.

B724 Andrew Saw. "No fuss as Eric Smith collects his Archibald Prize No. 3." *Weekend Australian*, 18-19 December 1982: 3.
Photo shows the prize-winning "semi-abstract" portrait of PS.
   Also announced: Terry Ingram, "Eric Smith could do it again," *AFR*, 15 Dec; and

"Archibald win fails to raise a single eyebrow," *SMH*, 18 Dec.

B725 Paul Griffiths. "Peter (Joshua) Sculthorpe." *The New Oxford Companion to Music*. 2 vols. Oxford: Oxford Univ. Press, 1983. Vol. 2, p. 1662.
Short entry identifies the composer, with birth date and names of Oxford teachers.

B726 Ava Hubble. *More Than an Opera House*. Sydney: Landsdowne, 1983.
(P. 19, 98-9:) PS's **Sun Music III** was the first work performed in the Opera House Concert Hall, to test the acoustics. Scenes from **Rites of Passage** are shown in color photos.

B727 K. S. Inglis. *This is the ABC: The Australian Broadcasting Commission 1932-1983*. Melbourne: Melbourne University Press, 1983.
PS is mentioned in connection with the **Sun Music IV** commission, the 1974 "Survey" documentary *Sun Music for Film*, and the 1974 SSO tour to Europe (p. 317, 354, 370).

B728 *The Macquarie Book of Events: 10,000 events that shaped Australia*. Devised and edited by Bryce Fraser. McMahons Point, NSW: Macquarie Library, 1983.
In "Music" section: listed for 1955 is the **Sonatina** performance at ISCM, and for 1965, the SSO's first extensive overseas tour and first performance of **Sun Music I** (p. 532). Caption for photo of PS, p. 534 , notes the influence of Asian music in his work.

B729 James Murdoch. *A Handbook of Australian Music*. Melbourne: Sun Books, 1983.
Book includes entries for: **Irkanda I-IV**; **Koto Music I, II**; *Notes on a Landscape*; **Port Essington**; **Quiros**; **Rites of Passage**; Sculthorpe; **Sun Music I-IV**; and **Tabuh Tabuhan**. Cover includes a photo of PS.

B730 Dr. Peter Sculthorpe. "Pancakes." *Fame & Flavour*. Sydney: Women's Committee of the Medical Foundation, University of Sydney, 1983.
PS's contribution to this celebrity cookbook is a recipe with four ingredients ("I hate cooking, so I go for something simple"), accompanied by a brief history of the pancake tradition and a 15th-century description of pancake-cooking.

B731 Malcolm Macdonald. "Australian Piano Music [**D47**]" *Gramophone* 60 (January 1983): 846.
PS's oddly-titled **Sonatina** is an undoubtedly Australian programme piece.

B732 Bill Zakariasen. "Aussie music, local bag ladies." *New York Daily News*, Tuesday 25 January 1983.
A downpour depleted the audience, but encouraged a few bag ladies to come in out of the inclement weather; and their running commentary seemed oddly appropriate. The program included one *bona fide* modern masterpiece, **Sun Music III**.

B733 Edward Rothstein. "Contemporary music: Juilliard concerts." *New York Times*, Tuesday 25 January 1983: C14.
The Juilliard Philharmonia (Jan 23) also presented the elegant Orientalism of PS's **Sun Music III** (1967), with its invocations of by-now-familiar Balinese patter.

B734 [Garden photo.] *Australian Home Beautiful*, March 1983: 108-9.
Color photo shows PS's back garden with sliding glass door to his studio beyond.

B735 Anne Boyd. "Nothing but best from Down Under." *South China*

Morning Post (Hong Kong), 31 March 1983.
The sombre **Lament for Strings** is a profound expression of grief. The ACO captured an inner stillness and desolation which was profoundly moving.

B736 "Time between works no hurdle for Peter." *Telegraph* [?], c5 April 1983.
"Have you got 23 minutes to hear my **Piano Concerto**?" asked PS. It's the first one he has written since he was twelve, and it has just been recorded [D40].

B737 Charles Shere. "Kronos Quartet's popularity and mastery continue to grow." *Oakland Tribune*, Monday 11 April 1983.
SQ 10 of PS (shown in photo) is a tight 17-minute piece moving through an arch-form of five connected movements. His music seems grounded in the Australian terrain. It's not unlively. There's a quiet turn to the subtler tunes in the *Sun Song* movements and an attractive grain to the harmonies of the chorales which reveal the innate interest of small familiar things.

B738 Heuwell Tircuit. "Kronos & Sculthorpe: fine duo." *SF Chronicle*, 11 April 1983.
The movements of this short "divertimento" (SQ 10) grow out of one another. The tune in the *Sun Song* movements is repeated over reiterative accompaniment; it is not, however, so-called *minimal music*. Sculthorpe has strength and freshness (will the local orchestras never get to him?).

B739 Dene Olding. "Australian Chamber Orchestra—an orchestra of the future." *Cadenza*, no. 1 (May/June 1983): 9.
We recognise our obligation to promote Australian music and have given first performances of Australian works by Sculthorpe, Butterley, and Conyngham.

B740 Ian Hunt. "Ideas in search of composition." *Australian*, 19 May 1983.
The atmospheric **Mangrove** has had the good fortune of three live performances in Melbourne in as many years. The cellos excelled in the warm, brooding passages.

B741 Stephen Whittington. "Interesting cello effect." *Advertiser*, 19 June 1983.
Mangrove contains a number of striking orchestral effects. But this performance is the solitary token of Australian content in this year's ASO subscription series.

B742 Marcia Ruff. "Winther's 50th birthday celebrated with a concert." *Canberra Times*, Monday 22 August 1983
The **Piano Concerto** is undemanding and pleasant, and should become a popular choice for orchestras looking to fill their Australian content quota.

B743 Fred Blanks. "Establishment stayed away in droves." *SMH*, 30 August 1983.
The Sculthorpe **Piano Concerto** can be welcomed by everyone but the avant garde, who will turn their noses up at its immediate appeal.

B744 Fred Blanks. "Seymour Group: Asian Interface concert." *SMH*, 20 September 1983.
Landscape II (1978) is full of melodic beauty with an Aboriginal undercurrent. Sculthorpe's verbal interludes were of helpful brevity. (*Publicity:* Jeremy Eccles, "Interface is where the twain has met," *Australian*, 15 Sept.)

B745 Helen Frizell. "The Asian interface." *Hemisphere* 28, no. 2 (September/October 1983): 108-115.
Frizell (former literary editor of the *SMH*) reviews the Asian influences on PS's style. Photo shows Sculthorpe and Hannan "preparing" the piano for **Koto Music.**

B746 Fred Blanks. "String quartet stakes its claim." *SMH*, 24 October 1983.
The Petra's abilities were heard to better advantage in Bartók than Mozart or Sculthorpe (SQ 8).

B747 [Art sale.] *Sun-Herald*, 31 October 1983.
PS has contributed a sheet of music drawn on ledger lines curved like rainbow serpents, to the Apmira art sale for Aboriginal land rights next week at Paddington Town Hall.

B748 "Peter Sculthorpe." *Baker's Biographical Dictionary of Musicians.* 7th edn.; rev. Nicolas Slonimsky. New York: Schirmer Books, 1984.
PS's music is often a battleground for European Expressionism and native ritualism. He has also been influenced by the physical environment of Australia. A paragraph of biography and a list of works through 1981 complete this updating of the 1978 edn.

B749 George Dreyfus. *The Last Frivolous Book.* Sydney: Hale & Iremonger, 1984. P. 63, 69, 70, 84.
In the sixties Meale, Sculthorpe, Butterley, and I were aware of each other, and envy was part of our awareness. (Book's title is Dreyfus's response to hearing Hannan on the radio describe his book [B702] as "the first serious book" on an Australian composer.)

B750 Robin Duffecy. "Self-indulgence." *Mode* (Sydney), January 1984.
"PS, composer," (shown in color photo), age 35, names his Thai elephant post as his favorite thing. The top elephant of the ten has a raised trunk, considered very lucky.

B751 June Epstein. *Concert Pitch: The Story of the National Music Camp Association and the Australian Youth Orchestra.* Melbourne: Hyland House, 1984. P. 86 (page from **W113** score), 89-90, 92, 159-160.
Music for Japan on tour in 1970 required two amplifiers which took two people nearly an hour to set up. In 1976, **Sun Music I** on the USA tour created a great deal of interest.

B752 Robert Treborlang. "Peter Sculthorpe: A personal profile." *2MBS-FM: The Monthly Programme Guide* 10 (February 1984): 10-11.
PS, in his fifties and famous, makes a conscious effort to be accessible for he has a kind democratic nature. His handwritten scores have the perfection of a printed page and the charm of a Miro painting, (Interview, with photo of Sculthorpe and Hannan, announces special programmes of PS's music, Feb. 5, 11, 18, 25, prepared by Treborlang and Belinda Webster.) Treborlang's review of Hannan's book [B702] follows, p. 18-19.

B753 Peter Sculthorpe. "Living with a garden." *Vogue Living* 18 (February 1984): 122-125.
"Perhaps you could say I am a man devoted to symmetry and planned colour." In the front and back gardens (shown in photos), symmetry abounds.

B754 Olive Lawson. "Peter Sculthorpe: The man and his music." *APRA Journal* 3 (March 1984): 2-6.
Lawson summarizes her impressions of Sculthorpe over nearly twenty years, quotes from critical responses to his music, and interviews him concerning performing right issues. Black-and-white photos are on the cover and p. 1, 2, and 4.

B755 John Rockwell. "Festival of moderns opens in California." *NY Times*, Sunday 11 March 1984: 60.
In **SQ 8, 2nd movt,** offered as an encore, outer skittery sections frame a solemn contemplative middle portion.

B756 John Colwill. "Conductor Mills, take a bow." *Courier-Mail*, 19 April 1984.
The fragmentary nature of the opening *grave* and the relentless repetitive piano figurations give an oppressive static quality to the **Piano Concerto** which presents as an incongruous mixture of the mechanical, the Oriental, and the romantic.

B757 Nicole Jeffery. "Music is in his blood." *Courier-Mail*, 25 April 1984: 2.
Sculthorpe is interviewed about his plans for music and a book.

B758 [Interview.] *Australian*, 15 May 1984.
Pianist Helen McAdam chose Sculthorpe's **Sonatina** "because it's nice and loud and it catches people's attention. And no one can really tell when you make mistakes." (Quote is reprinted in "Sayings of the week," *SMH*, 19 May.)

B759 [Concert review.] *Pravda*, Moscow (transl.), 18 May 1984.
The Moscow audience has undoubtedly received with enormous sympathy the work of Australian composer PS. His **SQ 6** riveted the attention of composers, conductors, art critics and performers from more than fifty countries of all continents.

B760 Peter Sculthorpe. "If I had a vast amount of power and money." *SMH*, Metro sect., 25 May 1984.
If I had the power and the money, I'd work to develop a truly national consciousness, not only in music, but in our whole society.

B761 John Rockwell. "Horizons: New-music festival ends." *New York Times*, 10 June 1984, sect. 1: 67, col. 1.
Mangrove, lush and pictorial, consisted of sharply defined sections that courted the charge of mere exoticism. But Mr. Sculthorpe's music in general coheres into a statement by a distinctive composer with something interesting and evocative to say.

B762 Bill Zakariasen. "A musical success from unusual marriage." *New York Daily News*, 12 June 1984: M10.
Mangrove by PS is full of the whoop-up imagery and impulsive zest inherent in so much Australian music—even Down Under, the sun always rises.

B763 Thor Eckert Jr. "New York Philharmonic finds promise on the musical horizon." *Christian Science Monitor*, 20 June 1984.
The works on the final program had little to offer. At least Tasmanian composer PS's **Mangrove** was an earnest attempt to evoke a specific mood and locale.

B764 Roger Covell. "The blacker, the more cheerful." *SMH*, 18 June 1984.
Sculthorpe, just back from warm appreciation of his music in the USSR and NY, was in the hall to hear Susan Blake perform his note-thrifty, strong-fibered **Requiem.**

B765 Tom O'Byrne. "Composer inspired by visit to Russia." *Examiner*, 21 June 1984: 7.
Says PS, "One of the most obvious components in Russian music is the emotional appeal by the composers to their audiences and this was one of the reasons why my **SQ 6** was so well received" in Moscow.

B766 Gregory Sandow. "Let the festivities begin." *Village Voice* (New York) 29 (26 June 1984): 92.
Australian composer PS had a triumph, too, with a smiling, entirely original, and deceptively simple piece called **Mangrove**.
Other reviews: Leighton Kerner, "Music as Will and Idea," ibid., 10 July: 67 (picturesque, sometimes incantatory nature piece); Edward Rothstein, "The return of romanticism," *New Republic*, 27 Aug: 25-30 ('nature' was a theme in the "New Romanticism" festival, as in the tropical **Mangrove**).

B767 Joan Tyson. "Moscow applauds master Sculthorpe." *Mercury*, 30 June 1984, Weekend sect., p. 5.
Glowing reviews and a eulogistic interview with Australian composer PS (shown in photo) appeared in *Pravda* [B759] after the recent performance of his **SQ 6**. He wrote from Moscow, "I'm exhilarated beyond all bounds and find Moscow a most noble city."

B768 [Garden photo.] *Australian Home Beautiful*, July 1984: 114-115.
Color photo of Sculthorpe's back garden shows brick paving, furniture, and vines.

B769 Jill Sykes. "Sculthorpe hears the music in Slav passion and American energy." *SMH*, Saturday 7 July 1984.
Sculthorpe has recently returned from his first trip to the Soviet Union and says "the euphoria of it all" has proved an inspiration. "It's all that Russian passion. I'd never heard my **sixth quartet** played the way I heard it in Moscow."

B770 "Australia's top 50 creative talents." *National Times*, 13-19 July 1984: 12.
Based on research by the *National Times* staff, and compiled by Kristin Williamson, the list includes Sculthorpe.

B771 Patricia Brown. "Take one solo cello, with relish." *SMH*, 8 August 1984.
The English cellist Timothy Hugh's account of PS's **Requiem** seemed the most thoroughly felt and technically well-realised to date. The work revealed itself as a deeply committed, tautly ordered and intensely enjoyable gem.

B772 Nicholas Kenyon. "Australian Youth Chamber Orchestra/Zollman." *Times*, 14 August 1984: 8.
Sun Music II—Ketjak is a splendid five-minute bash of percussion in a monkey-dance, full of lively colours, surrounded by the odd whining chord from the strings and even a little foot-stomping from the double basses.

B773 Geoffrey Norris. "Ardour from Australia." *Daily Telegraph*, 13 August 1984.
Sun Music II—Ketjak had an enthusiasm and vigour that aptly reinforced the AYO's cumulative energy

B774 Edward Seckerson. "Elizabeth Hall." *Guardian*, 13 August 1984.
Sun Music II is mercifully short, and thin—a short sharp shock of colourist dance music.

B775 David Johnson."Usher Hall: Australian Youth Orchestra." *Glasgow Herald*, 27 August 1984.
Sun Music II was a vivid jungle-noises piece, lasting a modest seven minutes. It was an exciting performance—fun to watch as well as to hear.

B776   John Martin. "Australian YO/Mackerras." *Guardian,* 27 August 1984.
Treated as a fun piece, Sun Music II was remarkably successful, but so short that one wished for a little more.

B777   Conrad Wilson. " 'Planets' as Holst requested." *Scotsman,* 27 August 1984.
Sun Music II conveyed an impression of a harsh, blistering landscape, which seemed at times on the point of eruption.

B778   Martin Long. "Evocative melding of the old and new." *Australian,* 24 September 1984.
Mangrove has a specious but fine-drawn atmosphere, suggestive of veiled distances and shimmering haze rather than the life-teeming density of a mangrove swamp. Does it matter? Not in the least. The audience was small.

B779   Fred Blanks. "Söderstrom and Britten eloquent about animals." *SMH,* 24 September 1984.
Music rich in philosophical and emotional emplications about the troubled relations between Man, Nature, and all living creatures made the concert a distinguished one. Mangrove is PS's finest, most approachable work for orchestra, depicting flocks of birds, distant horizons with the colours of sunset, and the mood of loneliness.

B780   "Portfolio of faces." *West Australian,* 26 September 1984.
A new portfolio of ten lithographs by Judy Cassab, with an introduction by the curator of the West Australia Art Gallery, was launched at the Holdsworth Galleries in Sydney by NSW Premier, Mr. Wran. A photo shows the lithograph of Sculthorpe. (The *Wentworth Courier* in Sydney also reports on the launch.)

B781   Derek Moore Morgan. "Ovation says it all to Callaway." *West Australian,* 22 October 1984: 14.
The concert overflowed with affection for Sir Frank Callaway. PS's colourful Sun Song for orchestra was one of the works written as a special tribute.

B782   Bernard Holland. "Concert: The Kronos String Quartet." *NY Times,* Friday 26 October 1984: C3.
In SQ 8 PS uses popular Balinese musical traditions to create his own kind of minimalism, and the results are highly expressive.

B783   Anthony Pople. "Sculthorpe, **Mountains; Requiem; Mangrove.** Score." *Music and Letters* 65 (October 1984): 434.
Mountains is evocative and brief. More frankly descriptive music is found in Mangrove. Requiem clearly requires a solo cellist of high calibre.

B784   Peter Sculthorpe. "Some thoughts upon the idea of a Pacific culture." *Canzona* 6, no. 18 (December 1984).
For some years I have believed that a high culture, which might be known as a Pacific culture, will arise from the countries bordering the Pacific basin. Although I am a composer in the Western European sense, as an Australian I feel free to draw upon musical traditions of the Pacific tradition. (The essay, written in 1976 for a Japanese magazine, is illustrated by a page from SQ 8, fourth movement.)

B785   [Requiem review.] Wellington (NZ) *Evening Post,* 7 December 1984.
The ideas of the **Requiem** are based on the plainsong Requiem Mass. The Sculthorpe magic brings them off movingly.

B786 [Mangrove review.] *Auckland Star,* 10 December 1984.
Mangrove possesses a timeless quality. Echoes of the distant past—the Aboriginal dreamtime—filter through to the present in search of the future. This performance revealed a work that must surely hold an important place in the world's music.

B787 [Mangrove review.] Wellington *Evening Post,* 11 December 1984.
Mangrove crystallizes in sound the overpowering presence of its designated landscape.

B788 *Directory of Australian Composers.* Sydney: Australian Music Centre, 1985.
Included are Sculthorpe's publisher and address (p. 51).

B789 Peter Dunbar-Hall, Annette Pollak, and Glendon Hodge. "Peter Sculthorpe." In "Musical Resource Notes." Typescript. Sydney: Educational Resource Materials, 1985.
Section on "Four Australian Composers" (PS, Butterley, Grainger, M. Sutherland) contains a short biography, description of musical style, list of works, and photo (p. 43-8).

B790 Andrew Pfeiffer. *Australian Garden Design: In Search of an Australian Style.* Melbourne: Macmillan, 1985.
A color photo (p. 80) shows the front garden of Sculthorpe's house.

B791 Joan Tyson. "Music book aims to fill big gap." *Mercury,* 5 Jan 1985: 14.
PS discusses the history of Australian music and the contents of his book in progress.

B792 [Mangrove review.] *The Listener* (Wellington, NZ), 19 January 1985.
Amidst the profusion of contemporary compositions (Dec broadcast), Mangrove shone.

B793 Stephen Pettitt. "Concerts: Lontano." London *Times,* 13 April 1985: 7.
Requiem is an exercise in deliberate simplification of dialectic which, though well-intentioned, fails to make an impact, perhaps because it is too personal a statement.

B794 Meirion Bowen. "Australian premieres." *Guardian,* 15 April 1985.
Requiem was played with great concentration by Margaret Powell. Lacking a larger context, its impact was elusive.

B795 Martin Pacey. "Concert notes." *The Strad* 96 (May 1985): 88-9.
The intensely devotional Requiem (April 15), clear, economical and simple, shows the influence of Britten (his three suites were also programmed) in some of its dark, brooding refrains. Most memorable was the *Qui Mariam* movement's elegant melody with throbbing pizzicato accompaniment.

B796 Fred Blanks, " 'Phoenix Quartet' a potential winner for Conservatorium," *SMH,* 21 June 1985.
The reconstituted Sydney SQ, making a bid for Con. support, understandably showed tension in performances of Sculthorpe 6, Haydn 76/1, and Beethoven 59/3.
Also: "Sykes on Sunday," *Sun-Herald,* 23 June (a persuasively atmospheric reading).

B797 "Music, young maestro, please." *Look & Listen,* July 1985: 31-2.
Sydney's Barker College recently hosted a special music camp for young musicians from NSW, Victoria, and Queensland. PS (shown with students in three photos) and other composers each spent a day. Final concert presented 20 student compositions.

B798 Reg Chapman. "Sculthorpe work feature of concert." *Mercury,*

Thursday 19 September 1985: 26.
Port Essington encompasses poignant humour and great beauty.

B799   Tim Toni. "My style: Peter Sculthorpe." *SMH*, 3 Oct 1985, Style sect.: 1.
PS's house is a testament to his talent for composition and arrangement—everything is painstakingly well organized. (A detailed description of the house follows.)

B800   Neil Jillett. "Composer who works for love and money." *Age*, 5 Oct 1985: Saturday Extra sect.
PS talks about **Burke and Wills**, composing habits, and plans in this lengthy interview. His **Piano Concerto**, which just won the APRA award for the year's most performed composition, was the background music to a television documentary on the Rainbow Warrior/Greenpeace drama in New Zealand. (Jillett's interview also appears, slightly changed, as: "Sculthorpe: Composing for love and money," *West Australian*, 16 Oct: 57, and "Saturday Profile: Peter Sculthorpe," *SMH*, 19 Oct: 44.)

B801   Caroline Baum. "Film also explores music limits." *Herald*, 31 Oct 1985, Arts Extra: 23.
PS talks about **Burke and Wills** and his current activities. (*Other publicity:* Kristin Williamson, *National Times*, 1-7 Nov: 38 [Graeme Clifford says he could *feel* Australia in PS's **Sun Music**]; and *Univ. of Sydney News* 17 [29 Oct]: 250.)

B802   Neil Jillett. "Worthy but disappointingly stolid homage to disaster." *Age*, 4 November 1985: 14.
Burke and Wills has an atmospheric, stirring but never obtrusive score by PS.
   Several film reviews praise the music: Harvey Mitchell, "Death in the desert," *National Times*, 8-14 Nov; Evan Williams, "Moving saga, but needs more anguish," *Weekend Australian*, 9-10 Nov, Magazine: 11; and Peter Gould and Frank O'Connell, "Where there's a Wills there's a way," *Catholic Weekly* (Sydney), 20 Nov; Plush, "Tosca's kiss," *Arts International* (ABC Radio), 7 Nov ("a huge Ivesian soundscape").

B803   T. H. Naisby. "Settling on the score for Burke and Wills." *Newcastle Herald*, 13 December 1985.
An arrangement of the film music for band was played before the film screening and for a dance band at supper afterwards.

B804   Peter Sculthorpe. "The Asian influence upon Australian music." In "The Asian Composers Conference Australia, 18-21 Sept 1985." Typescript. Strathfield, NSW: Fellowship of Australian Composers, 1986.
In a paper delivered to the Asian Composers League in Sydney on Sept 19, PS discusses Asian influences on Grainger, Glanville-Hicks, Boyd, Conyngham, Edwards, Meale, and others, and on himself.

B805   Trevor Hood. "Peter Sculthorpe." *Aspects of Music*. Sydney (Marrickville): Science Press, 1986.
Article (p. 26-27) includes a biography, a photo, and a quiz: "for each date, provide a biographical fact or name of a piece of music by PS": 1929, 1946, 1951, 1955, 1960, 1963, 1965, 1967, 1968, 1969, 1970, 1971, 1972/73, 1974, 1982. Answers are on p. 115.

B806   *Made in Australia: A Source Book of All Things Australian*. Sydney: Watermark Press, 1986. (First published, Richmond, VIC: William Heinemann Australia, 1986.)
(P. 137, 153:) PS today is internationally recognized for his hauntingly beautiful work.

B807 Therese Radic. *Bernard Heinze*. Melbourne: Macmillan, 1986.
Heinze conducted performances of **Sun Music III** (p. 196, 198, 200, 201, 206).

B808 Harvey Mitchell. "Fun and sadness help plug a gap." *Australian*, 20 January 1986.
Jeannie Marsh was irreproachable in PS's pleasing soliloquy on an Aboriginal fragment, **The Song of Tailitnama**.

B809 Harvey Mitchell. "Soviet defector brings a revelation of beauty." *Australian*, 27 January 1986: 5.
PS has mentioned the influence of Mahler on **The Stars Turn**, this soothingly rhapsodic piece. But the opening, at least, was strongly, and not disagreeably, reminiscent of Delius. (John Stapleton, "Time for a broader summer umbrella," *AFR*, 24 Jan: 37 mentions PS as among the better known composers heard at the Melbourne festival.)

B810 John Carmody. "An exultant blast." *National Times*, 14-20 March 1986.
Burke and Wills Suite was sometimes frankly revealing of its cinematic origins, sometimes witty. (The "blast" of the headline was Plush's *The Wakefield Chronicles*.)
Other reviews: Sam Hordern, "Nowhere to hide as unholy noise blasts cathedral," *Australian*, 7 March; and Elizabeth Silsbury, "Noisiest noise," *Advertiser*, 7 March.

B811 Will Crutchfield. "Music: of and by Australians." *NY Times*, Thursday 13 March 1986: C24.
PS's haunting and vibrant **SQ 8** leapt into relief--or was sprung into it by the dramatic performance of the Kronos Quartet.

B812 Brian Hoad. "Deep in cultural Skangaroovia, the Barnum and Boojum stir." *Bulletin*, 25 March 1986.
The quest for Australian identity is not so lonely as it was, as recognised at Adelaide by a new work [**Burke and Wills Suite**] from PS, now one of the older generations of Australian composers who years ago turned his back on European traditions.

B813 Andrew Clark. "New York hit for Sculthorpe." *Bulletin*, 8 April 1986: 76.
In New York. Crutchfield [**B811**] was "bowled over by" **SQ 8**, and Gregory Sandow, who writes for the *Wall Street Journal*, told *The Bulletin* he was "knocked out." Crutchfield took the composition home and played it on the piano to hear it again. Sandow said, "If Australians want to be proud of someone in music, they can be proud of him." (Salomon, "Classical," *Sunday Tasmanian*, 13 April: 39, reports the acclaim.)

B814 Richard Toop. "Music. Eureka Ensemble." *SMH*, 3 June 1986.
Song of Tailitnama for voice and piano made a strong impression, due not least to mezzo-soprano Jeannie Marsh.

B815 Barbara Yates Rothwell. "Passion from the peaks of Tasmania." *West Australian*, 6 June 1986.
The strong effective piece, **Mountains** [June 5], opens with dark and sombre moods and grows with a logical progression.

B816 Harvey Mitchell. "Collegium presents a rewarding repertoire." *Australian*, 26 June 1986.
Irkanda IV expresses deep, but restrained sorrow. Spiros Rantos and colleagues produced playing of refinement, sympathy, and insight, by understanding and matching Sculthorpe's economy of means and dignity of expression.

B817   Kenneth Hince. "Through the gloom, enjoyment." *Age*, 26 June 1986.
Irkanda IV was shot with melancholy. Through some alchemy which is often felt but
very hard to explain, the depression which can be triggered by music as sombre as this
was warded off by very good playing from the Rantos Collegum.

B818   Fred Blanks. "Quartet rises to increasing standards." *SMH*, 27 June
1986.
SQ 6 is a personal statement of lament, intense and strictly tonal. Its few fast sections
could have been played with more energetic sharpness, but the warmth of tone elsewhere was quite beautifully maintained. The cello managed to suggest a didgeridoo at
the end of the middle movement.

B819   Tom di Nardo. "Crickets & Hendrix." *Philadelphia Daily News*, Saturday 5 July 1986.
SQ 8 on the Kronos recording [D59] begins gloomily, finally intercut with slashing,
scraping daggers and agonizing utterances.
Also: David Hendricks, "Record reviews," San Antonio TX *Express News*, 31 May;
"New from Kronos Quartet," *Cincinnati Enquirer* (a most attractive piece); Tircuit,
"Recordings," *SF Chronicle*, 8 June (PS's snazzy SQ 8 takes the cake); James Wierz-
bicki, "Kronos String Quartet discovers Jimi Hendrix," *St. Louis Post-Dispatch*, 29 June
(deep-probing, often austere); Ginell, "Blending cultures," *LA Times (Daily News?)*, 4
July; Peter Goodman, "New releases," *Newsday*, 6 July (melancholy, a touch acerbic).

B820   "Top classical albums." *Billboard: The International Newsweekly of
Music and Home Entertainment*, 98 (5 July 1986): 38.
SQ 8 [D59] is #26 on the "chart" of the 30 top-selling classical albums, compiled from a
national US sample of retail store sales reports. [It climbs to #9 on 13 Sept, then falls
on 15 Oct to #10 after 18 weeks.] (News of the charts appears in *Fanfare* (Faber Music),
July/Aug: 366, and *Accent* (Boosey & Hawkes Australia), August.)

B821   Laurie Strachan. "Politics for Sculthorpe as he postpones the joy."
Australian, 14 August 1986: 9.
Earth Cry is a major departure for PS, the first time he has allowed politics in any
sense to have a say in his music. (Strachan reviews PS's current projects and ideas.)

B822   Fred Blanks. "Hopkins landmarks." *SMH*, 15 August 1986.
Particularly impressive was the performance (Aug 12) of **Mangrove**, a sometimes sultry
and always ingeniously scored though rather disjointed work .

B823   [Blanks?] "Down-to-earth heavenly sounds." *SMH*, 19 August 1986.
How the Stars Were Made, heard in a welcome revival, is simple music, perhaps, but
very effective. And it was nice to see Sculthorpe himself back in the public arena,
telling some good Takemitsu stories and being disarmingly vague about his own work.

B824   Stephen Whittington. "ASO turns on the power." *Advertiser*, 23
August 1986.
Earth Cry is a sombre, impressive score with many passages of striking and original
beauty. Haunting melodies, reiterated like some primitive incantation, seemed to
speak, in an indefinable way, with the authentic voice of this country.

B825   John von Rhein. "Kronos Quartet routs routine." *Chicago Tribune*, 24
Sept 1986.
PS's SQ 8 has become something of a Kronos signature piece, and it is hard to imagine
any quartet giving it a more highly charged reading.

B826 Fred Blanks. "Sydney pays tribute to Liszt." *SMH,* 7 October 1986.
PS's variation Djilile was slow and typically atmospheric. (*Announcements:* Blanks, "Composers' homage to Franz Liszt," *SMH,* 17 Sept; and in the *Australian,* 27 Sept.)

B827 Stephen Whittington. "Australian-made music." *Advertiser,* 9 October 1986: 26.
SQ 6 is a well-constructed and atmospheric work with an austere beauty. Its spare textures suggest a kind of lonely resignation, softened only by the final chords.

B828 Hans Forst. "Chamber ensemble with paprika spice." *Australian,* 30 October 1986.
The orchestra performed chorales of **Sonata for Strings** fine effect and helped the expertly-crafted score to a well-deserved success.

B829 Fred Blanks. "Sonata has an Aussie accent." *SMH,* 31 October 1986: 16.
Though PS's **Sonata for Strings** uses an American Indian fertility song, it had an unmistakable Australian accent in its throbbing phrases for low strings and in the dreamtime patience of drawn-out melodies, which can only be called—though the word is in disrepute among most contemporary composers—beautiful. This must be one of his most appealing works. (*Also:* "Sykes on Sunday," *Sun-Herald* [a "serious" work].)

B830 Neville Cohn. "Ensemble's rich percussion harvest." *Australian,* 4 November 1986.
Sonata for Viola and Percussion was given the most gently sensitive playing of the evening.

B831 Roger Covell. "Sculthorpe looks below life's hectic surface." *SMH,* 7 November 1986: 14.
Earth Cry is neither manifesto nor protest; it is a poet's reminder of the preoccupations that remain important below living's hectic surface.

B832 Martin Long. "Where simplicity loses its vitality." *Australian,* 7 November 1986.
In **Earth Cry**, one wished for more resourceful development of the rather plain thematic material.

B833 Jill Sykes. "Graeme's triumph." *Sun-Herald,* 9 November 1986.
I enjoyed the specific character of **Earth Cry** and the dynamism of the central sections.

B834 John Rockwell. "Music: Kronos Quartet." *NY Times,* Sunday 16 November 1986: 72.
On Friday, one of the "encores" was a favorite Kronos showpiece, the skittery, mysterious second movement from the Australian PS's **Quartet No. 8.**

B835 William Dart. "Ahead in programming." *NZ Listener* (Radio New Zealand programme guide) 6 December 1986.
PS's program note for **Earth Cry** suggested pessimism, but no: in this passionate work there was all that 'throbbing emotionally obsessive quality' that Roger Covell found in Sculthorpe's music almost 20 years ago. The effect of violas and trombones playing the opening theme over murmuring timpani is magical.

B836 Alan Kozinn. "Variety thrives on new-music disks." *NY Times,* Sunday 7 December 1986, sect. 2, p. 32.

There is a good deal of warmth in Mr. Sculthorpe's rhythmically vibrant, colorfully scored SQ 8 [D59], but getting at it requires a bit more of the listener than does Sallinen's quartet, for his style is more uncompromising and he ranges much farther afield.
  Other reviews (cont. from B819 July): David Sterritt and Madora McKenzie, "Soundtakes," *Christian Science Monitor*, 5 Nov: 23 (Kronos Quartet's virtuosity shines through), and mentioned 25 Nov: 29; Jon Pareles, "Recordings," *NY Times*, Sun. 9 Nov, sect. 2, p. 21, reprinted 20 Nov: 13H; Michael Walsh, *Time* (US edn), 17 Nov: 94 (the Balinese-influenced SQ 8 by the idiosyncratic Australian PS); Charles McCardell, "Kronos: On the cutting edge," *Washington Post*, Mon 24 Nov: C10 (an exchange of sorrowful melodies initiated by the cellist, and click-clacking bows and wispy glissandos by the other strings); Rockwell, "New glories in classical amid reissues," *NY Times*, Sun 28 Dec: sect. 2, p. 21.

B837   Robert Commanday. "Case of the missing harmony." *SF Chronicle*, 8 December 1986: 57.
  PS does his work effectively with rhythm, as was evident in SQ 8. Its fast movements, stressing strictly percussive playing, move with a certain intricacy and direction.

B838   Richard Pontzious. "Kronos Quartet at its best." *SF Examiner*, 8 December 1986: B1.
  PS's writes extremely well for strings, and he has a fine sense of line and form. All five movements of SQ 8 relate to each other in one way or another, so the piece has a cohesiveness not often found in large contemporary works.

B839   John Henken. "Kronos Quartet expresses its integrity in concert." *LA Times*, 15 Dec 1986: pt. 6, p. 2.
  PS based his **Eighth Quartet** [Dec 12] on Balinese music, and though not identifiably Asian, it has a sort of abstractly alien quality. Mournful movements featured the wonderfully expressive abilities of cellist Joan Jeanrenaud.

B840   Kenneth G. Brooks. *An Affirming Flame: Adventures in Continuing Education*. Hobart: William Legrand, 1987.
  (P. 57, 61-2:) PS, later famous, was involved with Tasmanian Adult Education programmes in the fifties. He has written to me that the Hobart conference in 1963 was "one of the most important events in the history of Australian music."

B841   Roger Covell. "Overtones of risk in commissioned scores are as it should be." *Vogue Australia Bicentennial Arts Guide*, 1987: 73-76.
  There should be limited capacity for disaster in PS's *Concerto Grosso* [**Second Sonata for Strings**]. The *Australian Music Celebration* [**Child of Australia**] is a collaborative effort. (Article is illustrated by a photo of a laid-back PS.)

B842   Beth Dean and Victor Carell. *Gentle Genius: A life of John Antill*. Arncliffe, NSW: Akron Press, 1987.
  (P. 176:) PS wrote a piece [actually, he did not] for Antill's 70th birthday [1974].

B843   John Schaefer. *New Sounds: A listener's guide to new music*. New York: Harper & Row, 1987.
  (P. 108:) SQ 8, based on Balinese rhythms, is the strongest work on the recording [D59].

B844   Peter Sculthorpe. "Letter, February 1987" In *A Lou Harrison Reader*, edited by Peter Garland. Santa Fe, NM: Soundings Press, 1987.
  (P. 104:) Harrison has established warm friendships in Australia, and is the only American composer to have named a piece after an Australasian city.

B845 Peter Sculthorpe. "Pancakes." *A Taste of Woollahra: A tasteful anthology of life in Australia's oldest suburb.* Produced in association with the Woollahra Bicentennial Community Committee; ed. Robin Brampton. Sydney: Media House, 1987. P. 75.
Recipe, with historical preamble, is reprinted from *Fame and Flavour* [**B730** above].

B846 Christopher Syms. *The Melbourne Symphony Orchestra: An introduction and appreciation.* Melbourne: MSO, 1987.
The orchestra regularly plays works of PS and other Australian composers (p. 92).

B847 Paolo Totaro. "Cultural diversity in music perspectives for Australian society." In *The Possum Stirs*, proceedings of the National Folklore Conference (1987): 285-34.
Paper for the Music Momentum Conference, Melbourne, 1984, mentions PS's work.

B848 Michael G. Nastos. "Dear Kronos—please come back soon." *Ann Arbor News*, Monday 19 January 1987.
PS's **SQ 8, 2nd movt,** featured percussive counterpoint and a serene pastoral section before returning to the rhythmic buzzing of the Aussie bush and the "kooks."

B849 Glenn Giffin. "Kronos Quartet unleashes dazzling sounds." *Denver Post*, Friday 6 February 1987.
In **SQ 8** the players give new meaning to the term *col legno.* The aggressive and percussive pizzicatos of the **2nd movt,** and its incredibly romantic middle, were dazzling.
    Other reviews on tour in Feb: James Wierzbicki, "Kronos fills theatre with young admirers," *St. Louis Post-Dispatch*, 16 Feb (**2nd movt** was "brief but substantial"); Robert Trussell, "Eclectic edge," *Kansas City Star*, 20 Feb (flawless playing of an extraordinarily challenging work); Rick Karr, "Kronos lives up to critical reputation, satisfies audience after three encores," *Purdue Exponent*, 26 Feb: 11 (a dizzying and entrancing rhythmic interplay, with harsh, angular tonality); and Ray Cooklis, "Kronos music pushes boundaries to outer limits," *Cincinnati Enquirer* (**SQ 8** made a fine opening display piece for the standing-room-only crowd).

B850 Patricia Kelly. "Performance of highest quality." *Australian*, 9 February 1987: 9.
The versatile QTO made an excursion into the present century in playing PS's **Irkanda IV,** with its tension-creating motifs, muted violins, ominous bass and accelerating tremolo creating a funeral mood before the work settles to a tranquil finish.

B851 K. Robert Schwarz. "Kronos Quartet" [**D59**]. *Musical America* 107 (March 1987): 64.
Balinese influence in **SQ 8** is especially apparent in the driving rhythmic ostinatos of the rapid movements, although the static, drone-like intervening sections are even more evocative.
    Other reviews: David Patrick Stearns, "The Kronos dazzles in five contemporary works," *Ovation*, May 1987: 45 (SQ8 is fun, even though it doesn't add up to much); Rockwell, "50 more CDs to tickle your laser," *NY Times*, Sunday 7 June, sect. 2, p. 29 (brief mention); Edward Rothstein, *New Republic*, 5 Oct.; McLellan, "The string masters," *Washington Post*, Sunday 10 Jan 1988: G1.

B852 Richard Buell. "Kronos String Quartet seduces the senses." *Boston Globe*, Sunday 15 March 1987: 42; reprinted 16 March: 22.
SQ 8 had its terse, piquant existence on the surface of things, and it was there that it

gave great satisfaction—a classy sort of Windham Hill-unto-ECM music.

B853 Roger Covell. "Asian views in Australia." *SMH,* 11 May 1987.
Sculthorpe's nine-year-old **Landscape II** spaces and highlights its characteristic lyricism with fastidious clarity and deliberation.

B854 James Cockington. "Music rooms: Striking the right chord." *SMH,* 21 May 1987, Style sect.: 1-2.
PS (and three other musicians) describe their work-rooms. PS's is tidy, enclosed, low-tech. "The acoustics are dull, the piano hammers muffled. The studio does tend to get a bit public, and I'm gregarious, yet my work requires a hermit-like existence."

B855 "Composer honoured." *University of Sydney News,* 2 June 1987: 101.
Composer Peggy Glanville-Hicks has been awarded an Honorary Doctorate in Music; photo is captioned with a one-sentence summary of the citation by PS.

B856 Martin Long. "Safety-first policy pays off." *Australian,* 15 June 1987.
The technical devices in **Sun Music I** and the static, impressionistic style it employs are now part of the stock-in-trade of the avant-garde; yet the piece has lost none of its impact as a vivid impression of parched land and hostile sun.

B857 Fred Blanks. "Safety first at the ABC?" *SMH,* Tuesday 16 June 1987: 12.
Sun Music I is an ingeniously scored mood piece with pictorial qualities that conjure up deserts with a shimmering heat haze, distant thunder, and searing winds. The work wears well and remains more daring than many later Sculthorpe pieces.

B858 Fred Blanks. "Vibrant Vivaldi from the ACO." Ibid.
Very beautifully played was the **Lament** by Sculthorpe in which controlled, decorous mourning suddenly splinters into two episodes of discordant tragedy.

B859 "SSO: Meet the Music 1987: **Piano Concerto.**" Teaching kit 2, Concert 3, 16 & 17 June 1987.
Materials are based on two ABC Radio National programs: "Peter Sculthorpe—The Assimilation of Traditions" by Anthony Fogg (26 June 1983); and PS's lecture, "The Contemporary Australian Concerto" on ABC radio, December 9, 1983.

B860 Peter McCallum. "Special applause for the SSO." *SMH,* 18 June 1987.
Much of the **Piano Concerto** sounded like the kind of thing one might tinker with in a bar after the customers had gone. Doing it in public, however, is quite another matter.

B861 Virginia Milson. "When work is play—Peter Sculthorpe: My favorite room." *Australian Home Beautiful,* July 1987: 144-5.
A large color photo shows PS at the piano in his studio with the garden courtyard beyond. The text describes the room and its contents and Sculthorpe's schedule.

B862 Jeffrey Lyons and Michael Medved. "Sneak Previews" (syndicated US national TV show of film reviews), 2 July 1987.
Everything about **Burke and Wills** is glorious—the music, cinematography. (Print reviews in the US begin in June; most only name PS as composer: Walter Goodman, *NY Times,* Fri 12 June: C10; Kevin Thomas, *LA Times,* Th 18 June, pt 6, p. 5.)

B863 Howard Reich. "Kronos Quartet liveliness at home in any era." *Chicago Tribune,* Tuesday 14 July 1987: 10.
The group's remarkable command of **SQ 8** made it immensely satisfying.

B864 Fred Blanks. "French pianism without a swoon." *SMH*, 20 July 1987.
Mountains brooded darkly.

B865 Martin Long. "A fitting tribute to Seymour." *Australian*, 21 July 1987.
Sydney Youth Orchestra gave a robust performance of Earth Cry. (Peter McCallum, "A champion is remembered," *SMH*, 21 July, does not mention Earth Cry.)

B866 Ülo Joasso. "Peter Sculthorpe." *Sydney Music Diary*, no. 41 (Oct 1987): 4.
PS's SQ 8 is popular in the US. He is not married, which gives him a chance to devote his life to music. He has very little time for hobbies. (PS's photo is on the cover.)

B867 Tristram Cary. "Empty seats greeting for a living composer." *Australian*, 12 October 1987: 9.
Though PS describes his Piano Concerto as "within a familiar European tradition", this rather withdrawn and gloomy score is Australian with nearby Pacific influences. The piano part is not demanding as concertos go, its small figuration set against expansive, slow-moving orchestral textures and exotic percussion. It was a convincing, thoughtful performance, obviously enjoyed by those subscribers who did turn up.

B868 Stephen Whittington. "Oz concerto a cause to celebrate." *Advertiser*, 12 October 1987: 12.
PS has written rather an odd Piano Concerto, unbelievably sombre from beginning to end. Nor is there any occasion for pianistic pyrotechnics.

B869 Roger Covell. "Tactile, fun, and irresistibly alive." *Sun-Herald*, 9 November 1987.
How the Stars Were Made [D13] represents the period of Australian composition of not so long ago when our composers were more inclined to ponder than to dance. Its sensitive response to an Aboriginal creation myth is characteristic of its greatly gifted composer.

B870 [News item.] *SMH*, 14 November 1987.
Controversy begins about Child of Australia (it is considered too long for the morning program and is moved to evening), and continues in: Murray Trembath, "Tribute hits sour note," *Sun*, 20 Nov; Leo Schofield, "Leo at Large", *SMH*, 28 Nov; and *SMH*, 3 Dec.

B871 "The Bicentennial awards: At the Grave of Isaac Newton." *Sounds Australian*, no. 16 (December 1987): 19-23.
The committee has commissioned an "extravaganza" [Child of Australia] from PS, and the ACO a "Concerto Grosso, provisionally titled At the Grave of Isaac Nathan.

B872 *Australopedia: How Australia works after 200 years of other people living here.* Fitzroy, VIC: McPhee Gribble, 1988. P. 304.
Young people's encyclopædia, section "When I was twelve," quotes PS (shown in boyhood photo): "Before I reached my teens, I decided that I was going to be a composer."

B873 John Cargher. *Bravo! Two Hundred Years of Opera in Australia.* South Melbourne: Macmillan (Australia), 1988.
Discussed are: Rites of Passage (color photo, p. 174-5), Quiros, and Eliza Fraser Sings.

B874 Ava Hubble. *The Strange Case of Eugene Goosens and Other Tales from the Opera House.* Sydney: Collins, 1988. P. 31, 32, 226.

Press officer of the Opera House mentions **Rites of Passage** premiere, and PS's views on programme notes [in 1981, **B684** above].

B875 Lou Klepac. *Judy Cassab: Artists and Friends*. Sydney: The Beagle Press, 1988.
Plate 59 is a portrait of PS, 1980, oil on canvas 120 x 97 cm. (An exhibition of the portraits in Brisbane is announced in "Briefs," *Courier-Mail*, 2 Sept 1988.)

B876 "Peter Sculthorpe." (Australian Composers Series, No. 5.) Sydney: Australian Music Centre, 1988.
Booklet contains a short biography and a list of works.

B877 Patricia Shaw. "New music in old lands." In *Ormond Papers*, vol. 5 (1988): 21-29.
Discussion mentions the work of PS. (Title appears in APAIS database.)

B878 Fred Blanks. "Inspiring words for rousing tune." *SMH*, 28 Jan 1988.
Child of Australia has all the right attributes of music for a specific ceremonial occasion, including music which is easy to follow, impressive to sing, and which ultimately delivers what used to be called a rousing good tune. Review includes a photo of PS and the full text. (Performance is also mentioned in *Daily Mirror*, 27 Jan: 3.)

B879 John Rockwell. "Concert: Australian Orchestra." *NY Times*, Sunday February 7, 1988, sect. 1, p. 68, col. 6.
Port Essington is an absolutely sterling score, accessible yet boldly original, conceptually fascinating and musically compelling.

B880 Joseph McLellan. "Australian Chamber Orchestra." *Washington Post*, 8 February 1988.
In **Port Essington** the ACO, playing in spiky, modern style, effectively portrayed the conquering bush, while the string trio in 19th-century style represented the settlers who never quite came to terms with the environment.

B881 Fred Blanks. "Our bicentennial birthright." *SMH*, 15 February 1988.
On program of music by Australian and near-Australian composers (Feb 10) PS's **Song of Tailitnama** was the only work that revealed an Australian origin.

B882 Roger Covell. "Quartet is of its time but ahead of its audience." *SMH*, 27 February 1988.
The rhythmic sections of **SQ 8** sounded exhilaratingly lean and bony; the lyrical and meditative moments were not so much performed as inhabited by the Kronos players. *Also:* "Sykes on Sunday," *Sun-Herald*, 28 Feb: 111 (exciting vitality).

B883 T. H. Naisby. "No gimmicks in string quartet's vibrant performance." *Newcastle Morning Herald*, 27 February 1988.
PS's **SQ 8** is beoming a classic in Australian music. Because the Kronos players have a profound understanding and affection for the work we should be grateful that they pioneer this composer in their own country, America.

B884 Mark Mobley. "Consort presents four from Toho Koto Society." Norfolk [VA] *Ledger-Star*, Tuesday 1 March 1988.
Tabuh Tabuhan is more ingenuous (picturesque sounds, repetitive patterns) than ingenious, but there are some clever things. And the languid sound of wind-chime-like little bells shaken by the wind players, brought to mind the film "Body Heat."

B885 Noel Sanders. "Not Drowning, Waving." *Canzona* (New Zealand Composers Association) 9, no. 29 (Autumn 1988).
It is Jan 26, 1988 and I've just been watching the ultimate puke-event on TV, namely the Bicentennial orgy of self-satisfaction. PS appears and announces that **Child of Australia** extols the unity of Australia—at all odds with all conceivable reason.

B886 Fred R. Blanks. "Sydney." *Musical Times* 129 (April 1988): 207.
Child of Australia is tuneful, optimistic and bright. Another bicentennial concert featured songs of Sculthorpe and other Australian composers.

B887 Roger Covell. "ACO hits fine touring form." *SMH*, 11 April 1988: 16.
Port Essington is already handsomely proved as a touring work and deserves to do so again. Self-renewing pleasures from it on this occasion were several.

B888 John Carmody. "Playing it safe: why the ABC is losing friends." *Australian Financial Review*, 11 April 1988: 12.
Less than one per cent of ABC-FM radio network time is devoted to Australian music, and if the "safe" names like Alfred Hill and Percy Grainger are deleted the residue is almost exclusively one composer, PS.

B889 John Colwill. "Mixed bag of clarinet for U. S." *Courier-Mail*, 11 April 1988: 24.
The mission hymn first heard in the piano in **Songs of Sea and Sky** is straight Charles Ives. The piece hangs together well; the form is an easy-to-read arch-shape, and the language suggests a sense of spaciousness.

B890 "Radio." *Newsday*, Sun 17 April 1988: 93.
Mondays at 9 pm, WNYC-FM: the avant-garde Kronos Quartet performs from a diverse repertoire. Interspersed with the music are interviews: PS introduces his [SQ 8].

B891 Tristram Cary. "Potential requires polish." *Australian*, 4 May 1988: 16.
PS's **SQ 8** sounds a little old-fashioned with its *col legnos*, tail-piece bashing, wrong side of the bridge and all that, but it has some warmly felt passages and was a good vehicle for the youthful Arioso Quartet to show its technical paces.

B892 Barbara Hebden. "Violin virtuoso at work." *Courier-Mail*, 4 May 1988: 45.
Alone is an atmospheric piece in which the violin, first in a high-pitched desolate sound and later as the accompaniment to the performer's gentle whistle, evokes an atmosphere of solitude.

B893 Leo Schofield. "Leo at Large." *SMH*, 21 May 1988.
Plans are underway for a Braidwood Festival, devoted to the music of PS, to be held in late September 1989. Contributions are needed; Vincent Plush has information.

B894 Roger Covell. "In search of an identity." *SMH*, 23 May 1988.
The Sydney SQ (shown in photo) gave a completedly studied interpretation of **SQ 10**.
Long, "Quartet returns full of promise," *Australian*, 23 May: 10, finds the quartet characteristically spare, relying for its appeal on rhythmic impulse.

B895 Arnold Whittall. "Sculthorpe. Chamber Music" [D35]. *Gramophone* 66 (June 1988): 44.
PS is a good composer to get to know during the Australian bicentennial. Though well-schooled in the musical ways of present-day Europe and America, he seeks to give his

compositions a high degree of local colour. This is intriguing and attractive.

B896   Stephanie Green. "Performance with gusto." *Canberra Times*, Monday 6 June 1988: 13.
Even the nine pieces by Australian composers tended to reflect a European heritage. In **Small Town**, a beautiful oboe solo is echoed by the strings.

B897   "Aussie notes." *Doncaster Free Press*, 16 June 1988.
The distinguished Anglo-Australian pianist Penelope Thwaites played some attractive, rarely heard Australian music. PS's often percussive early **Sonatina** seemed to have much in common with Aboriginal beginnings.

B898   Glenn Giffin. "Aspen Music Festival upholds its excellence." *Denver Post*, Sunday, 26 June, 1988: 6D.
Sonata for Strings is a good, strong piece that falls easily on the ear. In the *Sun Song* movements, which refer to Australia's unique skies and wide-open land, the harmony changes about as quickly as a Kansas landscape.

B899   Andrew Ford. "Kakadu is transplanted to Colorado, but where's Hoges?" *SMH*, Saturday 23 July 1988: 77.
PS's presence at the Aspen Music Festival as resident composer will be the highlight. Premiered tomorrow will be **Kakadu**. (Other announcements of Aspen and Telluride include: Angela Bennie, "Aspen hills to echo an Aussie hum," *Australian*, 7 July: 9; "Arts news," *SMH*, 5 Mar; and Covell, *SMH*, 11 Dec 1987.)

B900   Laurie Strachan. "Overnight sensation." *Bulletin*, 26 July 1988: 140-1, 143-4.
PS says he's too busy writing music these days to listen to it. After 40 years in the business, Australia's leading composer is enjoying international acclaim. Interview reviews his ideas and activities.

B901   John Colson. "They make the new music." *Aspen Times*, 28 July 1988, sect. B.
At the Aspen Festival last Sunday a packed house listened attentively to PS explain **Kakadu** and, at the end of the piece, stood for a prolonged ovation for the composer and the musicians. Photos show "Peter Sculthorpe, bowing" and Mester conducting a rehearsal of **Kakadu** while PS looks on.
Reports in Australia: "Composers bask in fame abroad." *West Australian*, 28 July: 5; "Australian composers win accolades in US." *Weekend Australian*, 27-28 Aug: 8.

B902   Glenn Giffin. "Despite top performers, Aspen Orchestra disappointing." *Denver Post*, 28 July 1988: 4C.
Kakadu made the greatest impression. This wonderful piece is a powerful evocation of a land that can exist as well in the imagination as in reality. Mester conducted with authority and got a machined performance from the orchestra.

B903   Shirley Stott Despoja. "Playing out a day in the life of Australia." *Advertiser*, 29 July 1988.
PS's **Piano Concerto**, used for part of the the the ballet *Once around the sun*, was poignant and beautiful, but opportunities in the music were rarely fulfilled on stage.
Other reviews: Patricia Laughlin, *Age*, 1 Aug; Tracey Jambor, *Sun*, 10 July (somewhat discordant score); and Greg Roberts, 29 July.

B904   Marc Shulgold. [Review.] *Rocky Mountain News*, Sunday 31 July 1988.

Kakadu was the highlight of the concert. Borrowing heavily from Aboriginal music and philosophy, PS has created a pleasantly colorful, descriptive 20-minute work filled with wisps of cricket and bird sounds and abundant drumming. *Also:* Shulgold interviews Sculthorpe in Aspen, "Australia's rhythms inspire composer," ibid., 65.

B905 Fred R. Blanks. "Sydney." *Musical Times* 129 (August 1988): 426.
SQ 10 (May 21), given its Sydney premiere at one of many bicentenary concerts, was typically well crafted, its idiom influenced by oriental and aboriginal suggestions.

B906 Hans Forst. "Cultural exchange rates rebalanced." *Australian*, 1 August 1988.
Songs of Sea and Sky is to be commended for expert handling rather than for personal commitment. Favourable audience response had to be greatly credited to Westlake's rendition. (Forst, "Music," *North Shore Times*, 10 Aug, repeats these views.)

B907 David Vance. "Loads of Gallic charm." *SMH*, 1 August 1988.
Nigel Westlake played the Torres Strait dance song in **Songs of Sea and Sky** with a transcendent beauty suggesting a Mahlerian peace with the world. The piano part's Messiaen-like bird calls and energetic dance rhythms were equally evocative of the work's origins.

B908 "Meet the Music," Concert 4, 9 & 10 August 1988. Teaching Kit 3. Sydney Symphony Orchestra, 1988. P. 14-16.
Material about Edwards' *Maninyas* for violin and orchestra includes three pages of **The Song of Tailitnama**, which had a subconscious impact on Edwards' maninya style. In the sixties, by contrast, when he was PS's assistant, he was quite modernist.

B909 Anne Kilstofte. "Kronos' performance refreshingly different." *Denver Post*, 11 August 1988: 3F.
PS's **Quartet No. 8** gave listeners something to sink their teeth into.

B910 Neville Cohn. "Voicing an emphasis on today." *Australian*, 15 August 1988: 7.
Sonata for Viola and Percussion was an instrumental high point of the concert in Perth (August 12). A work of substance, it uses rhythm in a contemporary idiom to make a strong and meaningful musical statement.
  Derk Moore Morgan, "Pastel view of modern music," *West Australian*, 15 August: 50, finds the *Sonata* "an interesting excursion into gentle timbres."

B911 Wes Blomster. "A community of outsiders." Boulder (CO) *Daily Camera*, 28 August 1988: 1D-2D.
At Telluride's annual "Composer-to-Composer" symposium last week PS spoke of the imprint of his native landscape upon his music. (Conference announcements naming PS include: "Composers are meeting at Colorado symposium," *LA Times*, 19 Aug.)

B912 [Article on Australian music.] *Music Today Quarterly* (Tokyo) 1, no. 2 (Autumn 1988): 019.
Article discusses Sculthorpe and other composers and includes a photo of him.

B913 Paul Carter, ed. *Performing Notes — 1988 Blue Mountain Arts Festival*. Katoomba: The Blue Mountains Festival, 1988. [P88-10]
Booklet includes, on p. 51-3, excerpts from some of PS's writings: notes on **Rites of Passage** (1974); "What is Australian music?" (1980); "Some Thoughts upon the Idea of a Pacific Culture" [B784]; and an introduction to the Japanese shakuhachi (1986).

B914   Peter Sculthorpe. Review of John Jenkins, 22 *Contemporary Australian Composers* (Melbourne: NMA Publications, 1988). *AMC News* no. 19 (Spring 1988): 31.
(PS's remarks are transcribed and edited by Warren Burt from a talk given on ABC Radio National's "Late Night Live" program:) The appearance of this book is really a major event. Very few important books on music ever appear in this country, let alone books on Australian music. (Sculthorpe is mentioned on p. 163 of the book as the teacher of Greg Schiemer.)

B915   Michael Hannan. "Concerts. Strings Story." *Australian Listener* (ABC), 17-23 September 1988: 40.
Discussion of **Port Essington** (to be broadcast Sept 17) covers the historical background and musical effects.

B916   Roger Covell. "Medieval drama in a split skirt." *SMH*, Friday 23 September 1988: 14.
The performance of **Eliza Fraser Sings** was the first I have seen to achieve something like a complete theatrical realisation. PS was present, and must have been pleased.

B917   Gail Brennan. "They said we'd never make it: The music of Australia." *SMH*, Saturday 24 September 1988: 81.
In a debate at National Composers' Conference on Thursday, composer Roger Smalley described Australian music in unintentionally devastating terms. "In Sculthorpe you have simple, extremely discrete blocks of material." By the time he got round to saying that this was not pejorative a number of jaws were hanging and someone giggled.

B918   Kevin Siddell. "Promising music at Uni." *Courier-Mail*, 18 Oct 1988: 4C.
The University Orchestra controlled the spirit of PS's **Lament for Strings** nicely throughout, the lower strings maintaining a solid support for its melodic features.

B919   Roger Covell. "Australians are finding their own musical path." *NY Times*, Sunday 23 October 1988, sect. 2, p. 23.
Article is part of the publicity for the SSO 1988 US tour. Similar articles include: Charles Buttrose, "Conducted tour of the USA." *Australian Listener*, 8-14 Oct 1988: 42-43; "At the Bushnell: Music from 'Down-Under,' " *Hartford* [CT] *Courant*, 17 Oct; and "A musical force from Down Under," Orange County [CA] *Register*.

B920   Richard Riley. "Symphony from Down Under serves up unappetizing fare." *Springfield [MA] Union News*, 25 October 1988.
Mangrove was more a series of ingeniously fashioned sonorities than a serious musical statement. It nevertheless evoked a sense of space and time that was quite magical.

B921   Gregory Hayes. "Australian orchestra lacks musical passion." *Daily Hampshire Gazette*, Northhampshire, MA, 25 October 1988.
The 18-minute **Mangrove** did not match its program note in eloquence and impact, but had moments of drama and eerie beauty, among them the imitation of bird calls.

B922   Steve Metcalf. "Australia exports youthful performers." *Hartford [CT] Courant*, Wednesday 26 Oct 1988: F6. Reprinted 27 Oct: 9, as "Sydney Symphony is a worthy and exuberant export."
Mangrove (Tuesday) was serviceable enough as an earnest, effect-filled curtain raiser, evoking thoughts of mangrove trees and other things Australian.

B923   Bruce I. Miller. "Aussie friends say it musically." *Worcester [MA] Evening Gazette*, 28 October 1988.
As a metaphor of love's relationship to life, which is one possible interpretation of **Mangrove** to be derived from PS's notes, the music succeeds only tenuously. But its use of tonal pallette is inventive and one might want to hear it again.

B924   Richard Duckett. "Sydney Symphony is superb." *Worcester [MA] Telegraph*, 28 October 1988.
Mangrove is unusual and one would like to hear it again. Ultimately, one felt that here was a work with heart and something powerful to say.

B925   John Noble. "Perihelion solar music true to intention." *Courier-Mail*, 31 October 1988: 19.
Sonata for Viola and Percussion reflects some of the **Sun Music** ideas with echoes of Australia's lonely, shimmering spaces.

B926   M. Renee Taylor. "A memorable evening with Sydney Symphony." *Journal Inquirer*, Monday 31 October 1988.
Mangrove mysteriously evoked a sense of this island tree's "extraordinary root system and life giving powers" (quoting from the composer's program note). The composer and conductor shared kudos from a spellbound audience.

B927   Tim Page. "An orchestral debut from Down Under." *New York Newsday*, 1 November 1988.
At first **Mangrove** seemed like a sound-piece, but its long middle section, a plaintive whole-tone chorale of sorts, belies this impression. It is both original and impressive.

B928   Dale Harris. "World-class debut." *New York Post*, 2 November 1988.
Mangrove was challenging and engaging. Lyrical introspection is blended with sounds of bird calls and Aboriginal tribal sounds, including the didjeridoo.

B929   Bill Zakariasen. "Sydney Symphony: A case of jet lag." *NY Daily News*, 2 November 1988.
Fragmented at the beginning, **Mangrove** hangs together better as it goes along, but it is hardly as instantaneously appealing as the **Sun Music** cycle.

B930   Bernard Holland. "No melody, just raw nature observed." *NY Times*, 2 November 1988: C20, col. 3-5.
Mangrove opens a slender but interesting new window of opportunity for the dwindling resources of so-called classical music. The medium is the standard symphony orchestra, but there is no development of ideas, no melody or harmony as such, no European symmetries of form—only a series of observed events, the aural impressions of looking around at raw nature.

B931   Robert V. Palmer. "RPO proves itself with Stravinsky." Rochester *Democrat and Chronicle*, 4 [?] November 1988.
Kakadu, though written this year, is as approachable as background music to a film, but it now and again entices, and is at least honest, if uncomplicated.
      Palmer's pre-concert interview of PS, "Two worlds of music," *Democrat and Chronicle*, 2 Nov, explains that this is the premiere of the revised score.

B932   Scott Cantrell. "Mester's worldly menu is served well by the RPO." Albany [NY] *Times-Union*, 4 November 1988: 16C.

Kakadu had a bracing, outdoorsy quality. Surrounding a lush central oasis (with haunting English horn solo) were aboriginal rites of hammering drums, insistent brass fanfares and repetitive string patterns. And PS's droll introduction was a delight.

B933   Ray Cooklis. "Tuckwell glamorizes CSO Australia night." *Cincinnati Enquirer*, 5 November 1988.
Sun Music III is evocative and combines Balinese ceremony and Asian atmospherics. One would like to hear some of his more recent music.

B934   Mary Ellyn Hutton. "Symphony hornist brightens a rainy night at Music Hall." *Cincinnati Post*, 5 November 1988.
The conductor crafted the work with utmost care.

B935   Hazel Hawke. "Making music and friends." *Australian Listener*, 5-11 November 1988.
The SSO on tour programmed an Australian work at each US concert—PS's **Mangrove** and works of Vine and Williamson. (The author, wife of Prime Minister Bob Hawke, travelled with the SSO.)
    Also: Ava Hubble, "Composers on tour: Three of the best," ibid. (announces the SSO broadcast on ABC on 12 Nov); and Geraldine O'Brien, "SSO scores a hit OS," *SMH*, 5 Nov: 93 (summarizes US reviews—reported in other Australian cities as well).

B936   Fred Blanks. "Festive restraint." *SMH*, 11 November 1988.
Child of Australia may retain respect and dignity after the official occasion for which it was written, Australia Day. PS starts with an Aboriginal theme and ends with an optimistic, inspiring tune which reflects the sentiments of the text.
    Long, "The open-air birth proved healthier," *Australian*, 10 Nov: 14, finds the work burdened with too much narrative.

B937   Bernard Holland. "Kronos Quartet stretches perimeters." *NY Times*, 28 November 1988: C23.
PS in **SQ 8** seems conscious of the past and at the same time cut off from it; and as a result, taps into the present using a few inherited tools.

B938   Andrew Porter. "Musical events." *New Yorker*, 28 November 1988: 118.
Australian music was represented, briefly but strongly, by a poetic account of PS's **Mangrove**. In a program note the composer disclosed that the tapping of an enormous tropical woodpecker while he was at Yaddo found its way into the colorful score.

B939   Barbara Hebden. "Con. a political pawn says an administrator." *Courier-Mail*, 6 December 1988.
PS, speaker at the 32nd Queensland Conservatorium of Music graduation ceremony, urged Australian composers to persuade students to play Australian works.

B940   Crossword puzzle. *Age*, 24 December 1988.
Question for 12 down: "What Australian composer is to have his 60th birthday specially honoured during the [Melbourne] orchestra's concert season of 1989? Picture F."

B941   John Rockwell. "Classical view: Good things from small labels." *NY Times*, Sunday 25 December 1988: sect. 2, p. 27.
This critic's 1988 best-records list, in the category of "Avant-Garde," includes "a riveting collection of music" by PS, on SC 1016 [D35].

B942   Max Harris. "Browsing." *Australian*, 31 December 1988.

It was Tom Keneally's usual good luck that the million-voice choir draped all over the Sydney Opera House made the words for Child of Australia incomprehensible.

B943   Roger Covell, "Fine imports and proud exports: Classical 88." *SMH*, 31 December 1988.
Kakadu drew an enthusiastic response from an ultra-knowledgeable Aspen audience.

B944   Elizabeth Gilliam. "Photographic portraits of Australians." 1989.
Collection of five photographs, 16.8 x 17 cm, includes portrait of PS (composer).

B945   Charles J. Hall, compiler. *A Twentieth-Century Musical Chronicle: Events 1900-1988*. (Music Reference Collection, Number 20.) Westport CT: Greenwood Press, 1989.
Musical events listed for 1929 include the birth of PS, April 29. Biographical highlights in 1960 include his return to Australia, and in 1972 his year at Yale [Sussex].

B946   *Our Place, Our Music*. Aboriginal Music: Australian Popular Music in Perspective, vol. 2, ed. Marcus Breen. Canberra: Aboriginal Studies Press, 1989. P. 137.
Sculthorpe uses drones and general imitations of tribal tunes, and Aranda texts; he wrote the music for **Manganinnie**, about Aborigines. (Book is reviewed in *Sounds Australian*, Winter 1991: 12.)

B947   Patrick White. *Patrick White Speaks*. Edited by Paul Brennan and Christine Flynn. Sydney: Primavera Press, 1989.
White's "Nine Thoughts from Sydney," no. 8, refers disparagingly to PS's music.

B948   Greg Schiemer. "Towards a living tradition." *NMA [New Music Articles]* 7 (1989): 30, 35.
When Schiemer studied with PS in 1969, the gamelan, like other Asian music, was respected as a useful source for western composers. (Helen Gifford, "Subliminal co-ordinates, drawing threads," ibid.: 8, recalls that she and PS and others studied counterpoint with A. E. H. Nickson.)

B949   Fred R. Blanks. "Sydney." *Musical Times* 130 (January 1989): 43.
During the euphoria of the bicentennial year I heard some 130 works by nearly 70 Australian composers. Among those that deserve permanency are PS's **Mangrove** and his **Child of Australia**, a celebratory work which is nationally inspiring.

B950   Roger Covell. "Luscious sounds from the tropics." *SMH*, 24 Jan 1989.
How the Stars Were Made can now be enjoyed in spotless sound on CD (**D14**).

B951   Barbara Hebden. "Sculthorpe tribute recalls greatness." *Courier-Mail*, Wednesday 8 February 1989: 30.
Tribute to PS in his 60th birthday year included a strong, musical account of his well-constructed SQ 10. Five Night Pieces were played with a fine understanding, **Mountains** with grandeur, and Songs of Sea and Sky brilliantly.

B952   W. L. Hoffmann. "CSO's commitment to Aust composers." *Canberra Times*, Monday 13 February 1989.
Performances of PS's music around Australia will mark his 60th birthday.

B953   Barbara Hebden. "Savage: accurate and quietly stylish artist." *Courier-*

Mail, 23 February 1989: 34.
In **Night Pieces**, PS has used the textural sonorities of the piano as an artist would use his brush. Savage, too, was richly inventive in his tone colors and dynamics.

B954 Peter Haley. "Symphony renders Australia in sound." Albany [NY] *Times Union,* 25 February 1989.
Sun Music I gave a reflection of the Australian landscape in unusual sound, too long by half. (*Publicity:* ibid., 24 Feb; *Berkshire Eagle,* 24 Feb; *Greenville Local,* 16 Feb; *News-Herald,* 16 Feb; etc.)

B955 B. A. Nilsson. "ASO's oboist shines in Tchaikovsky's 4th." *Schenectady [NY] Gazette,* 27 February 1989.
Sun Music I has a bright relentlessness about it.

B956 Barbara Hebden. "Back-shelf works given an airing." *Courier-Mail,* 3 March 1989: 29.
The conductor brought out the gamelan-like textures of **Sun Music III**.

B957 Meirion Bowen. "Waseda SO." *Guardian,* 15 March 1989: 37.
The City University SO (like the Waseda SO the next night) sported a UK premiere mingling Oriental and Occidental ingredients—PS's **Piano Concerto**. What failed to convince was the harmonic language, with numerous solecisms and inconsistencies.

B958 Meredith Oakes. "Opulence and ecstasy via the Orient." *Independent,* Wednesday 15 March 1989.
The **Piano Concerto** is simple, narrow, even dour: over-neat in its whipped-up frenzies, its ecstatic or nostalgic poses. But it is also uncompromising, communicative, and unfailingly skilful. There was warm applause.

B959 "First class air fare." *Hampstead & Highgate Express,* 17 March 1989: 114.
PS's **Piano Concerto** absorbs the music of the Pacific basin and then re-presents it in a form in which any European would feel at home. I would want to hear the piece again.

B960 Stephen Pettitt. "Concert: City University SO/Kess." *Times,* 20 March 1989: 20.
The **Piano Concerto** ruminates hypnotically, but its flavour and its repetitive patterns are worlds removed from East Coast minimalism; in fact its searching quality reflects Sculthorpe's preoccupation with Oriental music. The pianist is a non-combative, exploratory partner, though the part is technically challenging.

B961 Jillian McFarlane. "A feast of Sculthorpe." *Telegraph.,* 26 March 1989.
Sculthorpe is so busy—travelling for a documentary film, birthday concerts—he seems to be a little unnerved. Interview in this Sunday paper describes his activities.

B962 Roger Covell. "Parrots hit the note for Schumann." *SMH,* 29 March 1989.
At Mittagong, eight pieces or sets of pieces demonstrated how well PS's music has worn. He explained that he now hears some earlier works faster than the metronome marks he gave them—**Tabuh Tabuhan**, which seemed overlong here, is a case in point.
   Festival publicity includes: Ken Healey, "Mittagong opening: Season to salute Sculthorpe at 60." *AFR,* 23 March 1989, Weekend: 5.

B963 Barry Conyngham. "Profile: Peter Sculthorpe." *Vogue Australia* 33

(April 1989): 92.
I first met PS (shown in photo) in 1965. The passion of SQ 6 pushed me on towards a
desire to write music myself. No doubt there is a great range of opinion on the nature of
his contribution but very few would deny his uniqueness, his significance for the world
of Australian music. We can only look forward with excitement to what comes next.

B964   Belinda Webster. "Landscape and ritual: Peter Sculthorpe at sixty."
2MBS-FM Programme Guide 15 (April 1989): 4-5.
PS talks about his sources of inspiration, the influence of performers, his view of
musical form, and his work habits.

B965   Andrew Ford. "Sculthorpe at sixty." *24 Hours* 1 (new series) (April
1989): 6-7.
PS (shown in large photo) is something of an icon in Australian music. For many
people, here and overseas, Australian music begins (and too often ends) with Sculthorpe. But his modesty is geniune. Australian music will have to share its icon with
the rest of the world. And this is good for all of this country's composers.

B966   Ken Healey. "A selection of Sculthorpe." *Sun Herald*, 2 April 1989: 97.
PS (shown in photo), guest composer at Mittagong, deserved this recognition, and
emerged with his stature enhanced. **Songs of Sea and Sky** showed that his idiom has
refined what was already skilfully wrought.

B967   Joshua Kosman. "Symphony comes back to Oakland." *SF Chronicle*,
Monday 3 April 1989.
Mester conducted **Kakadu** with a rhythmic clarity and vibrancy of color that were
impressive, even in the slightly cavernous reaches of the Paramount. **Kakadu** is a
vivid and quite enjoyable work. Sculthorpe's flamboyant, sharply etched orchestration helps put the material across.

B968   Stephen Whittington. "String quartet hits the right note." *Advertiser*,
Tuesday 4 April 1989: 10.
The Arioso SQ gave PS's **SQ 6** an intensity and bite which made sense of its dramatic
gestures and carried through to the long, lyrical solo passages.

B969   Rodney Smith. "Contemporary Music Viva." *Advertiser*, 8 April 1989:
45.
SQ 9 was spectacularly successful. The rather conservative Musica Viva audience was
rivetted with the pulsating rhythms, searing Mahlerian romanticism, reiterated Bartokian ostinati, col legno effects and the all-pervading influence of Aboriginal music.

B970   Michael Hannan. Introduction to *Kakadu*. *SSO Orchestra Education
Program Teaching Kit. Twentieth Century Orchestra Open Rehearsal.
A Concert for Peter Sculthorpe's Sixtieth Birthday. Kakadu.* Sydney
Town Hall, 7 April 1989. Typescript, 47 leaves, and 1 sound cassette.
Kit contains: an introduction; transcription of an interview between Hannan and
Sculthorpe with Hannan's linking commentary; chart of the structure of main themes
in **Kakadu**; musical illustrations from Péron and Freycinet *Voyage de Découvertes aux
Terres Australes 1800-1804*; Ford's article in *SMH*, 23 July 1988; score extracts; and
acknowledgments.

B971   Robyn Harvey. "Today's people." *SMH*, 7 April 1989: 24.
Sculthorpe said yesterday that he had been overwhelmed by the number of birthday
concerts. What he really wants for his birthday is a compact disc player.

B972 Jill Sykes. "Sculthorpe takes his fancy to flight." *SMH*, Sat. 8 April 1989: 90. Reprinted as "Peter Sculthorpe at Sixty," *APRA Journal* 7 (October 1989): 5-7, with extra photos.
PS flies to Kakadu on Tuesday for the filming of a documentary. At home, his is essentially a simple life surrounded by articles of great beauty.

B973 Roger Covell. "Beautiful sounds, great invention." *SMH*, 10 April 1989.
Kakadu, heard for the first time in Australia, is a score full of beautiful sounds and striking invention.

B974 William Wilcox. "Birthday blockbuster." *Australian*, 10 April 1989: 9.
Kakadu, which the near-capacity audience probably came to hear, proved rather disappointing, with a soundtrack-like banal theme. Irkanda IV is PS's true voice.

B975 Kenneth Hince. "Sculthorpe's own Dreamtime." *Age*, 13 April 1989: 14.
A vague immobility (as in Takemitsu), a kind of incensed and perfumed navel-gazing, appears plainly in SQ 9, even if in the last two sections there are traces of melodic movement that are almost European. (*Also reviewed:* Bevan Leviston, "Promise of premium quality," *Australian*, 12 April [thematically sparse and atmospheric].)

B976 Fred Blanks. "Meditative Sculthorpe." *SMH*, Sat 22 April 1989: 85.
The Australia Ensemble concentrated on the meditative, lamenting, incantatory aspect of PS's music. Songs of Sea and Sky wove a haunting spell. Mountains is stark and craggy, and made an effective contrast to SQ 6, which manages to use entirely conventional material in a highly personal and emotionally intense way.

B977 Neville Cohn. "Ensemble makes Mozart sound simply glorious." *Australian*, 26 April 1989: 12.
SQ 6 is an exploration of the darker emotions—anguish, bereavement, yearning. The Arioso String Quartet's performance had many fine moments.

B978 John Carmody. "Sculthorpe inspires Australian creativity." *AFR*, 28 April 1989: 14.
Now the anti-intellectuals are in the ascendancy in our public life, so our dispirited creative people need encouragement, which the celebration of the achievements of a loved and valued sexagenarian can be.

B979 Candida Baker. "Searching for the sacred in nature." *Age*, 29 April 1989.
Sculthorpe is a man of contradictions: a loner who likes a party; an Australian, but a man of the world. All his work is founded on his belief in the world's spirituality.

B980 Editorial: "The sounds of Australia." *Advertiser*, 29 April 1989: 22. Birthday announcement: 17.
PS's music might not be widely appreciated until long after he, and today's accolades, are silent, but we should recognise an original voice such as his as worthy of homage.

B981 Marietta's column. *Weekend Australian*, 29-30 April 1989.
Last week, at one of the jolliest 60th-birthday parties, thrown by the Sydney International Piano Competition at the home of Senator Bronwyn Bishop, PS had to demolish an edible grand piano, complete with a sheet of his music delectably iced in every detail. (*Other coverage: Sun-Herald*, 23 April: 144 (with a photo of PS and Sen. Bishop); and *Sunday Telegraph*, 23 April (with a photo of PS and his mother, Edna).

B982 "Sunday afternoon with Peter Ross." ABC-TV broadcast, 30 April 1989.
Peter Ross interviews PS while showing him parts of earlier films and filmed tributes from friends and colleagues in Australia, Japan, the UK and the US. Film clips are from: PS and Conyngham performing **Landscape**; *They Found A Cave; Tabuh Tabuhan; Sun Music for Film; Essington; Burke and Wills*; and videotaped performances of **Mangrove, Earth Cry, Kakadu**. Tributes are by: Boyd, Conyngham, Edwards, Ford (with excerpt from *Parabola*); Fogg (playing **Piano** Concerto cadenza); David Matthews, Mester, Takemitsu, and John Coburn ("Sun Music" lithograph). (Taped on 16 April.)

B983 John Carmody. "Honouring Sculthorpe." *Sydney Review*, May 1989.
Kakadu (heard in Sydney) seems tailored to a *Biedermeyer* trans-Pacific taste.

B984 Felicia Chadwick. "*Kakadu* Teaching Kit—Years 5 to 8." Sydney: Fort Street High School, May 1989.
Kit includes class activities: learning the melodies and rhythmic patterns in **Kakdu**, listening for instruments, and composing and performing music based on these patterns.

B985 Keith Field. "MSO's inspiring tribute." *Herald*, 1 May 1989.
The mood of **Kakadu** is reflective, gentle and lyrical. Kakadu received the sustained applause of an enthusiastic audience which warmed to PS's conviction and dedication.

B986 Kenneth Hince. "Hardenberger gets chance to display talent." *Age*, 2 May 1989.
Kakadu is a score of handsome sound, quite conservative, using with polish the box or bracket techniques familiar in the 1960s, and expertly laid out for the orchestra. (*Preconcert publicity*: Michael Shmith. "Peter Sculthorpe's musical 60th." ibid., 28 April.)

B987 Roger Covell. "Sculthorpe eloquent and impressive." *SMH*, 8 May 1989.
Performance of the six chorales from **Rites of Passage** by silhouetted groups of singers and instrumentalists focused attention on the pedal notes and brightly floating soprano tones. Shorter, more popular part-songs served as a bridge to two Gershwin arrangements. (Concert is mentioned by Warrick Dobbie, *Sydney Music Diary*, June 1989: 4.)

B988 ———. "Bastille Day beckons percussion group." *SMH*, 10 May 1989: 18.
How the Stars Were Made is still an outstandingly successful combination of metrical excitement and imaginative use of colour and sonority.

B989 John Colwill. "Australian composer celebrated." *Courier-Mail*, 15 May 1989: 16.
A well-focused performance of **The Stars Turn** was a key to the program of PS's music; poem and music are filled with images of sun and stars and the inevitability of the turning of time. Soaring melodies are also abundant in **Songs of Sea and Sky**.

B990 Bernard Holland. "Kronos Quartet presents a program of sight and sound." *NY Times*, 18 May 1989: C26.
Each piece had its own visual environment. Mr. Sculthorpe's lushness in **SQ 8** was matched by trickling water that gradually filled a large transparent aquariumlike container. The long dark lines and vivid percussive effects had an exotic, almost tropical quality—one that is neither totally borrowed nor totally made up.

B991 Elizabeth Silsbury. "The joys of flawless music." *Advertiser*, 22 May 1989: 17.
Songs of Sea and Sky, arr. fl & pf, showed little evidence of the 30 years between it

and the Copland work.

B992   Richard Toop. Review of recording "Flute Australia" [D53]. *Ossia, A Journal of Contemporary Music*, no. 1 (Winter 1989): 27.
Songs of Sea and Sky is, for me, the most spontaneous and unselfconscious of PS's recent pieces.

B993   "Column 8." *SMH*, Saturday 3 June 1989: 1.
Liz Rouse of Newtown says her cat likes PS's music, and leaves the radiator to sit near the radio. Perhaps Sculthorpe's lower string chords resemble a cat's miao?
(Cont., June 10:) The Newtown cat that likes PS's music was like Tarzan, a black cat, who, when Wagner was played on the radio, would squat in front of the radio, ears laid back, not unlike Nipper, the HMV dog.

B994   Belinda Webster. "Interview with Peter Sculthorpe." Sound recording, recorded at Woollahra, NSW, on June 15 and June 16, 1989; *c*155 min.; 6 tape reels. National Library of Australia and Esso Australia: Esso Performing Arts and Oral History Archive Project. Transcript, 90 p., typescript. (Some restrictions on access.)
Sculthorpe speaks of his family background; education; early musical interests and composing; techniques, ideas, and approaches to composition; influences in his work; people he has worked with; and future directions.

B995   Ken Healey. "Repetition without waste." *Sun-Herald*, 18 June 1989: 112.
Two new CDs—"Landscapes" [D37] and "Flute Australia" [D53]—demonstrate PS's tightly disciplined, idiosyncratic style.

B996   Roger Covell. "In homage to Sculthorpe." *SMH* 1989
New CD, "Landscapes" [D37], shows how Sculthorpe draws his borrowings into his own world until we find it difficult to imagine them outside his lovingly spun context.

B997   "Rumour and gossip." *Sounds Australian*, July 1989: 11.
Before the world premiere of Sun Song in Paris, PS spoke briefly of the work, in French, including an explanation of the Australian coo-ee call. His full-throated *coo-ee* threw the house into hysterical laughter. In French "cuilles" means "testicles". (Story is reprinted in *Coo-ee!* (Western Australian Department for the Arts), Sept 1989: 4.

B998   Richard Toop. "Sharing Haydn's glory." *30 Hours*, July 1989: 30.
String Quartet No. 10 an elegant flirtation with minimalism.

B999   Stephen Whittington. "Well-balanced musical bargain." *Advertiser*, Monday 10 July 1989: 12.
Sun Music II is a boisterous and violent piece, quite impressive in its sheer volume of sound. This performance was delivered with gusto.

B1000   Clive O'Connell. "Australian works given with polish and subtlety highlight three-pianist concert." *Age*, Tuesday 11 July 1989.
Snow, Moon and Flowers makes demands, if nothing else, on the player's capacity to exercise restraint, suggesting a quiet and meditative world of sparse properties.

B1001   Laurie Strachan. "Poise, prowess . . . perfection." *Australian*, 21 July 1989.

SQ 9 cleverly maintains interest by beautifully judged tonal shifts and athletic ostinato rhythms. PS would have been happy with this performance.

B1002 "Two more honorary doctorates for Sculthorpe." *University of Sydney News* 21 (8 August 1989): 1-2.
Dr. Sculthorpe (photographed in academic regalia) received an Honorary Doctor of Music from the Univ. of Melbourne on July 29. On July 11, the Univ. of Sussex, UK, bestowed on him the degree of Honorary Doctor of Letters.

B1003 Clive O'Connell. "Honors to Sculthorpe, a sincere creator." *Age*, Tuesday 1 August 1989.
"Sculthorpe: A Celebration" (July 30) reminded the forgetful how much is owed to a sincere composer who has added a substantial quantity to our musical history, language and technique. Brenton Broadstock's impressionistic tribute to his one-time teacher, *In the Silence of the Night* mirrors Sculthorpe's gentle, urbane personality.

B1004 "The world is Peter's stage." *Examiner*, 1 August 1989: 17C.
Profile, with photo, is drawn from several Sydney pieces and covers childhood and career, including the many special programs for the 60th birthday.

B1005 Fred R. Blanks. "Sydney." *Musical Times* 130 (September 1989): 563.
Report mentions **Kakadu** by the SSO, the Mittagong festival, and other celebratory concerts for PS's 60th birthday.

B1006 Martin Buzacott. "Mod squad." *24 Hours* 1 (new series) (September 1989): 26-7.
New series called "Sonic Boom" on ABC FM this month explores developments in Australian music from the 1960s. PS's four **Sun Musics** are a landmark.

B1007 David Matthews. "Peter Sculthorpe at 60." *Tempo*, Sept 1989: 12-17.
Essay examines trends in PS's style from 1979 to 1989, with seven substantial musical illustrations. The personal preoccupations of **Requiem** —death, ritual—are a long way from his central theme of landscape. **Mangrove** is definitely a landscape piece, but is also concerned with death, in a more generalized way, and with love. In his sixtieth year, PS advances with confidence along the path he has most carefully chosen, and there will be many more pieces in the future, I am sure, to enrich our lives.

B1008 Roger Covell. "Startling contrast in the latest Synergy recital." *SMH*, 12 September 1989: 12.
The major new piece, PS's **Sun Song**, pays tribute to a historical intersection of French and Australian cultures with relaxed and unrhetorical amiability.

B1009 Laurie Strachan. "The play-safe policy that trumpets the past." *Weekend Australian*, 7 October 1989, Weekend: 21.
PS's **Sun Music** series of the sixties remains one of the great landmarks of the history of 25 years of Australian music. The ABC still emphasizes the older classics, though.

B1010 Roger Covell. "Tognetti's leadership provokes striking and compelling contrasts." *SMH*, 18 October 1989.
Second Sonata for Strings moved through alternations of driving rhythm and spellbound lyricism with telling resource and focus.

B1011 Denis Butler. "Musica Viva's dinner concert menu saved the best for last." *Newcastle Morning Herald*, Wednesday 18 October 1989.

Second Sonata for Strings brings together the modern European school and the most ancient music of all, that of the Aborigines. It is a stunning amalgam, by turns fiercely urgent and gossamer-light.

B1012 Peter McCallum. "Season without Vivaldi." *SMH*, 24 October 1989: 14.
The work that received the most spontaneous enthusiasm was Synergy's typically involving performance of **How the Stars Were Made**, fresh from success in Paris.
  The concert is mentioned by Carmody, "Unsystematic concert-goer's October," *Sydney Review*, Nov 1989.

B1013 John Noble. "ACO's subtleties delight." *Courier-Mail*, 25 October 1989.
Second Sonata for Strings is in an elegaic mood. There were ostinato effects, pungent harmonies, bass harmonics, and bow tapping (suggesting message sticks).

B1014 ———. "Concert shows musical agility." Ibid., Thursday 26 October 1989: 34.
The genial composer explained the inspiration for his **Nourlangie**. Mysterious and evocative, it uses the guitar as an extra color rather than in a virtuoso concerto role.

B1015 Denis Butler. "Rapturous reception for a work of striking originality." *Newcastle Herald*, Tuesday 31 October 1989.
Nourlangie, a mood piece, provoked something close to rapture from a Newcastle audience. In part the reception could be attributed to a disarming chat by Sculthorpe before the work was offered. But also there was superb playing.

B1016 Peta Koch. "Stage whispers." *Courier-Mail*, 1 November 1989: 28.
PS appeared on stage before **Nourlangie** (Brisbane) and said that someone had "wrecked his night" telling him about the huge thundersheet used the week before for Strauss' *Alpine Symphony*. The ACO percussionist had to use something smaller.

B1017 Roger Covell. "Pleasures of a peppery baton and an exquisite guitar." *SMH*, 1 November 1989.
The guitar part is often the continuum (even continuo) of **Nourlangie**. The opening string chords suggest a softly tumbling skyline, and a Torres Strait kind of pentatonic tune first appears shyly and then expands. The ending is exquisitely managed.

B1018 Ken Healey. "Triumphant climax to season." *Sun-Herald*, 12 November 1989.
Nourlangie sounded a little introverted. The guitar often blends with the string orchestra. With Sculthorpe's compositions one is left with the feeling of a spiritual reality expressed in sound. For a composer who is so inspired by the Australian landscape, I can think of few higher tributes.

B1019 "The A-to-Z of everything you've forgotten about the decade." *Bulletin*, December 5, 1989: 38 *et infra*.
Listed items include, under A, "Archibald Prize": winner of Australia's biggest portrait competition in 1982: *Peter Sculthorpe*, by Eric Smith.

B1020 Michael Atherton. *Australian Made, Australian Played: Handcrafted musical instruments from didjeridu to synthesizer*. Kensington: University of NSW University Press, 1990.
PS is named in the Acknowledgements; excerpts from the score of **Nourlangie** are printed on the front and back inside covers. (He also launched the book, according to a Sydney newspaper announcement on 11 November 1990.)

B1021 Andrew Ford. "Peter Sculthorpe at Sixty." In *Speaking of Music: A Selection of Talks from ABC Radio by Eminent Musicians, Composers and Conductors.* Edited by Jan Balodis and Tony Cane. Sydney: ABC Enterprises, 1990. P. 186-209.

Beginning a series of four talks in 1989, Ford notes that PS at 60 is "far from dead and shows every indication of moving in a striking new direction." Single-mindedness and uncluttered textures make his art aesthetically naive, but it is not technically naive. (Book review by Patricia Rolfe, "The virtuoso in history," *Bulletin,* 31 July 1990: 104-105, mentions the "long essay" about Sculthorpe.)

B1022 Deborah Hayes. *Peggy Glanville-Hicks: A Bio-Bibliography.* Westport CT: Greenwood Press, 1990: 33, 176, 189, 205, 207, 210, 225.

In 1978 PS's music was played at a sculpture exhibit that Glanville-Hicks organized. In 1986 she was featured on an ABC *State of the Arts* program where PS described her as a "mother figure" to Australian composers, a visionary composer. In 1987 he wrote the citation for her Honorary Doctorate in Music from the Univ. of Sydney.

B1023 Coralie Hinkley. *Innovisions: Expressions of Creativity in Dance.* Nedlands: Western Australia University Press, 1990. P. 53-7.

Hinkley's contemporary dance *Mangrove* to PS's **Mangrove** is an orchestration of dynamic movement changes for a large group (approximately 30), suggested by images in the mind of the composer. She quotes from his programme notes.

B1024 David Wright. *Faber Music: The First 25 years, 1965-1990.* London: Faber, 1990. P. 34-35.

Discussion, accompanied by photo of Sculthorpe, compares him to Janacek as the closest European comparison.

B1025 "Commitment to excellence earns the nation's respect." *Australian,* Friday 26 January 1990: 6.

PS (shown in photo) has been made an Officer of the Order of Australia (AO) for services to music. He is "naturally delighted," says Anne Jamieson, " 'Good run' for composer," ibid. (*Other reports: SMH,* 26 Jan: 4, *Daily Telegraph,* 26 Jan: 10; *Age,* 26 Jan; "Respected musician says he is 'just a simple man,' " *Advertiser,* 26 Jan; [no heading] *Univ. of Melbourne Gazette;* and "Musicians among Australia Day Honours recipients," *Univ. of Sydney News* 22 [20 Feb]: 13 [with photo].)

B1026 "There's no time." Videorecording. Patrick Taggart, director; Don Featherstone, producer. Produced with the assistance of the ABC. Melbourne: Australian Film Institute, 1990. 55 min. Broadcast Feb 8.

Documentary film, in "Creative Spirits" series, includes his early pieces and major compositions. He talks about his music and is shown at work in Sydney, Mittagong, Kakadu, and the US. The film is frequently re-broadcast. *Publicity:* "Peter's inspired by bush sounds," *Telegraph,* 31 Jan: 34. The film was broadcast on the British Satellite Broadcasting's NOW channel, according to "BSB announces major autumn arts schedule," Origin Universal News Servies Ltd, 31 Aug 1990.

B1027 ["Cataclysm" plans.] *Libretto* (3MBS-FM, Melbourne, Programme Guide). March 1990: 3, 35.

PS will be an April guest on the "Cataclysm" programme hosted by Michael Clark. Each programme of music and discussion runs a little under 90 minutes. What if, aeons after The Cataclysm, archeologists from another civilization discover six pieces of music from our world? What pieces would we choose? [For PS three are Asian.]

B1028   Tristram Cary. "Two quartets with singular excellence." *Australian*, 9 March 1990.
PS stepped up to introduce **Sun Song II [Djilile]**. Thunder sheet, tam-tam, etc., got it going, with the main statement quietly lyrical on marimba and vibraphone.

B1029   Steven Whittington, "Dynamic drums." *Advertiser*, 8 March 1990.
Synergy's sensitivity to tonal balance and dynamic nuance was apparent in Takemitsu's *Rain Tree* and again in the lilting melody of PS's **Sun Song II [Djilile]**.
   (*Publicity*: Raymond Chapman Smith, "Percussionists to hit off with premiere." *Advertiser*, Wednesday 7 March: 17.)

B1030   Roger Covell. "Sculthorpe opus conspicuously active." *SMH*, Monday 12 March 1990: 17.
PS's new SQ 11, premiered by the Kronos Quartet in a typically hypnotic recital, is one of the new kind of conspicuously active Sculthorpe works.
   Other reviews: Hince, "Kronos Quartet never short of brilliant," *Age*, 12 Mar (brief mention); Whittington, "Composer brings back Holocaust experiences," *Advertiser*, 12 March (an "attractive new string quartet"); William Weaver, "Avant-garde in Adelaide," *Financial Times* (London), 28 Mar ("coherent, flowing, thought-provoking").

B1031   "The great Australian balance sheet: Our top human assets; Our top human liabilities." *Bulletin*, 20 March 1990: 56.
In the list of 55 human assets is PS: perhaps our greatest classical composer, his work is exploratory, exciting and wide-ranging (like his other interests, which include red sports cars). (Then comes a list of 45 human liabilities.)

B1032   Paul Hertelendy. "Kronos charges Stanford with cutting-edge energy." *San Jose* [CA] *Mercury News*, 26 March 1990.
Jabiru Dreaming uses perpetual motion accompaniments reminiscent of minimalism. The Australian based it in part on Aboriginal chant, in part on tone-painting of the landscapes and the gait of the jabiru (stork).

B1033   Allan Ulrich. "Kronos shining like gold." *SF Examiner*, 26 March 1990: B-1, B-10.
In **Jabiru Dreaming** PS capitalizes on the Kronos' daredevil attacks with shared virtuoso passagework. It adds up to an electrifying 15 minutes.

B1034   Andrew Ford. "Cheerful in adversity, exhilarating in concert." *Australian Society*, April 1990: 42-44.
If the SQ 8 just happened to suit the up-front musical personalities of the Kronos Quartet, the new SQ 11 is tailor-made.

B1035   Peter Goodman. "The world voyages of the starship Kronos." New York *Newsday*, Monday 2 April 1990: pt. II: 2.
SQ 11, based to some extent on Aboriginal music, was restless and dark. There were some effective passages that recalled birds or bats, or perhaps some squeaking spirits.

B1036   Bernard Holland. "New works for new ears." *NY Times*, Tuesday 3 April 1990: C18.
Mr. Sculthorpe's **Quartet No. 11** continues this Australian's liberating experiments in instrumental writing. Its textures sidestep the tradition that leads back to Haydn.

B1037   Peter Cochrane. "Rainbow after the storm." *SMH*, 4 April 1990.
PS's first encounter with the SSO in 1965 was "pretty stormy," he recalled yesterday.

Yesterday, he spoke of his "favourite orchestra" at the launch of its new CD (D36).

B1038 Melinda Bargreen. "Sound and fury, signifying little." *Seattle Times*, 20 April 1990.
SQ 11 was given an evocative performance in which the cries of birds could be heard.

B1039 Richard Letts. "Address to Australian Society for Music Education, NSW Branch AGM, March 3, 1990." *Sydney Music Journal*, May 1990: 34-38.
From 1960, the works of Meale, Butterley and Sculthorpe, also Werder and Dreyfus, brought Australian composition into line with Europe (p. 36).

B1040 "Lim wins big award." *Opera Australia*, May 1990: 149.3.
The 1990 Sounds Australian Award for the best performance of an Australian vocal or choral work in 1989 was by Urizen (an Adelaide group) of **Song of Tailitnama**. Awards are given by the National Music Critics' Circle, critics drawn from seven major metropolitan newspapers.
Sun Song [P89-9] received the national award for the Best Performance of an Aust-ralian Instrumental/Orchestral Work, and the state award for Best Performance of an Australian Work by Performers Resident in New South Wales during 1989.

B1041 Jill Sykes. "Catalyst sets the pace." *SMH*, Monday 7 May 1990: 19.
Ballet *My Name is Edward Kelly* (photo shows dancers) uses music of Sculthorpe.
Other reviews: Paul McGillick, "New ballet has special whimsy," *AFR*, 11 May: 8; Hoad, "Dance to the music of time," *Bulletin*, 22 May: 116-117; John Lahey, "Lahey at large: Dancers find out just how game Ned Kelly was," *Age*, Wed 13 June: 5.

B1042 Roger Covell. "Drop the others, here is the standard reference for Sculthorpe." *SMH*, 8 May 1990.
New CD of Sculthorpe's orchestral music [D36] presents thoroughly realised inter-pretations of four major scores and one delectable idyll.

B1043 Chris Copas. "Sculthorpe captures Outback landscapes." *Examiner*.
Sculthorpe's orchestral music on new recording [D36] captures the Australian landscape, geographical or metaphysical.

B1044 Anno Mungen. "Zwischentone: Australische Musik im British Council." *Der Tagespiegel/Feuilleton*, Wednesday 16 May 1990.
(Transl. J. E. Wilkinson:) At the "Antipodes Festival" Djilile for piano had beauty of tone. Particularly impressive in SQ 8 were the two percussive middle movements.

B1045 Linda Hemsley. "Novel chamber for music." *Examiner*, Monday 28 May 1990: 1, 3.
Little Serenade was included at a picnic concert yesterday in an "immaculate shearing shed." Photos on p. 1, 3 and 28 accompany the report.

B1046 Neville Cohn. "The Song of Tailitnama, arr. voice and piano, CSM 15 [D50]." *Sounds Australian*, No. 26 (Winter 1990): 30-31.
The marriage of accompaniment and vocal line in the Aranda section has a fascinat-ing atavistic quality. And the close has the mood of a berceuse. (Review by Michael Shmith, *24 Hours*, March 1990: 31, only mentions **Song of Tailitnama**.)

B1047 Graeme Skinner. "Musical juggling act." *SMH*, 23 June 1990: 78.
As performed by AustraLYSIS, **Dream** was fleshed out in a manner uncharacteristic of

Sculthorpe (despite "borrowings" from his other works), yet to good effect.

B1048 Fred Blanks. "Soloists excel despite lack of intimacy." *SMH*, 25 June 1990: 14.
The ACO conveyed the evocative Aboriginal hues of PS's **Second Sonata for Strings** with much skill.

B1049 Stephen Pettitt. "Kronos Quartet." *Times*, 26 June 1990.
Jabiru Dreaming too often resorts to the repeated formulae beloved of the minimalists, which is a pity, for PS possesses abundant lyrical gifts and a fresh, innocent idealism.

B1050 Robert Maycock. "Better by design." *Independent*, 27 June 1990: 13.
SQ 11, after a promising start, got bogged down in the narrow confines of a born-again tonality from which it could take wing only in a couple of bouts of engaging squeals.

B1051 "The ARIA 20 best-selling classical titles," July 1990.
On Australian Recording Industry Awards (ARIA) classical "chart," #1 is *PS: Earth Cry* [D36], and #16 is *Australian Piano Concertos* [D41].

B1052 Margaret Moore and Louie Suthers. "Peter Sculthorpe: **Little Nourlangie**." *Sounds Great* (SSO newsletter), no. 1 (July 1990).
Sculthorpe answers some questions about being a composer, and about this work.

B1053 SSO Proms Orchestra, Years 2, 3, 4, Teaching Kit: *Kakadu*. 16 July 1990.
Kit contains a booklet of information and a tape.

B1054 Laurie Strachan. "Youthful vigour is well directed." *Australian*, 17 July 1990.
The AYO played **Kakadu** with enormous enthusiasm .

B1055 Peter McCallum. "Value of rehearsal shows." *SMH*, 18 July 1990.
Kakadu was enthusiastically received, with its evocatively pictorial orchestration.

B1056 "Piano recital." *Centralian Advocate* (Alice Springs), 27 July 1990.
With the recent appearance at Araluen of composer PS following the performance by the AYO of his work **Kakadu**, our young musicians should feel even more inspired.

B1057 Bob Crimeen. "Showbiz" column. *Sunday Sun* (Melbourne), 29 July 1990: 70.
Record of the week: ABC 426481-2 [D36]. Since being overwhelmed by PS's music in *My Name is Edward Kelly*, my estimation for his work has risen inestimably.

B1058 Dorothy Grimm. "Composer relates with nature." *Centralian Advocate* (Alice Springs), Friday, 3 August 1990.
Sculthorpe came to Alice Springs [in July] to meet the AYO which is performing **Kakadu** on their Australian tour. People in the audience were still looking for birds even though the violins were playing; few people knew with certainty that the man in jeans was the composer. (An informal photo shows Sculthorpe in jeans.)

B1059 Philip Nunn. "Grainger's genius can't be neglected." *Age*, 9 August 1990.
For the first-ever recording of Grainger's **Beautiful Fresh Flower** [D2], Sculthorpe has provided "sensitive orchestration."

B1060 "Pacific Music Festival." *The Monthly Music Magazine, Eumak Choon Chu*, 1990, no. 9 (September): 106.
On July 7 in Sapporo, in a talk at Art Park Museum, 1:00-3:00, PS (shown in a color photo) referred to a "feeling of family, a Pacific family" among composers.

B1061 Peter McCallum. *"Peter Sculthorpe: Earth Cry*, etc. [D36]." *Sounds Australian*, No. 27 (Spring 1990): 35.
PS's ideas about music and landscape seem to assert the existence of a cultural subconscious based on something reassuringly fundamental like the earth and beyond our control. For me, the emotionalism of a piece like Earth Cry is at odds with the "naive" formal design so that the phrase repetition starts to sound lacking in inspiration.

B1062 Roger Covell. [Australian Piano Concertos (D41).] *SMH*.
The synthesis in PS's **Piano Concerto** does not falsify his easily recognizable voice and uses the piano part to set up a groundswell of creative disaffection, so appearing to put familiar ideas in a special context of bleak endurance.

B1063 W. L. Hoffmann. "Concert one of the year's highlights." *Canberra Times*, Friday 7 September 1990: 8.
PS's own rescoring of **Irkanda IV** works very well, the flute's lamenting solo effectively set against the light textural background of the string trio.

B1064 Kenneth Hince. "Dullness creeps through." *Age*, 11 Sept 1990: 14.
PS's reworking of the original **Irkanda IV** was well and affectionately played.

B1065 Fred Blanks. "How to make friends." *SMH*, 21 Sept 1990: 12.
A feeling of incantation suffused the cello/piano arrangement of **Tailitnama Song**.

B1066 Fred Blanks. "Float like a butterfly, sing like a bee. *SMH*, 25 Sept 1990.
Irkanda IV, arr. fl & string trio (Sept 22), reminded us of Sculthorpe's impressive way of suggesting Aboriginal inflections in Western music.

B1067 Peter McCallum. "Synergy are on the way to new music's golden fleece." *SMH*, Monday 15 October 1990: 14.
Synergy gave an admirably precise performance of **Sunsong**, which is either naively or evocatively pictorial depending on your point of view (for me, the former).

B1068 Stephen Whittington. "Rhythmic revelry in choral blockbuster." *Advertiser*, Monday 15 October 1990: 19.
Sun Music for Voices and Percussion might have had a point to make in 1966, but now its obvious debts to Penderecki and Balinese ketjak chorus make it seem awfully thin.

B1069 Giacomo Pelliciotti. "Kronos Quartet jazz e rock sopra gli archi." *La Repubblica*, 18 October 1991.
Più risoluto e persuasivo il **Jabiru Dreaming** di PS, che fonde elementi esotici e folk, con influenze orientali e occidentali allo stesso tempo.
Other reviews from the Milan concert: Paolo Petazzi, "Il Kronos snobb i classici," *Il Giorno*; "Il Tempo divora il suoni del mondo," 18 Oct.

B1070 Richard S. Ginell. "Mester leads Pasadena Symphony opening." *LA Times*, Tuesday 30 October 1990: F8.
With its recurring tattoos of bongos and tom-toms, tense lyrical episodes, and teeming jungles of effects—the strings do terrific imitations of bird twitterings—PS's landscape in **Kakadu** evokes an uneasy combination of natural beauty and underlying fear.

B1071 Nancy Uscher. "Peter Sculthorpe: responding to nature." *Strings: The Magazine for Players of Stringed Instruments* 5 (November/December 1990): 49-52.
PS (shown on cover and in a smaller photo inside) discusses composing. Interview includes a classified listing of his works for strings, and several musical illustrations.

B1072 David Wright. "Inspired by Australia: diversity and dualism in Peter Sculthorpe's music." *The Listener*, 29 November 1990.
PS's music has qualities extending beyond national significance. **Earth Cry** and **Kakadu** show him seeking a universal musical language through an identity with "European" Australia and indigenous cultures of Australia and the Pacific Basin.

B1073 Peter McCallum. "Grainger, *Beautiful Fresh Flower*" [**D2**]. *Sounds Australian*, No. 28 (Summer 1990-91): 36.
Setting strings in relief against a pale background of tam-tam and vibraphone brushstrokes, the arrangement of **Beautiful Fresh Flower** mixes Grainger's *chinoiserie* with Sculthorpe's more sophisticated brand of orientalism.

B1074 Katherine Brisbane, ed. *Entertaining Australia.* Sydney: Currency Press, 1991.
(P. 19, 297, 299, 302, 340:) Mentioned are the ballets *Sun and Moon* and **Sun Music**, the Hobart seminar of 1963, and the ISCM recitals at the 1964 Adelaide Festival.

B1075 Andrew Ford. *Australian Classical Music: Selected works by Australian composers, described and analysed, with exercises in listening and composition.* (Sounds Australian Music Resource Series for Secondary Schools, no. 2.) Sydney: Sounds Australian, 1991.
Material on SQ 8 (p. 27-33) includes a short biography, musicological background, analysis (with score excerpts), and aural exercises.

B1076 Andrew Ford. *Inventing Music.* Sydney: Sounds Australian, 1991.
Personal musical style is like a voice print. PS's style is evident in **Koto Music, Sun Music III, Tabuh Tabuhan,** and **Kakadu,** even with their borrowed material, and in SQ 8, **How the Stars Were Made** and **Sun Music I-IV** (p. 25, 42, 49-50).

B1077 David Marr. *Patrick White: A life.* Milsons Point NSW: Random House Australia, 1991.
(P. 433-6:) In late 1963 White began to collaborate with PS on an opera about Mrs. Fraser. In late March 1964 Sculthorpe found the first pages of the libretto unacceptable. It was prose, not poetry, and read like the historical opera he had feared from the first. White, "shattered," conceived a passionate disapproval for Sculthorpe.

B1078 Michelle Potter. *A Full House: The Esso Guide to the Performing Arts Collections of the National Library of Australia.* Introduction by Robyn Archer. Canberra: National Library of Australia, 1991.
Two interviews with PS are in the oral history collection [**B214, B994**]. He is also mentioned in interviews with: dancer Cheryl Stock (1990), composers Mirrie Hill (1975), James Penberthy (1988), Simone de Haan (1986), Anne Boyd (1969, Ross Edwards (1973), Kim Williams (1972); and pianist Roger Woodward (1973). Sculthorpe correspondence is included among the papers of Margaret Sutherland.

B1079 SSO 1991 Education Program, K-8 Teaching Kit: *Kakadu.* Sydney: NSW Department of School Education and ABC.

Materials include a booklet of information and a tape.

B1080   Bruce Crossman. "The 1990 Pacific Composers' Conference: a report."
Canzona 14 (1991), no. 34: 90-91.
PS referred to himself as a "magpie composer"—not a "bird who talks a lot" but a bor-
rower. In SQ 8, rhythmic layering suggested by sounds in Bali achieved a very moving
Australasian sound with universal appeal.

B1081   John Henken. "Kronos Quartet offers eclectic versions of Schnittke
works at Wadsworth." *LA Times*, 14 January 1991: F3.
Jabiru Dreaming, a colorful pastoral in two movements, has a compelling gentleness
presented with real lyric charm.

B1082   Wilma Salisbury. "Committed ensemble brings intensity to modern
works." *Cleveland Plain Dealer*, Saturday 19 January 1991.
Jabiru Dreaming treated ethnic materials in a sophisticated manner. High pitches
sound like birds and rhythmic patterns relate to animals.
  Carlo Wolff, "The Kronos Quartet," *Billboard*, 2 March: 51, refers to a
"naturalistic" Jabiru Dreaming in Cleveland.

B1083   John von Rhein. "Transcendental journey: Kronos Quartet skillfully
crosses musical boundaries. *Chicago Tribune*, 22 January 1991.
Jabiru Dreaming sounded like a shorter sequel to PS's Eighth Quartet (the Kronos's
signature piece), with its sharply rhythmic treatment of an Australian Aborginal
chant. (Two pre-concert announcements also appeared in the *Tribune*.)

B1084   Betty Webb. "Kronos Quartet the 'new Fab Four' on KGNU public
radio series." Boulder [CO] *Daily Camera*, 24 January 1991: 3B.
What really turns these musicians on are compositions such as Jabiru Dreaming by PS,
who is called "the Australian Leonard Bernstein." A 1988 American Public Radio
series of 13 one-hour programs, "Radio Kronos," is now being rebroadcast.

B1085   Peter McCallum. "The formula is improving despite the wet
weather." *SMH*, 28 January 1991.
Nangaloar seemed on first hearing to repeat some ideas from Sculthorpe's highly
successful Kakadu. (Headline refers to the outdoor concert formula.)

B1086   Peter McCallum. "A little night music is just a peace offering." *SMH*,
4 February 1991.
PS told the audience (Feb 2) that his mournful and well-received lament Earth Cry
was about paying more attention to the cry of the Earth.

B1087   Philip Elwood. "Kronos explores the frontiers." *SF Examiner*, 4 February 1991.
Kronos, sensitive particularly in dynamics and in unison expressions, captures the
feeling of the vernacular as well as the disciplined scoring of Jabiru Dreaming.

B1088   Larm Kelp. "Kronos Quartet's world tour on a single stage." *Oakland
Tribune*, Monday 4 February 1991.
Jabiru Dreaming was more in the string quartet tradition than were the other pieces.

B1089   Joshua Kosman. "Kronos Quartet mixes it up at Cal." *SF Chronicle*, 4
February 1991: F2.

Jabiru Dreaming included some agreeable material but did not hold my attention.

B1090 Kenneth Herman. "Down Under theme fails to surface." *LA Times,*
San Diego County sect., 10 February 1991: F1, F3.
Songs of Sea and Sky, though based on a Saibai tune, sounded like Aaron Copland
dressing up an American folk tune in Sunday-go-to-meeting duds.

B1091 Dorea Richards. "Varied delights from orchestra." *Examiner,* Friday
15 February 1991.
Tomorrow's program features Overture for a Happy Occasion by Launceston-born
composer PS. (Report, with photos: "1000 flock to free concert," ibid., 18 Feb.)

B1092 Philip Nunn. "Top team plays definitive Sculthorpe." *Age,* 28 February 1991, Green Guide: 9.
Here [D39] is what must be considered the definitive recording of PS's **piano music.**

B1093 Peter McCallum. "*Peter Sculthorpe: Piano Music.*" *Sounds Australian,* No. 29 (Autumn 1991): 45.
The disc [D39] should be of interest to piano teachers and my guess is that it will also
be heard at the odd dinner party as well.

B1094 Daniel Buckley. "Kronos concert was a classic hoot." *Tucson* [AZ]
Citizen, 5 March 1991.
Jabiru Dreaming by PS, composer in residence for the Festival in the Sun, was in many
ways the best work in an excellent program.

B1095 James Reel. "Kronos pursues new, lively path." *Arizona Daily Star,* 5
March 1991.
Last night's finest work was Jabiru Dreaming by PS, who was in attendance. It uses
rhythms and chants indigenous to the Kakadu National Park area. Like most of the
program's works, it is rooted in tonality, with much color and variety.

B1096 Linda Terhune. "Australia sculpts Sculthorpe's music." Colorado
Springs *Gazette Telegraph,* Friday 15 March 1991: D8.
Says PS, now visiting composer at Colorado College, "Music must have a sense of
place in the beginning and leap up from there."

B1097 Stephen Pettitt. "Shiva Nova." *Times,* Wednesday 27 March 1991.
Neil Heyde gave with considerable passion PS's Requiem, a ripe exploration of and
reaction to the original plainsong.

B1098 Andrew Porter. "Musical events." *New Yorker,* 8 April 1991: 81.
Port Essington is modest, imaginative, and moving in a poetic and colorful performance. The score (described) confirms the refinement, subtlety, and originality.

B1099 Ronald Hambleton. "Master clarinettist's recital." *Toronto Star,*
Thursday 11 April 1991: D11.
Nothing could equal the beauty that Stoltzman and Vallecillo discovered in PS's
Songs of Sea and Sky, a fantasia that sounded to the ear like nature itself.

B1100 Martin Stevenson. "Maestro returns to open music school." *Examiner,* Friday 12 April 1991.
PS is here, and his mother is, too, in spite of having broken her arm two weeks ago.

B1101 ———. "Composer had sport ambition." Ibid., 13 April 1991: 6.
PS (shown in photo with several officials) returned Thursday to open the Launceston Church Grammar School's $300,000 Henrietta Cooper Music School. As a student there, he rode a bike from St. Leonards, but then became a boarder. During his visit he spoke with students, and spoke at the concert of his works.

B1102 Katherine Tulich. "Australia's midnight oil on fire at 5th ARIA awards." *Billboard*, 20 April 1991: 64.
Dateline: Australia. At the fifth annual Australian Record Industry Association awards, held March 25 at the Darling Harbour Convention Centre, award for best classical recording went to PS, for his *Orchestral Works* (D36).

B1103 Bernadette Cruise. "Flute recital displays impressive talent." *Canberra Times*, Saturday 11 May 1991.
In **Songs of Sea and Sky** PS imaginatively creates a seascape bounded within one continuous movement.

B1104 Jeremy Vincent. "The best reeds don't sway." *Australian*, 3 June 1991.
Sun Music I presented a rather eclectic sound. PS certainly has the knack of picture-writing and Hopkins was eloquent in his reading between the lines.

B1105 Philip Percival. " 'Little Nourlangie': The pipe organ in the Australian landscape." *Sydney Organ Journal* 22 (June-July 1991): 10-13.
The deep pedal 'C' of the Sydney Town Hall organ represents the fundamental, brooding aspect of the landscape which underlies any activity above it.

B1106 Stephen Whittington. "Choir left gasping." *Advertiser*, 4 June 1991.
Lament for Strings is both unobjectionable and unexceptional—a well-shaped and crafted work almost instantly forgettable, especially next to a masterwork like Brahms' *A German Requiem*, the main work of the concert.

B1107 Joshua Kosman. "Marvelous melting pot at Stern Grove." *SF Chronicle*, Monday 17 June 1991: E2.
Rice Pounding Music was vividly pictorial; it set a slow, sweetly elegiac centerpiece within matching musical bookends, each a rhythmically catchy collection of plinks and scratches.

B1108 [News item.] *SMH*, 27 June 1991.
During rehearsal at Government House a kelpie pup named Scarlett howled during PS's quartet [no. 9]. She was securely kennelled for the actual performance that night.

B1109 Graeme Skinner. "Haiku music." *Sydney Review*, July 1991.
PS, in one of his rare public appearances as a raconteur, talked about Japan for the Seymour Group last month. He learned about the haiku not from the Zen masters, to whose tradition it belonged, but from a rather more down-market Shinto abbott.

B1110 Stephen Whittington. "Intricate path leads to a well performed musical delight." *Advertiser*, 17 July 1991.
Second Sonata for Strings showed this country's best-known composer as a master of economical yet highly expressive music in a finely controlled performance.

B1111 Warren Bourne. "New wine tastes fine." *Australian*, 19 July 1991.
Second Sonata for Strings and two other pieces by experienced composers were the most memorably and precisely focused, incisive and sensitive.

B1112   Wilfrid Mellers. "New worlds and old wildernesses: Peter Sculthorpe and the ecology of music." *The Atlantic* 268/2 (Aug 1991): 94-8.
Australian music is beginning to find the universal within the topical and local. In
this respect, PS may be one of the most important living composers, wherever he may
stand in the greatness stakes. **Mangrove** has claim to being his masterwork. It seems
to embrace every aspect of his experience—Australian, Japanese, and "thoughts of a
New Guinea tribe that believe men and women to be descended from mangroves." The
rudimentary themes are literally aboriginal in springing from the acoustical bases of
melody. In **Kakadu**, the accommodation between modern man and his remote prede-
cessors leads to a consummation. (Mellers plans to include this material in a chapter,
"Wilderness Music," in a book in preparation.)

B1113   Margaret Legge-Wilkinson. "Stunning, fulfilling recital of works by
men alive today." *Canberra Times*, Saturday 10 August 1991.
Night Pieces relied heavily on repeated motifs to achieve a sweet calm.

B1114   Roger Covell. "It was all thanks to Eric." *SMH*, 12 August 1991.
Among the offerings of current colleagues, PS's memorable little idyll, **A Sunny Song
for Eric**, was delightful.

B1115   Tristram Cary. "Youthful spirits triumph all round." *Australian*, 15
August 1991.
Some of the effects in **Sun Music III** certainly showing their age, but Sculthorpe's
voice is always authentically his own.

B1116   David E. Sanger. "Bernstein is a palpable absence at a festival in
Japan." *NY Times*, Saturday 17 August 1991: 11.
(Dateline: Sapporo.) Early in the Pacific Music Festival Mr. Thomas conducted a
concert featuring the works of composers who were clearly influenced by the music of
the Far East, including PS, whose **Mangrove** has resonance of Japanese court music.

B1117   "Sculthorpe: **Songs of Sea & Sky**." *Clarinet & Saxophone*, Sept 1991.
Songs of Sea and Sky makes no great demands on the player for flashy finger dexteri-
ty, but an expansive legato control is required and a sensitive application of tonal
nuances. This is a haunting work, which grows on one, and for once is not a piece that
can be fitted neatly into some comparable idiomatic category.

B1118   Derek Moore Morgan. "Thoroughly modern militants." *Australian*,
Tuesday 17 September 1991.
Irkanda IV provided the most significant and logically integrated music on the
Kronos Quartet program (in Perth).
    David Hough, "A taste acquired," *Bulletin*, 1 Oct, reports that a smallish audience
was carried away by **Irkanda IV**.

B1119   Graeme Skinner. "Kronos's impressive struggle against consumer
resistance." *SMH*, 19 September 1991.
SQ 11, Jabiru Dreaming has that strong, open-air, major-key feeling typical of a
whole series of works since **Kakadu**. There's notably more steel to it than its pre-
decessors, with irony and even sadness. The third encore was most sombre music,
Irkanda IV, in a surprisingly successful new arrangement by the composer.

B1120   Rodney Smith. "Precise, pulsating magic." *Advertiser*, 21 Sept 1991.
Irkanda IV provided the more traditionally chromatic European-inspired modernism
(in contrast to the new wave American works) in the Kronos Quartet's program

B1121 Fred Blanks. "Steady as she goes." *SMH*, 24 September 1991.
The new version of **Lament** proved Wallfisch a musician of admirable qualities. If Australia ever needs an equivalent of Barber's *Adagio* or Elgar's *Nimrod* variations to play for hours on the radio when a high dignitary dies, **Lament** will do.

B1122 W. L. Hoffmann. "Quartet returns with pop hype." *Canberra Times*, 25 September 1991.
A deeply-felt lament, **Irkanda IV** seemed to gain in intensity of expression in this new form, and the performance displayed the Kronos Quartet at its best.

B1123 Chris Boyd. "Kronos calls its own tune." *AFR*, 27 September 1991.
Jabiru Dreaming was the highlight of the concert (in Melbourne). PS's works reward a repeat hearing. **Jabiru Dreaming** has a discreet magnificence.

B1124 Laurie Strachan. "Vivaldi smooth as velvet, Bartok simply brilliant." *Australian*, Friday 27 September 1991.
(Sydney:) The celebrity was English cellist Raphael Wallfisch. In PS's **Lament** he was not asked for any pyrotechnics, as the style appeared to be broodingly lyrical.
Other reviews: Live Entertainment, Sept: 14; and David Brown, "ACO and Wallfisch in top form," *Australian Jewish News*, Sydney edn, 4 Oct (the dignity and soulfulness of the cello part was admirably brought to the fore).

B1125 Margaret Legge-Wilkinson. "Better exposure for Australian composers in general programming." *Canberra Times*, 28 Sept 1991.
Unfortunately, during Sculthorpe's intense and brooding **Lament**, the melancholy phrases by the solo cello were often lost in the haze of harmonies surrounding it.

B1126 Stuart Thomas. "Peter Sculthorpe: Piano Music" [D39]. *Melbourne Report* 7 (October 1991): 46.
Covering all phases of the career of this gifted musical ambassador, this disk is well-played throughout and essential listening.

B1127 Margaret Berketa, compiler. *Famous People's Favourite Books.* Brighton NSW: Brighton City Library, November 1991. P. 265.
Sculthorpe names Joseph Conrad's *Lord Jim* as his favourite book, with its themes of primeval terror of wilderness, anguish of alienation and hazards of colonization.

B1128 Vincent Plush. "Pacific Overtures" and "Activity on the Oz-US Exchange." *24 Hours*, November 1991: 30-33, 35.
Plush examines the relationship of Australian music with the world's music, particularly that other New World country across the Pacific, mentioning PS's 1988 visits to the US. Small photos of Sculthorpe and 16 other composers are on the cover.

B1129 W. L. Hoffmann. "Reflective sounds in the afternoon," *Canberra Times*, 5 November 1991.
Night Pieces, brief aphoristic statements, were played with quiet expressiveness.

B1130 Mark Kanny. "Kronos plays weak music with style." *Pittsburgh Post-Gazette*, 12 November 1991.
Jabiru Dreaming is an attractive interplay of simple melody and modern timbral experimentation. (*Publicity*: Kanny, "Kronos lights up the Fulton," ibid., 11 Nov.)

B1131 Donald Rosenberg. "Kronos Quartet outplays weak program."

Pittsburgh Press, 12 November 1991.
Jabiru Dreaming is a lovely two-movement work of eclectic inspiration, its tradition-al, almost folkloric scenes of nature blending with episodes of Bartokian intensity.

B1132   Richard Dyer. "The savvy sound of Richard Stoltzman." *Boston Globe*, Mon 18 November 1991: 29.
Songs of Sea and Sky (Nov 17) is a colorful and attractive work. The piano's memory of the hymn tune while the clarinet twitters and soars aloft is a magical moment.

B1133   Marilyn Tucker. "Jenkins' 'Sightings' a sight to behold in Oakland." *SF Chronicle*, Monday 18 November 1991: E2.
For the world premiere of *Sightings* (shown in photo) the music was an alluring assist, PS's **Jabiru Dreaming**, played live by the Kronos Quartet.
   Other reviews: Ulrich,"Oakland troupe finally at home," *SF Examiner*, 16 Nov, Arts and Leisure; David Gere, *Oakland Tribune*, 18 Nov: B-2 ; and Renee Renouf, "Oakland Ballet seems ready for a longer season," *Piedmonter*, 26 Nov: 14.

B1134   Dorothy Grimm. "Orchestral manœuvres in bush surroundings." *Centralian Advocate* (Alice Springs), 3 December 1991: 5.
Photos show musicians at the Darwin SO concert at Simpson's Gap. Andrew Langford played didgeridoo at the start and joined in **Earth Cry**.
   Also: Grimm, "Australia's Mozart: Sculthorpe's **Earth Cry** is a light in musical wilderness," ibid., 10 Dec: 15 (interview); and "Full of enthusiasm," *Weekend Australian*, 18/19 Jan 1992 (3,000 attended; the tam-tam was halfway up the chasm).

B1135   Christy Vena. "National treasure visits." Townsville *Advertiser*, 5 December 1991.
PS will visit Townsville this weekend for the 10th Anniversary Barrier Reef Piano Competition. (Also announced in Robin Rattray-Wood, "Composer takes musical lead from Australian land," *Townsville Bulletin*, Monday 9 Dec.)

B1136   "Peter Sculthorpe elected to Academy." *University of Sydney News*, 17 December 1991: 287.
On November 13, PS was one of 13 Australian scholars elected Fellows of the Austral-ian Academy of the Humanities for their distinguished contributions to research.

B1137   Deborah Jones. "Musical family mourns Challender." *Weekend Australian*, 21-22 December 1991.
More than 2000 people (PS is shown in photo) gathered yesterday for the memorial service. David Pereira played PS's "Stuart Challender in Memoriam" [**Threnody**].
   PS is quoted in the Sat. *Mercury*, 14 Dec: 1, 9, and mentioned by Michael Shmith, "Australia: Music poorer for Challender's death," *Age*, 14 Dec.

B1138   Fred Blanks. "State of the big league stats after Wolfie's super year." *SMH*, 27 December 1991.
In 1991, there were 222 Mozart performances in Australia. The Australian composers most performed are: PS, Grainger, Williamson, and Banks.

B1139   Alison Broinowski. *The Yellow Lady: Australian Impressions of Asia.* Melbourne: Oxford University Press, 1992.
PS,'s work with Asian materials, and his ideas about Asia, are reviewed in several contexts: p. 49, 95-8, 134, 137, 146-7, 151, 199.

B1140   Anne Edgeworth. *The Cost of Jazz Garters: A History of Canberra*

Repertory Society, 1932 to 1982. Acton ACT: Canberra Repertory Society, 1992.

In 1956 PS came to Canberra to oversee the recording of the music for **Twelfth Night** (p. 106). For **Ulterior Motifs**, he turned out some catchy tunes (p. 267).

B1141 Wendy Beckett. *Peggy Glanville-Hicks.* Pymble NSW: CollinsAngus & Robertson, 1992.

Mentioned are the sculpture exhibit (p. 195) and Glanville-Hicks's seventy-fifth birthday party at Sculthorpe's house, with his mother, Edna (p. 201-202).

B1142 Peter Sculthorpe. Foreword to *Australian Alphabet,* by Timoshenko Aslanides. Springwood NSW: Butterfly Books, 1992.

For contemporary Australians, this is a lyric poetry which celebrates what we are. (In *Zeitgeist* (p. 53), the poet mentions the influence of his teacher, Sculthorpe.)

B1143 "Peter Sculthorpe." In: Julian Faigan. *Uncommon Australians: Towards an Australian Portrait Gallery.* Sydney: Art Exhibitions Australia Ltd, 1992. P. 109.

Portrait is by Eric Smith (b. 1919), oil on canvas 107.5 x 107.5 cm. 1975. Caption and brief paragraph describe Sculthorpe's work.

B1144 "Peter Sculthorpe." *Baker's Biographical Dictionary of Musicians.* 8th edn.; rev. Nicolas Slonimsky. New York: Schirmer Books, 1992.

Updating the 1984 edn, the entry (on p. 1675) includes a paragraph of biography and a classified list of titles through 1989.

B1145 Thérèse Radic. "Rites of Passage" and "Peter (Joshua) Sculthorpe." *New Grove Dictionary of Opera,* ed. Stanley Sadie. 4 vols. London: Macmillan, 1992. Vol. 3, p. 1351, and vol. 4, p. 277-8.

Entries summarize Hannan [B702] concerning PS's aims and style. **Quiros** is mentioned.

B1146 Daniel Cariaga. "Kronos returns with new works." *LA Times,* 27 January 1992.

Jabiru Dreaming was the most disturbing work on the program. It is a 13-min. work of strong, compacted, and wide-ranging emotions that demands further hearings.

B1147 Adam Prasser. "Lackluster show for an unspoiled Kronos." *La Jolla Light,* 2 February 1992: C1.

Jabiru Dreaming develops Aboriginal material in a Western, post modern manner. It was one of the three most profound works on the program. (Pre-concert publicity: Thomas Arne, "Quartet for the end of time," *San Diego Reader,* 30 Jan: 1, 3.)

B1148 H. M. "Australia—a land of music?" *Wiener Zeitung* (transl.), 4 February 1992.

In **Irkanda IV, arr. flute and SQ,** a three-note motive plays the essential role. The flute alternates with the strings and the sound is minor, with chromatic tones.

B1149 Gunter Duvenbeck. "With sweeping gesture, Australia Ensemble presents itself in Bonn." *General-Anzeiger Bonn,* 14 February 1992.

It was interesting to hear a work of the Australian PS, whose **Irkanda IV, arr. fl & SQ,** moved from atonal desperation to comforting harmony.

B1150 "Personal Chair promotions." *Univ. of Sydney News,* 18 Feb 1992.

Peter Sculthorpe is among those promoted to Personal Chair, as of Jan 1, 1992. According to the University Senate resolution of Nov 1990, "A Personal Chair is created as an extraordinary appointment to recognize the achievements of a member of the academic staff who has attained exceptionally high distinction in his or her field."

B1151   SSO 1992 Education Program, K-8 Teaching Kit, p. 61-69: **From Uluru.** Richard Gill, adviser. Sydney: NSW Dept. of School Education and ABC.
Materials include a description of the piece, tape, listening guide, and excercises.

B1152   Peter Dickinson. "Sculthorpe: Piano Works" [**D39**]. *Gramophone* 69 (March 1992): 70-71.
This is a fascinating collection—a composer's source-book and an introduction to one of the leading personalities in Australian music.

B1153   Graeme Skinner. Review of "Until I Saw ... Contemporary Australian Choral Music" [**D3**]. *Sounds Australian*, no. 33 (Autumn 1992): 50.
The highlight among the shorter works is **The Birthday of Thy King**, written for the King's College Choir, which shows that even a self-sufficient musical nationalist like PS can still have his (to borrow a phrase from Mellers) 'Vision of Albion'.

B1154   Benjamin Thorn. "Bent Perspectives: State of euphoria year 12 certificate, Australian music examination." Ibid.: 4.
Sculthorpe and his works are mentioned in all twelve multiple choice questions and both essay questions of this tongue-in-cheek quiz.

B1155   Wilfrid Mellers. "Peter Sculthorpe." (Repertoire Guide No. 24.) *Classical Music*, 7 March 1992.
Mellers presents to UK readers much of the material of his *Atlantic* essay (**B1112**) and adds discouraging information about the availability of recordings in the UK.

B1156   W. L. Hoffmann. "Remarkable recital from a venerable composer." *Canberra Times*, 8 April 1992.
Pianist-composer Miriam Hyde (at age 79) gave a crisp and sprightly performance of the **Sonatina** by her younger contemporary, Peter Sculthorpe.

B1157   "Married at Longford." *Examiner*, 10 April 1992.
A feature of the wedding reception for Anne Sculthorpe and Malcolm Wilson was the performance of a piece of music written by the bride's uncle, composer PS. [*See* **W218**.]

B1158   Steve Metcalf. "Kronos Quartet fuses unique attitude, new music into theater." *Hartford Courant*, 25 April 1992: E4.
There were some fairly straight-ahead pieces, including PS's truly beautiful and evocative **Jabiru Dreaming**, inspired by a natural vista in his native Australia.

B1159   David Denton. "From America—without love." *The Strad* 103 (May 1992): 458-9.
Jabiru Dreaming [P91-12] is a work of immense happiness. Sculthorpe must be one of the most important creators of 20th-century quartets, an impression that has been confirmed by the appearance of each new work.

B1160   Daniel Cariaga. "Kronos Quartet at the Wadsworth." *LA Times*, 11 May 1992: F6

To replace Pascoal the Kronos offered an old specialty, PS's **Eighth Quartet**, here given a hair-raising reading of immaculate profile.

B1161 Shirley Apthorp. "Youthful vigour electrifies work." *Australian*, 18 May 1992.
PS's **Piano Concerto**, an unrelentingly dark work, full of murky harmonies and bleak emotions, is powerful and mesmeric. Cislowski chose an interpretation of driving anger, with immense forward momentum, resulting in great dramatic tension.

B1162 Peter Platt. "Songs of Sea and Sky" [D52]. *Sounds Australian*, no. 34 (Winter 1992): 45-6.
PS's beautiful **Songs of Sea and Sky** could be described as a meditation on the conditions (and plight?) of the Saibai islanders.

B1163 Roger Covell. "Poppies to the horizon." *SMH:* 12.
The new Tall Poppies CD gets underway superlatively with **Songs of Sea and Sky** [D52], of all Australian pieces the one that seems to me to evoke most vividly and refreshingly the vast horizons of small islands in an ocean setting.

B1164 John von Rhein. "Pianist does tradition of Dame Myra Hess proud." *Chicago Tribune*, 4 June 1992: 28.
Victor Sangiorgio (Sicilian-born, Australian-trained, London-based pianist) then moved on to PS's **Sonatina**, a concise, attractively wrought work in three linked movements culminating in a toccata-like finale of nervous rhythmic propulsion.

B1165 David Wright. "Cry of the Earth." *Musical Times* 133 (July 1992): 339-341.
Wright finds many reasons for more sustained interest in PS's work in Britain, describing recent works such as **Mangrove**, **Earth Cry**, **Nangaloar**, and **Kakadu**.

B1166 Whitney Smith. "Who needs big city? Kronos performs in Cordova." Memphis TN *Commercial Appeal*, 1 August 1992.
Jabiru Dreaming was pastoral and imagistic. Some passages attempted to emulate sounds of buzzing insects and the gait of a *Jabiru*, a type of stork.

B1167 Richard Dyer. "The Kronos Quartet: cosmetically cutting edge." *Boston Globe*, Saturday 1 August 1992.
PS has been among the most interesting composers promoted by Kronos. **Jabiru Dreaming** is a characteristic mixture of Aboriginal themes, nature-painting and transcendental optimism, with an element of cloying sweetness that is less attractive.

B1168 Clifton J. Noble, Jr. "Kronos Quartet wildly eclectic." *Springfield [MA] Union-News*, 1 August 1992.
Positive and heartening in its unpretentious simplicity, **Jabiru Dreaming** was a highlight of the concert (Tanglewood). PS integrated Aboriginal sounds into his larger musical conceptions.

B1169 Andrew L. Pincus. "Lightweight Kronos Quartet performs at Tanglewood." *Berkshire Eagle*, 1 August 1992: B11.
Pleasantly but inconsequentially picturesque, **Jabiru Dreaming** is another of PS's travelogues of the Australian outback.
Publicity: Pincus, "Modern music crosses the continental divide," *Berkshires Weekly*, 24 July; Tim Page, "Exciting new sounds at Tanglewood," *NY Newsday*, 29 July; Whitney Smith, "Kronos stretches limits of chamber music," *Boston Herald*, 30 July.

B1170   Andrew Clements. "BBC Philharmonic Orchestra—London Promenade Concerts." *Financial Times*, 14 August 1992: 9.
As a well-crafted string meditation, **Lament** is effective enough, but it left neither a lasting impression nor a distinctive flavour.

B1171   Robert Maycock. "The art of profound exhaustion." *Independent*, Friday 14 August 1992: 13.
Lament for Strings is a little double concerto: haunting melody in dialogue over distinctly flavoured harmonies, with a central episode of freely revolving figures. No doubt PS's music has seemed too lush and approachable for critical correctness here, but times have caught up.

B1172   Barry Millington. "Schumann with a spring in his step." *Times*, 14 August 1992.
PS's music has an identifiably Australian voice, evoking the vast open spaces of the outback in a way that is most attractive to the harassed modern city dweller. **Lament for Strings** begins with spare solos for cello and violin, but moves towards a more neo-Romantic mode of expression, beseeching and melancholy. (*Other reviews:* Anne Branigan, "ACO wins over Poms at Proms," *Australian*, 14 Aug [reports Millington's praise]; Paul Driver, "Worth waiting up for," *Sunday Times*, 16 Aug; Peter Brown, "Concerts," *The Strad* 103 (Dec): 1200 [stunningly beautiful, moving, significant].)

B1173   Malcolm Hayes. "Schumann helps to set the record straight." *Weekend Telegraph*, 15 August 1992.
Dubious tuning at the start of PS's darkly soulful **Lament for Strings** was a technical accident, which a harsh judge would insist shouldn't happen at this level.

B1174   Tom Sutcliffe. "Laments." *Guardian*, 15 August 1992.
Lament for Strings was a real highlight of the season—miniature, economical with resources, but perfectly judged. The piece was contained—a sort of washed out pain.

B1175   Peter McCallum. "No tears at this wake." *SMH*, 17 August 1992.
Jabiru Dreaming for percussion [Sun Song] came across as rather thin, I thought. In their up-tempo mode, however, Synergy were consistently scintillating.

B1176   Kenneth Hince. "Athletic show of percussion." *Age*, 19 August 1992.
There was a monotonous sameness of metre to this Synergy concert. To a degree the one movement of **Jabiru Dreaming [Sun Song]** escaped from this straitjacket.

B1177   Jeremy Vincent. "Contemporary punch displaces classic image." *Australian*, 19 August 1992
Jabiru Dreaming [Sun Song] presented itself as a delightfully melodic episode, rich in resonance from the vibraphone and marimba.

B1178   Andrew Ford. "Barry Conyngham." *24 Hours*, Sept 1992: 51-52, 58.
Conyngham recalls PS's support of his student work and explains his own rejection, then reconsideration, of the landscape idiom in music.

B1179   Fred Blanks. "Gain, not pain, in a dash of Oz." *SMH*, 14 Sept 1992.
SQ 8 could be subtitled "Bloch in Bali." Its touch of Biblical modality marks much of the music from the days when PS was still a nine-days wonder (more like nine years).

B1180   "Sculthorpe may tackle opera." *SMH*, 19 September 1992.
The director of a new opera house being built at Huddersfield has asked PS to write

an opera for 1994. PS believes 1995 is more likely.

B1181 Roger Covell. "Richness in talent, relaxation in direction." *SMH,* Monday 28 September 1992.
Tropic has a streaming lyricism as refreshing as a sea breeze on a hot day—although the piece may be a minute or two too long for its own good. (Attacca pre-concert publicity includes: Gail Brennan, "Music from the real world," ibid., 24 Sept; and Nicolas Soames, "Strings but no labels," London *Daily Telegraph,* 2 June: 16.)

B1182 "Meet the Music Teaching Kit 5: **Earth Cry**, etc." SSO Education Program. Concerts on October 14 and 15, 1992.
Materials, written by Neil Aubrey (Gorokan HS), include a description of the work, with musical illustrations, and quotes from PS's preface to the score.

B1183 Alexius Pereira, "Shame and passion." *Straits Times,* 8 Oct 1992.
The fine performance of the highly evocative **Second Sonata for Strings** was intentionally exposed and pungent.
Other reviews: Andrew Lim, "Mature artistry from 12-year-old," *Business Times* (Singapore), 9 Oct (fascinating musical painting, presented with fine virtuosity); and Panya Panicharfauk, "The best from Australia," Bangkok newspaper, Oct.

B1184 Tim Smith. "Orchestra plays Beethoven, modern works." Ft. Lauderdale *Sun-Sentinel,* 29 Oct: 3E.
Kakadu is rich in color and atmosphere. (*Other Florida reviews:* James Roos, "Philharmonic makes surprising news with gracious Beethoven," *Miami Herald,* 3 Nov: 5E; Charles Passy, "Nature inspires Philharmonic pieces, *Palm Beach Post,* 3 Nov; Herbert Perez-Vidal, "Beethoven headlines Philharmonic Celebrity Series," *Palm Beach Daily News,* 4 Nov: 2 [composer, conductor accepted well-deserved applause].)

B1185 Jenny Dawson. "Peter (Joshua) Sculthorpe." *Contemporary Composers,* ed. Brian Morton and Pamela Collins. Chicago and London: St. James Press, 1992. P. 844-7.
Entry presents brief biography, list of works and recordings, and description of style.

B1186 "Digging music." Text: Rosa Shiels; editor: Amana Finlay; photography: George Seper. *Vogue Living* 26 (Dec 92/Jan 93): 84-88.
"Sculthorpe's small city garden harmonises white, red and green within a classical structure." Three and one-half pages of photos show the front and back gardens.

Dissertations, theses, and papers

B1187 Joanne O'Brien. "Peter Sculthorpe: His life, music, development and future position as a composer." Thesis for Diploma in Music, NSW State Conservatorium of Music, 1968.

B1188 Michael Hannan. "The Piano Music of Peter Sculthorpe." Unpublished Bachelor's thesis, University of Sydney, 1971.

B1189 Diana Blom. "An Analysis of **Music for Japan**." Unpublished Master's thesis, University of Sydney, 1972.

B1190 Michael Hannan. "The Music of Peter Sculthorpe: An analytical appraisal with special reference to those social and cultural forces

which have influenced the formulation of an Australian vision."
Ph.D. thesis, University of Sydney, 1977.

B1191 Barbara Janet Wilson. "Select Vocal Works for Female Voices by Six
Australian Composers." B. Mus. (Hons.) thesis, University of
Queensland, 1979. [One chapter is about PS.]

B1192 Hugh De Ferranti. *"Gagaku* and the Works of Richard Meale and
Peter Sculthorpe: A study of the significance of non-Western resources within the Western compositional tradition." B. Mus. (hons)
thesis, University of Sydney, 1983.

B1193 Geoffrey Mark Trim. "Peter Sculthorpe's **Piano Concerto**: A perspective." B. Mus. (Honours: Composition) thesis, University of Sydney,
November 1984. Typescript (iv, 60 p.).

B1194 Nerida Jane Tyson. "Music for Film: A special study of Peter Sculthorpe's score for the film **Manganinnie**." B. Mus. thesis, University
of Sydney, 1986.

B1195 Terry Moran. "Peter Sculthorpe: A contemporary Australian composer and artist." Undergraduate paper, School of Creative Arts, University of Wollongong, 1986.

B1196 Chu Wang-Hau. "Folio of Composition; Folio of Analysis." M. Mus.
thesis, University of Melbourne, 1986. [Analyzes SQ 9.]

B1197 Jana Skarecky. "The System of Harmony Developed by Karel
Janecek." Unpublished paper for the University of Sydney Music
Department Research Seminar, March 30, 1987. [Analyzes SQ 10 *Chorale.*]

B1198 Patricia Shaw. "The Development of a National Identity in Australian Contemporary Music." B. Mus. (hons) thesis, University of Melbourne, 1988. [Chapter 2 ("Reactions to Indigenous Music"), sect. 2 ("Peter
Sculthorpe"), chapter 3 ("The Australianism of Peter Sculthorpe"), *et infra.*]

B1199 Kathryn Tibbs. "East and West in the Music of Anne Boyd." B. A.
(Honours) thesis, University of Sydney, 1989. [PS was an influence.]

B1200 Philip Percival. "Linear Unity in Peter Sculthorpe's Kakadu Cycle."
Bachelor of Arts (Honours) thesis, Department of Music, University
of Sydney, 1991.

Appendix I:
Classified List of Works

WORKS FOR ORCHESTRA
Irkanda IV, arr. strings and
 percussion **W90**
Sun Music I **W94**
Sun Music III (Anniversary Music)
 W100
Sun Music IV **W101**
From Tabuh Tabuhan **W108**
Sun Music II (Ketjak) **W110**
Music for Japan **W113**
Overture for a Happy Occasion
 W117
Lament for Strings **W135**
Small Town **W136**
The Stars Turn, arr. string orchestra
 W137
Port Essington **W143**
Mangrove **W152**
Little Suite for Strings **W169**
Sonata for Strings **W170**
Sun Song (orchestra) **W172**
The Dream (string orchestra) **W178**
Earth Cry **W181**
Autumn Song, arr. string orchestra
 W184
Second Sonata for Strings **W191**
Kakadu **W192**
Two Grainger Arrangements **W200**
Nangaloar **W208**
From Uluru **W216**

**WORKS FOR SOLO INSTRU-
 MENT AND ORCHESTRA**
Irkanda IV **W80**

Piano Concerto **W167**
Nourlangie **W201**
Little Nourlangie **W206**
Lament **W211**

WORKS FOR ENSEMBLE
The Loneliness of Bunjil **W60**
Sonata for Viola and Percussion
 W77
String Quartet No. 6 **W91**
String Quartet No. 7 **W99**
Tabuh Tabuhan **W106**
String Quartet No. 8 **W111**
Dream **W114**
Morning Song, arr. string quartet
 W115
How the Stars were Made **W121**
Crimson Flower (gamelan) **W126**
String Quartet No. 9 **W132**
Sun Song (recorder quartet) **W134**
Little Serenade **W141**
Dua Chant **W144**
Landscape II **W145**
Cantares **W154**
Small Town, arr. David Matthews
 for string quartet **W156**
Tailitnama Song, arr. chamber
 ensemble **W163**
String Quartet No. 10 **W168**
The Burke and Wills Waltzes, arr.
 David Matthews **W174**
Djilile ('cello and piano) **W182**
Songs of Sea and Sky **W185**
Songs of Sea and Sky, arr. flute and

(WORKS FOR ENSEMBLE, CONT.)
piano W186
Tailitnama Song, arr. 'cello and
piano W194
Sun Song (percussion ensemble)
W196
Djilile, for percussion ensemble of
four players W203
String Quartet no. 11 (Jabiru
Dreaming) W204
Irkanda IV, arr. flute and string trio
W207
Irkanda IV, arr. string quartet W209
A Sun Song for Eric W210
Tailitnama Song, arr. violin &
piano W212
Kooee W214
Hill-Song No. 1 W218
Irkanda IV, arr. flute and string
quartet W219
Jabiru Dreaming for percussion
W220
Dream Tracks W221
Tropic W222
Awake, Glad Heart, arr, two
trumpets and strings W223

INSTRUMENTAL WORKS
Irkanda I W62
Alone W138
Night Pieces, arr. harp W150
Koto Music, arr. harp W151
Requiem W153
Nocturne (guitar) W159
Overture for a Happy Occasion
(organ) W160
Threnody W217
Simori W224

WORKS FOR PIANO
Sonatina W59
Left Bank Waltz W70
Haiku W93
Two Easy Pieces W104 (Sea Chant,
W103, arr. piano, and Left Bank
Waltz W70)
Night Pieces W118
Landscape W119
Koto Music W127

Koto Music II W133
Colonial Dances, arr. two pianos
W140
Four Little Pieces for Piano Duet
W149
Mountains W162
Three Pieces for Prepared Piano
W166
Djilile W183
Callabonna W197
Nocturnal W198
The Rose Bay Quadrilles W199
Second Impromptu W213
National Country Dances W215

CHORAL WORKS
Night Piece W95
Sun Music for Voices and
Percussion W96
Morning Song for the Christ Child
W98
Sea Chant W103
Autumn Song W105
Music for Mittagong or Fun Music I
W107
Ketjak W124
Sea Chant, arr. unison voices and
orchestra W131
The Stars Turn, arr. David Mat-
thews for mixed chorus W148
Saibai W179
Child of Australia W188
Anthem from Child of Australia
W189
The Birthday of Thy King W193
It's You W195
Child of Australia, arr. symphonic
band W202
Haughty Sortie W205

VOCAL WORKS
Three Songs W81
Two Shakespeare Songs W83
Love 200 W112
The Stars Turn, arr. high voice and
piano W122
The Stars Turn, arr. high voice,
strings, and percussion W123
The Song of Tailitnama W129

(VOCAL WORKS, CONT.)
Eliza Fraser Sings **W146**
Boat Rise, arr. Michael Hannan for
high voice and piano **W157**
East of India **W165**
The Song of Tailitnama, arr.
medium voice and piano **W171**
Ballad (The Dream) **W187**

WORKS FOR THE STAGE
Sun Music (ballet) **W109**
Rites of Passage **W125**
Quiros **W164**

WORKS FOR BAND
Burke and Wills Suite, arr.
symphonic band **W175**
The Croquet Waltz, arr. big band
W176
O Mistress Mine, arr. symphonic
band **W177**
Burke and Wills Suite, arr. brass
band **W180**

INCIDENTAL MUSIC
Much Ado About Nothing **W52**
The Miser **W54**
The Girl Who Couldn't Quite **W57**
Life With Father **W58**
Junius on Horseback **W63**
Twelfth Night **W64**
Ulterior Motifs **W65**
Cross Section **W68**
Some New Moon **W72**
King Lear **W78**

FILM MUSIC
Documentary films
The Splendour and the Peaks **W84**
El Alamein Fountain **W88**
The Troubled Mind **W89**
Exploration North **W147**

Feature films
They Found a Cave **W82**
Age of Consent **W102**
Essington **W128**
Manganinnie **W155**
Burke and Wills **W173**

**MUSIC FOR RADIO AND
TELEVISION**
Sons of the Morning **W66**
Don't Listen Ladies **W67**
The Fifth Continent **W87**
News Theme **W97**
Alpine **W130**
The Body is a Concert of Sensation
W139
Love Thoughts of a Lady **W142**

EARLY WORKS (1945-1954)
Nocturne (no. 1) **W1**
It's dark down the street **W2**
Falling Leaves **W3**
Short Piece for Pianoforte No. 1 **W4**
Short Piece for Pianoforte No. 2 **W5**
Slow Movement from Sonata no. 1
W6
Short Piece for Piano (No. 1) **W7**
Aboriginal Legend **W8**
Evocation **W9**
Chamber Suite **W10**
Sonatina no. 1 **W11**
New Hampshire **W12**
Epigram **W13**
Gardener Janus Catches a Naiad
W14
Siesta **W15**
Come Sleep **W16**
The Olive **W17**
Elegy for a Clown **W18**
Siesta, arr. bassoon and piano **W19**
Monsieur Miroir **W20**
In the morning **W21**
Wenn zwei voneinander scheiden
W22
To Meadows **W23**
Song **W24**
Hughley Steeple **W25**
Aspatia's Song **W26**
Jack and Joan **W27**
To Meadows, arr. soprano and
strings **W28**
Elegy **W29**
Jack and Joan, arr. soprano and
strings **W30**
Two Reveries **W31**

Appendix II:
Awards, Degrees, Positions

1942-45	Magistrates' Scholarship, Launceston Church Grammar School
1946	Royal Schools of Music Scholarship [not able to use]
	J. A. Steele Composition Prize (B2)
1947-50	University of Melbourne Examinations Board Scholarship (B3)
1948	Victorian School Music Award (B5)
1950	Graduated B. Mus., The University of Melbourne
1950-56	Lecturer in Music, Adult Education Board, Tasmania
1953-	Director, Sculthorpe's Pty. Ltd., Launceston
1956-58	Freelance composer, Canberra and Sydney
1958-60	Lizette Bentwich Travelling Scholarship (B26)
	Candidate for the Degree D. Phil. (Oxon.) [Unable to remain in England to complete work for degree]
1959	Royal Concert Trust Fund Composers' Award (B28)
	German Government Scholarship (B28) [not able to use]
1960	Royal Concert Trust Fund Composers' Award (B32)
1963	First Alfred Hill Memorial Award (W91, B61, B67)
1963-65	Lecturer in Music, The University of Sydney (B61, B67, B89n)
1965	Appointed Life Fellow, International Institute of Arts and Letters (B135)
1965-67	Harkness Fellowship (B90, B195)
	Composer in residence, Yale University (B119, B195)
	Guest at Yaddo artists' colony, Saratoga Springs, NY (B463).
1965-68	Senior Lecturer and Sydney Moss Lecturer in Music, The University of Sydney
1967	First John Bishop Memorial Award (W106)
	Appointed Life Fellow, Branford College, Yale University
1968	Encyclopædia Britannica Australia Award for the Arts (B280-281)
	Radcliffe Music Award (W111, B271)
1968-91	Reader in Music, The University of Sydney (B278)
1970	Appointed MBE (B356)
1972-73	First Visiting Professor of Music, The University of Sussex (B427, B449)
1975-77	First Australia Council Composers' Award (B472).

	Freelance composer, Special Leave from The University of Sydney
1977	Appointed OBE (**B546**)
	Queen's Silver Jubilee Medal (**B550**)
1980	Australian Film Institute Award and "Sammy" Award (**B673**)
	The Degree Honorary Doctor of Letters conferred by The University of Tasmania (**B654**). Upon an invitation from the Chancellor, Sir John Cameron, Sculthorpe delivered an address, "On Being Tasmanian"
1984	USSR Medal for Peace and Freedom
1985	1985 APRA Award, for most-performed work (**B800**)
1989	The Degree Honorary Doctor of Music conferred by The University of Melbourne (**B1002**). Hon. D. Mus. oration, "Peter Sculthorpe," was written by Barry Conyngham and delivered by Ronald Farren-Price
	The Degree Honorary Doctor of Letters conferred by The University of Sussex (**B1002**). Sir Leslie Fielding, Vice-Chancellor, delivered the Hon. D. Litt. oration, "Peter Sculthorpe"
1990	Appointed AO (**B1025**)
	Sounds Australian awards (**B1040**)
1991	Elected Fellow of the Australian Academy of the Humanities (**B1136**)
	ARIA Award for best classical recording **B1102**
	Promoted to Personal Chair, The University of Sydney (**B1150**)
1992-	Professor in Musical Composition (Personal Chair), The University of Sydney

Appendix III:
Works Dedicated
to Sculthorpe

Kirsty Beilharz: *Flexus II: Fire and Water*, for violin and piano (1992)

Anne Boyd: *P. S.*, for solo pianoforte (1979) **[P79-4]**

Colin Bright: *String Quartet* (1977)
                         Music for Contrabass Octet and Didjeridu (1986)

Brenton Broadstock: *In the Silence of the Night*, for piano (1989). "For Peter
                         Sculthorpe and Linda Kouvaras" **[P89-7]**

Alice Cohen: *P.S. for P.S.*, for piano (1991)

Adrian Connell: *String Quartet no. 2* (1990)

Barry Conyngham: *Five Windows*, for orchestra (1969)
                         Three, for string quartet and percussion (1970)
                         PPP, for piano (1979) **[P79-4]**

Ian Cugley: *Pan the Lake*, for orchestra (1967) **[P67-2]**
                         Little Adagio for Strings (1979) **[P79-4]**

Ross Edwards: *Duet for Two Flutes* (1979) **[P79-4]**
                         Maninya V, for voice and piano (1986)
                         Dance, for percussion ensemble (1989)

Andrew Ford: *Parabola*, theatre piece for two voices and chamber
                         ensemble (1989). Text: Barbara Blackman

Eric Gross: *Song 424/50*, for chamber ensemble (1979) **[P79-4]**

Michael Hannan: *Garland Piece*, for small orchestra (1979) **[P79-4]**
                         Earth Song, for piano (1987). "To Peter and Eve"
                         Misterious Flowers I, for piano (1990)

Michael Irik: *Music for Orchestra* (1975)

Melissa Irwin: *The Late Rains,* for piano (1993)

Jacqueline Lasdauskas: *Violin Sonata no. 6,* for violin and piano (1981)

David Matthews: *String Quartet no. 2* (1980)
                         Green, for mixed chorus (1989). Text: D.H. Lawrence

Peter Platt: *Aetat 50: gaudeamus,* for two-channel tape (1979)
                      [P79-4]

Vincent Plush: *Little Orchestra Piece: PS for PS,* for small orchestra
                        (1979) **[P79-4]**
                        Concord/Eendracht, for orchestra (1990)

Howard Skempton: *From Scratch,* for string quartet (1989)

Roger Smalley: *The Southland,* for chorus, didjeridu, gamelan
                        ensemble, folk group and large orchestra (1988). Text:
                        Jack Davis; Taufiq Ismail; Charles Thatcher; Chief
                        Seattle; traditional. "To Sir Frank Callaway and Peter
                        Sculthorpe, pioneers of Australian music"

Caroline Szeto: *Energy,* for symphony orchestra (1990)

Kelly Trench: *I met Morton Feldman in Glenmore Road,* for string
                       quartet (1986)

Martin Wesley-Smith: *P.S.* (Variations on a theme by Peter Sculthorpe), for
                     percussion ensemble (1989)

Nigel Westlake: *H. Birthday P.S.,* for percussion ensemble (1989)

Gillian Whitehead: *Oue: from a White Northumbria,* for small orchestra
                            (1979) **[P79-4]**

Also: various short pieces on greeting cards from Don Banks, Peter Maxwell
Davies, Michael Hannan, Mirrie Hill, Christopher Hogwood, David
Matthews, Nicholas Maw, Toru Takemitsu and others.

Title Index

This is an index to Sculthorpe's works by title. Titles in **boldface** are works with **W** numbers in the "Works" catalog; for each of these the **W** number is given, followed by D numbers ("Discography") and page numbers in the "Bibliography" chapter. Further references to **P** listings ("Performances") and **B** listings ("Bibliography") are in the "Works" catalog. Titles in *italics* are movements and alternate titles, while titles in quotation marks are provisional titles.

Subject Index

This index lists authors, book and periodical titles, composers, performers, institutions, and other significant categories. References to the "Biography" are indicated by the actual page number; items located in the other chapters are identified with the relevant mnemonic (W, D, P, B) and catalog number. B numbers with a letter *n* (=*note*) refer to citations listed at the end of the annotation.

Hiscocks, Wendy, P83-10
H.M., B1148
Hoad, Brian, B486, B679, B812, B1041n
Hobart Drama Festival, W63, W72
Hobart Repertory Theatre, P55-12
Hobart conference/seminar (1963), 20, 23,
  B59-59n, B60, B388, B545, B840
Hobcroft, Rex, W162
Hockley, Dot, 33, B597
Hoddinott, Alun, B176
Hodge, Glendon, B789
Hoffmann, Andrew, vn, P63-7
Hoffmann, W. L., B214, B401-402, B584,
  B952, B1063, B1122, B1129
Hogan, Christine, B673
Hogwood, Christopher, App III
Holden, Ray, cond., P89-9
Holdsworth Galleries, B780
Holford, Franz, B18, B37, B95, B116
Holland, Bernard, 32, B782, B937, B930,
  B990, B1036
Holland, Dulcie, B78
Hollier, Donald, D20
Holloway, Daniel, vc, P89-7, P90-7
Holmes, James, cond., P88-4
Holowell, Elizabeth, vn, D16, P89-10
Honey, John, W155, B705
Hong Kong Academy Orchestra, P89-7
Hong Kong Philharmonic Orchestra, P90-11
Hong Kong Standard, B641
Honi Soit (Univ. of Sydney), B91, B101
Honolulu Symphony, P91-3
Hood, Trevor, B805
Hopkins, John, cond., 26, W94, W110, W112,
  W113, W116, W125, W129, W131, W206,
  D23, D30-31, D34, D42, D62, D68, P66-2,
  -10, P67-2, -3, -11 (x3), P68-2, -3, P69-5,
  -10, P70-2, -7, -9, P71-2, -3, P72-3, P74-2,
  P75-9, -10, P79-9, P81-6, P82-3, P83-5 (x3),
  P84-2, P85-4, P91-1, -3, -5, B327
Hordern, Sam, B810n
Horne, Donald, B627
Horner, John, B76, B201, B239-240
Hornsby Advocate, P91-6
Hornung, Richard, va, P89-10
Horton, Andrew, B664
Horwitz, Sonia, vc, P50-10
Hough, David, B1119n
Housman, A. E., W17, W21, W25
Houstoun, Michael, pf, P87-9, P87-10
Hove, Mark van, perc, P64-8
Howard, Brian, D24
Howard, John, W188
Howat, Roy, pf, P86-6, P87-7, P92-5
Hubble, Ava, B684, B726, B874, B935n
Hubert, Karl, B651
Huddersfield Examiner, P90-11

Huddersfield Festival, P90-11, P91-10,
  B1180
Hudson, W.J., B461
Hugh, Timothy, vc, P83-1, P84-8, P85-4
Hughes, Anthony, B707, B714
Hughes, Robert (composer), D11
Hughes, Robert (critic), B25, B247
Hughes, Tony, P88-1
Humble, Keith, cond., P84-3, -4
Humphries, Barry (Dame Edna Everage),
  P91-1
Hunt, Ian, B740
Hunt, Terence A., cond., P71-5
Hunter Orchestra, P92-12
Hush, David, B623
Hutchens, Frank, 12, P45-5, -9
Hutton, Geoffrey, B265n
Hutton, Mary Ellyn, B934
Hyde, Miriam, pf, 15, P88-10, P92-4, P92-8

I Do (dance), P88-4
I Lotring, W100
Illing, Rosamund, sop., P88-11
In the Making, 27, B287
Independent, The (London), B958, B1050,
  B1171
Indian Ocean Arts Festival (Perth), P79-9
Indonesia, 9, 10: Bali: music and dance, 7,
  10, 24-25, 28, 32, W100, W111, W126,
  B269, B382, B388, B451, B455, B457, B495,
  B528, B533-534; Java (*Udan mas*), W116
Inglis, K.S., B727
Ingram, Robert, vn, P83-9
Ingram, Terry, B724
Instrumentenbau Musik International, B587
Invisible Barrier, P91-11
Irik, Mike, as cond., P89-10; as composer,
  App III
Irwin, Melissa, App III
Isaacs and Martin, *Dictionary of Music*,
  B703
Isaacs, Ike, P87-1
Ise no Umi ("The Sea of Umi"), W142,
  W155
Island Moving Company, P91-9
ISCM: Adelaide, W90, W96, B208; Baden-
  Baden festival, 2, 15, W59, B11-12, B16,
  B81; London festival, P71-6; Madrid, B92;
  Sydney, 21, 23, 25, W114, P64-8
ISME Congress, P80-6
ISO Dance Theatre, P88-4
Ives, Charles, 8, B266, B889
Iwaki, Hiroyuki, cond., P76-8, -9, P80-9,
  P86-4, -9, P89-4, P90-10, P91-6
Iwamoto, Mari, String Quartet, D55

Jackson, George (critic), P91-9

About the Author

DEBORAH HAYES is Associate Professor, Musicology, at the University of Colorado. She is author of *Peggy Glanville-Hicks: A Bio-Bibliography* (Greenwood Press, 1990) and editor of Keyboard Sonatas by Bayon (1769) and Lebrun (1780). She has also contributed chapters to several edited volumes.